THE LITTLE
SLOW COOKER
COOKBOOK

Quarto is the authority on a wide range of topics.

Quarto educates, entertains and enriches the lives of our readers—enthusiasts and lovers of hands-on living.

www.QuartoKnows.com

© 2016 Quarto Publishing Group USA Inc.

First published in the United States of America in 2016 by
Fair Winds Press, an imprint of
Quarto Publishing Group USA Inc.
100 Cummings Center
Suite 406-L
Beverly, Massachusetts 01915-6101
Telephone: (978) 282-9590
Fax: (978) 283-2742
QuartoKnows.com
Visit our blogs at QuartoKnows.com

All rights reserved. No part of this book may be reproduced or utilized, in any form or by any means, electronic or mechanical, without prior permission in writing from the publisher. All images in this book have been reproduced with the knowledge and prior consent of the artists concerned, and no responsibility is accepted by producer, publisher, or printer for any infringement of copyright or otherwise, arising from the contents of this publication. Every effort has been made to trace the copyright holders and ensure that credits accurately comply with information supplied. We apologize for any inaccuracies that may have occurred and will resolve inaccurate or missing information in a subsequent reprinting of the book.

20 19 18 17 16   1 2 3 4 5

ISBN: 978-1-59233-733-0

Digital edition published in 2016
eISBN: 978-1-63159-176-1

Library of Congress Cataloging-in-Publication Data available

Cover Image and Photography: Bill Bettencourt; shutterstock.com and istock.com
Page Layout: Leanne Coppola

Printed in China

THE LITTLE
SLOW COOKER
COOKBOOK

500 of the Best Slow Cooker Recipes Ever

Subtly Spicy Peanut Fondue (see page 35)

From-the-Pantry Pot Pie (see page 129)

Strawberry-Lime Granita (see page 245)

Coquito Eggnog (see page 262)

CONTENTS

PANTRY BASICS
6

APPETIZERS
24

BREAKFASTS
38

BREADS AND SANDWICHES
54

MAIN DISHES
76

SALADS AND SOUPS
142

SIDE DISHES
176

DESSERTS
210

BEVERAGES
246

CREDITS
267

INDEX
268

PANTRY BASICS
See pages 10-11, 14-15, and 22-23 for Pantry Basics photos.

BEEF STOCK
What's the difference between broth and stock? Broth is meat simmered with water and vegetables, while stock is meaty bones that are browned and simmered, which produces a richer, more flavorful broth. This recipe produces stock that can be diluted before using. It cooks easily in a slow cooker and gives you a good quantity of stock.

1½ pounds (680 g) meaty beef bones
1 cup (160 g) sliced onion
1 cup (130 g) sliced carrot
1 cup (100 g) sliced celery
1½ cups (355 ml) water
½ teaspoon black pepper
1 teaspoon thyme

Preheat the oven to 350°F (180°C, or gas mark 4).
    In a roasting pan, place the bones and vegetables in a single layer. Roast for about 1 hour, or until browned.
    Transfer the mixture to a slow cooker. Cover with water. Add the pepper and thyme. Cook on low 8 to 9 hours.
    Remove the beef and bones from the pot and let cool until easy to handle. Remove the meat from the bones and save for another use.
    Strain the vegetables from the stock and discard.
    Chill the stock in the fridge and remove the fat from the top.

Yield: 8 servings

CHICKEN STOCK
This produces a richer, more flavorful broth that can be diluted before using. It cooks easily in a slow cooker and gives you a good quantity of stock. You can use chicken bones that have most of the meat removed. Mix this stock with equal amounts of water and use it in any recipe calling for chicken broth.

1½ pounds (680 g) meaty chicken bones
1 cup (160 g) sliced onion
1 cup (130 g) sliced carrot
1 cup (100 g) sliced celery
1½ cups (355 ml) water
½ teaspoon black pepper
1 teaspoon thyme

Preheat the oven to 350°F (180°C, or gas mark 4).
    In a roasting pan, place the bones and vegetables in a single layer. Roast for about 1 hour, or until browned.
    Transfer the mixture to a slow cooker. Cover with water. Add the pepper and thyme. Cook on low 8 to 9 hours.
    Remove the chicken and bones from the pot and let cool until easy to handle. Remove the meat from the bones and save for another use.
    Strain the vegetables from the stock and discard. Chill the stock in the fridge and remove the fat from the top.

Yield: 8 servings

FRESHEST VEGETABLE BROTH
Broth is a highly concentrated form of nutrients, distilling everything wonderful from the vegetables into a rich liquid. Homemade broth is the best. It's fresher tasting, it doesn't have added sodium, and you control the quality of the ingredients. A slow cooker is absolutely the best tool ever for making perfect broth because all you do is prep it and leave it.

4 ribs celery with leaves, quartered
4 carrots, unpeeled and quartered (with greens, if possible)
3 parsnips, unpeeled and quartered
1 large yellow onion, unpeeled and quartered
1 large leek, well rinsed and coarsely chopped
2 portobello mushrooms, including stems (Use 6 or 8 cremini mushrooms if you prefer a lighter-colored broth.)
1 small zucchini, coarsely chopped
2 cabbage leaves, optional
1 bunch Italian parsley, thicker stems removed
4 cloves garlic, unpeeled and crushed
2 star anise, optional
½ teaspoon green peppercorns or ½ teaspoon black pepper

In a 6-quart (5.7 L) slow cooker, combine all of the ingredients. Cover with water to about 2 inches (5 cm) from the top of the insert. Cover and cook on low for 9 to 10 hours (or overnight).
    Cool slightly and strain the mixture through a double-mesh sieve into one or two large storage containers. Reserve the vegetables for another use or discard.
    Store the broth in the fridge or in pintsize containers in the freezer for later use. Place a layer of microwave-safe plastic wrap on the surface of the cold soup and under the lid before freezing to keep it airtight.

Yield: 3 to 4 quarts (2.8 to 3.7 L)
▶ *Recipe Variation*
An easy and economical way to make vegetable broth is to hang on to all the peels, cores, and ends of your vegetables from the week and use them over the weekend to make broth. Just keep them fresh in a container in the refrigerator.

Different herbs and vegetables lend different qualities to your broths. Many peels, such as onion skins, tend to darken the color. You can also sweat chopped veggies in a skillet on the stove for 5 to 10 minutes before adding to the slow cooker to further concentrate their flavors.

▶ *Did You Know?*
Even though broth and stock are different, many people use them in recipes interchangeably.

ONION SOUP MIX
Some of these recipes call for onion soup mix. You can easily make your own mix that is even lower in sodium. You can use this in the same way as you would a one-serving envelope of one of the commercial brands. Some brands make multiple servings per envelope.

1 tablespoon (15 g) dried minced onion
1 teaspoon sodium-free beef bouillon
½ teaspoon onion powder
⅛ teaspoon black pepper
⅛ teaspoon paprika

In a bowl, stir all of the ingredients together.
  Store the mixture in an airtight jar or bag.

Yield: 1 serving

▶ *Recipe Tip!*
Mix this Onion Soup Mix with a pint of sour cream. It makes a great dip.

CONDENSED CREAM OF MUSHROOM SOUP
Many slow cooker recipes call for mushroom soup. Here's a homemade version that's low-sodium to boot! It makes an amount that can be substituted for one can of the condensed soup.

1 cup (70 g) sliced mushrooms
½ cup (80 g) chopped onion
½ cup (120 ml) low-sodium chicken broth
1 tablespoon (1 g) dried parsley
¼ teaspoon garlic powder
⅔ cup (160 ml) skim milk
2 tablespoons (16 g) cornstarch

In a saucepan, cook the mushrooms, onion, broth, parsley, and garlic powder until the vegetables are soft.
  Transfer the mixture to a blender and blend until well puréed.
  In an airtight container, shake together the milk and cornstarch until the cornstarch is dissolved. Pour the mixture into a saucepan. Cook over medium heat, stirring, until thick. Stir in the vegetable mixture.

Yield: 6 servings

CITRUS RUM BBQ SAUCE
Tired of having to read labels with words on them that have little or nothing to do with food? Make your own barbecue sauce at home. This one is slightly sweet from the rum and orange juice, and it's seasoned with thyme, allspice, and ginger. Freeze the leftovers in ice cube trays, and defrost a cube or two the next time you crave a sandwich.

2 tablespoons (30 ml) olive oil
1 onion, minced
2 cloves garlic, minced
1 teaspoon grated ginger
1 can (14½ ounces, or 406 g) tomato sauce
1 can (6 ounces, or 170 g) tomato paste
½ cup (120 ml) orange juice
Juice of ½ lime
½ cup (120 ml) rum (amber or dark, if possible)
2 tablespoons (30 ml) apple cider vinegar
2 tablespoons (30 ml) agave nectar or maple syrup
3 tablespoons (45 g) brown sugar
1 teaspoon dried thyme
½ teaspoon allspice
½ teaspoon paprika
Pinch of ground cloves

In a skillet, cook the oil over medium heat for 3 to 5 minutes, or until translucent. Add the garlic. Cook for about 1 minute more.
  In a slow cooker, combine all of the ingredients. Cook on low for 8 to 10 hours. If the sauce is still too thin, turn the slow cooker to high and prop the lid up with the handle of a wooden spoon to allow some of the liquid to evaporate.
  Store the sauce in an airtight container in the fridge for 1 week or in the freezer for up to 6 months.

Yield: 3 to 4 cups (750 to 1,000 g)

▶ *Serving Suggestion*
You can make super easy pulled chicken, pork, or meatless sandwiches with this sauce. After the sauce has been cooked, add chicken, pork, or shredded seitan or tofu. Cook in a slow cooker on low for 6 to 8 hours. Serve on toasted buns.

HOMEMADE SMOKY KETCHUP

Most people love ketchup and always have it on hand. Try making your own. It's really easy in a slow cooker because it cooks while you're away. This recipe has a smoky flavor, but you can make your own signature ketchup by omitting some or all of the spices in the recipe and adding curry powder or roasted garlic instead. You are only as limited as your imagination.

2 tablespoons (30 ml) olive oil
½ small onion, minced
2 cloves garlic, minced
1 can (20 ounces, or 560 g) crushed tomatoes (fire-roasted, if possible), drained
2 tablespoons (32 g) tomato paste
½ cup (115 g) packed brown sugar
½ cup (120 ml) apple cider vinegar (or white vinegar or rice vinegar)
½ teaspoon salt
¼ teaspoon chipotle chile powder
¼ teaspoon allspice
¼ teaspoon celery seed
⅛ teaspoon dry mustard
⅛ teaspoon ground cloves
⅛ teaspoon ground ginger

In a skillet, heat the oil over medium heat. Sauté the onion for 3 to 5 minutes, or until it's translucent. Add the garlic and cook for about 1 minute more.
    In a slow cooker, combine all of the ingredients. Cook on low for 8 to 10 hours. If the ketchup is still too thin, turn the slow cooker to high and prop the lid up with the handle of a wooden spoon to allow some of the liquid to evaporate.

Yield: 2 to 2½ cups (500 to 625 g)

▶ Recipe Tips!
- Only keep the amount of ketchup you will use in a week in the fridge. Store the rest in the freezer for up to 6 months.

- You can use Preserve-the-Harvest Diced Tomatoes on page 17 instead of canned crushed tomatoes. Just purée them first, or purée the batch of ketchup after cooking.

CHILI SAUCE

You'll likely prefer this sauce to the bottled chili sauce you can buy in stores. There are enough vegetables in it to give it something more than a glorified ketchup taste. It keeps well in the refrigerator for weeks.

2 cups (360 g) canned diced tomatoes
1 can (8 ounces, or 225 g) tomato sauce
½ cup (80 g) onion, chopped
½ cup (100 g) sugar
½ cup (50 g) celery, chopped
½ cup (75 g) green bell pepper, chopped
1 tablespoon (15 ml) lemon juice
1 tablespoon (15 g) brown sugar
1 tablespoon (20 g) molasses
¼ teaspoon hot pepper sauce
⅛ teaspoon cloves
⅛ teaspoon cinnamon
⅛ teaspoon black pepper
⅛ teaspoon basil
⅛ teaspoon tarragon
½ cup (120 ml) cider vinegar

In a large saucepan, bring all of the ingredients to a boil. Reduce the heat. Simmer uncovered for 1½ hours, or until the mixture is reduced to half of its original volume.

Yield: 48 servings

BLUEBERRY-BALSAMIC MEATBALL SAUCE WITH ROSEMARY

This savory sauce has sweet flavors of blueberries and raspberries that are balanced out with rosemary.

12 ounces (340 g) fresh or frozen blueberries
2 tablespoons (30 ml) agave nectar or maple syrup
1 tablespoon (16 g) tomato paste
½ cup (120 ml) raspberry or plain balsamic vinegar
½ cup (120 ml) red wine
½ cup (120 ml) water
1 clove garlic, minced
2 sprigs fresh rosemary

In a blender, purée the blueberries, agave, paste, vinegar, wine, water, and garlic.
    Oil the crock of a 1½- to 2-quart (1.4 to 1.9 L) slow cooker. Add the purée and the rosemary. Cook on low for 3 to 4 hours, or on high for 1½ to 2 hours. (Many small slow cookers have no temperature control, so they cook everything on low.)
    Remove the rosemary and discard. Switch to warm or low to keep the sauce warm for a party.

Yield: 12 servings

VEGETARIAN SPAGHETTI SAUCE
Chock-full of fresh veggies, this sauce is a real winner.

4 cups (328 g) eggplant, peeled and cut into 1-inch (2.5 cm) cubes
1 cup (160 g) chopped onion
2 cups (300 g) chopped red bell pepper
4 teaspoons (12 g) minced garlic
1 can (28 ounces, or 785 g) crushed tomatoes, undrained
1 can (28 ounces, or 785 g) diced tomatoes, undrained
1 can (6 ounces, or 170 g) tomato paste
2 tablespoons (30 g) brown sugar
2 tablespoons (12 g) Italian seasoning
¼ teaspoon red pepper flakes

In a slow cooker, combine all of the ingredients. Cover and cook on low for 10 to 12 hours or on high for 5 to 6 hours.

Yield: 6 servings

▶ *Garnish this flavorful sauce with fresh oregano sprigs and Parmesan cheese. You can store extra sauce in the fridge for up to 3 days or freeze for later.*

EASY PASTA SAUCE
Quick and easy to make, this pasta sauce has great taste. Make a big batch and freeze the extra for future use.

2 teaspoons olive oil
1 cup (160 g) finely chopped onion
1½ teaspoons minced garlic
2 cans (28 ounces, or 785 g) crushed tomatoes
2 teaspoons basil
1 teaspoon oregano
½ teaspoon black pepper
1 tablespoon (13 g) sugar
1 tablespoon (4 g) fresh parsley

In a saucepan, heat the oil over medium heat. Sauté the onion and garlic for about 10 minutes, or until the onion becomes very soft.
 In the slow cooker, combine of all the ingredients except for the parsley. Cover and cook on low 6 to 8 hours. Add the parsley. Cook for an additional 30 minutes.

Yield: 8 servings

SLOW COOKED TWO-TOMATO AND SPICY TURKEY SAUSAGE SAUCE
If you're new to the pleasures of slow cooking, you'll be a convert after you make this sauce. The slow cooking brings out the subtle flavors in a way no other kind of cooking can. You'll love how the color of the tomatoes subtly blends with the colors of the red peppers and carrots. This sauce is great over traditional whole-grain pasta. For a low-carb option, serve it over zucchini "noodles." To make them, thinly slice 4 to 6 zucchinis lengthwise using a vegetable peeler or mandoline and sauté them in a little olive oil until they are just tender.

½ cup (55 g) sundried tomato strips in olive oil, drained, oil reserved
2 yellow onions, chopped
2 ribs celery, finely chopped
1 cup (110 g) grated carrot
1 red bell pepper, seeded and finely chopped
4 cloves garlic, minced
4 links (4 ounces, or 112 g each) spicy Italian turkey sausage, chopped or skinned and crumbled
2 cans (28 ounces, or 784 g each) crushed tomatoes
1 teaspoon dried oregano
¾ teaspoon Sucanat
¾ teaspoon salt
½ teaspoon black pepper
½ teaspoon dried thyme
½ teaspoon ground fennel

In a large skillet, heat 1½ tablespoons (23 ml) of the reserved olive oil from the sundried tomatoes over medium heat. Sauté the onions, celery, carrot, and bell pepper for 6 to 8 minutes, or until the onions are softened but not browned. Add the garlic and cook for 30 seconds.
 Transfer the mixture to the slow cooker and add the sun-dried tomatoes, sausage, crushed tomatoes, oregano, Sucanat, salt, pepper, thyme, and fennel. Stir gently to combine. Cook on low for 6 to 8 hours to the desired consistency. To thicken the sauce, remove the lid, increase the temperature to high, and cook for 30 minutes longer.

Yield: 6 to 8 servings

▶ *Health Bite*
Slow cooking this sauce even has some salutatory health benefits—for example, increasing the availability of lycopene, which is an important plant chemical that has been linked to a lower risk of prostate cancer. *But the real flavor breakthrough comes from the turkey sausage. If you buy one of the better organic turkey sausages, they are much lower in calories than traditional sausage.*

1 Beef Stock

2 Chicken Stock

MEGA OMEGA PIQUANT ARTICHOKE, OLIVE, AND ANCHOVY SAUCE

This pungent sauce has "Greek" written all over it. We all know anchovies from the local pizzeria, and this lowly little fish delivers a knockout nutritional punch. We love this tangy sauce. You and your family will too. This sauce is great over grilled white fish for a Mediterranean main dish, tossed with whole-grain pasta or over baked chicken.

1 tablespoon (15 ml) olive oil
1 large yellow onion, finely chopped
1 jar or can (12 or 14 ounces, 336 or 392 g) artichoke hearts in water, drained and chopped
4 cloves garlic, minced
1 can (28 ounces, or 784 g) crushed tomatoes
4 anchovy fillets, minced
⅓ cup (33 g) pitted and sliced black olives
1 tablespoon (8.6 g) capers, drained
1 teaspoon dried thyme
½ teaspoon salt
½ teaspoon black pepper

In a large skillet, heat the oil over medium heat. Sauté the onion and artichokes for 6 to 7 minutes, or until the onion is tender. Add the garlic and cook for 1 minute.

Transfer the mixture to a slow cooker. Add the tomatoes, anchovies, olives, capers, thyme, salt, and pepper. Stir gently to combine. Cover and cook on low for 7 to 8 hours or on high for 3 to 4 hours.

Yield: 4 to 6 servings

▶ *Health Bite*

One 3-ounce (84 g) portion of anchovies delivers an incredible 24.5 grams of protein and more than 1,600 milligrams of combined EPA and DHA, which are the critically important omega-3 fats that are found in fish and fish oil.

Black olives are a rich source of important polyphenols, plant chemicals with multiple health benefits, including the ability to help fight certain pathogens. Also they're loaded with heart-healthy monounsaturated fat. Add some liver-cleansing artichokes—rich in the plant chemical silymarin, which is enormously supportive to the liver—and you're in business.

The tomato base is rich in lycopene, which is a powerful antioxidant that has also been linked to a reduced risk of prostate cancer.

MEMORABLE GINGERED PEACHES AND BLUES SAUCE

This peachy-blue sauce is all fruit, with no added sweeteners. It doesn't need them! Enjoy! Use prepared ginger juice, run fresh ginger through a juicer, or simply grate a large handful of shavings and squeeze. This fruity sauce is great in the morning over pancakes or French toast, mixed into cottage cheese for a tasty snack, or served over low-sugar vanilla ice cream or Rice Dream for dessert.

4 medium fresh, ripe peaches, peeled, pitted, and chopped
8 ounces (225 g) fresh blueberries
¼ cup (60 ml) pear nectar (or apple juice concentrate or water)
2 teaspoons ginger juice
¾ teaspoon dried ginger
2 tablespoons (30 g) minute tapioca

In a slow cooker, combine all of the ingredients. Stir gently until well mixed. Cook, uncovered, on low for 4 to 5 hours, stirring occasionally, or until the sauce reaches the desired consistency.

Yield: 3 to 4 cups (720 to 960 g)

▶ *Health Bite*

Blueberries are a true "memory" food. Animal studies have demonstrated that daily consumption of blueberries dramatically slows impairments in motor coordination and memory. And they have one of the highest "ORAC" scores of all time, meaning they score high on a standardized test for antioxidant power.

PESTO

This makes a fairly typical pesto but without the usual added salt. It's good in recipes or just over warm pasta.

2 cups (80 g) fresh basil, packed, divided
3 tablespoons (27 g) pine nuts, divided
1 teaspoon garlic, finely minced, divided
¼ cup (20 g) Parmesan cheese, divided
½ cup (120 ml) olive oil, divided

In a food processor, pulse one-third of the basil until well chopped. Add about one-third of the pine nuts and garlic. Blend again. Add about one-third of the cheese. Blend while slowly adding about one-third of the oil, stopping to scrape down sides of the container. Process the pesto until it forms a thick, smooth paste. Repeat until all of the ingredients are used. Mix all of the batches together well.

Store the pesto in an airtight container for 1 week in the fridge or for a few months in the freezer.

Yield: 12 servings

COCONUT LEMON CURD

Love lemon? You'll adore this homemade lemon curd–with coconut added for flavor and crunch. Just for good measure we reduced the sugar to about half that in a classic curd. Lemon curd is wonderful on light, whole-grain toast with a little butter; stirred into yogurt, cottage cheese, or fresh ricotta cheese; or drizzled over berries.

½ cup (120 g) unrefined coconut oil
Juice and zest of 4 lemons
½ cup (120 g) erythritol
½ cup (120 g) Sucanat (Replace with erythritol for brighter lemon color.)
4 eggs, beaten

In a small pan, melt the oil over low heat.
  Remove from the heat. Whisk in the juice, zest, erythritol, and Sucanat. Allow the mixture to cool. Whisk in the eggs until well combined and pour into a small, shallow casserole dish with a lid or cover with foil. Cover and place the casserole in a 6- or 7-quart (5.7 or 6.6 L) slow cooker. Add water to come halfway up the sides of the casserole.
  Cover the slow cooker and cook on low for 4 to 4 1⁄2 hours, whisking very well once at about 2 hours. Unplug the slow cooker and remove the covers to cool enough to remove the casserole dish from the hot water.
  Whisk well, cool completely, and store in sterilized jars in the fridge for up to 4 weeks. (To sterilize the jars, run the jars and lids through the hottest cycle of your dishwasher, or submerge in a pot of boiling water for at least 2 minutes and allow them to air-dry.)

Yield: about 3 cups (960 g)

▶ *Health Bite*
Though considered an "acid" fruit, lemons actually have the exact opposite effect on the body, acting more like an alkalizing agent. Because our standard diet tends to be pretty acidic, we can use all the help we can get to reach a more balanced state, and lemons do the job nicely. One of the countless reasons why vegetables and fruits are so good for you is that virtually all of them are highly alkalizing to the body.)
  Coconut oil hits the trifecta for cooking oils: tastes terrific, stands up well to heat, and is good for you. (We particularly like the Barlean's brand of coconut oil, which is widely available and of superb quality.) Coconut oil contains particular fatty acids, such as lauric acid, that are antimicrobial, thus supporting the immune system. The fat in coconut oil is a kind of fat known as medium-chain triglycerides, or MCTs, which the body prefers to use for energy rather than turning it into a spare tire.
  Just for good measure we reduced the sugar to about half that in a classic curd. You'll love this!

LIGHTLY SWEETENED AUTUMNAL FRUIT BUTTER

Fruit butters have no fat or sugar, and the best ones are almost entirely made of fruit with just a smattering of other minor ingredients. You're essentially buttering your toast, or anything else you want to butter, with "essence of apple" (or whatever fruit butter you're using). This version is only lightly sweetened using cider, molasses, and a tiny bit of Sucanat. And this one is even healthier because we leave the skins on, and the skins are where so many nutrients (and fiber) are often concentrated. Note: This recipe has a long cooking time, but who cares? The prep is quick!

3 large McIntosh apples, unpeeled, cored, and sliced
4 large Bartlett pears, unpeeled, cored, and sliced
¼ cup (36 g) raisins
1 cup (235 ml) pear nectar (for sweeter butter) or apple cider
2 tablespoons (40 g) blackstrap molasses
⅓ cup (80 g) Sucanat
1 tablespoon (8 g) grated fresh ginger
½ teaspoon ground cinnamon
½ teaspoon ground nutmeg

In the bottom of a 4-quart (3.7 L) slow cooker, combine the apples, pears, and raisins.
  In a medium bowl, whisk together the nectar, molasses, Sucanat, ginger, cinnamon, and nutmeg until well combined. Pour the mixture over the fruit, cover, and cook on low for 8 to 10 hours. Remove the cover, stir gently, and cook uncovered for 6 to 8 hours more, or until very thick and most of the juices have evaporated. Using an immersion blender, purée the mixture until smooth.
  (Or cool and purée in a regular blender or food processor.)
  Store in tightly sealed glass containers in the fridge for up to 1 month.

Yield: about 3 quarts (2.8 L)

3 Freshest Vegetable Broth; 4 Onion Soup Mix; 5 Condensed Cream of Mushroom Soup; 6 Citrus Rum BBQ Sauce; 7 Homemade Smoky Ketchup; 8 Chili Sauce

9 Blueberry-Balsamic Meatball Sauce with Rosemary; 10 Vegetarian Spaghetti Sauce; 11 Easy Pasta Sauce; 12 Slow Cooked Two-Tomato and Spicy Turkey Sausage Sauce; 13 Mega Omega Piquant Artichoke, Olive, and Anchovy Sauce; 14 Memorable Gingered Peaches and Blues Sauce; 15 Pesto; 16 Coconut Lemon Curd

PERFECT PUMPKIN PUREE
Each fall, pie pumpkins are sprinkled in with the larger jack-o'-lantern pumpkins.

1 pie pumpkin that will fit in your slow cooker

Wash the pumpkin. Poke holes in it for the steam to escape.

Place the pumpkin in the slow cooker and cook on low for 6 to 8 hours, or until a fork easily slides through the skin and the flesh.

Let the pumpkin cool. Move it to a cutting board, and slice it in half. Remove the seeds and pumpkin guts. Scrape the flesh into a food processor or blender and purée until smooth.

Yield: 3 to 6 cups (735 to 1,470 g)

▶ *Recipe Tips*
- Use this purée in any recipe that calls for cooked or canned pumpkin in the same proportion.
- Freeze the purée in 1½-cup (368 g) portions, so you can thaw the same amount that's in one 12-ounce (368 g) can.

APPLE BUTTER
Apple butter is traditionally slow-cooked in huge tubs, but you can make it right in your slow cooker.

12 apples, preferable Jonathan or winesap
2 cups (475 ml) apple juice
5 cups (1 kg) sugar
2 tablespoons (14 g) cinnamon
1 tablespoon (6 g) allspice
1 tablespoon (6.6 g) cloves

Wash, core, and quarter the apples. (There's no need to peel them.) Coat the crock of a slow cooker with nonstick cooking spray.

In the slow cooker, combine the apples and juice. Cover and cook on low for 6 to 8 hours or on high for 2 to 4 hours, or until the apples are tender.

Using a slotted spoon, remove the apples from the slow cooker.

In a food mill, remove the peel from the apples.

Measure the cooked apples and return them to the slow cooker. For each pint of cooked fruit, add 1 cup (200 g) sugar, 1 teaspoon cinnamon, ½ teaspoon allspice, and ½ teaspoon cloves; stir well. Cover and cook on high for 6 to 8 hours, stirring about every 2 hours.

After 3 hours, remove the cover to allow the fruit and juice to cook down.

Yield: 80 servings

FALL HARVEST FRUIT BUTTER
Serve up a bit of fall all winter long by freezing some of this recipe. It's perfect on toast, English muffins, or bagels. The spices scent your house while it's cooking, which is a bonus. No fresh pumpkin on hand? Use 1 can (15 ounces, or 420 g) pumpkin purée or 2 cups (490 g) Perfect Pumpkin Purée at left.

6 large pears, peeled, cored, and chopped
4 large apples (or about 6 medium ones), peeled, cored, and chopped
2 cups (300 g) cubed fresh pumpkin or butternut squash
Juice of 2 lemons
½ cup (115 g) packed brown sugar (You can substitute 1½ cup (120 ml) agave nectar or maple syrup.)
1 teaspoon cinnamon
½ teaspoon allspice
½ teaspoon cardamom
½ teaspoon ground ginger
¼ teaspoon ground cloves

Coat the crock of a slow cooker with nonstick cooking spray.

In the slow cooker, combine all of the ingredients. Prop the lid open by placing the thin edge of a wooden spoon handle across the crock to allow the liquid to evaporate. Cook on low for 8 to 10 hours, or until most of the liquid has evaporated.

If you need to evaporate more liquid, switch the slow cooker to high, leave the lid propped up, and cook for 1 to 2 hours longer.

Using an immersion blender, purée the mixture. (Or purée it in batches using a countertop blender.) Let cool completely.

Transfer the mixture to freezer bags or special freezer containers for preserves. Store it in the freezer for up to 4 months.

Yield: 6 to 8 cups (1,920 to 2,560 g)

▶ *Serving Suggestion*
Want to make a fast and fancy dessert? Combine about 1 cup (320 g) of the Fall Harvest Fruit Butter with 1 container (12 ounces, 336 g) silken tofu in a food processor. Blend until very smooth, stopping periodically to scrape down the sides with a spatula. Serve chilled in martini glasses as a mousse, or put in a graham cracker crust for a super easy Thanksgiving pie.

BALSAMIC ONION MARMALADE

In this spread, the sweetness of the cooked onions contrasts nicely with the balsamic vinegar. This is not the marmalade to spread on your morning toast. Instead, use it on crostini, on top of pizza, or anywhere else you think it will be appreciated.

4 large onions, sliced
½ cup (120 ml) water
¼ cup (60 ml) balsamic vinegar
2 tablespoons (30 ml) olive oil
2 tablespoons (25 to 30 g) sugar (or agave nectar or maple syrup)
1 sprig fresh rosemary
½ to 1 teaspoon salt

In a slow cooker, combine all of the ingredients. Cook on low for 6 to 8 hours. Remove and discard the rosemary. Let cool completely before using or storing.
Store in the fridge for up to 1 week or in the freezer for up to 2 months.

Yield: 2 to 3 cups (500 to 750 g)

▶ *Serving Suggestion*
Use this Balsamic Onion Marmalade on pizzas, in pastas, or on hot dogs. You can use it to top bruschetta or on top of spreads, such as hummus.

ALL-OCCASION ROASTED GARLIC

This is a great no-fuss treat that's good for you and your waistline. Once it's cooked, squeeze the cloves, or use a knife to get them out from the skins. It's true you use no water. It really is as easy as it seems. You can spread it on bread instead of olive oil or butter or use it on pizzas and in pastas.

4 to 6 heads garlic

Cut off the top of each garlic head (the pointy side) to expose the cloves. Place the garlic in the slow cooker cut sides up. Cook on low for 3 to 4 hours. Let cool completely before squeezing the cloves from the skins.
Store in the fridge for up to 1 week.

Yield: 4 to 6 heads garlic

▶ *Recipe Variation*
You can also cook 1 or 2 heads of garlic in a 1 to 1½-quart (940 ml to 1.4 L) slow cooker.

PRESERVE-THE-HARVEST DICED TOMATOES

Here's an easy, free-form recipe. Give it a try, and you'll get that satisfied feeling when you use your handiwork in soups and stews later in the year. If possible, cook the tomatoes on the same day you buy or pick them.

Tomatoes to fill your crock

Rinse the tomatoes. To determine how many tomatoes will fit in your slow cooker, place tomatoes in the slow cooker one at a time until it is filled to the rim.
Remove the tomatoes. If desired, peel the tomatoes. Remove the top of the stem and any bruised or mushy parts. Dice the tomatoes. Place the tomatoes and their juice in the slow cooker. Cook on low for 6 to 8 hours or on high for about 3 hours. Let the tomatoes cool completely.
Transfer the tomatoes to freezer-safe containers or freezer-safe zip-top bags, carefully push the air out, and close.
If using bags, to prevent the bags from sticking together, wipe off the outside of the bags to make sure they're dry. So the bags will freeze flat, stack them in the freezer on top of one another.
To defrost, thaw overnight in the fridge. Or run cold water over the bag.

Yield: Depends on the size of the slow cooker

▶ *Recipe Note*
At the farmers' market, select tomatoes that are not overripe or mushy. They're sometimes called "ugly," "seconds," or another creative word to let you know why they cost less per pound than the perfect tomatoes. Many times you can buy these at one-third of the perfect tomato price, making it even more of a bargain.

If you use organic tomatoes, you don't need to peel the tomatoes. But if yours aren't organic, you can drop them in boiling water for a couple of minutes after making a small X in the bottom of each with a knife. Once they're cool enough to handle, the skins will slide right off. Dice and proceed as indicated.

PANTRY BASICS • 17

DRY BEANS FROM SCRATCH

If you're picky about what goes into your food, making beans from scratch is perfect for you. You can control how much salt, if any, goes into them. Even better, dry beans cost three to six times less than canned, so you're saving money, too! Use any kind of bean other than lentils or split peas. They cook much quicker than other beans, so you cook them in a dish, not in advance.

1 pound (454 g) dried beans

Rinse the beans. Remove any little rocks.
   Place the beans in a slow cooker. Add water to cover the beans by about 3 inches (7.5 cm). Cook on low for 6 to 8 hours or up to overnight. (After you cook the beans once in your slow cooker, you'll know if you need to use less water (about 2 inches [5 cm], instead of 3 inches [7.5 cm]). It will vary depending on how hot your slow cooker runs.)
   Using a slotted spoon, remove the beans.

Yield: 4½ to 5 cups (788 to 875 g)

▶ *Recipe Notes*
- Cook extra beans and freeze in bags to use later. You can freeze them in 1½-cup (340 g) portions so that it's easy to switch out a bag for a can of beans.

- Though all dry beans may look alike, beans that have been on the shelf (or in your pantry) a long time can take up to twice as long to cook completely. However, there is nothing wrong with eating them once they're cooked.

- Split peas and lentils cook much faster than larger beans such as pinto, black, and white. They're often added to a recipe dry, while the larger beans are cooked before they are added to other recipes.

- You can cook any beans in the slow cooker, but be aware that kidney beans can have a toxin called phytohaemagglutinin and need to be brought up to a boiling temperature to destroy the toxin. So boil them for 10 minutes before cooking in the slow cooker. This step is not necessary for other types of beans.

BUTTER CHICK'N

This full-flavored curry sauce can be served traditionally over a protein such as tofu, tempeh, or seitan. It also works great over steamed vegetables, beans, or rice.

2 tablespoons (30 ml) olive oil
1 large onion, minced
4 cloves garlic, minced
2 tablespoons (16 g) grated ginger
1 can (28 ounces, or 784 g) diced tomatoes or 3 cups (540 g) fresh chopped
1½ to 2 tablespoons (11 to 14 g) garam masala
1½ teaspoons cumin
⅛ teaspoon turmeric
Salt, to taste
¼ cup (60 ml) water
1 package (15 ounces, or 420 g) tofu, drained and cubed
3 tablespoons (42 g) butter
¼ cup (60 ml) milk
Chopped fresh cilantro
Brown basmati rice

In a skillet, heat the oil over medium heat. Sauté the onion for 3 to 5 minutes, or until it's translucent. Add the garlic and sauté for 2 minutes.
   In a slow cooker, combine the onion, garlic, ginger, tomatoes, garam masala, cumin, turmeric, salt, water, and tofu. Cook on low for 6 to 8 hours.
   Just before serving, add the butter and milk. Stir to combine and melt the butter. Taste and adjust the seasonings. Top with cilantro and serve over rice.

Yield: 6 servings

CHICK'N SEITAN

Making your own seitan takes less work than you might think. Plus, you can control everything that goes into it. This seitan is wetter than what you buy in the store. It's made especially for cooking again in a slow cooker recipe. It's not good for grilling, but it can be used in other recipes that call for gluten.

FOR THE BROTH:
7 cups (1645 ml) water
2 cloves garlic, crushed
2 bay leaves
1 stalk celery, minced
1 sprig parsley
1½ tablespoons (9 g) vegan chicken-flavored bouillon

FOR THE SEITAN:
1½ cups (352 ml) water
1½ cups (150 g) vital wheat gluten
⅓ cup (32 g) nutritional yeast
1 tablespoon (16 g) tomato paste

¼ teaspoon salt
1 tablespoon (4.3 g) dried thyme, optional
1 tablespoon (9 g) garlic powder, optional

To make the broth: In a slow cooker, combine all of the broth ingredients. Cook on high while you make the seitan.

To make the seitan: In a large bowl, combine all of the seitan ingredients. Mix until combined and knead for 5 minutes. You can use a mixer with a dough hook, or mix in a bread machine on the dough cycle for about 5 minutes. Let the dough rest for about 5 minutes.

Stretch the dough out to the desired thickness. Cut it into the desired sizes, such as 4 chicken breast–size pieces about the size of your palm or strips, nuggets, or medallions.

Drop the seitan pieces into the slow cooker with the broth. Cook on high for 2 to 3 hours, or until the pieces float to the top. It may look like they all stuck together, but once you take them out of the broth, they'll easily come apart.

Store in the fridge submerged in the broth, or freeze in the broth in recipe-size portions.

Yield: 1¾ pounds (795 g)

▸ *Serving Suggestions*
Use the chicken breast–shaped pieces in Chick'n Mushroom Casserole (see page 112).

Remember, you can make any shape you want. Try making them nugget shaped, then bread them and bake them in the oven for a perfect lunch box treat.

BEEFY SEITAN

This is great for the Veggie New Orleans Po' Boy (see page 70), pepper steak, and other traditional beef recipes. Grate it for barbecue or use like you would ground meat. It freezes well, and you can use any leftover broth in other dishes.

FOR THE BROTH:
7 cups (1,645 ml) water
2 tablespoons (30 ml) soy sauce
2 sprigs fresh rosemary

FOR THE SEITAN:
1½ cups (352 ml) water
2 cups (240 g) vital wheat gluten
⅓ cup (32 g) nutritional yeast
1 tablespoon (16 g) tomato paste
½ teaspoon garlic powder
¼ teaspoon black pepper
1 tablespoon (15 ml) soy sauce
2 tablespoons (30 g) ketchup (To make your own, see "Homemade Smoky Ketchup" on page 8.)
1 tablespoon (15 ml) Worcestershire sauce

1 tablespoon (16 g) hoisin sauce
2 tablespoons (30 ml) Kitchen Bouquet, optional (for color)

To make the broth: In a slow cooker, combine all of the broth ingredients. Cook on high while you make the seitan.

To make the seitan: In a large bowl, combine all of the seitan ingredients. Mix until combined and knead for 10 minutes. You can use a mixer with the dough hook, or mix in a bread machine on the dough cycle for about 10 minutes. Let the dough rest for about 5 minutes.

Stretch the dough out to the desired thickness. Cut it into the desired sizes, such as 4 steak-size pieces, or chunks, squares, or medallions. Or roll it into a small roast to shred for sandwiches.

Drop the seitan pieces into the broth in the slow cooker. Cook for 3 hours, or until the pieces float to the top. If you make very large steak or roast pieces, you'll need to turn them over with tongs, because their weight will make them sink to the bottom of the slow cooker, and they aren't likely to float up. It may look like they're all stuck together, but once you take them out of the broth, they'll easily come apart.

Store in the fridge in the broth or freeze in the broth in recipe-size portions.

Yield: 1⅔ pounds (754 g)

▸ *Did You Know?*
Kitchen Bouquet is a product that's used to add color to gravies. It works great on seitan as well.

APPLE SAGE SAUSAGE

This is a great way to make your own meatless sausage to use in other recipes. The texture is similar to Gimme Lean. You can cook it in the slow cooker in one large piece and crumble it in a food processor, or make patties with the uncooked mixture, and then cook on the stove top or in the oven. The crumbles and the cooked patties freeze great. This is great in the From-the-Pantry Pot Pie (see page 129), the Meatless Sausage and Mushroom Ragu (see page 134), or in any recipe with sausage crumbles.

1½ cups (248 g) cooked brown rice
1 cup (110 g) walnut pieces
1 cup (120 g) vital wheat gluten
2 tablespoons (12 g) nutritional yeast
1 cup (250 g) applesauce
2 tablespoons (14 g) ground flaxseed mixed with 2 tablespoons (30 ml) warm water
1 tablespoon (6 g) chicken-flavored bouillon
2 tablespoons (4 g) sage
1 teaspoon thyme

1 teaspoon oregano
1 teaspoon Hungarian paprika
½ to 1 teaspoon salt (Use less if your bouillon is salty.)
Black pepper, to taste

Coat the crock of a slow cooker with nonstick cooking spray.
    In a food processor, pulse the rice and walnuts until the mixture is coarsely ground but not puréed.
    In the slow cooker, combine the walnut mixture with the rest of the ingredients. Cook on high for 1½ to 2 hours.
    Transfer the mixture to a food processor. Break it down into small pieces and process until it crumbles.
    Store in the fridge for up to 1 week and longer in the freezer.

Yield: 6 to 8 servings

▶ *Gluten-Free Alternative*
Make this gluten-free by changing three things in the recipe. Leave out the vital wheat gluten and use 1½ cups (165 g) walnuts and 2 cups (330 g) brown rice instead of the amounts listed.
    Do not try to cook the gluten-free version in the slow cooker. Instead of using the slow cooker, oil a baking sheet and form the mixture into patties. Bake in a 350°F (180°C or gas mark 4) oven for about 15 minutes, and then turn them over and cook for 10 to 15 more minutes.

TEA-SCENTED TOFU

Here's an easy way to make a uniquely flavored tofu. Use your favorite marinades to design your own bold flavors. Lapsang souchong tea is a smoked tea, but you can use blackberry, jasmine, or any flavored tea you have on hand. Don't have any loose tea on hand? Tear open tea bags and use the tea in those instead.

1 package (15 ounces, or 420 g) firm tofu
4 tablespoons (14 g) loose black tea
4 tablespoons (12 g) uncoooked rice
4 tablespoons (60 g) brown sugar

Drain the tofu, and cut the block in half widthwise. Cut each half into 3 pieces, for a total of 6 pieces. On a clean dish towel, place 2 of the tofu pieces side by side and roll the towel over. Add 2 more on top of that and roll the towel again. Repeat one more time, and place on a flat surface. Place a large pan on top, and put something heavy in it, such as a bag of flour or rice, to press the tofu. Let the tofu sit for 10 to 15 minutes, and then unroll.
    Line the slow cooker crock with foil so the sugar doesn't burn on the crock and ruin it. Tear 2 to 4 long pieces of foil and arrange them like crosses inside the crock, so the pieces overlap.
    Spread the tea, rice, and sugar on top of the foil. Place a metal vegetable steamer basket into the crock over the smoking ingredients. Place the tofu slices on the steamer in a single layer, if possible. Cook on high for at least 2 hours. Reduce the heat to low and cook for 6 to 10 more hours. Turn the tofu over about halfway through.
    The longer you cook the tofu, the denser it will be. You can keep cooking it until it's almost a jerky consistency, so check it after 8 hours to decide whether you want to cook it longer.
    Store in the fridge for up to 1 week or freeze for up to 2 months.

Yield: 6 servings

▶ *Recipe Tip*
Try adding other flavors to the smoking mixture, such as anise, citrus zest, chiles, or cinnamon sticks. Get adventurous and smoke tempeh, seitan, and mushrooms to add a punch of flavor to your favorite dishes

VERSATILE LEAN AND EASY CHICKEN BASE

This recipe is an excellent and easy way to use the slow cooker to best advantage. It provides the bonus benefit of having cooked chicken on hand all of the time.

½ cup (120 ml) chicken broth or water
4 shallots, peeled and crushed
1 bay leaf
½ teaspoon black peppercorns
1 teaspoon salt
1 or 2 chickens (3 to 4 pounds, or 1,362 to 1,816 g each)

In the bottom of a 6- or 7-quart (5.7 or 6.6 L) slow cooker, combine the broth, shallots, bay leaf, and peppercorns.

Lightly salt the chicken all over and place in the slow cooker. Cover and cook on low for 7 to 9 hours, or until the chicken is cooked through.

Remove the chicken and allow to cool enough to handle. Remove the meat from the carcasses and discard all skin, cartilage, and bone. Dice or shred the chicken or cut away in whole pieces. Refrigerate or freeze the chicken in small portions. Remove and discard the bay leaf.

Yield: 3 to 4 cups (1,120 to 1,400 g) per chicken

▶ *Serving Suggestion*
Use cooked chicken to quickly make enchiladas, tostadas, tacos, wraps, hot barbecue chicken salads, cold mayo or tahini salads, quick chilis, and more. It's great with our Citrus Rum BBQ Sauce on page 7.

DUMPLINGS

Feel free to use this with other meat-and-gravy dishes if you like!

Gravy
¾ cup (71 g) ground almonds, or almond meal
½ cup (80 g) rice protein powder (Get this at your health food store. If they don't have it, they can order it.)
¼ cup (30 g) wheat gluten
2 tablespoons (28 g) butter
2 tablespoons (28 g) coconut oil
½ teaspoon salt
2 teaspoons baking powder
½ teaspoon baking soda
¾ cup (175 ml) buttermilk

In a large saucepan, bring the gravy to a boil.
In the food processor with the S-blade in place, pulse the almonds, protein powder, gluten, butter, oil, salt, baking powder, and baking soda to cut in the butter and evenly distribute it in the dry ingredients.

Transfer the mixture to a bowl.

Once the gravy is boiling, pour the buttermilk into the dry ingredients. Stir it in with a few swift strokes until the mixture is evenly damp and forms a soft dough. Don't overmix.

Drop the mixture by spoonfuls over the boiling gravy, cover the pot. Cook for 25 to 30 minutes.

Yield: 12 servings

17 Lightly Sweetened Autumnal Fruit Butter; 18 Perfect Pumpkin Purée; 19 Apple Butter; 20 Fall Harvest Fruit Butter; 21 Balsamic Onion Marmalade; 22 All-Occasion Roasted Garlic; 23 Preserve-the-Harvest Diced Tomatoes; 24 Dry Beans from Scratch

22 • THE LITTLE SLOW COOKER COOKBOOK

25 Butter Chick'N; 26 Chick'N Seitan; 27 Beefy Seitan; 28 Apple Sage Sausage; 29 Tea-Scented Tofu; 30 Versatile Lean and Easy Chicken Base; 31 Dumplings

PANTRY BASICS • 23

APPETIZERS

See pages 26-27, 32-33, and 36-37 for Appetizer recipe photos.

CHEESY SPOONBREAD

This is a moist, wheat-free (and therefore gluten-free) bread that you can actually eat with a spoon. It's warm, soothing, and satisfying and just begs to be enjoyed either on its own or as a side dish.

2 eggs
¾ cup (105 g) high-quality stone-ground cornmeal
1¼ cups (163 g) fresh corn kernels (or frozen, thawed)
⅔ cup (75 g) low-fat cottage cheese
2 tablespoons (30 ml) corn oil (or olive oil)
1 tablespoon (15 g) Sucanat or xylitol
2 teaspoons baking powder
Several dashes of hot pepper sauce, optional
½ teaspoon salt
½ cup (58 g) shredded sharp Cheddar cheese

Spray the insert of a 2-quart (1.9 L) slow cooker with nonstick cooking spray.

In a large bowl, beat the eggs. Add the cornmeal, corn, cottage cheese, oil, Sucanat, baking powder, hot pepper sauce, if using, and salt. Mix to combine.

Transfer the batter to the prepared slow cooker, cover, and cook on low for 2 to 2½ hours, or until the center is set. Sprinkle an even layer of cheese on top, cover, and cook for 5 to 10 minutes longer, or until the cheese melts.

Yield: 8 servings

▶ **Health Bite**

If this is the first time you've encountered the term gluten-free, a word of explanation is in order. Gluten is a protein, and it's found in grains such as wheat, rye, and barley. And it's a big problem for many people. When it becomes a huge problem, it's diagnosed as celiac disease, which is a condition in which the intestinal villi (tiny little projections that come out from the walls of the small intestine) are seriously damaged when they come into contact with gluten.

One in 133 people has full-blown celiac disease, but many more are affected with a much lesser version of this syndrome, which is usually called gluten sensitivity or gluten intolerance.

Symptoms of gluten intolerance can range all over the map, but when people who are sensitive to gluten stop eating it, their symptoms, which can include bloating, brain fog, aches, and pains, clear up almost immediately. Hence the huge explosion of gluten-free products on the market. Here we've created one of our own.

The cottage cheese in this recipe adds a nice protein boost! Hint: Just to be safe, avoid the GMO cornmeal and go for organic.

WHOLE-GRAIN CRUNCHY PARTY MIX

Party mix is a slow cooker favorite. This recipe has all of the spicy, satisfying crunch of the classic version.

2 cups (62 g) whole-grain Chex-style cereal
2 cups (62 g) whole-grain oat Chex-style cereal
2 cups (56 g) whole-grain "O's"-style cereal
1 pound (454 g) roasted mixed nuts, unsalted
1 cup (30 g) whole-grain mini pretzel twists or sticks
¼ cup (55 g) unsalted butter, melted
2 teaspoons Worcestershire sauce
1 teaspoon granulated garlic
1 teaspoon curry powder
¾ teaspoon garlic salt
½ teaspoon onion powder
½ teaspoon cayenne pepper

In a 6-quart (5.7 L) slow cooker, combine the cereals, nuts, and pretzels. Stir gently to combine.

In a small bowl, whisk together the butter, Worcestershire, garlic, curry, garlic salt, onion powder, and cayenne pepper. Drizzle over the cereal mixture. Fold very gently to coat without breaking the cereal. Cover and cook on low for 3 hours, frequently stirring gently. Remove the lid for the last hour of cooking time to aid with the drying. Or cook uncovered on high for 2 hours, stirring frequently.

Yield: about 2 quarts (775 g) or 16 servings

▶ **Health Bite**

Unfortunately party mix is usually made from conventional cereals. If that sugar hit weren't enough, most commercial mixes use refined white flour and high-fructose corn syrup. You can make your party mix better by buying natural and/or organic cereals.

We added nuts for their fiber, minerals, and monounsaturated fat (great for the heart), and we eliminated a whole lot of calories by halving the usual amount of butter (with virtually no sacrifice in taste or texture).

24 • THE LITTLE SLOW COOKER COOKBOOK

DARK CHOCOLATE TRAIL MIX FOR A CROWD
Trail mix is one of those really good-for-you things that you can easily get kids to eat–just don't tell them it's "health food." This recipe makes a really big batch, so get ready to share with friends!

1½ pounds (680 g) highest quality dark chocolate bark
12 ounces (336 g) highest quality dark chocolate
1½ pounds (680 g) roasted mixed nuts
6 ounces (168 g) juice-sweetened tart cherries
4 ounces (112 g) mini twist pretzels or Chex-style cereal, optional

In a slow cooker, layer the chocolates on the bottom. Pour the nuts on top and cover. Cook on low for 1½ to 2½ hours, or until the chocolate is fully melted. Start checking at 90 minutes. Stir gently to thoroughly mix.

Remove the insert from the cooker, uncover, and let cool for 30 minutes. Fold in the cherries. Gently fold in the pretzels, if using, and turn carefully with a spoon to coat all without breaking the pretzels.

Lay out two 2-foot (61 cm) lengths of waxed paper. Drop the mixture by tablespoonsful onto the paper. Allow to cool and harden completely.

Store in the fridge.

Yield: about 4 pounds (1.8 kg) (about 30 servings)

▶ *Health Bite*
Trail mix is a common item in every grocery store and comes with every possible mix of nuts, raisins, dried fruit, chocolate, and pretzels that you can imagine. We've even seen it in prepackaged "100-calorie snack" packs perfect for lunchboxes.

We use cocoa-rich dark chocolate because of the health-promoting flavanols in cocoa, which have been shown to support heart health and blood pressure. We also use tart cherries, which is a fruit that has gained a ton of attention from studies showing that it helps control body weight (in animals) and helps reduce inflammation (in people).

Use any nuts you like–all of them contain minerals and fiber and a dollop of protein for good measure. Remember, though, that this is, after all, a "candy," so it's higher in sugar and calories than many other treats. Moderation is the key to enjoying this wonderfully healthy mix of treats.

SWEET AND SPICY NUTS
These spicy little nuts will be a big hit. They'll keep for several weeks at room temperature, but we bet they won't last that long.

1 cup (140 g) cashews
1 cup (145 g) almonds, toasted
1 cup (100 g) pecan halves, toasted
½ cup (100 g) sugar
⅓ cup (75 g) butter, melted
1 teaspoon ground ginger
½ teaspoon cinnamon
¼ teaspoon cloves
¼ teaspoon cayenne pepper

In a slow cooker, place the nuts.

In a small bowl, combine the sugar, butter, ginger, cinnamon, cloves, and cayenne. Transfer the mixture to the slow cooker, stirring to coat the nuts. Cover and cook on low for 2 hours, stirring after 1 hour.

Lay out a large piece of foil and spray with nonstick cooking spray. Spread the nuts in a single layer on the foil. Let cool for at least 1 hour.

Yield: 22 servings

CINNAMON WALNUTS
These exquisite nuts are the perfect complement to fresh peaches, pears, apples, and strawberries. They're good together, and they're good for you.

FOR THE CINNAMON SUGAR:
½ cup (100 g) granulated sugar
2 tablespoons (14 g) ground cinnamon

FOR THE CINNAMON WALNUTS:
4 cups (1 pound, or 455 g) walnut halves
8 tablespoons (1 stick, or 112 g) butter, melted
½ cup (95 g) Cinnamon Sugar (see above)

To make the Cinnamon Sugar:
In a small bowl, stir the sugar and cinnamon together to combine.

Store the mixture in an airtight container in a cool place.

To make the Cinnamon Walnuts:
In a slow cooker, combine the walnuts and butter. Add the Cinnamon Sugar and stir until the walnuts are evenly coated. Cover and cook on high for 15 minutes. Reduce the heat to low and cook uncovered for another 1½ to 2 hours, or until the nuts are coated with a glaze, stirring occasionally.

Transfer the nuts to a bowl to cool completely.

Yield: 16 servings

1 Whole-Grain Crunchy Party Mix

APPETIZERS • 27

SPICED NUTS

These nuts have just enough heat to make them interesting. They make a great nibble while watching TV or when you need a little something while you prepare dinner.

½ pound (255 g) pecan halves
½ pound (255 g) cashews
¼ cup (55 g) butter, melted
1 tablespoon (7.5 g) chili powder
1 teaspoon dried basil
1 teaspoon dried oregano
1 teaspoon dried thyme
½ teaspoon onion powder
¼ teaspoon garlic powder
¼ teaspoon cayenne pepper

In a slow cooker, combine all of the ingredients. Cover and cook on high for 15 minutes. Reduce the heat to low and cook uncovered, stirring occasionally, for 2 hours.

    Transfer the nuts to a baking sheet to cool completely.

Yield: 32 servings

SUGARED PECANS

Many people have a special fondness for spiced and sugared nuts. This is about the easiest recipe ever, but it doesn't give up a thing in taste.

1 pound (455 g) pecan halves
¼ cup (55 g) butter, melted
½ cup (63 g) confectioners' sugar
¼ teaspoon ground cloves
1½ teaspoons ground cinnamon
¼ teaspoon ground ginger

Preheat a slow cooker on high for about 15 minutes.
    In the slow cooker, stir together the nuts and butter. Add the sugar, stirring to blend and coat evenly. Cover and cook on high for 15 minutes. Reduce the heat to low and cook uncovered, stirring occasionally, for about 2 to 3 hours, or until the nuts are coated with a crisp glaze. Transfer the nuts to a bowl to cool.
    In another small bowl, combine the cloves, cinnamon, and ginger. Sift the spice mixture over the nuts, stirring to coat evenly. Let cool completely.

Yield: 24 servings

CURRIED ALMONDS

Are you a party nut? Or do you just like serving them? Curried Almonds are a crunchy addition to chicken salad, curried rice, or your party table.

8 tablespoons (1 stick, or 112 g) butter, melted
1 tablespoon (6 g) curry powder
1 teaspoon salt
8 cups (2 pounds, or 910 g) blanched whole almonds

In a slow cooker, combine the butter, curry powder, and salt. Add the almonds and stir to coat evenly. Cover and cook on low for 2 to 3 hours. Increase the heat to high and cook uncovered for another 1½ to 2 hours, stirring occasionally.

Yield: 32 servings

▶ **Health Bite**
Almonds have almost as much calcium as milk. If that isn't enough to drive you to the store for a bag o' nuts, almonds are also high in the antioxidants selenium and vitamin E.

PARTY MEATBALLS

Variety is the spice of life. At your next party, treat your guests to this tasty twist on an old favorite–sweet-and-spicy meatballs.

1½ cups (480 g) raspberry jelly
½ cup (169 g) chili sauce
One 1-pound (455-g) bag frozen fully cooked meatballs, completely thawed

In a slow cooker, stir the jelly and sauce together. Add the meatballs. Stir to coat them with the sauce. Cover and cook on low for 3 1/2 to 4 1/2 hours or on high for 1 1/2 to 2 1/2 hours, or until the mixture is hot. Before serving, stir the meatballs to coat them with sauce again.

Yield: 6 servings

▶ **Recipe Tip**
You can easily double this recipe for a party or big crowd.

SPINACH ARTICHOKE DIP
If you're serving this at a party, once it's hot, turn the slow cooker to warm or low, and it will stay warm through the party. You may need to stir it every once in a while to prevent the top of the dip from turning brown and drying out. Serve it with fresh veggies, crackers, or toast points.

FOR THE CASHEW SOUR CREAM:
¾ cup (100 g) raw cashews
½ cup (120 ml) water
Juice of ½ lemon

FOR THE SPINACH ARTICHOKE DIP:
2 tablespoons (30 ml) olive oil
1 small onion, minced
1 clove garlic, minced
8 cups (10 ounces, or 280 g) fresh baby spinach, washed
1 recipe Cashew Sour Cream (see above)
Splash of water
1 can (14 ounces, or 392 g) artichoke hearts, packed in water, not marinated
⅓ cup (37 g) nutritional yeast
¼ teaspoon smoked paprika or plain paprika and a few drops liquid smoke
¼ teaspoon nutmeg (freshly grated, if possible)
Salt, to taste
Black pepper, to taste

To make the Cashew Sour Cream:
In a blender, purée the cashews, water, and juice until fairly smooth.
Store leftovers in an airtight container in the fridge.

To make the Spinach Artichoke Dip:
In a skillet, heat the oil over medium heat. Sauté the onion for 3 to 5 minutes, or until translucent. Add the garlic and spinach and sauté for 5 to 10 minutes, or until the spinach is reduced.
Coat the crock of a slow cooker with nonstick cooking spray. Add the spinach mixture, Cashew Sour Cream, water, artichokes, yeast, paprika, and nutmeg. Season with salt and pepper. Mix well. Cook on low for 1 to 1½ hours or on high for 30 minutes to 1 hour, or until thoroughly heated through.

Yield: 8 servings

▶ *Serving Suggestion*
Serve leftovers as a topping for pasta as a grown-up mac and cheese variation.

CRANBERRY MEATBALLS
The cranberries make this appetizer great for holiday parties. It's tasty enough for the rest of the year, too.

One 16-ounce (455-g) can whole-berry or jellied cranberry sauce
¾ cup (169 g) chili sauce
¼ cup (60 ml) water
Two 1-pound (455-g) bags frozen fully cooked meatballs, completely thawed

In a slow cooker, stir the cranberry sauce, chili sauce, and water together. Add the meatballs and stir to coat them with the sauce. Cover and cook on low for 3 to 4 hours. Stir the meatballs again, and serve them warm from the slow cooker.

Yield: 8 servings

▶ *Add It!*
Add 2 packed tablespoons (28 g) brown sugar and 1 teaspoon lemon juice to the sauce.

LOW-CARB SESAME TURKEY MEATBALLS
This recipe features kudzu, which one of the most interesting ingredients to come down the pike in a while. It's a plant that's native to China and Japan. Kudzu grows so fast, especially in the southern United States, that it's been nicknamed "the vine that ate the South." The sesame seeds and miso give this low-calorie turkey meatball recipe Japanese flair.

1½ pounds (680 g) ground turkey
1 egg, beaten
⅓ cup (5 g) finely chopped cilantro
2 tablespoons (16 g) toasted sesame seeds
1 tablespoon (6 g) minced fresh ginger
3 cloves garlic, minced
¼ teaspoon cayenne pepper
2 cups (470 ml) chicken broth
½ cup (120 ml) tamari
½ cup (120 ml) mirin
½ cup (125 g) white miso paste
1½ tablespoons (12 g) kudzu dissolved in 2 tablespoons (30 ml) chicken broth or water, optional

In a large bowl, combine the turkey, egg, cilantro, seeds, ginger, garlic, and cayenne. Mix gently and form 1½-inch (3.8 cm) meatballs. Do not over handle the meat.
Transfer the meatballs to a slow cooker.
In another bowl, whisk together the broth, tamari, mirin, and miso. Pour the mixture over the meatballs. Cover and cook on high for 3 to 3½ hours, or until the meatballs are cooked through and no pink remains.
Using a slotted spoon, remove the meatballs.

Transfer the liquid to a medium saucepan. Bring the mixture to a boil, add the dissolved kudzu, and stir for 1 to 2 minutes, or until thickened.
Serve the meatballs with the sauce.

Yield: 8 servings

SWEET AND SOUR HOT DOG BITES
These tasty little hot dog slices are always a hit as an appetizer. Serve them directly out of the slow cooker with toothpicks to use for retrieving them.

1 cup (340 g) grape jelly
½ cup (88 g) mustard
1 pound (455 g) hot dogs, sliced
8 ounces (225 g) pineapple tidbits

In a large microwave-safe bowl, microwave the jelly for about 30 seconds, or until thin. Stir in the mustard, hot dogs, and pineapple.
Transfer the mixture to a slow cooker. Cover and cook on low for 2 hours.

Yield: 16 servings

HONEY CHICKEN WINGS
These wings are sweet, with a sort of almost barbecue flavor. They're always popular, especially with people who don't like the heat of Buffalo wings.

3 pounds (1.4 kg) chicken wings
1 cup (340 g) honey
½ cup (120 ml) soy sauce
2 tablespoons (28 ml) olive oil
2 tablespoons (30 g) ketchup (To make your own, see "Homemade Smoky Ketchup" on page 8.)
½ teaspoon minced garlic

Rinse the wings and pat dry. Cut off and discard the wing tips. Cut each wing into 2 parts.
Transfer the wings to a slow cooker.
In a bowl, combine the remaining ingredients and mix well. Pour the sauce over the wings. Cover and cook 6 to 7 hours on low.

Yield: 16 servings

ASIAN CHICKEN WINGS
Asian-flavored wings cook easily in the slow cooker, soaking up lots of flavor in the process.

3 pounds (1.4 kg) chicken wings
1 cup (160 g) chopped onion
1 cup (235 ml) soy sauce
1 cup (225 g) brown sugar
2 teaspoons ground ginger
½ teaspoon minced garlic
¼ cup (60 ml) sherry

Lightly oil a broiler pan.
Rinse the wings and pat dry. Cut off and discard the wing tips. Cut each wing at the joint to make two sections. Place the wings on the prepared pan. Broil about 4 inches from the heat for 10 minutes on each side, or until the wings are nicely browned.
Transfer the wings to a slow cooker.
In a bowl, combine the onion, soy sauce, sugar, ginger, garlic, and sherry. Pour the sauce over the wings. Cover and cook on low for 4 to 5 hours or on high for 2 to 2½ hours. Stir the wings once about halfway through cooking.
Serve the wings directly from the slow cooker, keeping the temperature on low.

Yield: 16 servings

SWEET AND SOUR CHICKEN WINGS
These are a nice sweet and hot combination if you use the full teaspoon of hot pepper sauce. If you like them milder, feel free to reduce the amount.

3 pounds (1.4 kg) chicken wings
¼ cup (60 ml) balsamic vinegar
1 cup (330 g) apricot preserves
1 cup (240 g) ketchup (To make your own, see "Homemade Smoky Ketchup" on page 8.)
3 tablespoons (45 g) horseradish
1 cup (160 g) finely chopped onion
1 teaspoon hot pepper sauce

Rinse the wings and pat dry. Transfer the wings to a slow cooker.
In a bowl, mix together the remaining ingredients. Taste and adjust the seasonings. Pour the sauce over the wings. Cover and cook on low for 4 to 5 hours, or until the wings are tender.

Yield: 16 servings

QUESO DIP
This is a moderately spicy cheese dip. It's perfect with either vegetables or corn chips.

1 cup (160 g) chopped onion
2 tablespoons (28 g) butter
4 ounces (115 g) jalapeños, chopped
2 cups (360 g) chopped tomatoes, undrained
4 ounces (115 g) pimientos, chopped and drained
¾ cup (90 g) grated Cheddar cheese

In a medium saucepan, sauté the onion in the butter. Add the jalapeños, tomatoes, pimientos, and cheese and heat through.
    Transfer the mixture to a slow cooker. Cover and cook on low for 2 hours.

Yield: 12 servings

SPINACH DIP
This tasty Spinach Dip is a great appetizer. Or you can make a meal of it, serving it fondue-style with bread cubes and vegetables such as mushrooms and broccoli.

8 ounces (225 g) cream cheese, cubed
¼ cup (60 ml) whipping cream
1 cup (190 g) frozen chopped spinach, thawed and squeezed dry
2 tablespoons (24 g) pimiento, diced
1 teaspoon Worcestershire sauce
¼ teaspoon garlic powder
2 tablespoons (10 g) grated Parmesan cheese
2 teaspoons finely chopped onion
¼ teaspoon thyme

In a slow cooker, combine the cream cheese and cream. Cover and cook on low for about 1 hour, or until the cheese is melted. Add the remaining ingredients. Cover and cook on low 30 to 45 minutes.

Yield: 12 servings

TACO DIP
This creamy Mexican-flavored dip is great with corn chips. For a treat that's just as tasty and much healthier, try it with broccoli or other vegetables.

16 ounces (455 g) cream cheese
1 teaspoon onion soup mix (To make your own, see "Onion Soup Mix" on page 7.)
1 pound (455 g) ground beef
2 teaspoons Mexican seasoning
½ cup (58 g) shredded Cheddar cheese
¼ cup (38 g) finely chopped green bell pepper

In a bowl, combine the cream cheese and soup mix. Spread in the bottom of slow cooker.
    In a skillet, brown the beef and seasoning over medium-high heat. Place on top of the cheese mixture. Sprinkle with the Cheddar cheese and pepper. Cover and cook on low 2 to 3 hours.

Yield: 10 servings

MEXICAN DIP
Here's a great Mexican layered dip, made easy by the slow cooker. This is especially good with tortilla chips.

1 pound (455 g) ground beef
1 cup (160 g) chopped onion
2 cups (476 g) refried beans
1 tablespoon (7 g) Mexican seasoning
1 cup (230 g) sour cream
½ cup (58 g) shredded Cheddar cheese

In a skillet, brown the beef and onion over medium-high heat. Stir in the beans and seasoning.
    Transfer the mixture to a slow cooker. Spread the sour cream on top. Sprinkle with the cheese. Cover and cook on low for 1½ to 2 hours.

Yield: 20 servings

▶ *Serving Suggestion*
Sprinkle this Mexican Dip with jalapeno rings if you wish.

2 Dark Chocolate Trail Mix for a Crowd; 3 Sweet and Spicy Nuts; 4 Cinnamon Walnuts; 5 Spiced Nuts; 6 Sugared Pecans; 7 Curried Almonds

8 Spinach Artichoke Dip; 9 Party Meatballs; 10 Cranberry Meatballs; 11 Low-Carb Sesame Turkey Meatballs; 12 Sweet and Sour Hot Dog Bites; 13 Asian Chicken Wings; 14 Honey Chicken Wings; 15 Sweet and Sour Chicken Wings

GOURMET MUSHROOMS
Long, slow cooking gives these mushrooms great flavor.

1 pound (455 g) mushrooms
¼ cup (55 g) butter
1 cup (235 ml) chicken broth
¼ cup (60 ml) white wine
1 tablespoon (1.7 g) marjoram
1 tablespoon (3 g) chives

Place the mushrooms in a slow cooker.
 In a saucepan, melt the butter. Add the remaining ingredients. Stir until thoroughly blended. Pour the mixture over the mushrooms. Cook on high for 4 hours.

Yield: 8 servings

WINE-BRAISED ARTICHOKES
Don't let the looks of artichokes intimidate you. They are worth the extra effort to prepare them.

FOR THE ARTICHOKES:
4 whole, fresh artichokes
1 cup (235 ml) dry red wine
1 cup (235 ml) vegetable broth (or water)
1 teaspoon dried oregano
¼ teaspoon black peppercorns
¼ cup (25 g) chopped celery

FOR THE DIP:
¼ cup (60 g) plain Greek yogurt
¼ cup (60 g) mayonnaise
2 teaspoons lemon juice
2 teaspoons Dijon mustard
2 tablespoons (6 g) minced fresh chives
1 shallot, minced
¼ teaspoon salt
¼ teaspoon white pepper

To make the artichokes: Rinse the artichokes and trim off any thorny leaf ends. Slice off the stems at the base and remove any small leaves on the base.
 In a slow cooker, combine the wine, broth, oregano, peppercorns, and celery. Place the artichokes, bases down, into the cooker. Cover and cook for 4½ to 5 hours on low, or until the lower leaves pull away easily and the base is fork-tender.

To make the dip: Meanwhile, in a small bowl, whisk together the yogurt, mayonnaise, juice, mustard, chives, shallot, salt, and pepper until well incorporated. Adjust the seasonings to taste. Chill in the fridge for the flavors to develop while the artichokes cook.
 Serve the artichoke with the dip.

Yield: 4 servings

▶ *Artichokes 101*
To choose a fresh artichoke, look for a firm, heavy, medium green one with compact center leaves.
 To eat a steamed artichoke, pull the leaves off, dip lightly, and drag the base ends through your teeth, scraping off the tender pulp and discarding the tougher parts of the leaves.
 When all of the leaves are gone, scoop out the thistly fibers (choke) and enjoy the tender "heart" (base) and stem.

MEDITERRANEAN STUFFED GRAPE LEAVES
This beautiful dish tastes as great as it looks. The gentle heat of the slow cooker is absolutely perfect for cooking tender, delicate grape leaves. This dish would be right at home at a beach resort on the Greek Isles.

1 pound (454 g) ground lamb
1 small red onion, finely chopped
2 cloves garlic, minced
1 cup (165 g) cooked brown rice (Golden rose brown rice or brown basmati work well.)
⅓ cup (50 g) raisins
1 teaspoon salt
½ teaspoon black pepper
½ cup (48 g) chopped fresh mint
⅓ cup (80 ml) lemon juice, divided
About 48 grape leaves, drained and rinsed
2 teaspoons olive oil
1½ cups (353 ml) vegetable broth

Coat the crock of a slow cooker with nonstick cooking spray.
 In a large skillet over medium-high heat, cook the lamb, onion, and garlic for 5 to 6 minutes, stirring frequently, or until the lamb is cooked through with no pink remaining.
 Remove from the heat, drain off the excess fat, and fold in the rice, raisins, salt, pepper, mint, and 2 tablespoons (30 ml) of the juice.
 Place one grape leaf, shiny side down on a clean countertop. Place a heaping tablespoon (15 g) of the lamb mixture on the leaf, near the bottom on the stem side. Fold in the sides of the leaf over the filling and roll it from the wide bottom side upward.
 Place the roll, seam side down, against the side of the slow cooker insert.
 Continue to fill each leaf and pack them close together to prevent unrolling, stacking them in layers.
 In a bowl, whisk the remaining juice and the oil into the broth. Pour the mixture evenly over the stuffed leaves. Cover and cook on low for about 4 hours, or until the stuffed leaves are tender.

Yield: 12 servings

CLEAN AND TASTY PIZZA FONDUE

Fondue is back in style again and oh-so-cosmopolitan and vaguely European. Regular fondue is all cheese, and not even necessarily very good cheese. This modern, urbane "fondue" is very flavorful yet way lighter on the cheese, and spiked with ground turkey and tasty tomato sauce.

8 ounces (225 g) ground turkey
1 small yellow onion, finely chopped
4 cloves garlic, minced
1 can (28 ounces, or 784 g) crushed tomatoes
1 can (6 ounces, or 168 g) tomato paste
½ cup (120 ml) hot water
1 tablespoon (1.3 g) dried parsley
1 teaspoon Sucanat
1 teaspoon salt
1 teaspoon dried basil
1 teaspoon dried oregano
½ teaspoon red pepper flakes, optional
¼ cup (20 g) shredded Parmesan cheese
8 ounces (225 g) mozzarella cheese, cut into 1¼2-inch (1.3 cm) cubes
2 cups (480 g) baby carrots
½ loaf whole-grain or sourdough bread, cut into 1-inch (2.5 cm) cubes

In a large skillet, cook the turkey, onion, and garlic over medium heat for about 8 minutes, or until the meat is cooked though and no pink remains.
    Transfer the mixture to a slow cooker. Add the tomatoes, paste, water, parsley, Sucanat, salt, basil, oregano, red pepper, and Parmesan. Stir well to mix. Cover and cook on low for 3 to 4 hours, or until hot and melted.
    Stir and serve with the mozzarella, carrots, and bread for dipping.

Yield: 16 servings

▶ *Time-Saver Tip*
To save time, use 2 cans (15 ounces, or 420 g each) high-quality pizza sauce in place of the homemade (crushed tomatoes through oregano). If you do that, you may also want to add 2 crumbled links (4 ounces, or 112 g each) of Italian chicken sausage to the turkey for more flavor.

PIMIENTO CHEESE FONDUE

Serve this cheesy goodness with veggies and toast points for dipping. Or serve over whole pieces of toast to make an English main dish called rarebit. The recipe is easy to double (or even triple), if you have a large slow cooker.

1 can (15 ounces, or 420 g) white beans, drained and rinsed
¾ cup (180 ml) water
2 tablespoons (12 g) chicken bouillon
1 jar (2 ounces, or 56 g) diced pimientos, drained
2 cups (225 g) shredded Cheddar cheese
2 tablespoons (28 g) mayonnaise
½ teaspoon stone-ground mustard
Salt, to taste
Black pepper, to taste

In a food processor, purée the beans and water until smooth.
    Coat the crock of a slow cooker with nonstock cooking spray.
    Place the bean mixture and the remaining ingredients in the slow cooker. Cover and cook on low for 1 to 1½ hours, or until the cheese is fully melted, stirring the mixture about every 20 minutes during cooking to fully incorporate the cheese as it melts.
    If you prefer a thinner fondue, add water until it's the desired consistency.

Yield: 4 servings

▶ *Serving Suggestion*
Use leftovers as a sandwich filling, and grill your sandwich for a traditional Southern treat.

SUBTLY SPICY PEANUT FONDUE

Serve this fondue with crispy pan-fried tempeh strips, firm tofu cubes, tiny boiled potatoes, and lightly steamed veggies. You can leave it in the slow cooker, and it will stay warm during your party.

½ cup (130 g) peanut butter
1 can (14 ounces, or 392 g) coconut milk
1 clove garlic, minced
1½ tablespoons (12 g) fresh grated ginger
½ to 1 teaspoon soy sauce
¼ to ½ teaspoon ground chile (chipotle, cayenne, etc.)
½ to 1 teaspoon garam masala
1 tablespoon (8 g) cornstarch, as needed

Spray the crock of a slow cooker with nonstick cooking spray.
    In the slow cooker, combine the peanut butter, milk, garlic, ginger, soy sauce, ground chile, and garam masala. Cover and cook on low for 1½ to 2 hours, or until the dip is heated through.
    If the fondue is too thin, add the cornstarch and cook for 15 minutes longer.

Yield: 4 servings

▶ *Serving Suggestion*
Serve leftovers over rice and tofu for an easy meal.

16 Queso Dip; 17 Spinach Dip

36 • THE LITTLE SLOW COOKER COOKBOOK

18 Taco Dip; 19 Mexican Dip; 20 Gourmet Mushrooms; 21 Wine-Braised Artichokes; 22 Mediterranean Stuffed Grape Leaves; 23 Clean and Tasty Pizza Fondue; 24 Pimiento Cheese Fondue

APPETIZERS • 37

BREAKFASTS
See pages 40-41, 46-47, and 52-53 for Breakfasts recipe photos.

BASIC GRANOLA
Basic granola–or designer granola! Keep this recipe simple for a plain but delicious granola, or pump it up with antioxidants by tossing in your favorite combination of dried fruits, nuts, and seeds.

4 cups (300 g) old-fashioned rolled oats
½ cup (113 g) honey
3 tablespoons (45 ml) vegetable oil

Spray the crock of a slow cooker with nonstick cooking spray. In the slow cooker, stir the oats, honey, and oil together. Partially cover, propping the lid open with a twist of foil or a wooden skewer to allow the moisture to escape. Cook on low for 2½ to 3½ hours, or until the oat morsels are roasted dry and golden brown, stirring every 30 minutes.

Let cool. Store in an airtight container in the fridge.

Yield: 5 servings

▶ Recipe Notes
- When the granola has cooled, add in a total of 1 to 2 cups of raisins, shredded unsweetened coconut, chopped walnuts, slivered almonds, or shelled pumpkin or sunflower seeds. Mix and match your favorites!
- It's not easy to get a full day's requirement of vitamin E through food sources. Fortunately, manufacturers are starting to enrich vegetable oil with vitamin E. Enriched oil is a smart way to get your E because the body absorbs this fat-soluble vitamin best when it's consumed along with foods containing a fat such as vegetable oil. Vitamin E and vegetable oil. It's a natural.

MAPLE PECAN GRANOLA
Tired of burning granola when you make it in the oven? Making it in the slow cooker helps cook it just right. You still need to be around for a few hours to stir it, so it's perfect for a day when you are cooking other staples.

4 cups (320 g) rolled oats
1 cup (110 g) chopped pecans
3 tablespoons (21 g) ground flaxseed
¼ cup (60 ml) maple syrup
¼ cup (60 ml) olive oil
1 teaspoon vanilla extract

Coat the crock of a slow cooker with nonstick cooking spray. In the slow cooker, stir all of the ingredients together. Cook on high, uncovered, for 3 to 4 hours, or until the oats are no longer soft and are a golden brown. Stir every 15 to 20 minutes and every 10 minutes during the last hour.

Let cool completely.

Yield: 8 to 10 servings

MIXED BERRY AND ALMOND GRANOLA
This sweet, crunchy granola is delicious sprinkled onto yogurt or ice cream. You can eat it plain by the handfuls when you can't fix a proper breakfast. Use your favorite dried berries or raisins in this recipe.

3 cups (240 g) rolled oats
½ cup (55 g) slivered almonds
½ cup (60 g) dried berry blend
3 tablespoons (21 g) ground flaxseed
¼ cup (60 ml) agave nectar
¼ cup (60 ml) olive oil
1 teaspoon almond or vanilla extract
¼ teaspoon cardamom
¼ teaspoon nutmeg

Coat the crock of a slow cooker with nonstick cooking spray. In the slow cooker, stir all of the ingredients together. Cook on high, uncovered, for 3 to 4 hours, or until the oats are no longer soft and are a golden brown. Stir every 15 to 20 minutes and every 10 minutes for the last hour. Let cool completely before storing.

Yield: 8 servings

BREAKFAST APPLE CRUNCH

Apple Crunch for breakfast is appealing when the weather turns cold. The crunchy topping makes it all the more satisfying. Serve this crunch with milk or a dollop of whipped cream.

One 21-ounce (595-g) can cinnamon-and-spice apple pie filling
2 cups (244 g) Basic Granola plus a smidge more for garnish (See page 38.)
½ cup (60 ml) water
4 tablespoons (56 g) butter, cut into pieces

Coat the crock of a slow cooker with nonstick cooking spray.
    In the slow cooker, stir the pie filling, Basic Granola, water, and butter together. Cover and cook on low for 5 to 6 hours or on high for 2 to 3 hours.
    Sprinkle each serving with extra Basic Granola for added crunch.

Yield: 5 servings

▶ *Recipe Notes*
The Golden Delicious apple is one of the best apples for cooking and baking. Interestingly enough, it's not related to the Red Delicious, which is the best apple for snacking. Other common cooking and baking apples are the Jonathan, Granny Smith, and Rome.

BREAKFAST GRAINS

This great multigrain hot cereal cooks overnight while you sleep.

¼ cup (46 g) barley
¼ cup (25 g) bulgur
¼ cup (20 g) rolled oats
¼ cup (29 g) wheat germ
¼ cup (25 g) chopped almonds
1 teaspoon cinnamon
1 apple, chopped
3 cups (705 ml) apple juice
1 cup (235 ml) water

In a slow cooker, stir all of the ingredients together. Cover and cook on low for 10 to 12 hours.

Yield: 4 servings

▶ *Serving Suggestion*
Serve with milk and fruit, if desired. Or, switch grains or change the proportions as long as you have about a cup of grains total.

APPLE OATMEAL BREAKFAST PUDDING

Put this in the slow cooker before you go to bed, and you'll have a hot breakfast waiting for you when you get up.

2 cups (160 g) rolled oats
3 cups (705 ml) water
½ cup (115 g) brown sugar
1 teaspoon cinnamon
5 apples, peeled and sliced
2 tablespoons (28 g) butter, melted

In a slow cooker, combine all of the ingredients. Cover and cook on low for 8 to 12 hours.

Yield: 6 servings

EGGY SPICY WHOLE-GRAIN BREAKFAST BREAD PUDDING

This is a bread pudding with a difference. It's filled with healthful ingredients, plus, it actually tastes like bread pudding. As a bonus: It's incredibly easy to make!

1 teaspoon butter or coconut oil, softened
9 slices whole-grain bread
3 teaspoons ground cinnamon, divided
1 can (12 ounces, or 353 ml) evaporated milk
5 eggs
2 tablespoons (14 g) toasted wheat germ
2 tablespoons (40 g) maple syrup
¾ teaspoon vanilla stevia (such as NuNaturals)
¼ teaspoon ground cardamom
¼ teaspoon ground allspice
¼ teaspoon ground cloves

Lightly coat a slow cooker insert with the butter. Arrange the bread in layers, sprinkling 1 teaspoon of the cinnamon on top of each layer.
    In a medium bowl, whisk the milk, eggs, wheat germ, syrup, stevia, the remaining 1 teaspoon cinnamon, the cardamom, allspice, and cloves together until smooth. Pour the mixture evenly over the bread. Cover and cook on low for 6 to 8 hours, or until set. Remove the cover for the last 45 minutes of cooking time to evaporate the excess liquid.

Yield: 8 servings

▶ *Health Bite*
If you use whole grain bread, preferably sprouted grains such as Ezekiel brand bread, it will boost the fiber and nutrients in this dish. Using a generous helping of five eggs converts this into a high-protein breakfast. You can use evaporated skim milk instead of regular, which provides creaminess without the calories and adds even more protein to the mix. Cinnamon is well known to reduce the glycemic (sugar) impact of food. The only sweetener we use is a touch of syrup.

BREAKFASTS • **39**

1 Basic Granola; 2 Maple Pecan Granola; 3 Mixed Berry and Almond Granola; 4 Breakfast Apple Crunch; 5 Breakfast Grains; 6 Apple Oatmeal Breakfast Pudding; 7 Eggy Spicy Whole-Grain Breakfast Bread Pudding; 8 Strawberry Sourdough Bread Pudding

9 Pick-Your-Pleasure Breakfast Rice Pudding; 10 Fruit 'n Nutty Overnight Breakfast Groats; 11 Peach Almond Breakfast Polenta; 12 Breakfast Risotto; 13 Cranberry Vanilla Quinoa; 14 Big Pot of Oatmeal; 15 Carrot Cake and Zucchini Bread Oatmeal; 16 Pumpkin Pie Oatmeal

STRAWBERRY SOURDOUGH BREAD PUDDING
This sourdough bread pudding is filling and sweet, but it contains far less sugar and fewer calories than standard-issue bread puddings. You might want to finish this off with a dollop of Cinnamon Yogurt.

FOR THE BREAD PUDDING:
4 cups cubed slightly stale sourdough bread (¾- to 1-inch (2 to 2.5 cm) cubes)
⅓ cup (37 g) toasted sliced almonds
1 can (12 ounces, or 353 ml) evaporated milk
4 eggs
⅔ cup (160 g) Sucanat
1 teaspoon vanilla stevia (such as NuNaturals)
1 teaspoon ground cinnamon
½ teaspoon ground coriander
1½ tablespoons (11 g) toasted wheat germ
2 cups (340 g) sliced fresh strawberries

FOR THE CINNAMON YOGURT:
¼ cup (60 g) plain, low-fat Greek yogurt
¾ teaspoon ground cinnamon, optional
2 teaspoons honey

To make the bread pudding: Coat the crock of a slow cooker with nonstick cooking spray.
  In the slow cooker, place the bread and sprinkle with the almonds.
  In a medium bowl, whisk the milk, eggs, Sucanat, stevia, cinnamon, and coriander together. Pour the mixture evenly over the bread. Toss gently to coat. Sprinkle the wheat germ over all. Cover and cook on low for 4 to 5 hours, or until the pudding is mostly set. The pudding will set as it cools. Allow to cool to the desired thickness.

To make the cinnamon yogurt: In a small bowl, whisk the yogurt, cinnamon, if using, and honey together until very well mixed.
  Serve the bread pudding topped with the strawberries and a dollop of Cinnamon Yogurt, if using.

Yield: 10 servings

▶ *Health Bite*
All bread is not created equal. Researchers at the University of Guelph in Canada studied four types of bread, trying to determine the differences in health effects. They fed subjects either white bread, whole wheat bread, whole wheat bread with barley, or sourdough bread, and then measured indicators of how efficiently their bodies metabolized the carbohydrates, checking, for example, blood sugar and insulin levels. The results were dramatic: The people who ate the sourdough showed the most positive responses (i.e., blood sugar control) and— best of all—those positive responses continued after

eating a second meal later in the day that didn't include bread!
  Our sourdough bread pudding is filling and sweet with way less sugar (and fewer calories) than standardissue bread puddings. We added four eggs to beef up the protein content. The wheat germ adds extra fiber and vitamin E. Finish it off with a dollop of Cinnamon Yogurt

PICK-OUR-PLEASURE BREAKFAST RICE PUDDING
In this delicious breakfast pudding, nutritious brown rice cooks down into a creamy, sweet breakfast that's perfect to take to work in a Thermos. Change out the flavorings and fruit to match your favorites. The combinations are endless! A favorite is vanilla extract with raisins.

½ cup (85 g) short- or long-grain brown rice
1 cup (235 ml) milk
1 cup (235 ml) water
½ teaspoon vanilla, almond, or orange extract
½ cup (60 g) dried cranberries or raisins or chopped fresh apple or other fruit (See note below.)
2 tablespoons (30 g or ml) brown sugar, agave nectar, stevia, or maple syrup

Coat the crock of a 1½- to 2-quart (1.4 to 1.9 L) slow cooker with nonstick cooking spray.
  In the slow cooker, combine the rice, milk, water, extract, dried fruit (if using fresh, you can add it at the end), and sugar. Cover and cook on low for 6 to 8 hours. Stir and adjust the sweeteners to taste. Top with fresh fruit if using.

Yield: 2 servings

▶ *Recipe Note*
If using raisins or dried cranberries, replace the milk with another 1 cup (235 ml) water. Some raisins and dried cranberries contain ascorbic acid, which curdles milk.

FRUIT'N NUTTY OVERNIGHT BREAKFAST GROATS
Check out the combination of spices in this breakfast dish. If you like spice, these groats will quickly become one of your breakfast faves.

¾ cup (60 g) whole oat groats
¼ cup (20 g) whole wheat or rye berries
4 cups (940 ml) water
½ cup (75 g) whole raw almonds
½ cup (75 g) raw sunflower seeds
¼ cup (36 g) sesame seeds (raw or toasted)
1 cinnamon stick, optional
¼ teaspoon ground cardamom, optional

¼ teaspoon ground nutmeg, optional
¾ cup (110 g) fresh or dried berries of your choice (Try fresh blueberries or dried goji berries.)

In a 2-quart (1.9 L) slow cooker, combine the oats, wheat berries, water, almonds, sunflower seeds, sesame seeds, and, if using, the cinnamon stick, cardamom, and nutmeg. Cover and cook on low for 9 hours or overnight. Stir in the berries and let warm for 5 minutes.

Yield: 4 to 6 servings

▶ *Recipe Notes*
- If you can't find whole oat groats, use steel-cut oats (steel-cut oats are just chopped groats), which are readily available at most supermarkets, but you may need to decrease the cooking time—start checking at 6 hours.

- For sweeter oatmeal, stir in half a mashed banana or ½ to ¾ cup (123 or 185 g) unsweetened applesauce before serving. To sweeten with no added sugars, add ¼ cup (60 g) xylitol (or to taste) or 1½ teaspoons NuNaturals vanilla stevia.

- Oat groats also work as a savory dish: simply omit the sweet spices when cooking and season to taste with a small amount of tamari sauce before serving.

- They're also great with chopped chives or scallion stirred in, even for breakfast! To add a little more calcium and some friendly intestinal flora, stir 2 to 3 tablespoons (30 to 45 g) plain yogurt into individual portions of either the sweet or the savory version.

PEACH ALMOND BREAKFAST POLENTA

Move over, cream of wheat, it's time to add polenta on the breakfast menu. Try it as written—with almond meal and peaches—and then make up your own variations. Try cooking up pear and ginger polenta or berries and basil polenta to take advantage of the freshest fruit of the season.

½ cup (70 g) polenta
2 cups (470 ml) milk
¼ cup (25 g) almond meal
¼ cup (60 g) applesauce (See note.)
¼ teaspoon almond extract
2 sprigs thyme, optional
2 large peaches, peeled, cored, and chopped
2 to 4 tablespoons (30 to 60 ml) agave nectar or maple syrup
Minced thyme, for garnish, optional

Coat the crock of a 1½- to 2-quart (1.4 to 1.9 L) slow cooker with nonstick cooking spray.
   In the slow cooker, combine the polenta, milk, almond meal, applesauce, almond extract, thyme sprigs, and peaches. Cover and cook on low for 6 to 8 hours.
   Remove the thyme sprigs. Stir the polenta and add the agave to taste. (The amount of sweetener needed will vary with how sweet the peaches are.) Top with minced thyme, if using

Yield: 4 servings

▶ *Recipe Note*
Some applesauces contain ascorbic acid. Ascorbic acid, like lemon juice, will curdle milk. If yours contain it, replace the milk with water.

▶ *Recipe Variation*
Pour leftovers into an oiled pan and chill. Once it has set up, cut into triangles. Grill the triangles until warm. Serve with fresh fruit and additional agave nectar or maple syrup for brunch or dessert.

BREAKFAST RISOTTO

This delightful fruit-flavored rice dish is perfect for breakfast when you're looking for something a little different.

¼ cup (55 g) butter, melted
1½ cups (345 g) Arborio rice
3 apples, cored and cubed
1½ teaspoons cinnamon
⅛ teaspoon nutmeg
⅛ teaspoon cloves
⅓ cup (75 g) brown sugar
2 cups (475 ml) apple juice
2 cups (475 ml) milk

Coat the crock of a slow cooker with nonstick cooking spray.
   Pour the butter into the slow cooker. Add the rice and stir it around to coat it. Add the apples, cinnamon, nutmeg, cloves, and sugar. Stir in the juice and milk. Cover and cook on low 6 to 9 hours. Stir before serving.

Yield: 6 servings

CRANBERRY VANILLA QUINOA

Quinoa is a nice change of pace from plain old oatmeal. Did you know that quinoa is not a grain, but rather it's a seed? Plus, it's a complete protein, so it's a perfect way to start your day.

½ cup (86 g) quinoa
2½ cups (588 ml) vanilla-flavored almond milk, plus more as needed
¼ cup (30 g) dried cranberries (See note.)
½ cup (123 g) unsweetened applesauce (See note.)
½ teaspoon vanilla extract (or scrape 1¼ teaspoon vanilla paste from a split whole vanilla bean)
⅛ teaspoon stevia, optional
Slivered almonds

In a mesh strainer, rinse the quinoa to remove the bitter coating.
 Spray the crock of a 1 1½2- to 2-quart (1.4 to 1.9 L) slow cooker.
 In the slow cooker, combine the quinoa, milk, cranberries, applesauce, vanilla, and stevia, if using. Cover and cook on low for 6 to 8 hours. Stir the quinoa. Taste and adjust the seasonings and add more liquid if needed. Top with the almonds.

Yield: 2 servings

▶ *Recipe Note*
Some dried cranberries and applesauces contain ascorbic acid. Ascorbic acid, like lemon juice, will curdle milk. If yours contain it, replace the milk with water.

▶ *Recipe Tips*
- Try switching out different flavors of apple or pear sauce, or using fruit butters or purées.

- Some quinoa is pre-rinsed, but some is not. If you're using a new-to-you brand, always assume it is not rinsed, and rinse it yourself. There is nothing worse than throwing away a whole dish because it's too bitter to eat!

BIG POT OF OATMEAL

Oatmeal is underestimated in our opinion. It is full of nutrition, inexpensive, and as versatile as your imagination. Give it a little extra respect and feature it at your next brunch. Keep it warm in your slow cooker and add water as necessary to keep it loose. Set out a buffet of toppings, including fresh fruit, maple syrup, vanilla-flavored nondairy milk, chocolate shavings, toasted nuts, and dried fruit. It makes for a beautiful table and will satisfy your guests' appetites.

1 cup (80 g) steel-cut oats
5 cups (1,175 ml) water, plus more if needed
Milk
Fresh fruit or your favorite topping

Coat the crock of a slow cooker with nonstick cooking spray.
 In a slow cooker, combine the oats and water. If you will cook it longer than 8 hours or if your slow cooker runs a little hot, add more water. Cover and cook on low for 6 to 10 hours.
 Stir the oatmeal to get a consistent texture. Serve topped with milk and fresh fruit.

Yield: 6 servings

▶ *Recipe Variation*
If your slow cooker is older and cooks at a lower temperature, use 4 cups (940 ml) of water.

CARROT CAKE AND ZUCCHINI BREAD OATMEAL

This oatmeal is chock-full of vegetables, and it takes elements from carrot cake and zucchini bread. If you're trying to get rid of your zucchini surplus, or just sneak in some veggies into the kids, this is the oatmeal for you. You can use only carrots, or only zucchini, but the combination is the best. If you have picky eaters, you may want to peel the zucchini to get rid of any green specks they might notice.

½ cup (40 g) steel-cut oats
1½ cups (355 ml) vanilla-flavored almond milk, plus more if needed
1 small carrot, grated
¼ small zucchini, grated
Pinch of salt
Pinch of nutmeg
Pinch of ground cloves
½ teaspoon cinnamon
2 tablespoons (30 g or ml) brown sugar or maple syrup
¼ cup (28 g) chopped pecans

Coat the crock of a 1½- to 2-quart (1.4 to 1.9 L) slow cooker with nonstick cooking spray.
 In the slow cooker, combine the oats, milk, carrot, zucchini, salt, nutmeg, cloves, cinnamon, and sugar. Cover

44 • THE LITTLE SLOW COOKER COOKBOOK

and cook on low for 6 to 8 hours. Stir the oatmeal. Taste and adjust the seasonings, and add more milk, if needed. Top with the pecans.

Yield: 2 servings

PUMPKIN PIE OATMEAL
Do you love pumpkin? This oatmeal gets a nutritional boost from the pumpkin, but still tastes like dessert for breakfast!

½ cup (40 g) steel-cut oats
2 cups (470 ml) unsweetened vanilla-flavored almond milk
½ cup (125 g) pumpkin purée
½ teaspoon cinnamon
¼ teaspoon allspice
Pinch of ground cloves
Brown sugar
Chopped pecans

Coat the crock of a 1½- to 2-quart (1.4 to 1.9 L) slow cooker with nonstick cooking spray.
    In the slow cooker, combine the oats, milk, pumpkin, cinnamon, allspice, and cloves. Cover and cook on low for 6 to 8 hours. Stir the oatmeal to get a consistent texture. Top each serving with sugar and pecans.

Yield: 2 servings

▶ **Recipe Variation**
You can use any winter squash you have on hand in place of the pumpkin. Try acorn or butternut squash. They are the closest in flavor.

RASPBERRY YOGURT OATMEAL
Getting up early for a quick morning walk or run? Have this hot but refreshing breakfast waiting when you arrive home.

1½ cups (360 ml) water
¾ cup (56 g) old-fashioned rolled oats
¼ teaspoon salt
One to two 8-ounce (245-g) containers raspberry yogurt
1 cup (110 g) fresh raspberries

In a slow cooker, stir the water, oats, and salt together. Cover and cook on low for 7 to 8 hours.
    To serve, stir the oatmeal and divide it among 4 cereal bowls. Fold one-fourth of the yogurt into each serving. Top each serving with ¼ cup (25 g) of the raspberries.

Yield: 4 servings

▶ **Recipe Tips**
- *Add it!* Fold 2 tablespoons (16 g) slivered almonds into each serving of cooked oatmeal along with the yogurt.

- *Note:* Raspberries are an excellent source of vitamin C and potassium. In addition, studies show raspberries contain a phytochemical, ellagic acid, which may help prevent cancer. They also taste pretty good.

BIG POT OF GRITS
Grits are a staple in any Southern household. Everyone has his or her favorite variation. But contrary to popular belief, grits aren't just used in the South. If you are in an area where you can't easily buy grits, look for yellow polenta. Often they will be sub-labeled as corn grits. If you haven't tried grits before, don't be scared. They're very similar to polenta; in fact, the yellow ones are polenta. Serve this at a brunch with an assortment of toppings, such as bacon crumbles, Cheddar cheese, spicy pickled peppers, and roasted garlic. (To make your own, see "All-Occasion Roasted Garlic" on page 17.) Everyone loves mix-ins.

1 cup (140 g) white or yellow grits
5 cups (1,175 ml) water, plus more if needed
2 tablespoons (28 g) butter or 2 tablespoons (30 ml) olive oil
Salt, to taste
Black pepper, to taste
Shredded Cheddar cheese, optional

Coat the crock of a slow cooker with nonstick cooking spray.
    In the slow cooker, combine the grits, 5 cups (1,175 ml) of the water, and the butter. Season with salt and pepper. Add more water if you'll cook it longer than 8 hours or if your slow cooker runs a little hot. Cover and cook on low for 6 to 10 hours. Taste and adjust the seasonings. Top with the cheese, if using.

Yield: 4 to 6 servings

▶ **Recipe Variation**
Try putting leftovers in a shallow oiled pan and store them in the fridge. Later you can slice them into triangles and grill them. It makes a great meal topped with black beans and salsa.

17 Raspberry Yogurt Oatmeal

18 Pear and Cardamom French Toast Casserole; 19 Broccoli Egg Casserole; 20 Breakfast Casserole; 21 Mexican Egg Scramble; 22 Weekend Tofu and Hash Brown Breakfast Casserole

BREAKFASTS • 47

PEAR AND CARDAMOM FRENCH TOAST CASSEROLE

This is similar to bread pudding in texture, but the sausage and fruit add a breakfasty twist. Wake up and throw this together in the slow cooker. You'll have time to take a walk or read the paper while it cooks. It's a perfect weekend treat.

4 links breakfast sausages, cut into half moons, or 1 to 2 cups (110 to 220 g) crumbled precooked Apple Sage Sausage (See page 19.)
2 cups (470 ml) milk
3 tablespoons (45 g) unsweetened applesauce (See note.)
½ teaspoon cardamom
½ teaspoon cinnamon
½ loaf whole wheat bread, cubed (approximately 6 cups [300 g])
3 medium pears, peeled, cored, and chopped
Maple syrup

In a nonstick skillet, cook the sausage for 10 to 12 minutes, or until browned.

Coat the crock of a slow cooker with nonstick cooking spray.

In the slow cooker, stir the milk, applesauce, cardamom, and cinnamon together. Place the bread, pears, and sausage on top. Press down into the wet mixture. Cover and cook on high for 1½ to 2 hours. After 1 hour, press the bread into the wet mixture again to help it cook more thoroughly. Serve drizzled with syrup.

Yield: 4 servings

▶ *Recipe Note*
Some applesauces contain ascorbic acid. Ascorbic acid, like lemon juice, will curdle even nondairy milks. If yours contains it, cook with water instead of nondairy milk.

BROCCOLI EGG CASSEROLE

Eggs and veggies are a favorite breakfast combination. So this easy recipe is a popular favorite.

24 ounces (680 g) cottage cheese
10 ounces (280 g) frozen broccoli, thawed and drained
1½ cups (355 ml) egg substitute
⅓ cup (40 g) flour
¼ cup (55 g) butter, melted
3 tablespoons (30 g) finely chopped onion
2½ cups (288 g) shredded Cheddar cheese, divided

Coat the crock of a slow cooker with nonstick cooking spray.

In a large bowl, combine the cottage cheese, broccoli, egg substitute, flour, butter, onion, and 2 cups (225 g) of the cheese. Pour the mixture into the slow cooker. Cover and cook on high for 1 hour. Stir. Reduce the heat to low. Cover and cook for 2½ to 3 hours. Sprinkle with the remaining ½ cup (58 g) cheese.

Yield: 6 servings

BREAKFAST CASSEROLE

Breakfast is the most important meal of the day. After you taste this easy-to-make casserole once, you'll never skip breakfast again. It's addictively satisfying.

One 1-pound (455-g) bag frozen hash browns, partially thawed, divided
3 cups (338 g) shredded Cheddar or provolone cheese, divided
12 large eggs
1 cup (240 ml) water
½ teaspoon salt
¼ teaspoon black pepper

Coat the crock of a slow cooker with nonstick cooking spray.

In the slow cooker, spread out half of the hash browns. Top the hash browns with half of the cheese. Repeat with the remaining hash browns and cheese.

In a large bowl, beat the eggs with a whisk. Mix in the water, salt, and pepper. Pour the egg mixture into the slow cooker over the hash browns and cheese. Cover and cook on low for 8 to 9 hours.

Yield: 8 servings

▶ *Recipe Tips*
- *You don't have to thaw the hash browns unless they're rock-solid from sitting in your freezer. As long as you can sprinkle them into the slow cooker, you're good to go.*

- *Tip: Leftover Breakfast Casserole is excellent served sandwich-style between two slices of toasted bread. Cheese lovers can add a slice of melted cheese.*

- *Add it! Combine 12 ounces (120 g) bacon, cooked and crumbled, or 12 ounces (225 g) sausage, sliced and browned, with ½ cup sautéed chopped onion, and mix with the uncooked hash browns. For a richer casserole, substitute 1 cup milk for the water.*

MEXICAN EGG SCRAMBLE

These Mexican-accented eggs and sausage cook overnight while you sleep.

1 pound (455 g) breakfast sausage, cooked and drained
1 cup (160 g) chopped onion
1 cup (150 g) chopped green bell pepper
4 ounces (115 g) canned chopped green chilies, drained
2 cups (230 g) grated Monterey Jack cheese
4 cups (960 ml) egg substitute

Coat the crock of a slow cooker with nonstick cooking spray.
In the slow cooker, layer some of the sausage, onion, peppers, chilies, and cheese, repeating the layering process until all of the ingredients are used. Pour the egg substitute on top. Cover and cook on low 7 to 8 hours.

Yield: 12 servings

WEEKEND TOFU AND HASH BROWN BREAKFAST CASSEROLE

This is a breakfast worth waiting for. Go do some yard work, take a walk, or just relax while your breakfast is cooking. These cheesy potatoes are covered with a light tofu custard.

1 package (16 ounces, or 454 g) frozen hash browns (no oil added, if possible)
½ cup (58 g) shredded Cheddar cheese
1 package (12 ounces, or 340 g) silken tofu
½ cup (120 ml) plain coconut creamer or other nondairy creamer or milk
2 tablespoons (12 g) chicken-flavored bouillon
¼ teaspoon turmeric
⅛ teaspoon garlic powder
½ teaspoon salt
Black pepper, to taste
Paprika, to taste

Coat the crock of a slow cooker with nonstick cooking spray.
In the slow cooker, spread the hash browns over the bottom. Sprinkle the cheese on top.
In a blender, combine the tofu, creamer, bouillon, turmeric, garlic powder, and salt until smooth. Pour the mixture over the hash browns. Season with pepper and paprika. Cover and cook on high for 1½ to 2 hours, or until set, but still a little jiggly in the middle.

Yield: 4 servings

▶ *Try adding a layer of vegan sausage, leftover pesto, or some Italian seasoning to keep it interesting.*

SCRAMBLED TOFU WITH PEPPERS

Imagine waking up in the morning and having breakfast waiting for you. That's the real reason to make this quick dish in the slow cooker. Vary the veggies with onions, broccoli, and carrots for a change of pace.

1 package (15 ounces, or 420 g) tofu, drained and crumbled
½ to 1 cup (120 to 235 ml) water
1 clove garlic, minced
½ bell pepper, seeded and chopped
1 teaspoon turmeric
½ teaspoon chili powder
Dash of liquid smoke, optional
Dash of hot pepper sauce, optional
Salt, to taste
Black pepper, to taste
Fresh herbs of choice, minced, optional
Salsa, optional

In the slow cooker, stir the tofu, ½ cup (120 ml) of the water, the garlic, bell pepper, turmeric, chili powder, and liquid smoke and hot sauce, if using, together. Add the other ½ (120 ml) water if you'll cook it longer than 8 hours or if your slow cooker runs a little hot. Cover and cook on low for 6 to 10 hours. Drain any excess water from the mixture. Season with salt and pepper and top with fresh herbs or salsa, if using.

Yield: 4 servings

▶ *Recipe Variation*
Add leftover veggies, black beans and salsa, or even diced onion to make your own variation.

WESTERN OMELET

This makes big batch of breakfast. It's great if you have a number of people staying over because you can put it in the night before and have a nice hot breakfast with no work.

32 ounces (1 kg) frozen hash brown potatoes, divided
½ cup (75 g) chopped ham, divided
¾ cup (120 g) chopped onion, divided
½ cup (75 g) chopped green bell pepper, divided
12 eggs
1 cup (235 ml) milk

In a slow cooker, layer half of the potatoes, ham, onion, and peppers. Repeat with the other half. In a bowl, beat together the eggs and milk. Pour the mixture over the potato mixture. Cover and cook on low for 8 to 10 hours.

Yield: 10 servings

SLOW COOKER POACHED EGGS
It's amazing the things you can do with a slow cooker. Don't have an egg poacher or have trouble getting them cooked just right? Here's the slow cooker to the rescue!

2 eggs

Into a slow cooker, pour about ½ inch (1.3 cm) of tap water, as hot as possible. Cover and cook on high for 20 to 30 minutes.
　Coat two custard cups, one for each egg, with nonstick cooking spray. Break 1 egg into each cup. Place the cups in the cooker in a single layer. Cover and cook on high for 12 to 15 minutes if you like your yolks runny. You can test them by pressing each egg yolk gently with a spoon. When the white is firm but the yolk is still soft, they're done.

Yield: 2 servings

BREAKFAST BURRITOS
Here are some breakfast rollups, courtesy of the slow cooker.

4 eggs
⅓ cup (60 g) chopped and seeded tomatoes
¼ cup (25 g) chopped green onions
1 cup (115 g) shredded Monterey Jack cheese
4 flour tortillas

In a slow cooker, combine the egg substitute, tomatoes, and onions. Cover and cook on low for 2 hours. Add the cheese and cook for another 30 minutes to 1 hour, or until the cheese is completely melted and the eggs are set.

　Fill the tortillas with the egg mixture. Roll up to serve.

Yield: 4 servings

▶ *Serving Suggestion*
For even more Mexican flavor, top the burritos with salsa and sour cream or add a 4-ounce (115 g) can of chopped green chilies to the mixture.

EGGS FLORENTINE
Why should you cook eggs in your slow cooker? Sometimes you want a brunch dish that you can put in to cook and forget about while you do other things—and that will stay warm while people serve themselves. And it's also because eggs aren't just for breakfast anymore.

2 cups (225 g) shredded Cheddar cheese, divided
1 package (10 ounces, or 280 g) frozen chopped spinach, thawed and drained
1 can (8 ounces, or 225 g) mushrooms, drained
¼ cup (25 g) chopped onion
6 eggs, beaten
1 cup (235 ml) heavy cream
1 teaspoon black pepper
½ teaspoon Italian seasoning
½ teaspoon garlic powder

Coat a slow cooker with nonstick cooking spray. Spread 1 cup (115 grams) of the cheese on the bottom of the slow cooker. Layer the spinach, mushrooms, and onion on top.
　In a bowl, combine the egg, cream, pepper, Italian seasoning, and garlic powder. Pour the mixture into the slow cooker. Top with the remaining 1 cup (115 grams) cheese. Cover and cook on high for 2 hours, or until the center is set.

Yield: 4 servings

BROCCOLI-BACON-COLBY QUICHE

This crustless quiche is wonderful, but feel free to make any quiche recipe you have, minus the crust, in the same way. This recipe uses broccoli cuts that are bigger than chopped broccoli but smaller than florets.

2 cups (312 g) frozen broccoli florets, thawed and coarsely chopped, or a bag of broccoli cuts
2 cups (225 g) shredded Colby cheese
6 slices cooked bacon
4 eggs
2 cups (475 ml) Carb Countdown dairy beverage
1 teaspoon salt
1 teaspoon dry mustard
2 teaspoons horseradish
¼ teaspoon black pepper

Coat a 1½-quart (1.4 L) glass casserole dish with nonstick cooking spray.
Put the broccoli in the bottom of the casserole dish. Spread the cheese evenly on top of the broccoli. Crumble the bacon evenly over the cheese.
In a bowl, whisk together the eggs, Carb Countdown, salt, dry mustard, horseradish, and pepper. Pour the mixture over the broccoli in the casserole dish.
Place the casserole dish in a slow cooker. Carefully pour water around the casserole dish to within 1 inch (2.5 cm) of the rim. Cover the slow cooker and cook on low for 4 hours. Turn off the slow cooker, uncover it, and let the water cool until you can remove the casserole dish without risk of scalding your fingers. Serve hot or at room temperature.

Yield: 6 servings

SPICY HASH BROWNS

If you're looking for something to wake you up, try these spicy hash browns. They are heated up with pepper jack cheese and canned jalapeños. This dish will definitely help get you going in the morning.

5 cups (1 kg) frozen hash brown potatoes
1 cup (133 g) shredded pepper jack cheese, plus more if desired
½ cup (80 g) chopped onion
½ cup (75 g) chopped red bell pepper
4 ounces (115 g) canned sliced jalapeños
2 cups (475 ml) water

In a slow cooker, place the hash browns.
In a bowl, combine the cheese, onion, bell pepper, jalapeños, and water. Pour the mixture over the potatoes. Cover and cook on low for 8 to 9 hours or on high for 4 to 5 hours. If desired, top with additional cheese.

Yield: 8 servings

BREAKFAST COBBLER

Here's a simple and easy breakfast recipe. Depending on the size of your slow cooker and the number of people you are feeding, this can easily be doubled.

2 cups (220 g) sliced apple
2 cups (250 g) granola
1 teaspoon cinnamon
¼ cup (85 g) honey
2 tablespoons (28 g) butter, melted

In a slow cooker, combine all of the ingredients. Cover and cook on low for 8 to 10 hours.

Yield: 4 servings

▶ *Serving Suggestion*
This cobbler is great served with milk.

23 Western Omelet

24 Slow Cooker-Poached Eggs; 25 Breakfast Burritos; 26 Eggs Florentine; 27 Broccoli-Bacon-Colby Quiche; 28 Spicy Hash Browns; 29 Breakfast Cobbler

BREAKFASTS • 53

BREADS AND SANDWICHES

See pages 56-57, 60-61, 66-67, and 73-75 for bread and sandwiche recipe photos.

WHITE BREAD
This bread is plain and simple. It's a great base for toast or sandwiches.

Nonstick baking spray that contains flour
2¾ teaspoons (7 g) yeast
1¼ cups (295 ml) warm water, divided
¼ cup plus 1 teaspoon (55 g) sugar, divided
¼ cup (60 ml) egg substitute
¼ cup (60 ml) canola oil
3½ cups (438 g) flour, divided

Coat a 2-pound (900 g) coffee can with the nonstick baking spray.
  In a bowl, dissolve the yeast in ¼ cup (60 ml) of the water with 1 teaspoon of the sugar. Let it stand until bubbles form. Add the egg substitute, oil, the remaining 1 cup (235 ml) water, the remaining ¼ cup (50 g) sugar, and 2 cups (250 g) of the flour until well mixed. Stir in the remaining flour until the dough is workable.
  Place the dough in the prepared can. Place the can in a slow cooker. Cover and cook on high for 2 to 3 hours. Wearing oven mitts, carefully remove the can from the slow cooker. Let it stand for 5 minutes before removing the bread from the can.

Yield: 12 servings

ITALIAN QUICK BREAD
This bread is good with soups or salads. It's an easy way to get that Italian flavor without the usual work of traditional breadsticks.

FOR THE BAKING MIX:
6 cups (750 g) flour
3 tablespoons (41 g) baking powder
⅓ cup (75 g) butter

FOR THE ITALIAN QUICK BREAD:
1½ cups (180 g) Baking Mix (see above)
¼ cup (60 ml) egg substitute
½ cup (120 ml) milk
1 tablespoon (10 g) minced onion
1 tablespoon (13 g) sugar
1 teaspoon Italian seasoning
½ teaspoon garlic powder
¼ cup (25 g) grated Parmesan cheese

To make the baking mix:
In a bowl, stir the flour and baking powder together. Using a pastry blender or two knives, cut in the butter until the mixture resembles coarse crumbs.
  Store leftovers in a container with a tight-fitting lid in the fridge.

Yield: 12 servings

To make the Italian Quick Bread: Coat the crock of a slow cooker with nonstick cooking spray. In a bowl, combine all of the ingredients except for the cheese.
  In the bottom of the slow cooker, spread the mixture. Sprinkle with the cheese. Cover and cook on high for 1 hour.

Yield: 8 servings

WHOLE WHEAT BREAD
This is tasty bread, great for sandwiches or morning toast. 2 cups (475 ml) milk, warmed to 115°F (46°C)

2 tablespoons (28 ml) canola oil
¼ cup (60 g) brown sugar
2¾ teaspoons (7 g) yeast
2½ cups (300 g) whole wheat flour, divided
1¼ cups (171 g) bread flour, divided

Coat a bread or cake pan with nonstick cooking spray. Spray a sheet of foil with nonstick cooking spray to cover the pan.
  In a bowl, using an electric mixer, mix together the milk, oil, sugar, yeast, and half of each flour. Stir in the remaining flour.
  Place the dough in the prepared pan. Cover with the prepared foil. Place in a slow cooker. Cover and cook on high for 2½ to 3 hours. Let stand for 10 minutes before removing from the pan.

Yield: 8 servings

WHOLE GRAIN BREAD
This makes just about enough for a family meal. With just a little preparation time, you can have fresh bread even if you don't have a bread machine.

Nonstick baking spray that contains flour
½ cup (120 ml) water
1 tablespoon (12 g) yeast
¼ cup (60 ml) warm water
1 cup (235 ml) milk, warmed to 115°F (46°C)
½ cup (40 g) rolled oats

2 tablespoons (28 ml) oil
2 tablespoons (40 g) honey
¼ cup (60 ml) egg substitute
¼ cup (29 g) wheat germ
2¾ cups (330 g) whole wheat flour

Coat a deep metal or glass bowl or 1-pound (455 g) coffee can with nonstick baking spray.

In the bottom of a slow cooker, place the ½ cup (120 ml) water and a trivet or some crumpled foil. Preheat the slow cooker on high.

In a bowl, dissolve the yeast in the ¼ cup (60 ml) warm water.

In a separate bowl, combine the milk, oats, oil, honey, egg substitute, and wheat germ. Add the yeast mixture. Mix in the flour. Knead for about 5 minutes, or until smooth and elastic.

Turn the dough into the prepared bowl or can. Cover loosely with foil.

Wearing oven mitts, carefully place the bowl or can in the slow cooker on top of the trivet or crumpled foil. Cover and cook on high for 3 hours.

Yield: 8 servings

GRANOLA BREAD
This is a sweet bread that's good for breakfast or snacking.

2¾ cups (344 g) flour
¾ cup (150 g) sugar
4 teaspoons (18.4 g) baking powder
1 teaspoon cinnamon
½ cup (120 ml) egg substitute
1⅓ cups (315 ml) milk
¼ cup (60 ml) canola oil
½ teaspoon vanilla
1 cup (125 g) granola
¾ cup (131 g) chopped prunes

Coat a 3-pound (1⅓ kg) shortening can with nonstick cooking spray.

In a bowl, stir the flour, sugar, baking powder, and cinnamon together.

In a separate bowl, combine the egg substitute, milk, oil, and vanilla. Add to the flour mixture. Stir just until moistened. Fold in the granola and prunes.

Turn into the prepared can. Cover loosely with foil to allow for expansion of the dough.

Place the can in a slow cooker. Cover and cook on high for 3½ hours.

Wearing oven mitts, carefully remove the can from the slow cooker. Allow the bread to cool for 10 minutes in the can.

Yield: 12 servings

OAT BRAN BREAD
This is a really easy and delicious bread. It's good toasted, with cream cheese, or for sandwiches.

Nonstick baking spray that contains flour
2 cups (250 g) all-purpose flour
⅓ cup (67 g) sugar
1 teaspoon baking soda
1½ cups (120 g) rolled oats
1 cup (90 g) bran cereal, such as Kellogg's All-Bran
½ cup (75 g) raisins
½ cup (120 ml) egg substitute
1½ cups (355 ml) buttermilk
½ cup (170 g) molasses

Coat two 1-pound (445 g) coffee cans, a 2-quart (1.9 L) mold, or a 2-pound (900 g) can with nonstick baking spray.

In a bowl, mix the flour, sugar, baking soda, oats, cereal, and raisins. Add the egg substitute, buttermilk, and molasses. Mix well.

Pour the mixture into the prepared cans.

Place the cans in a slow cooker. Cover with 2 or 3 paper towels. With the slow cooker cover slightly ajar, cook on high for 3 hours, or until done. Let the bread stand in the can for 10 minutes and then turn it out onto a rack to cool completely.

Yield: 12 servings

TOMATO-HERB BREAD
This is a great bread to serve with soup or Italian food.

1 tablespoon plus 1 teaspoon (17 g) sugar, divided
⅓ cup (80 ml) water, warmed to 115°F (46°C)
2¾ teaspoons (7 g) yeast
4 cups (500 g) flour, divided
¼ cup (40 g) finely chopped onion
1 cup (245 g) tomato sauce
¼ cup (30 g) grated Cheddar cheese
¼ teaspoon black pepper
½ teaspoon dried oregano

Coat the crock of a slow cooker with nonstick cooking spray.

In a large, warmed bowl, stir 1 teaspoon of the sugar into the water. Sprinkle the yeast on top. Let stand for 10 minutes. Stir to dissolve the yeast. Add 3 cups (375 g) of the flour and the onion, sauce, cheese, pepper, oregano, and the remaining 1 tablespoon sugar. Using an electric mixer on low, beat the mixture to moisten, and then beat on high for 2 minutes. Add the remaining 1 cup (125 g) flour.

Turn the dough into the slow cooker. Using a spatula, smooth the top. Cover and cook on high for about 2½ hours. Using a knife, loosen the sides. Turn the bread out onto a rack to cool.

Yield: 12 servings

1 White Bread; 2 Honey Wheat; 3 Italian Quick Bread; 4 Whole Wheat Bread; 5 Whole Grain Bread; 6 Granola Bread; 7 Oat Bran Bread

8 Tomato-Herb Bread

CARROT BREAD

For people who like carrot cake but feel guilty eating it for breakfast, this is the solution. It's a great, easy-to-make bread that tastes like carrot cake.

Nonstick baking spray that contains flour
1 cup (125 g) all-purpose flour
1 cup (200 g) sugar
1 teaspoon baking powder
1 teaspoon ground cinnamon
½ cup (120 ml) egg substitute
½ cup (120 ml) canola oil
2 cups (260 g) grated carrots
½ cup (55 g) chopped pecans

Coat a 2-quart (1.9 L) mold with nonstick baking spray.

In a medium bowl, combine the flour, sugar, baking powder, and cinnamon.

In a separate bowl, using an electric mixer, beat the egg substitute until frothy. Drizzle in the oil. With the beater on low, add the flour mixture a little at a time. Fold in the carrots and pecans. Pour the mixture into the prepared mold.

Place the mold in the slow cooker. Cover loosely with a plate. Cover the slow cooker and prop the lid open a little to let excess steam escape. Cook on high for 2½ to 3½ hours.

Yield: 8 servings

CRANBERRY ORANGE NUT BREAD

This flavorful breakfast bread with cranberry and orange is great with cream cheese.

Nonstick baking spray that contains flour
2 cups (220 g) cranberries
½ cup (60 g) chopped walnuts
2 cups (250 g) all-purpose flour
1 cup (200 g) sugar
1½ teaspoons baking powder
½ teaspoon baking soda
6 tablespoons (85 g) butter
¼ cup (60 ml) egg substitute
1 tablespoon (6 g) grated orange zest
½ cup (120 ml) orange juice

Coat a 2-quart (1.9 L) mold or coffee can with nonstick baking spray.

Preheat a slow cooker on high.

In a food processor, grind the cranberries and walnuts with a coarse blade.

In a large bowl, combine the flour, sugar, baking powder, and baking soda. Using a pastry blender or two knives, cut in the butter to form a coarse mixture. Make an indent in the mixture. Add the egg substitute, zest, and juice. Beat only until lumps disappear. Add the cranberries and walnuts. Stir until evenly mixed.

Pour the batter into the prepared pan.

Wearing oven mitts, carefully place the pan in the slow cooker. Cover and cook for 3 hours. Let the bread cool in the pan for 15 minutes, and then remove and cool completely.

Yield: 12 servings

COCONUT BREAD

This sweet bread can be eaten as a dessert or spread.

Nonstick baking spray that contains flour
3 cups (375 g) all-purpose flour
1 tablespoon (13.8 g) baking powder
1 cup (200 g) sugar
1 cup (85 g) flaked coconut
¼ cup (60 ml) egg substitute
1 cup (235 ml) milk
1 teaspoon vanilla extract

Coat two 1-pound (455 g) coffee cans with nonstick baking spray.

In a bowl, mix the flour, baking powder, and sugar together. Add the coconut and mix thoroughly.

In a separate bowl, combine the egg substitute, milk, and vanilla. Stir the mixture into the dry ingredients. Mix well.

Press the batter into the prepared cans.

Place the cans in a slow cooker and cover the cans with 3 paper towels. Cover the slow cooker and cook on high for 3 hours, or until done.

Wearing oven mitts, carefully remove the cans from the slow cooker. Cool the bread on a wire rack for 10 minutes before removing it from the cans.

Yield: 8 servings

ZUCCHINI BREAD

This is a good sweet bread for breakfast or snacking.

½ cup (120 ml) egg substitute
⅔ cup (160 ml) canola oil
¼ cup (50 g) sugar
1⅓ cups (160 g) peeled and grated zucchini
2 teaspoons vanilla extract
2 cups (250 g) all-purpose flour
½ teaspoon baking powder
1 teaspoon cinnamon
½ teaspoon nutmeg
½ cup (55 g) chopped pecans

Coat a 2-pound (900 g) coffee can or 2-quart (1.9 L) mold with nonstick cooking spray.

In a bowl, using an electric mixer, beat the egg substitute until light and foamy. Add the oil, sugar, zucchini, and vanilla. Mix well.

In a separate bowl, combine the flour, baking powder, cinnamon, nutmeg, and pecans. Add the mixture to the zucchini mixture. Mix well.

Pour the batter into the prepared can or mold.

Place the can or mold into a slow cooker. Cover the top with 3 paper towels. Cover the slow cooker and cook on high for 3 to 4 hours.

Yield: 8 servings

BANANA BREAD
Have a few bananas that are past their peak? This bread is a good way to use them.

Nonstick baking spray that contains flour
3 bananas, mashed
½ cup (112 g) butter, softened
½ cup (120 ml) egg substitute
1 teaspoon vanilla extract
1 cup (200 g) sugar
1 cup (125 g) all-purpose flour
1 teaspoon baking soda

Coat a 2-pound (900 g) coffee can with nonstick baking spray.

In a bowl, combine all of the ingredients. Using an electric mixer, beat for 2 minutes.

Pour the batter into the prepared can. Cover the can with foil.

Place the can in a slow cooker. Cover and cook on high for 2 to 2½ hours. Let the bread cool before removing it from the can.

Yield: 8 servings

WHOLESOME CHOCOLATE CHIP BANANA BREAD
This traditional sweet banana bread is full of chocolaty goodness. It's great for a decadent breakfast or an easy dessert.

2 cups (240 g) whole wheat pastry flour
1 tablespoon (8 g) baking powder
½ teaspoon baking soda
2 tablespoons (14 g) ground flaxseed mixed with 2 tablespoons (30 ml) water
½ cup (120 g) applesauce
½ cup (100 g) sugar
2 tablespoons (30 ml) olive oil
1 teaspoon vanilla extract
3 bananas, mashed
1 cup (175 g) chocolate chips (Mini chips work great for this.)

Coat the crock of a slow cooker or a loaf pan with nonstick cooking spray.

In a large bowl, combine the flour, baking powder, and baking soda.

In a separate bowl, combine the flaxseed mixture, applesauce, sugar, oil, vanilla, and bananas. Add the dry mixture to the wet. Using a wooden spoon, stir until just combined. Stir in the chocolate chips.

Pour the mixture into the prepared loaf pan and place the pan into a slow cooker. Or pour the mixture directly into the slow cooker.

Cover the slow cooker, propping the lid up with a wooden spoon to allow the condensation to escape. Cook for 1½ to 2½ hours if cooked in the crock or 2½ to 3½ hours if cooked in a loaf pan, or until the center feels springy when touched. (If you cook it in a loaf pan, it will continue to cook a little more after you remove it from the slow cooker.)

Yield: 1 loaf

LEMON BREAD
This is a sweet bread with just enough lemon flavor. It's good for breakfast or just as a snack. Try it with cream cheese.

Nonstick baking spray that contains flour
½ cup (112 g) butter, softened
¾ cup (150 g) sugar
½ cup (120 ml) egg substitute
½ cup (120 ml) milk
1½ teaspoons baking powder
1⅔ cups (208 g) all-purpose flour
½ cup (55 g) chopped pecans
1 tablespoon (6 g) grated lemon zest

Coat a 2-pound (900 g) coffee can with nonstick baking spray.

In a bowl, using an electric mixer, cream together the butter and sugar. Add the egg substitute and beat well. Stir in the milk.

In a separate bowl, stir the baking powder and flour together. Add the dry ingredients to the wet ingredients. Stir in the pecans and zest.

Spoon into the mixture into the prepared can. Cover with foil.

Place the can in a slow cooker. Cover and cook on high for 2 to 2½ hours.

Yield: 6 servings

9 Carrot Bread

10 Cranberry Orange Nut Bread

CRANBERRY BREAD
You'll love this bread for breakfast, with nothing at all on it. It also makes a good companion to a salad with cranberries or other fruits.

1 cup (255 g) cottage cheese
½ cup (120 ml) egg substitute
1 cup (200 g) sugar
¾ cup (175 ml) milk
1 teaspoon vanilla extract
2¾ cups (345 g) Baking Mix (See page 54–Italian Quick Bread)
½ cup (60 g) dried cranberries

Coat the crock of a slow cooker with nonstick cooking spray. In a bowl, combine all of the ingredients. Spread the mixture in the bottom of the slow cooker. Cover and cook on high for 2 hours.

Yield: 8 servings

CITRUSY ROSEMARY BREAKFAST BREAD
Start the morning with an orangey treat that has a touch of pine from the rosemary. This bread is made with whole wheat pastry flour, so it's healthier than your average quick bread. This recipe uses sugar, but you can substitute agave nectar or maple syrup if you prefer. You'll just need to add a few more tablespoons of flour to make up for the extra moisture.

½ cup (100 g) sugar
2 cups (240 g) whole wheat pastry flour
1 tablespoon (8 g) baking powder
½ teaspoon baking soda
1 tablespoon (2 g) minced fresh rosemary
2 tablespoons (14 g) ground flaxseed mixed with 2 tablespoons (30 ml) water
½ cup (120 g) applesauce
2 tablespoons (30 ml) olive oil
½ cup (120 ml) orange juice
Juice of ½ lemon
1 teaspoon vanilla extract
1 teaspoon orange or lemon extract

Coat the crock of a slow cooker or a loaf pan with nonstick cooking spray.

In a large bowl, combine the sugar, flour, baking powder, baking soda, and rosemary.

In another bowl, combine the flaxseed mixture, applesauce, oil, orange juice, lemon juice, vanilla, and orange extract. Add the wet ingredients to the dry ingredients. Using a wooden spoon, stir until just combined.

Pour the mixture into the prepared pan or slow cooker crock. Cover the slow cooker, propping the lid up with a wooden spoon to allow the condensation to escape. Cook on high for 1½ to 2½ hours if cooked in the crock or for 2½ to 3½ hours if cooked in the loaf pan, or until a knife inserted into the center comes out almost clean. (If you cook it in a loaf pan, it'll continue to cook a little more after you remove it from the slow cooker.)

Yield: 1 loaf

▶ *Make half the recipe and put into silicon muffin cups. In a 5½- to 6-quart (5.2 to 5.7 L) oval slow cooker, you can fit 6 muffins. The cooking time will shorten to 1 to 1½ hours.*

BOSTON BROWN BREAD
This is the traditional accompaniment to Boston baked beans, but it's also good for breakfast with a little cream cheese.

½ cup (64 g) rye flour
½ cup (60 g) whole wheat flour
½ cup (70 g) cornmeal
3 tablespoons (39 g) sugar
1 teaspoon baking soda
½ cup (60 g) chopped walnuts
½ cup (75 g) raisins
1 cup (235 ml) buttermilk
⅓ cup (113 g) molasses

Coat the inside of three 1-pound (445 g) vegetable cans with nonstick cooking spray. Coat three pieces of foil with cooking spray to cover the cans.

In a bowl, combine the flours, cornmeal, sugar, and baking soda. Stir in the walnuts and raisins. In a separate bowl, stir the buttermilk and molasses together. Stir the wet ingredients into the dry ingredients until well mixed.

Spoon the batter into the prepared cans. Cover each can with a prepared piece of foil and fasten with a rubber band.

Place the cans in a slow cooker. Pour boiling water into the slow cooker to come halfway up the cans. Cover the slow cooker and cook on low for 4 hours.

Yield: 12 servings

▶ *Recipe Tip*
Rolling the cans on the counter and tapping on the sides will help to release the bread.

CORNBREAD

If you're trying to avoid last-minute preparation for a dinner party or holiday, make your cornbread in the slow cooker. It'll bake while you prepare the rest of the meal.

1¼ cups (156 g) all-purpose flour
¾ cup (105 g) cornmeal
¼ cup (50 g) sugar
4 teaspoons (18.4 g) baking powder
¼ cup (60 ml) egg substitute
1 cup (120 ml) milk
⅓ cup (80 ml) canola oil

Coat a greased 2-quart (1.9 L) mold with nonstick cooking spray.

In a bowl, stir the flour, cornmeal, sugar, and baking powder together.

In a separate bowl, combine the egg substitute, milk, and oil. Stir the mixture into the dry ingredients until just moistened.

Pour the batter into the prepared mold. Place on a rack or on top of crumpled foil in a slow cooker. Cook on high for 2 to 3 hours.

Yield: 6 servings

CHOCK-FULL-OF-VEGGIES CORNBREAD

This is a traditional Southern cornbread. It doesn't have any wheat flour in it, only cornmeal. The moisture of the zucchini replaces the oil to make it easy on your waistline, too. Cooking it in the slow cooker will make it extra moist. To make this a meal, serve thick and hearty, home-style beans over the cornbread.

1 tablespoon (15 ml) apple cider vinegar
1½ cups (355 ml) milk
2 cups (275 g) cornmeal
½ teaspoon salt
1½ teaspoons baking powder
½ teaspoon baking soda
1 tablespoon (7 g) ground flaxseed mixed with 3 tablespoons (45 ml) warm water
1 cup (132 g) fresh or frozen corn kernels
½ cup (75 g) chopped bell pepper
½ cup (60 g) shredded zucchini

Coat the crock of a slow cooker or a loaf pan with nonstick cooking spray.

In a bowl, combine the vinegar and milk. Set aside for 5 minutes.

In a large bowl, combine the cornmeal, salt, baking powder, and baking soda. Add the milk mixture, flaxseed mixture, corn, pepper, and zucchini to the bowl. Mix until combined.

If the zucchini is not providing enough moisture to combine the mixture, add 1 tablespoon (15 ml) water and mix again.

Pour the mixture into the prepared slow cooker crock or pan. Place the pan in the slow cooker. Cook on high for 2½ to 3½ hours if cooking in the crock or for 3½ to 4½ hours if cooking in the pan, propping up the lid with a wooden spoon to allow the condensation to escape. After 2 hours, stick a fork in the center and see if it comes out clean; if not, cook longer and check again. The center will still stay moister than it would if it were oven baked, but you will see a difference on the fork as it continues to cook. (If you cook it in a loaf pan, it'll continue to cook a little more after you remove it from the slow cooker.)

Yield: 1 loaf

SCRUMPTIOUS STRAWBERRY CORNBREAD

This sweet cornbread is great for breakfast. Like most baked goods cooked in the slow cooker, it's very dense and moist. You can substitute blueberries if you'd like.

1 cup (140 g) cornmeal
1 cup (132 g) whole wheat pastry flour
1½ teaspoons baking powder
½ teaspoon baking soda
½ teaspoon salt
6 ounces (170 g) yogurt
1 tablespoon (7 g) ground flaxseed mixed with 3 tablespoons (45 ml) warm water
3 to 5 tablespoons (45 to 75 ml) maple syrup or agave nectar
3 tablespoons (45 ml) olive oil
12 ounces (340 g) fresh or frozen strawberries, chopped

Coat the crock of a slow cooker or a loaf pan with nonstick cooking spray.

In a large bowl, combine the cornmeal, flour, baking powder, baking soda, and salt.

In a separate bowl, combine the yogurt, flaxseed mixture, syrup, oil, and strawberries. Add the wet ingredients to the dry ingredients. Stir to combine. If the strawberries don't provide enough moisture to combine the mixture, add 1 tablespoon (15 ml) water and mix again.

Pour the mixture into the prepared slow cooker crock or loaf pan. Cook on high for 2½ to 3½ hours if cooking in the crock or for 3½ to 4½ hours if cooking in the loaf pan, propping up the lid with a wooden spoon to allow the condensation to escape. After 2 hours, stick a fork in the center and see if it comes out clean; if not, cook longer and check again. The center will still stay moister than it would if it were oven baked, but you will see a difference on the fork as it continues to cook. (If you cook it in a loaf pan, it'll continue to cook a little more after you remove it from the slow cooker.)

Yield: 1 loaf

SAVORY CHEDDAR SAUSAGE BREAD
This savory quick bread has a nice herb flavor that's complemented by the bite of Cheddar cheese.

2 cups (240 g) whole wheat pastry flour
1 tablespoon (8 g) baking powder
½ teaspoon baking soda
¼ teaspoon salt
Black pepper, to taste
2 tablespoons (14 g) ground flaxseed mixed with 2 tablespoons (30 ml) water
2 tablespoons (30 ml) olive oil
1 cup (235 ml) milk
1½ cups (153 g) sausage, cooked, or Apple Sage Sausage (See page 19.)
1 cup (115 g) shredded Cheddar cheese

Coat the crock of a slow cooker or a loaf pan with nonstick cooking spray.

In a large bowl, combine the flour, baking powder, baking soda, and salt. Season with pepper.

In a separate bowl, combine the flaxseed mixture, oil, and milk. Add the dry ingredients to the wet ingredients. Using a wooden spoon, stir until it's just combined. Stir in the sausage and cheese.

Pour the mixture into the prepared slow cooker crock or loaf pan. Cover the slow cooker, propping the lid up with a wooden spoon to allow the condensation to escape. Cook for 1½ to 2½ hours if cooked in the crock or 3 to 3 1½2 hours if cooked in the loaf pan, or until the middle feels springy when touched. (If you cook it in a loaf pan, it'll continue to cook a little more after you remove it from the slow cooker.)

Yield: 1 loaf

WHOLE WHEAT PUMPKIN GINGERBREAD
This gingerbread gets a nutrition boost and fall flavor from the addition of pumpkin.

2 cups (240 g) whole wheat pastry flour
1 tablespoon (8 g) baking powder
½ teaspoon baking soda
1½ tablespoons (8 g) ground ginger
1 teaspoon cinnamon
½ teaspoon ground cloves
½ teaspoon allspice
¼ teaspoon nutmeg
¼ teaspoon salt
2 tablespoons (14 g) ground flaxseed mixed with 2 tablespoons (30 ml) water
1 cup (245 g) pumpkin purée
½ cup (170 g) molasses
½ cup (170 g) agave nectar or maple syrup
¼ cup (60 ml) olive oil
1 teaspoon vanilla extract

Coat the crock of a slow cooker or a loaf pan with nonstick cooking spray.

In a large bowl, combine the flour, baking powder, baking soda, ginger, cinnamon, cloves, allspice, nutmeg, and salt.

In a separate bowl, combine the flaxseed mixture, pumpkin, molasses, agave, oil, and vanilla. Add the dry ingredients to the wet ingredients. Using a wooden spoon, stir until just combined.

Pour the mixture into the prepared slow cooker crock or pan. Cover and cook on high, propping the lid up with a wooden spoon to allow the condensation to escape, for 1½ to 2½ hours if cooked in the crock or for 2½ to 3½ hours if cooked in the loaf pan, or until a knife inserted into the center comes out almost clean. (If you cook it in a loaf pan, it'll continue to cook a little more after you remove it from the slow cooker.)

Yield: 1 loaf

HONEY WHEAT BREAD
This makes great sandwich bread. It's soft and full of flavor.

2 cups (475 ml) milk, warmed to 1150F (460C)
2 tablespoons (28 ml) canola oil
¼ cup (85 g) honey
2¾ teaspoons (7g) yeast
3 cups (360 g) whole wheat flour, divided
¾ cup (86 g) wheat bran
¼ cup (29 g) wheat germ

Preheat a slow cooker on high for 30 minutes. Coat a baking pan with nonstick cooking spray. In a bowl, combine the milk, oil, honey, yeast, and half of the flour. Using an electric mixer, beat well for about 2 minutes. Add the remaining flour and the wheat bran and wheat germ. Mix well.

Place the dough in the prepared pan; cover.

Wearing oven mitts, carefully place the pan in the slow cooker. Cover and cook on high for 3 hours.

Yield: 8 servings

FOOLPROOF FOCACCIA

Bread and pizza aren't the first things most people think of when they think of using a slow cooker, but it's perfect for hot summer months, plus you can run errands while the dough is rising or the bread is cooking. This focaccia recipe is easy because it requires no kneading, and the dough lasts for 7 days. You can use a 5½-quart (5 L) oval slow cooker for this, but a round one will work, too. The size and shape of the slow cooker will determine the thickness of the focaccia.

1 tablespoon (12 g) or 1 packet dry yeast
1½ cups (355 ml) warm water (105° to 115°F (40.5° to 46°C))
½ teaspoon agave nectar or maple syrup
2 tablespoons (30 ml) olive oil, plus more for drizzling
2 cups (240 g) whole wheat flour
1 cup (120 g) white whole wheat or unbleached white flour
1¼ teaspoons salt
Coarse salt, optional
Dried or fresh rosemary, optional

In a large bowl, combine the yeast, warm water, and agave nectar. Let it sit for 5 to 10 minutes, or until you can see the difference in the mixture as the yeast grows, expands, and looks almost foamy. Add the oil, flours, and salt. Using a wooden spoon, stir until combined, or use a mixer with a dough hook. The batter will be very sticky.

Turn the dough out onto a floured cutting board. Separate the dough, depending on what you plan on making. This recipe makes one thick focaccia, but you can split it in half to make two thinner ones or into quarters to make four pizzas. (See "Perfect Pizza from Your Slow Cooker" on page 138.) Store any extra dough in a covered bowl in the fridge for up to 1 week.

Coat the crock of a slow cooker with nonstick cooking spray.

Shape the dough to fit the shape of the slow cooker. Place the shaped dough into the slow cooker. For focaccia, make indentions with your fingers or a fork, drizzle with more oil, and sprinkle with coarse salt and rosemary, if using. Cover and let the dough rise for about 1 hour with the slow cooker off.

Place a clean dish towel under the lid to absorb the condensation that will otherwise drip down onto your bread and increase the cooking time. Cover and cook on high for 1½ to 2 hours, or until the middle feels springy.

Yield: Dough for 2 focaccias or 4 pizzas

▶ *Serving Suggestion*
Top with All-Occasion Roasted Garlic on page 17 or your favorite marmalade or chopped fresh herbs.

FAJITAS

Get away from the frying and make fajitas the easy way with the slow cooker. The long cooking makes the meat both more tender and more flavorful.

1½ pounds (680 g) flank steak
1 can (14 ounces, or 400 g) diced tomatoes, undrained
1 jalapeño, seeded and chopped
½ teaspoon minced garlic
1 teaspoon coriander
1 teaspoon cumin
1 teaspoon chili powder
2 cups (320 g) sliced onion
2 cups (300 g) sliced green bell pepper
2 cups (300 g) sliced red bell pepper
1 tablespoon (1 g) fresh cilantro

Thinly slice the steak across the grain into strips. Place in a slow cooker. Add the tomatoes, jalapeño, garlic, coriander, cumin, and chili powder. Cover and cook on low for 7 hours. Add the onion, peppers, and cilantro. Cover and cook 1 to 2 hours longer, or until the meat is tender.

Yield: 6 servings

▶ *Serving Suggestion*

Serve on flour tortillas with sour cream and salsa.

FRENCH DIP

This recipe makes quite a bit. You can freeze the leftovers, or serve this when you're entertaining and impress everyone.

3 pounds (11/3 kg) beef round roast
2 cups (475 ml) beef stock (To make your own, see "Beef Stock" on page 6.)
2 tablespoons (15 g) onion soup mix (To make your own, see "Onion Soup Mix" on page 7.)
12 ounces (355 ml) beer

In a slow cooker, place the beef, stock, soup mix, and beer. Cover and cook on low for 7 hours. Slice the meat on the diagonal to serve.

Yield: 12 servings

11 Coconut Bread; 12 Banana Bread; 13 Wholesome Chocolate Chip Banana Bread; 14 Lemon Bread; 15 Cranberry Bread

66 • THE LITTLE SLOW COOKER COOKBOOK

16 Citrusy Rosemary Breakfast Bread; 17 Boston Brown Bread; 18 Chock-Full-Of-Veggies Cornbread; 19 Scrumptious Strawberry Cornbread; 20 Foolproof Focaccia

BREADS AND SANDWICHES • 67

SHREDDED BEEF
Use this versatile beef to make sandwiches, stir-fries, soups, and other savory meals.

3 pounds (1⅓ kg) boneless beef chuck
2 small onions, cut into thin wedges
1 teaspoon minced garlic
1¾ cups (410 ml) beef stock (To make your own, see "Beef Stock" on page 6.)
1 tablespoon (15 ml) Worcestershire sauce
2 teaspoons dry mustard
1 teaspoon dried thyme, crushed
¼ teaspoon cayenne pepper

Trim the fat from the beef. If necessary, cut the beef to fit in the slow cooker.
    In the slow cooker, place the onions and garlic. Top with the beef.
    In a medium bowl, combine the stock, Worcestershire, mustard, thyme, and cayenne. Pour the mixture over the beef in the slow cooker. Cover and cook on low for 11 to 12 hours or on high for 5 to 6 hours.
    Remove the beef and onion from the slow cooker, reserving the juices.
    In a bowl, using two forks, shred the beef, discarding any fat. Using a spoon, skim the fat from the juices. Add the onion to the beef along with enough juices to moisten the beef.

Yield: 12 servings

GREEK SANDWICH FILLING
Similar in flavor to a number of Greek and Middle Eastern dishes such as gyros, this sandwich filling is always popular. This recipe makes a large batch that's perfect for entertaining.

4 tablespoons (60 ml) olive oil, divided
4 pounds (1.8 kg) beef round steak, cut in ½-inch (1.3 cm) cubes, divided
2 cups (320 g) chopped onions
½ teaspoon minced garlic
1 cup (235 ml) dry red wine
1 can (6 ounces, or 170 g) tomato paste
1 teaspoon dried oregano
1 teaspoon dried basil
½ teaspoon dried rosemary
Dash of salt
Dash of black pepper
1 tablespoon (8 g) cornstarch
2 tablespoons (28 ml) water

In a skillet, heat 1 tablespoon (15 ml) of the oil. Brown 1 pound (455 g) of the beef. Remove the cooked beef to a plate. Repeat with the remaining oil and beef. Reserve the drippings.
    Transfer the beef to a slow cooker.
    In the skillet, sauté the onion and garlic in the drippings until tender.
    Transfer the onion and garlic to the slow cooker. Add the wine, paste, oregano, basil, rosemary, salt, and pepper. Cover and cook on low 6 to 8 hours. Increase the heat to high.
    In a small bowl, combine the cornstarch and water until smooth. Stir into the beef mixture. Cook until bubbly and thickened, stirring occasionally.

Yield: 16 servings

SIMPLEST BEEFY TACOS
You'll love these simple beef tacos.

1 pound (454 g) ground beef
1 yellow onion, finely chopped
4 cloves garlic, minced
2 serrano chiles, seeded and finely chopped
1 can (16 ounces, or 454 g) refried beans
1 cup (115 g) shredded sharp Cheddar cheese
1 jar (16 ounces, or 454 g) salsa
12 corn tortillas, warmed
2 tomatoes, chopped
2 cups (110 g) shredded lettuce
⅓ cup (77 g) sour cream
⅓ cup (5 g) chopped fresh cilantro

In a large skillet, sauté the beef and onion over medium-high heat for about 6 minutes, or until no pink remains. Add the garlic and cook for 1 minute, stirring frequently. Drain any excess oils.
    Transfer the contents to a slow cooker. Stir in the chiles, refried beans, cheese, and salsa. Cover and cook on low for 5 to 6 hours or on high for 3 to 4 hours, or until the mixture is cooked through and bubbling. Stir.
    Serve over the warmed tortillas with the tomatoes, lettuce, sour cream, and cilantro.

Yield: 6 servings

LOADED SLOPPY JOE WITH A KICK

Canned sloppy Joes? With unidentifiable meat, high-fructose corn syrup, and enough sodium to choke an artery? You can do better! You'll love these Sloppy Joes, featuring a fabulous mix of spices that evokes the Southwest and one of the healthiest sweeteners on Earth, blackstrap molasses. This unique, healthy slow-cooked Joe mix will knock your socks off!

1 pound (454 g) ground beef
1 yellow onion, finely chopped
6 cloves garlic, crushed and chopped
1 red bell pepper, cored, seeded, and finely chopped
1 jalapeño pepper, seeded and minced
1 chipotle pepper in adobo sauce, minced
1 can (14 ounces, or 392 g) black beans, drained and rinsed
1 can (14 ounces, or 392 g) fire-roasted diced tomatoes, drained
1 can (14 ounces, or 392 g) tomato sauce
1½ tablespoons (30 g) blackstrap molasses
1½ tablespoons (23 ml) apple cider vinegar
1 teaspoon ground cumin
1 teaspoon dried oregano
1 teaspoon chili powder (use ancho chile powder, if you have it)
1 teaspoon salt
½ teaspoon ground allspice

In a large skillet, sauté the beef and onion over medium-high heat for about 6 minutes, or until the beef is completely browned, with no pink remaining. Add the garlic and cook for about 1 minute, stirring frequently. Drain any excess oils.

Transfer the beef and onion to a slow cooker. Add all of the remaining ingredients and stir well to combine. Cover and cook on low for 5 to 6 hours or on high for 3 to 4 hours, or until the vegetables are tender.

Yield: 6 servings

▶ *Recipe Tips*
- *Use gloves when working with hot chile peppers, and be careful not to touch your eyes!*

▶ *Serving Suggestions*
A favorite healthy and delicious way to serve sloppy Joes is to ditch the bun and stuff the mix into crisp, raw or blanched red bell peppers or hollowed-out heirloom tomatoes (use a melon baller to empty them quickly). It's also great served over a bed of crisp, fresh hardy green lettuce such as chopped romaine hearts garnished with raw red onion. This Joe mix has a kick, so the extra raw veggies also help cool the bite.

QUICK SESAME TERIYAKI LETTUCE WRAPS

The prep time for these wraps is just a few minutes, and the slow cooker does the rest. It uses prepared teriyaki sauce, but there are dozens of high-quality, all-natural options in the prepared teriyaki sauce department. If you choose wisely, you'll have the best of both worlds– convenience and nutrition.

¾ cup (180 ml) teriyaki sauce
¼ cup (60 ml) water
1 teaspoon ground ginger
6 boneless, skinless chicken thighs
1 package (12 ounces, or 336 g) slaw mix (broccoli, carrots, and cabbage)
2 tablespoons (16 g) toasted sesame seeds
1 small head red-leaf or Bibb lettuce

In a small bowl, whisk together the teriyaki sauce, water, and ginger.

In a slow cooker, place the chicken. Pour the sauce evenly over the top. Cover and cook on low for 3 to 4 hours or on high for 2 to 3 hours, or until the chicken is cooked through and very tender. Using two forks, shred the chicken. Stir in the slaw mix. Cover and cook for 10 minutes. Stir in the sesame seeds.

Serve over individual lettuce leaves.

Yield: 6 servings

▶ *Health Bite*
The most wonderful thing about this "slow-cooked fast food" is that it is absolutely loaded with nearly raw veggies. It's also wrapped in lettuce, which is the classic low-carb alternative to those doughy flour wraps that sometimes pass for "healthy" because they've got a tiny bit of green coloring in them. Go with the lettuce, get some vitamin K in the bargain, and save a bunch of useless calories.

ASIAN TEMPEH LETTUCE WRAPS

In this case, iceberg lettuce can be your friend. Its mild flavor really lets the Asian filling stand out. This is the perfect food to make for a light summer dinner because the slow cooker doesn't heat up your house. You can have it ready and waiting for an after-work cocktail party.

1 package (8 ounces, or 225 g) plain soy tempeh, cubed
1 large stalk celery
2 medium carrots
1 can (8 ounces, or 225 g) water chestnuts, drained

FOR THE SAUCE:
2 cloves garlic, minced
1 tablespoon (8 g) grated ginger, plus more as needed
1½ cups (355 ml) water

¼ cup (60 ml) soy sauce
¼ cup (60 ml) seasoned rice vinegar (or plain rice vinegar mixed with 1 teaspoon sugar)
¼ teaspoon red pepper flakes or sriracha
Whole iceberg or butter lettuce leaves

In a steamer basket, steam the tempeh for 10 minutes. (This takes out some of the bitterness.) Meanwhile, mince the celery, carrots, and water chestnuts.

To make the sauce: In a large bowl, combine all of the sauce ingredients. In a slow cooker, combine the tempeh, celery mixture, and sauce. Using a spoon, smash the tempeh until it crumbles. Cover and cook on low for 6 to 8 hours. Taste and adjust the seasonings. Add an additional 1 teaspoon ginger if its flavor has dulled. Serve with whole lettuce leaves to wrap the filling in.

Yield: 6 servings

▶ *Serving Suggestion*
Use the filling to make a banh mi sandwich. Serve on a toasted sub roll with fresh bean sprouts, shredded carrots, cilantro, and some jalapeños.

VEGGIE NEW ORLEANS PO'BOY

Po' boys are a staple in New Orleans cuisine. But if you want a veggie one, it's time to make your own. This recipe re-creates the messy po' boy experience.

3 cups (330 g) cubed beef-flavored seitan or Beefy Seitan, divided (See page 19.)
2 cloves garlic, minced
2 cups (470 ml) water or broth from homemade seitan, plus more as needed
2 tablespoons (12 g) vegetarian beef-flavored bouillon
½ teaspoon Cajun seasoning, optional
Salt, to taste
Black pepper, to taste
2 to 4 tablespoons (16 to 32 g) flour or 1 to 1½ tablespoons (8 to 12 g) cornstarch, as needed
French bread

Thinly slice half of the seitan.
In a food processor, grate or pulse the remaining half until you have small ragged bits.
In a slow cooker, combine the seitan, garlic, water, bouillon, and Cajun seasoning. Season with salt and pepper. Cover and cook on low for 6 to 8 hours. About 20 minutes before serving, add extra water if the mixture has become dry. Add 2 tablespoons (16 g) of the flour or 1 tablespoon (8 g) of the cornstarch to the slow cooker and mix well. Cook for 20 more minutes. This should thicken the gravy. If it's not thick enough, add the remaining 2 tablespoons (16 g) flour or ½ tablespoon (4 g) cornstarch.
Serve on French bread.

Yield: 4 servings

▶ *Serving Suggestion*
Serve the Po' Boy on a soft French baguette. Add vegan mayo, lettuce, and tomato to make it "dressed."

PHILADELPHIA-STYLE CHEESY PORTOBELLO SANDWICH

This is a quick and easy sandwich filling that's ready when you get home. Add a salad or some pasta salad, and you have a casual dinner for friends with almost no work.

2 tablespoons (12 g) beef- or chicken-flavored bouillon
½ cup (120 ml) water
1 medium onion, cut into strips
2 large bell peppers, seeded and cut into strips
4 large Portobello mushrooms, sliced
Salt, to taste
Black pepper, to taste
1 tablespoon (8 g) cornstarch
6 whole wheat hoagie rolls, toasted
Shredded Cheddar cheese

Coat the crock of a slow cooker with nonstick cooking spray.
In a small bowl, mix the bouillon with the water. Pour the mixture into the slow cooker. Add the onion, bell peppers, and mushrooms. Season with salt and pepper. Cover and cook on low for 6 to 8 hours. About 20 minutes before serving, stir the cornstarch into the gravy and mix well. Cook for 20 more minutes to thicken the gravy. Taste and adjust the seasonings.
Spoon some of the hot sandwich mixture onto each toasted roll and top with the cheese.

Yield: 6 servings

TEMPEH TORNADO

Okay, so this is really just a Sloppy Joe, Manwich, or whatever they call a hearty meat sauce sandwich in your part of the world. It's easy to throw together in the morning before work and can easily cook all day. If you will be gone more than 9 hours, add a little more water. You can make half of the recipe in a 1½- or 2-quart (1.4 or 1.9 L) slow cooker if you don't want to make this much.

2 packages (8 ounces, or 225 g each) plain soy tempeh, cubed
3 cloves garlic
½ bell pepper
4 or 12 buns, for serving

FOR THE SAUCE:
1 can (28 ounces, or 784 g) diced tomatoes
½ cup (120 ml) water
1 tablespoon (6 g) chicken-flavored bouillon
1 tablespoon (16 g) tomato paste
1 tablespoon (15 ml) agave nectar or maple syrup
1 tablespoon (15 ml) apple cider, white, or wine vinegar
1 teaspoon molasses
1 teaspoon Worcestershire sauce
½ teaspoon liquid smoke
½ teaspoon cumin
½ teaspoon chipotle chile powder or smoked paprika
½ teaspoon pasilla chile or regular chili powder
½ teaspoon salt
¼ to ½ teaspoon hot pepper sauce

In a steamer basket, steam the tempeh for 10 minutes to take out some of the bitterness.

Meanwhile, mince the garlic and bell pepper.

To make the sauce: In a large bowl, stir all of the sauce ingredients together.

In a slow cooker, combine all of the ingredients. Cover and cook on low for 6 to 8 hours. Taste and adjust the seasonings.

For open-faced sandwiches, split 4 buns and top each of the 8 slices with one-eighth of the mixture.

For regular sandwiches, split 12 buns, top each bottom half with a smaller dollop of the mixture, and replace the top half.

Yield: 12 regular sandwiches or 8 open-faced sandwiches

TEXAS-STYLE TOFU TACO FILLING

Tex-Mex food is simple, nutritious, and filling. These tacos are easy to throw together, and you can use the filling for burritos, nachos, or any of your favorites. Depending on how much liquid is left, you may want to serve with a slotted spoon so you don't disintegrate your taco.

1 package (15 ounces, or 425 g) firm tofu, cubed
1 clove garlic, minced
Zest and juice of 1 lime
3 tablespoons (50 g) salsa
½ teaspoon chili powder
¼ teaspoon chipotle chile powder or smoked paprika
¼ teaspoon cumin
Hot pepper, to taste
Salt, to taste
6 hard corn tortilla taco shells, warmed

Coat the crock of a 1½- to 2-quart (1.4 to 1.9 L) slow cooker with nonstick cooking spray.

In the slow cooker, combine all of the ingredients, except for the taco shells. Cover and cook on low for 6 to 8 hours. Taste and adjust the seasonings. Serve in warmed corn tortilla shells.

Yield: 6 servings

▶ *Serving Suggestion*
Serve this with your favorite burrito.

MASHED POTATO AND EDAMAME BURRITO FILLING

Your family will love this healthied-up potato burrito.

4 large russet potatoes, peeled and cut into chunks
1 cup (235 ml) water
1½ cups (390 ml) mild salsa
1 pound (454 g) mix of corn, chopped red bell pepper, and edamame (Such as frozen mix from Trader Joe's.)
Salt, to taste
6 to 8 tortillas

Coat the crock of a slow cooker with nonstick cooking spray.
   In the slow cooker, combine the potatoes, water, and salsa. Cover and cook on low for 6 to 8 hours. About 1 hour before serving, using a potato masher or immersion blender, mash the potatoes. Add the vegetables. Season with salt. Cover and cook until heated through. Taste and adjust the seasonings. Serve the filling wrapped in tortillas.

Yield: 6 to 8 servings

▶ *Recipe Tip*
If you buy low-fat tortillas, it helps to steam them before rolling the filling in them. You can put them on top of the filling while it's in the slow cooker for a few seconds to soften.

BURST OF FLAVOR BUTTERNUT SQUASH AND PESTO PANINI FILLING

For this dish, select a butternut squash that's small enough to fit in your slow cooker whole. This recipe was inspired by a butternut squash panini that was made by Toast restaurant for the Bull City Vegan Challenge. Be sure to visit them if you are ever in Durham, North Carolina.

1 medium butternut squash
3 or 4 fresh sage leaves
4 fresh rosemary leaves
Leaves from 1 thyme sprig
½ cup (60 g) walnuts
2 tablespoons (15 ml) olive oil
¼ cup (48 g) nutritional yeast
12 slices bread

Poke holes in the squash. Cook it in the slow cooker on low for 6 to 8 hours, or up to overnight. No water or oil is needed.
   Remove the squash from the slow cooker and let cool for about 30 minutes, then store in the fridge.
   When ready to serve, remove the squash from the fridge and cut it in half. Scrape out the seeds. Scoop out 1½ to 2 cups (385 to 510 g) of the flesh to use for this recipe. Store or freeze the rest for another dish or to remake this one at a later date.
   In a food processor, pulse the herbs, walnuts, and oil until grainy but not puréed.
   In a bowl, combine the pesto, yeast and squash.
   Spread the mixture on 6 slices of bread. Top each with the remaining 6 slices of bread.
   Cook the sandwiches in a panini pan. Alternately, cook the sandwiches in a pan, setting a smaller, heavy skillet on top of the sandwichs to press them. You can also cook the sandwiches on a grill, setting a heavy object on top of the sandwiches to press them.

Yield: 6 servings

21 *Fajitas*

22 French Dip; 23 Shredded Beef; 24 Greek Sandwich Filling; 25 Simplest Beefy Tacos; 26 Loaded Sloppy Joe with a Kick; 27 Quick Sesame Teriyaki Lettuce Wraps; 28 Asian Tempeh Lettuce Wraps

74 • THE LITTLE SLOW COOKER COOKBOOK

29 Veggie New Orleans Po'Boy; 30 Philadelphia-Style Cheesy Portobello Sandwich; 31 Tempeh Tornado; 32 Texas-Style Tofu Taco Filling; 33 Mashed Potato and Edamame Burrito Filling; 34 Burst of Flavor Butternut Squash and Pesto Panini Filling

BREADS AND SANDWICHES • 75

MAIN DISHES

See pages 78-79, 84-85, 88-89, 94-95, 100-101, 106-107, 110-111, 114-115, 118-119, 124-125, 132-133, and 140-141 for main dishes recipe photos.

REAL DEAL BEEF STEW WITH ORANGE AND CLOVE
This recipe calls for chuck. It's a fattier meat, but you need that extra fat because it really helps the meat hold up better to the long cooking time. This rich and aromatic stew has a tender bite, enhanced by the delicious taste and texture of the molasses, and it will gratify your taste buds with its subtle hints of orange and clove.

1 red onion, left whole, peeled
8 whole cloves
1 pound (454 g) baby carrots
3 large parsnips, peeled and sliced
1 sweet onion, chopped
1½ pounds (680 g) leanest chuck (shoulder roast), cut into 1½ to 2-inch (4 to 5 cm) cubes
¾ teaspoon salt
½ teaspoon black pepper
1 can (14 ounces, or 392 g) sliced stewed tomatoes, drained
1 cup (235 ml) beef broth
2 tablespoons (40 g) blackstrap molasses
1½ tablespoons (23 ml) apple cider vinegar
3 cloves garlic, crushed and chopped
2 teaspoons orange zest
1 teaspoon ground coriander
¼ teaspoon ground cinnamon
⅓ cup (50 g) raisins

Stud the red onion evenly with the cloves and place it in a slow cooker. Add the carrots, parsnips, and sweet onion.

Season the beef with the salt and pepper and place it on top of the vegetables. Pour the tomatoes over the beef.

In a medium bowl, whisk together the broth, molasses, vinegar, garlic, zest, coriander, and cinnamon. Pour the mixture over the beef. Cover and cook on low for 5 to 6 hours or on high for 3 to 4 hours, or until the vegetables and beef are tender. During the last 30 minutes of cooking time, add the raisins. Remove the studded red onion before serving.

Yield: 6 servings

▶ Health Bite
You haven't lived till you've tasted real beef stew made in a slow cooker. We always recommend grass-fed meat because it is free of hormones, steroids, and antibiotics, and the fat is much higher in omega-3s (and much lower in inflammatory omega-6s), resulting in a far healthier meat. If you can't get grass-fed, at least go for organic, and if neither is available, choose the shoulder roast because it has the least fat of the chuck.

Beef remains the best source of iron as well as vitamin B12, which is critical for the metabolism of every single cell in your body! This rich and aromatic stew has a tender bite, enhanced by the delicious taste and texture of the iron-rich molasses, and will gratify your taste buds with its subtle hints of orange and clove.

Onions are one of the best sources of a terrific anti-inflammatory, anticancer plant compound called quercetin.

TANGY TOMATO GRASS-FED POT ROAST
When you make pot roast in a slow cooker, the extra fat slowly tenderizes the meat, making it "fall apart" tender. This pot roast uses a tangy, flavorful tomato sauce to jazz up the meat. The acid in the tomatoes and vinegar is a great tenderizer! And the flavors permeate the orange vegetables too. The veggies make the sauce so succulent you'll want to sop up every juicy bite.

1 large sweet onion, quartered
4 medium carrots, peeled, halved, and quartered lengthwise
1 large sweet potato, peeled and coarsely chopped
2 cups (300 g) peeled, seeded, and cubed butternut squash
1 can (14.5 ounces, or 406 g) tomato sauce
3 tablespoons (48 g) tomato paste
¼ cup (60 ml) apple cider vinegar
1 tablespoon (11 g) Dijon mustard
4 cloves garlic, minced
2 teaspoons minced fresh ginger
1 tablespoon (15 g) xylitol (or 2 teaspoons [10 g] Sucanat)
½ teaspoon salt
½ teaspoon black pepper
½ teaspoon ground cumin
½ teaspoon ground turmeric
¼ teaspoon cayenne pepper
⅛ teaspoon ground cloves
2 to 2½ pounds (910 to 1,135 g) boneless chuck roast

In a slow cooker, combine the onion, carrots, potato, and squash.

In a medium bowl, whisk together the sauce, paste, vinegar, mustard, garlic, ginger, xylitol, salt, pepper, cumin, turmeric, cayenne, and cloves until well combined.

Place the roast on top of the vegetables. Carefully pour

76 • THE LITTLE SLOW COOKER COOKBOOK

the sauce over all. Cover and cook on low for 6 to 8 hours or on high for 4 hours, or until the roast is tender and cooked through.

Yield: 6 to 7 servings

▶ *Serving Suggestion*
Try this dish served over hot jasmine rice.

▶ *Health Bite*
Everything you ever heard about meat being bad for you came from studies where people ate processed meat (such as bologna, salami, hot dogs, and other deli specialties) and regular factory-farmed meat (loaded with antibiotics, steroids, and hormones). Grass-fed beef is raised on its normal diet of pasture, has a completely different fat makeup, has no hormones, steroids, or antibiotics, and tastes 100 percent better.
  As far as availability, you can usually find it at farmers' markets, although more and more health-conscious grocery stores (at least in big cities) are now carrying it as well.
  You can also order online from companies like U.S. Wellness Meats at www.grasslandbeef.com. Grass-fed has a higher concentration of omega-3 fats, its CLA content (conjugated linolenic acid–a fat that has anticancer activity), and its lack of all the stuff that makes conventional meat unhealthy.

BEEF WITH BUTTERNUT SQUASH AND CHERRIES
Beef and cherries? It's an unusual–but delicious–combination. When you cook inexpensive tougher cuts of meat in a slow cooker, they almost magically become fall-apart tender. It's delightful that delicious gravies and sauces develop on their own while the meat cooks.

12 ounces (336 g) frozen dark cherries
1 medium butternut squash, peeled, seeded, quartered, and sliced
1 large sweet onion, sliced
½ cup (60 g) dried, juice-sweetened tart cherries
1¼ pounds (568 g) cubed stew beef
1 can (14 ounces, or 392 g) diced tomatoes, undrained
2 tablespoons (30 g) quick-cooking tapioca
2 teaspoons tart cherry or apple butter, unsweetened, optional
¾ teaspoon salt
½ teaspoon black pepper
¼ teaspoon ground cinnamon

In a slow cooker, combine the frozen cherries, squash, onion, and dried cherries. Top with the beef.
  In a medium bowl, stir the tomatoes, tapioca, cherry butter, if using, salt, pepper, and cinnamon together to thoroughly combine. Pour the mixture over the beef in the slow cooker. Cover and cook on low for 5 to 6 hours or on high for 4 to 5 hours, or until the beef is cooked through but still moist and the squash is tender.

Yield: 6 servings

MUSHROOM POT ROAST
The slow cooker reigns supreme when it comes to preparing meats and meaty stews. In this recipe, if the meat were cut up, we'd call this more of a stew than a pot roast. Whatever you call it, the onion flavoring and beer make a great-tasting meal.

1 pound (455 g) mushrooms, sliced
3 pounds (1⅓ kg) beef round roast
2 tablespoons (15 g) onion soup mix (To make your own, see "Onion Soup Mix" on page 7.)
12 ounces (355 ml) beer
½ teaspoon black pepper

In a slow cooker, place the mushrooms. Set the beef on top of the mushrooms. Sprinkle the soup mix over the beef and pour the beer over everything. Season with the pepper. Cover and cook on low 9 to 10 hours, or until the beef easily pulls apart with a fork.

Yield: 9 servings

BEEF BURGUNDY IN HUNTER SAUCE
This is a simple yet elegant roast beef coddled in a sensational onion-wine sauce. Enjoy it with garlic potatoes and dinner rolls.

One 3- to 4-pound (1.4- to 1.8-kg) beef roast
¾ cup (175 ml) water
½ cup (120 ml) dry red wine
One 1.1-ounce (31-g) envelope hunter sauce mix or onion soup mix (To make your own, see "Onion Soup Mix" on page 7.)

In a slow cooker, place the beef.
  In a small bowl, combine the water, wine, and sauce mix. Pour the mixture over the beef in the slow cooker. Cover and cook on low for 8 to 10 hours, or until the beef is cooked.

Yield: 12 servings

1 Real Deal Beef Stew with Orange and Clove; 2 Tangy Tomato Grass-Fed Pot Roast; 3 Beef with Butternut Squash and Cherries; 4 Mushroom Pot Roast; 5 Beef Burgundy in Hunter Sauce; 6 Orange Onion Pot Roast; 7 Beef Biryani; 8 Braised Beef in Red Wine

9 Steak Rollups with Asparagus; 10 Savory Slow-Cooked Meat Loaf; 11 Swiss Steak; 12 Smothered Steak; 13 Beef with Gravy; 14 Quick Stroganoff; 15 Barbecued Short Ribs; 16 Short Ribs

MAIN DISHES • 79

ORANGE ONION POT ROAST

Here's a classic pot roast with a twist. Beef and orange are great flavor buddies, and the onions make a tasty accompaniment. The slow cooker captures the abundance of juices and tasty bits of meat as the roast is slowly cooked to perfection.

3 medium onions, thinly sliced
2 tablespoons (60 ml) olive oil
1 beef pot roast (about 3 pounds or 1365 g)
Salt, to taste
Black pepper, to taste
1 cup (320 g) orange marmalade
½ cup (120 ml) water

In a slow cooker, place the onions.
    In a sauté pan, heat the oil over medium-high heat. Season the beef with salt and pepper. Sear in the sauté pan on all sides to brown.
    Transfer the beef to the slow cooker. Spread the marmalade over the beef. Add the water. Cover and cook on low for 8 hours.
    Remove the beef from the slow cooker and slice thin. Serve the beef with the onions and pan juices.

Yield: 4 to 6 servings

BEEF BIRYANI

You'll love the rich taste that beef imparts to Indian biryani, which is already filled with savory spices. Slow cooking lets the meat infuse with those multilayered flavors, and cool yogurt is the perfect accompaniment.

1 large yellow onion, quartered
4 cloves garlic, crushed
1-inch (2.5 cm) cube fresh ginger, peeled
2 teaspoons olive oil
¾ teaspoon ground cumin
¾ teaspoon ground coriander
½ teaspoon ground cardamom
½ teaspoon ground cloves
½ teaspoon ground cinnamon
½ teaspoon salt
½ teaspoon black pepper
1 pound (454 g) top round beef, cut into 2 by ½-inch (5 by 1.3 cm) pieces
1 cup (130 g) frozen peas
⅔ cup (150 g) plain Greek yogurt
⅓ cup (50 g) toasted cashews, optional

In a food processor, process the onion, garlic, and ginger into a purée.
    In a small sauté pan, heat the oil over medium heat. Cook the cumin, coriander, cardamom, cloves, cinnamon, salt, and pepper for 1 to 2 minutes, stirring constantly, or until the spices are very fragrant. Pour the spice mixture into the food processor. Pulse briefly to combine.
    In a slow cooker, combine the onion-spice mixture and beef. Stir to coat. Cover and cook on low for 4 to 5 hours, or until the beef is cooked through but still tender. During the last 15 minutes of cooking time, stir in the peas and yogurt. Garnish with the cashews, if using.

Yield: 4 servings

▶ *Time-Saver Tip*
Omit the spice sauteing step, and add the spices directly to the onion mixture.

BRAISED BEEF IN RED WINE

This braised beef is the perfect grown-up comfort food. If you wish, stir in ⅔ cup (80 g) grated Cheddar cheese.

1 beef pot roast, such as chuck eye (3 to 4 pounds or 1365 to 1820 g)
Salt, to taste
Black pepper, to taste
2 cups (470 ml) red wine
6 or 7 cloves garlic, peeled

Into a slow cooker, place the beef. Season with salt and pepper. Add the wine and garlic. Cover and cook on low for about 8 hours.
    Remove the beef from the slow cooker and keep it warm.
    Transfer the cooking juices to a saucepan. Reduce the juices over high heat until you have about 1½ cups (355 ml). Slice the beef thin and serve it moistened with the reduced pan juices.

Yield: 4 to 6 servings

STEAK ROLLUPS WITH ASPARAGUS
This dish is the essence of elegance, yet it's very simple to prepare and cook. Serve it with Caesar salad, French bread, and herbed butter.

6 cube steaks
¼ teaspoon salt
½ teaspoon black pepper
18 baby asparagus spears, trimmed
12 very small new potatoes, scrubbed
24 toothpicks

Season the steaks with the salt and pepper. Position three spears of asparagus on top of each cube steak, and then roll up the steaks jelly-roll style. Secure the ends of the rolled-up steaks with toothpicks.

In a slow cooker, place the potatoes. Place the rolled-up steaks seam sides down on top of the potatoes. Cover and cook on low for 5 to 7 hours.

Yield: 6 servings

▶ *Serving Suggestion*
Substitute adobo seasoning for the salt and pepper.

SAVORY SLOW-COOKED MEAT LOAF
Using half ground turkey cuts the calories of this normally high-cal dish. Cooking meat loaf in the slow cooker is incredibly easy, and it also gives you a deliciously tender meat loaf. The leftovers freeze exceptionally well. Keep some handy for a quick, protein-rich snack.

1 pound (454 g) baby carrots
1 egg
1½ tablespoons (23 ml) Worcestershire sauce
¾ cup (180 g) ketchup or barbecue sauce, divided (To make your own, see "Homemade Smoky Ketchup" or "Citrus BBQ" on pages 7 and 8.)
½ cup (40 g) whole rolled oats
½ sweet onion, finely chopped
½ medium green or red bell pepper, seeded and finely chopped
1 pound (454 g) ground beef
1 pound (454 g) ground turkey
1 teaspoon salt
½ teaspoon black pepper

In a slow cooker, place the carrots in one layer in the center.

In a large bowl, beat the egg lightly. Add the Worcestershire, ½ cup (120 g) of the ketchup, the oats, onion, and bell pepper. Mix well to combine.

Break up the beef and turkey and add them to the bowl. Evenly sprinkle the salt and pepper over all. Using your hands, gently but thoroughly mix to combine well. Do not overwork the meat or your meatloaf will be tough. Shape the mixture into a loaf to fit your slow cooker.

Place the loaf on top of the carrots in the slow cooker. (This will prevent a soggy bottom and allow any excess fats to drain into the carrots and flavor them deliciously). Cover and cook on low for 4 to 6 hours, or until the meatloaf is cooked though.

At the end of the cooking time, turn up the heat to high, brush the top of the loaf with the remaining ¼ cup (60 g) ketchup, cover, and cook for 15 to 30 minutes longer, or until the sauce is set.

Yield: 6 to 8 servings

▶ *Recipe Tips*
• If using a larger slow cooker, form two longer, thinner loaves and cook them on high for 1½ hours and then on low for 1½ to 2 more hours, or until cooked through.
• For a flavorful alternative to the more classic meat loaf, substitute a fruit chutney for the ketchup or barbecue sauce. Try a high-quality jarred version, such as pineapple pepper.

SWISS STEAK
This classic dish is wonderful served with spaetzle, noodles, or boiled potatoes.

2 pounds (910 g) round steak, cut about 1 inch (2.5 cm) thick
Salt, to taste
Black pepper, to taste
1 cup (125 g) all-purpose flour
¼ cup (60 ml) cooking oil
1 (12-ounce or 340-g) can diced tomatoes with celery and onion

Cut the steak into 4 equal-size pieces.

Using a meat tenderizer, pound the steak lightly. Season the steak with salt and pepper.

Place the flour in a shallow dish. Dredge the steak in the flour.

In a sauté pan, heat the oil over medium-high heat. Sauté the steak until well browned, and then turn and brown the other side.

Transfer the steak to a slow cooker. Add the tomatoes. Cover and cook on low for 6 hours or on high for 3 hours.

Serve the steak with the sauce poured over it.

Yield: 4 servings

SMOTHERED STEAK

The slow cooker can turn what's usually a tough cut of beef into something fork-tender. This steak, covered in a mushroom and onion sauce, is excellent with mashed potatoes.

2 pounds (900 g) beef round steak
2 tablespoons (15 g) onion soup mix (To make your own, see "Onion Soup Mix" on page 7.)
¼ cup (60 ml) water
10 ounces (280 g) cream of mushroom soup (To make your own, see "Cream of Mushroom Soup" on page 7.)

Cut the steak into 6 pieces. Place the steak in a slow cooker. Add the soup mix, water, and soup. Cover and cook for 6 to 8 hours.

Yield: 6 servings

BEEF WITH GRAVY

This is a very quick meat course for a comfort food kind of meal.

10 ounces (280 g) cream of mushroom soup (To make your own, see "Cream of Mushroom Soup" on page 7.)
2 tablespoons (28 g) onion soup mix (To make your own, see "Onion Soup Mix" on page 7.)
1 pound (455 g) beef round steak, cut into 1-inch (2.5 cm) cubes

Coat the crock of a slow cooker with nonstick cooking spray.
In the slow cooker, combine the soup and soup mix. Stir in the beef. Cover and cook on low for 6 to 8 hours, or until the meat is tender but not dry.

Yield: 3 servings

▶ *Serving Suggestion*
Serve this dish over cooked noodles or mashed potatoes.

QUICK STROGANOFF

Meals don't get any easier than this tasty three-ingredient recipe.

1 pound (455 g) beef round steak, cubed
1 can (10 ounces, or 280 g) cream of mushroom soup (To make your own, see "Cream of Mushroom Soup" on page 7.)
1 cup (230 g) sour cream

In a slow cooker, place the beef. Pour the soup on top of the beef. Cover and cook on low for 8 hours or on high for 4 to 5 hours. Before serving, stir in the sour cream.

Yield: 4 servings

▶ *Serving Suggestion*
Serve this stroganoff over cooked rice, pasta, or baked potatoes.

BARBECUED SHORT RIBS

In this slow cooker dish, short ribs simmer all day in a fairly traditional barbecue sauce, becoming fork-tender in the process.

⅔ cup (83 g) all-purpose flour
½ teaspoon black pepper
4 pounds (1.8 kg) beef short ribs
¼ cup (60 ml) olive oil
1 cup (160 g) chopped onion
1½ cups (355 ml) beef broth (To make your own, see "Beef Stock" on page 6.)
¾ cup (175 ml) red wine vinegar
¾ cup (170 g) packed brown sugar
½ cup (140 g) chili sauce (To make your own, see "Chili Sauce" on page 8.)
⅓ cup (80 g) ketchup (To make your own, see "Homemade Smoky Ketchup" on page 8.)
⅓ cup (80 ml) Worcestershire sauce
1½ teaspoons minced garlic
1½ teaspoons chili powder

In a large resealable plastic bag, combine the flour and pepper. Add the ribs in batches and shake the bag to coat the ribs with the flour mixture.
In a large skillet, heat the oil over medium-high heat. Brown the ribs on both sides.
Transfer the ribs to a slow cooker.
In the same skillet, combine the remaining ingredients. Cook, stirring, until the mixture comes to a boil. Pour the mixture over the ribs in the slow cooker. Cover and cook on low for 9 to 10 hours, or until the ribs are tender.

Yield: 10 servings

SHORT RIBS

This recipe will give you both the most tender and the most flavorful short ribs you've ever had.

⅔ cup (83 g) all-purpose flour
½ teaspoon black pepper
4 pounds (1.8 kg) beef short ribs
¼ cup (60 ml) olive oil, divided
1 cup (160 g) chopped onion
1½ cups (355 ml) beef broth (To make your own, see "Beef Stock" on page 6.)
½ cup (120 ml) dry red wine
¼ cup (60 g) brown sugar
½ cup (140 g) chili sauce (To make your own, see "Chili Sauce" on page 8.)
½ cup (120 g) ketchup (To make your own, see "Homemade Smoky Ketchup" on page 8.)
¼ cup (60 ml) Worcestershire sauce
1½ teaspoons minced garlic

In a large resealable plastic bag, combine the flour and pepper. Add the ribs in batches and shake the bag to coat the ribs with the flour mixture.

In a skillet, heat half of the oil over medium-high heat. Brown half of the ribs and transfer them to a slow cooker. Repeat with the remaining oil and ribs.

In the skillet, combine the remaining ingredients. Cook, scraping up the browned bits, until the mixture comes to a boil. Pour the sauce over the ribs in the slow cooker. Cover and cook on low for 9 to 10 hours.

Yield: 8 servings

▶ *Serving Suggestion*
Serve the ribs with mashed potatoes or noodles.

STUFFED PEPPERS WITH BEEF AND CORN

Stuffed peppers are incredibly easy to make in the slow cooker, and they are a family favorite.

6 green bell peppers
1 pound (455 g) ground beef, browned
½ cup (80 g) chopped onion
¼ teaspoon black pepper
12 ounces (340 g) frozen corn
1 tablespoon (15 ml) Worcestershire sauce
1 teaspoon mustard
1 can (10 ounces, or 280 g) tomato soup

Cut the top off of each pepper. Remove the core, seeds, and white membrane from each.

In a small bowl, combine the beef, onions, pepper, and corn. Divide evenly among the peppers. Stand the peppers up in a slow cooker.

In a bowl, combine the Worcestershire, mustard, and soup. Pour the sauce over the peppers. Cover and cook on low for 5 to 6 hours.

Yield: 6 servings

HAMBURGER CASSEROLE

This is a simple casserole of hamburger and potatoes.

3 potatoes, sliced
1 cup (130 g) sliced carrots
1 cup (160 g) sliced onion
½ teaspoon black pepper
1 pound (455 g) ground beef, browned and drained
2 cups (475 ml) tomato juice

In a slow cooker, combine all of the ingredients. Cover and cook on low for 6 to 8 hours.

Yield: 4 servings

▶*Add It!*
Add a 1 pound (455 g) bag of frozen green beans and make it a whole meal.

17 Stuffed Peppers with Beef and Corn; 18 Hamburger Casserole; 19 Comfort Food Casserole; 20 Three-Alarm Chili; 21 Firehouse Chili; 22 Pineapple Pepper Chili; 23 Slow-Cooked Shepherd's Pie; 24 New England Corned Beef and Cabbage

84 • THE LITTLE SLOW COOKER COOKBOOK

25 New England Boiled Dinner; 26 Maple Glazed Corned Beef with Vegetables; 27 Corned Beef and Cabbage; 28 Luscious, Leanest Lamb Chops; 29 Moroccan Braised Lamb Shanks in Fresh Tomatoes and Red Wine; 30 Lamb Shanks with Lentils; 31 Pomegranante Lamb; 32 Lamb Cassoulet

MAIN DISHES • 85

COMFORT FOOD CASSEROLE
This is one of those meal-in-a-bowl sort of things that just seem—well, comforting. Slow cooking really brings out the best in turnips. They end up remarkably like potatoes.

1½ pounds (680 g) ground beef
1 tablespoon (15 ml) olive oil
1 medium onion, chopped
4 cloves garlic, crushed
4 stalks celery, diced
1 cup (235 ml) beef broth
1 teaspoon beef bouillon concentrate
½ teaspoon salt
1 teaspoon black pepper
2 teaspoons dried oregano
1 teaspoon dry mustard
2 tablespoons (32 g) tomato paste
4 ounces (115 g) cream cheese
3 turnips, cubed
¾ cup (86 g) shredded Cheddar cheese

In a big, heavy skillet, brown and crumble the beef over medium-high heat. Pour off the fat.

Transfer the beef to a slow cooker.

In the skillet, heat the oil over medium-low heat. Sauté the onion, garlic, and celery until they're just softened. Stir in the broth, bouillon, salt, pepper, oregano, dry mustard, and paste. Add the cream cheese, using the edge of a spatula to cut the cream cheese into chunks. Simmer, stirring occasionally, until the cream cheese is melted.

Meanwhile, add the turnips to the slow cooker.

When the cream cheese has melted, pour the sauce into the slow cooker. Stir until the beef and turnips are coated. Cover and cook on low for 6 hours.

Serve with Cheddar cheese on top.

Yield: 6 servings

THREE-ALARM CHILI
When it turns cold and wet outside, there's nothing better to warm the bones than Three-Alarm Chili. Serve this firey chili with your choice of shredded cheese and plenty of beverages to quench the fire.

2 pounds (910 g) beef chuck, cut into 1-inch (2.5-cm) cubes
½ teaspoon salt, plus more to taste
¼ teaspoon black pepper, plus more to taste
One 2.25-ounce (63-g) envelope French's Texas-style Chili-O Seasoning Mix
One 14½-ounce (413-g) can Mexican-flavored stewed tomatoes with jalapeños, garlic, and cumin

In a slow cooker, season the beef on all sides with the salt and pepper. Sprinkle the beef with the seasoning mix. Pour the tomatoes on top. Cover and cook on low for 6 to 8 hours.

Before serving, stir the chili and season it with additional salt and pepper.

Yield: 8 servings

▶*Add It!*
Add 5 to 10 drops Tabasco sauce along with the seasoning mix and stewed tomatoes—if you dare!

FIREHOUSE CHILI
Here's a crowd-pleaser! You could halve this, but you'd be left with a half can of soybeans, and you know you'll eat it up, so why bother? This is good with shredded cheese and sour cream. What chili isn't? But it also stands on its own very well.

2 pounds (900 g) ground beef
1½ cups (240 g) chopped onion
4 cloves garlic, crushed
3 tablespoons (24 g) chili powder
3 teaspoons (7 g) paprika
4 teaspoons (10 g) ground cumin
¼ cup (60 g) ketchup (To make your own, see "Homemade Smoky Ketchup" on page 8.)
2 tablespoons (32 g) tomato paste
1 can (14½ ounces, or 410 g) diced tomatoes
12 ounces (355 ml) light beer
1 teaspoon Splenda
2½ teaspoons (15 g) salt
1 can (15 ounces, or 425 g) black soybeans

In a big, heavy skillet, brown and crumble the beef over medium-high heat. Drain the beef.

Transfer the beef to a slow cooker. Add the onion, garlic, chili powder, paprika, cumin, ketchup, paste, tomatoes, beer, Splenda, salt, and soybeans. Stir to combine. Cover and cook on low for 8 hours.

Yield: 10 servings

PINEAPPLE PEPPER CHILI

Sweet tropical notes from the pineapple make this delicious chili stand out from the crowd.

1 pound (454 g) navy beans, soaked overnight, rinsed, and drained
1 large sweet onion, chopped
1 red bell pepper, seeded and chopped
1 orange bell pepper, seeded and chopped
1 serrano chile, seeded and finely chopped
4 cups (940 ml) vegetable broth, plus enough to cover (To make your own, see "Freshest Vegetable Broth" on page 6.)
1 can (14.5 ounces, or 406 g) fire-roasted diced tomatoes, undrained
1 can (6 ounces, or 168 g) tomato paste
1 can (8 ounces, or 225 g) diced pineapple in juice or water, drained
2 tablespoons (15 g) chili powder
1½ teaspoons ground cumin
¾ teaspoon ground coriander
1 teaspoon salt
½ teaspoon black pepper

In a slow cooker, combine the beans, onion, bell peppers, and chile. Pour the broth on top, plus more if needed to cover. Stir gently to combine. Cover and cook on low for 6 to 7 hours or on high for 3 to 4 hours, or until the beans are tender. Turn the heat to high, if necessary. Stir in the tomatoes, paste, pineapple, chili powder, cumin, coriander, salt, and pepper. Cover and cook for 45 minutes longer.

Yield: 8 to 10 servings

▶*Time Saver Tip*

In lieu of soaking the beans overnight, you can also bring them to a rapid boil in water to cover. Cook them for 10 minutes, remove the pan from the heat, and let it sit, covered, for 1 hour. Drain the cooking water and follow the recipe as directed.

SLOW-COOKED SHEPHERD'S PIE

Shepherd's pie is actually a variation on an old traditional dish called "cottage pie," which was basically a meat pie made with beef topped with a mashed potato crust. Fun fact: The term shepherd's pie first appeared in the 1870s. The "Cumberland pie" is a version of shepherd's pie with a layer of bread crumbs on top. These days, shepherd's pie tends to mean a meat dish where the meat is actually mutton or lamb—the thinking being that shepherds deal with sheep, not beef! Regardless, it's a delicious dish, and the slow cooker is an ingenious way to cook it.

1 pound (454 g) ground lamb
1 large white onion, diced
6 cloves garlic, minced
1 can (15 ounces, or 420 g) small white beans, drained and rinsed
1½ tablespoons (16 g) Dijon mustard
1 tablespoon (1.7 g) minced fresh rosemary (or 1 teaspoon dried, chopped)
1¼ teaspoons salt, divided
1 teaspoon black pepper, divided
⅓ cup (27 g) shredded Parmesan cheese
3 cups (675 g) cooked mashed potatoes
½ cup (24 g) chopped chives
2 teaspoons garlic powder

In a large skillet over medium-high heat, cook the lamb and onion for about 7 minutes, or until no pink remains. Drain the oils, stir in the garlic, and cook for 1 minute, stirring frequently.

Transfer the contents to a slow cooker and add the beans, mustard, rosemary, ¾ teaspoon of the salt, and ½ teaspoon of the pepper, stirring well to combine. Sprinkle evenly with the cheese.

In a medium bowl, combine the potatoes, chives, garlic powder, the remaining ½ teaspoon salt, and the remaining ½ teaspoon pepper. Mix well. Spread the potatoes evenly over the lamb and smooth out.

Cover and cook on high for 3 to 4 hours, or until heated through. During the final 20 to 30 minutes of cooking time, remove the lid to allow for the evaporation of any excess moisture before serving.

Yield: 6 servings

▶*Health Bite*

In this dish we used lean ground lamb, and we lowered the starch (and the carbohydrate load) by swapping out the traditional corn for white beans. The white beans add a nice amount of fiber and extra protein, and they also create a really creamy dish.

This dish is absolutely terrific for leftovers and even works for a nontraditional (but very filling and energizing) breakfast! Seriously!

33 Lemon Lamb Shanks

34

34 Caribbean Slow Cooker Lamb

MAIN DISHES

NEW ENGLAND CORNED BEEF AND CABBAGE
Corned beef is actually just salt-cured beef, and the dish itself has nothing to do with corn. The word corn comes from Old English. It's used to describe hard particles or grains—in this case, the coarse grains of salt used for curing. Corned beef does beautifully slow cooked. Here it's paired with cabbage.

4 baby turnips, unpeeled and quartered
4 carrots, peeled and thickly sliced on the diagonal
1 yellow onion, quartered
2 cups (470 ml) vegetable broth
1 to 2 cups (235 to 470 ml) pure apple cider
One 3-pound (1,362 g) corned beef brisket, fat trimmed
2 tablespoons (22 g) hot mustard
½ teaspoon black pepper
1 small head green cabbage, cored and cut into 8 equal wedges

In the bottom of a 6- or 7-quart (5.7 or 6.6 L) slow cooker, combine the turnips, carrots, and onion. Pour the vegetable broth and cider over all, using 1 cup (235 ml) of cider for a 6-quart (5.7 L) slow cooker and 2 cups (470 ml) for a 7-quart (6.6 L) slow cooker. Place the brisket on top and coat with the mustard. Sprinkle on the pepper. Lay the cabbage wedges on top of the brisket. Cover and cook on low for 8 to 9 hours, or until the meat is cooked through and tender.

Yield: 6 servings

▶Health Bite
The common practice of salting beef as a way of preserving it figures prominently in many cultures, from Jewish to Caribbean to Irish.
   Here we paired corned beef with cabbage, which is one of the great health foods of all time because of its generous helping of cancer-fighting chemicals called indoles. Cabbage is also loaded with powerful antioxidants like sulforaphane, which can disarm damaging free radicals and help fight carcinogens.
   We replaced the traditional white potatoes in this dish with turnips, which are actually in the same vegetable family as cabbages (the Brassica family, also known as Vegetable Royalty!). Turnips are a "highfoluve"food, which means it fills you up without costing you a lot of calories. They provide 3 grams of fiber, more than 250 milligrams of potassium, 18 milligrams of vitamin C, and 51 milligrams of calcium, all for a miserly 35 calories per cup.
   If a recipe could be a poster child for "a healthy dish," this one would be it!

NEW ENGLAND BOILED DINNER
This is a traditional St. Patrick's Day dinner, but it's a simple, satisfying one-pot meal on any chilly night. It's easy to make, but it takes a long time to cook. Do yourself a favor and assemble it ahead of time. If you wish, you can add a few little red boiling potatoes still in their jackets.

6 small turnips, peeled and quartered
2 large stalks celery, cut into chunks
2 medium onions, cut into chunks
3 pounds (1.4 kg) corned beef
1 packet Corned Beef Seasoning Mix
½ head cabbage, cut into wedges
Spicy brown mustard
Horseradish
Butter

In a slow cooker, combine the turnips, celery, and onions. Set the corned beef on top and add water to cover. Scatter the contents of the corned beef seasoning packet on top. Cover and cook on low for 10 to 12 hours. (You can cook it on high for 6 to 8 hours, but it won't be as tender.)
   Using a fork or tongs, remove the corned beef from the slow cooker to a platter and cover to keep warm.
   Place the cabbage in the slow cooker with the other vegetables. Re-cover the slow cooker and cook on high for ½ hour.
   Using a slotted spoon, remove the vegetables and pile them around the corned beef on the platter. Serve with the mustard and horseradish as condiments for the beef and butter for the vegetables.

Yield: 8 servings

MAPLE GLAZED CORNED BEEF WITH VEGETABLES
This is a trifle less traditional than, but just as good as, the New England Boiled Dinner above. The pancake syrup and mustard, plus last-minute glazing under the broiler, give it a new aspect.

6 medium turnips, cut into chunks
2 medium carrots, cut into chunks
1 medium onion, quartered
5 pounds (2.3 kg) corned beef brisket
1 packet Corned Beef Seasoning Mix
2 cups (475 ml) water
1 medium head cabbage, cut into wedges
3 tablespoons (60 g) pancake syrup
1 tablespoon (11 g) brown mustard
Horseradish

In a slow cooker, combine the turnips, carrots, and onion. Place the corned beef on top. Scatter the contents of the corned beef seasoning packet on top. Pour the water over all. Cover and cook on low for at least 9 to 10 hours. Carefully remove the corned beef and place it on a broiler rack, fatty side up. Using a slotted spoon, skim out the vegetables, put them on a platter, cover, and keep in a warm place.

Place the cabbage in the slow cooker. Cover and cook on high for 15 to 20 minutes, or until just tender. (Or you can pour the liquid from the pot into a saucepan and cook the cabbage in it on your stovetop, which is faster.)

Meanwhile, in a bowl, combine the pancake syrup and mustard. Spread the mixture over the top of the corned beef. When the cabbage is almost cooked, broil the corned beef for 2 to 3 minutes, or until glazed.

Using a slotted spoon, transfer the cabbage to the platter. Slice the corned beef across the grain.

Serve with horseradish.

Yield: 12 servings

CORNED BEEF AND CABBAGE
Here's a no-muss, no-fuss way to make your St. Patrick's Day favorite. (Leprechauns and shamrocks not included.)

1 corned beef (about 4 pounds or 1820 g)
1 small head green cabbage (about 2 pounds or 910 g), cut into wedges
6 medium boiling potatoes (about 2 pounds or 910 g), peeled

In a slow cooker, place the corned beef and any spice package that came with it. Add water to barely cover the meat. Cover and cook on low for 6 hours. Add the cabbage and potatoes and cook for 2 to 3 hours more.

Remove the corned beef from the slow cooker. Slice it thin. Remove the cabbage and potatoes from the cooker pot and allow the cabbage to drain.

Yield: 6 servings

▶*Add It!*
We like to pour a little malt vinegar over our cabbage for a zesty kick.

LUSCIOUS, LEANEST LAMB CHOPS
The loin chop is the leanest of lamb cuts. In this recipe, the slow cooker blends the flavors of the onion and fresh herbs beautifully with the rich taste of the meat. This dish also has a lovely finishing kick of balsamic vinegar. If desired, you can transfer the onions and juices to a large skillet and cook over medium-high heat for a few minutes until the sauce is slightly reduced and thickened before serving.

1 large yellow onion, sliced and separated into rings
2 tablespoons (30 ml) balsamic vinegar
2 tablespoons (30 ml) chicken broth
1 tablespoon (14 g) butter, melted
1 tablespoon (11 g) Dijon mustard
2 cloves garlic, minced
1 tablespoon (1.7 g) minced fresh rosemary (or 1 teaspoon dried)
1 tablespoon (2.4 g) minced fresh thyme (or 1 teaspoon dried)
½ teaspoon dried oregano
½ teaspoon salt
½ teaspoon black pepper
8 loin lamb chops
Fresh mint leaves, optional

In a slow cooker, layer the onion. Pour the vinegar, broth, and butter on top.

In a small bowl, stir the mustard, garlic, rosemary, thyme, oregano, salt, and pepper together. Rub the mixture evenly over the lamb. Place the lamb on top of the onion. Cover and cook on low for 4 to 6 hours, or until the lamb is cooked to the desired doneness.

Remove the lamb and stir the onion and juices before serving. Garnish with the mint, if using.

Yield: 4 servings

▶*Health Bite*
Lamb is an excellent source of high-quality protein, and it's also a good source of iron and B vitamins. And lamb provides about 45 percent of the daily requirement for zinc, which is essential for growth, healing, and a healthy immune system. Plus the zinc and iron found in lamb are easily absorbed by the body.

MOROCCAN BRAISED LAMB SHANKS IN FRESH TOMATOES AND RED WINE
Braising is a great technique for the slow cooker because of the low controlled temperature. This recipe makes fallapart-tender lamb–utterly delicious!

1½ tablespoons (23 ml) olive oil
6 lamb shanks
1 large sweet onion, chopped
½ cup (55 g) shredded carrot
1 rib celery, finely diced
1 clove garlic, minced
2 cups (470 ml) dry red wine
3 or 4 medium ripe heirloom tomatoes, chopped (about 3 cups [540 g])
1 cinnamon stick
½ teaspoon ground cloves
½ teaspoon ground allspice
1 tablespoon (20 g) honey
½ teaspoon salt
½ teaspoon black pepper

In a large skillet, heat the oil over medium-high heat. Add the lamb and cook for 7 to 9 minutes, or until lightly browned on all sides.

Transfer the lamb to a slow cooker.

In the skillet, cook the onion, carrot, and celery for 7 to 8 minutes, stirring frequently, or until just beginning to brown. Add the garlic and cook for 30 seconds. Add the wine, tomatoes, cinnamon stick, cloves, and allspice. Bring to a simmer, stirring well to incorporate all of the browned bits in the pan. Stir in the honey, salt, and pepper. Pour the mixture carefully over the lamb in the slow cooker. Cover and cook on low for about 7 hours or on high for about 4 hours, or until the lamb is tender and easily comes off the bone.

Remove the cinnamon stick before serving.

Yield: 6 servings

LAMB SHANKS WITH LENTILS
Most folks tend to relegate lentils to the sproutsy crowd, and that's a shame. They're a classic item in French cooking, as this delicious dish attests.

2 cups (400 g) lentils, picked over and rinsed
4 lamb shanks (about 3 pounds or 1365 g)
Salt, to taste
Black pepper, to taste
2 tablespoons (60 ml) olive oil
2 cups (470 ml) red wine
1 cup (235 ml) water, plus more if needed

In a slow cooker, place the lentils. Season the lamb with salt and pepper.

In a sauté pan, heat the oil over medium-high heat. Sear the lamb, in batches if necessary, to brown on all sides.

Transfer the lamb to the slow cooker.

Deglaze the sauté pan with the wine and add to the slow cooker. Add the water. Cover and cook on low for 8 hours. Check after 4 hours or so and add more water, if needed.

Yield: 4 servings

▶*Add It!*
Several peeled garlic cloves added to the slow cooker will give this dish a definite kick.

POMEGRANATE LAMB
Pomegranate juice continues to be a culinary darling, and with good reason. This combination provides a piquant and delicious meal.

3 medium onions, cut into ¼ inch- (6 mm) thick slices
1 boneless leg of lamb (about 3 pounds or 1365 g)
Salt, to taste
Black pepper, to taste
1 cup (235 ml) pomegranate juice

In a slow cooker, break up the onions.

Trim as much fat as possible from the lamb and cut it into 2-inch (5-cm) chunks. Add it to the slow cooker. Season with salt and pepper. Pour the juice over the lamb. Cover and cook on low for 6 to 7 hours.

Yield: 6 servings

LAMB CASSOULET
This cassoulet uses lamb in place of the sausage or chicken.

2 cups (364 g) great northern beans, cooked or canned
1 cup (235 ml) dry white wine
1 cup (245 g) tomato sauce
2 bay leaves
½ teaspoon minced garlic
1 tablespoon (4 g) fresh parsley
½ teaspoon thyme, crushed
2 tablespoons (28 ml) olive oil
8 ounces (225 g) lean lamb, cut in ½-inch (1.3 cm) pieces
¾ cup (120 g) chopped onion
¼ cup (60 ml) cold water
2 tablespoons (16 g) all-purpose flour

In a slow cooker, combine the beans, wine, sauce, bay leaves, garlic, parsley, and thyme.

In a saucepan, heat the oil over medium-high heat. Cook the lamb and onion until the lamb is well browned on all sides; drain.

Transfer the lamb and onion to the slow cooker. Stir to combine. Cover and cook on low for 5 to 6 hours. Turn the heat to high. Heat until bubbly, without lifting the cover.

In a small bowl, slowly blend the water into the flour. Stir into the meat-bean mixture. Cover and cook until slightly thickened.

Before serving, remove the bay leaves.

Yield: 6 servings

LEMON LAMB SHANKS
Lemon brings out the best in lamb. Serve this dish with a salad with plenty of cucumbers and tomatoes.

2 tablespoons (28 ml) olive oil
4 pounds (1.8 kg) lamb shank
1 teaspoon lemon pepper
½ teaspoon dry mustard
½ cup (120 ml) chicken broth (To make your own, see Chicken Stock on page 6.)
1 teaspoon beef bouillon concentrate
½ teaspoon grated lemon zest
2 tablespoons (28 ml) lemon juice
1 teaspoon dried rosemary
2 cloves garlic, crushed
Cornstarch

In a sauté pan, heat the oil. Sear the lamb all over in the oil.
　Transfer the lamb to a slow cooker.
　In a bowl, mix together the lemon pepper and mustard. Sprinkle the mixture evenly over the lamb.
　In the same bowl, mix together the broth, bouillon, zest, juice, rosemary, and garlic. Pour the mixture over the lamb in the slow cooker. Cover and cook on low for 8 hours.
　Remove the lamb to a platter. Add cornstarch a teaspoon at a time to thicken the liquid in the slow cooker.

Yield: 6 servings

CARIBBEAN SLOW COOKER LAMB
Lamb and goat are very popular in the Caribbean, and this is a slow cooker interpretation of a Caribbean lamb dish. Look for tamarind concentrate in a grocery store with a good international section. If you can't find it, you could use a tablespoon (15 ml) of lemon juice and a teaspoon of Splenda instead.

2- to 3-pound section (0.9 to 1.4 kg) of a leg of lamb
½ medium onion, chopped
½ teaspoon minced garlic or 1 clove garlic, crushed
1 teaspoon tamarind concentrate
1 tablespoon (11 g) spicy brown mustard
1 cup (180 g) canned diced tomatoes
1 teaspoon hot sauce (preferably Caribbean Scotch Bonnet sauce)
Cornstarch, optional
Salt, to taste
Black pepper, to taste

In a slow cooker, place the lamb.
　In a bowl, stir together the onion, garlic, tamarind, mustard, tomatoes, and hot sauce.
　Pour the mixture over the lamb in the slow cooker. Cover and cook on low for 8 hours.
　Remove the lamb to a serving platter. Add cornstarch to thicken the juices if necessary. Season with salt and pepper.

Yield: 6 servings

ROAST VEAL SHOULDER
Veal shoulder makes a delicious slow cooker roast. The bacon adds flavor and needed moisture to this lean meat. You can discard the bacon after cooking, if you wish. For an added flavor dimension, sprinkle the roast with some chopped fresh rosemary.

1 boneless rolled veal shoulder roast (3 to 4 pounds or 1365 to 1820 g)
Salt, to taste
Black pepper, to taste
4 slices bacon
½ cup (120 ml) white wine

In a slow cooker, place the veal roast into the slow cooker. Season the veal with salt and pepper.
　Drape the bacon on top of the veal. Pour the wine over all. Cover and cook on low for 6 to 8 hours.
　Remove the veal from the cooker. Remove and discard the bacon if you wish. Remove the twine from the roast and slice.
　You can reduce the cooking liquid to make a simple sauce, or it can be a base for gravy.

Yield: 6 to 8 servings

35 Roast Veal Shoulder; 36 Osso Buco; 37 Easy Pork Roast;
38 Hawaiian Pork Roast; 39 Apple Cranberry Pork Roast; 40 Asian Pork Roast

41 **42**

43 **44** **47**

45 **46** **48**

41 Pork and Sweet Potato Dinner; 42 Slow Cooker Shredded Pork, 43 Easy Maple Barbecue Pulled Pork Shoulder; 44 Pork Loin with Honey Mustard; 45 Stuffed Pork Chops; 46 Barbecued Pork Chops; 47 Pork Chops and Vegetables in Mushroom Gravy; 48 Southern Stuffed Pork Chops

MAIN DISHES • 95

OSSO BUCO

This classic Italian dish is traditionally served with risotto and topped with gremolata, which is a sprightly garnish made of minced garlic, lemon zest, and parsley.

4 pounds (1820 g) veal shanks, cut about 2 inches (5 cm) long
Salt, to taste
Black pepper, to taste
2 tablespoons (60 ml) olive oil
1 cup (250 g) garlic marinara sauce
½ cup (120 ml) white wine

Season the veal with salt and pepper.
In a sauté pan, heat the oil over medium-high heat. Sear the veal on each side until browned, working in batches, if necessary, to avoid crowding the pan.
Transfer the veal to a slow cooker. Add the sauce and wine. Cover and cook on low for 8 hours. Carefully remove the veal from the slow cooker. Serve the shanks topped with the sauce.

Yield: 4 to 6 servings

▶*Add It!*
Add several handfuls of baby carrots, along with a small, diced onion, to deepen the flavor.

EASY PORK ROAST

This is basic, which is a strength, not a weakness. It would be a great supper with a big salad.

3 pounds (1.4 kg) boneless pork loin
2 tablespoons (28 ml) olive oil
1 can (8 ounces, or 225 g) tomato sauce
¼ cup (60 ml) soy sauce
½ cup (120 ml) chicken broth (To make your own, see Chicken stock on page 6.)
½ cup (12 g) Splenda
2 teaspoons dry mustard
Cornstarch (optional)

In a big, heavy skillet, brown the pork on all sides in the oil. Transfer the pork to a slow cooker.
In a bowl, mix together the tomato sauce, soy sauce, broth, Splenda, and dry mustard. Pour the mixture over the pork in the slow cooker. Cover and cook on low for 8 to 9 hours.
When the time's up, remove the pork to a serving platter. Thicken the pot liquid, if needed, with cornstarch. Serve the juice with the pork.

Yield: 8 servings

HAWAIIAN PORK ROAST

In this dish, pork loin roast cooks to tender perfection with island flavors.

1½ pounds (680 g) pork loin roast
1 cup (235 ml) pineapple juice
¼ cup (60 ml) sherry
2 tablespoons (28 ml) soy sauce
1 teaspoon ground ginger
1 tablespoon (13 g) sugar

In a slow cooker, place the pork.
In a bowl, combine the remaining ingredients. Pour the mixture over the pork in the slow cooker. Cover and cook on low for 4 to 5 hours, or until done, but not dry.

Yield: 4 servings

▶*Serving Suggestion*
Serve over rice.

APPLE CRANBERRY PORK ROAST

This flavor of this roast really says fall, with its apple and cranberry combination. Try it with sweet potatoes. You can even put them in the cooker to cook with the roast if you like.

1 tablespoon (15 ml) canola oil
3 pounds (1⅓ kg) pork loin roast
2 cups (475 ml) apple juice
3 cups (330 g) sliced apples
1 cup (100 g) cranberries
¼ teaspoon black pepper

In a skillet, heat the oil over medium-high heat. Brown the pork on all sides.
Transfer the pork to a slow cooker. Add the remaining ingredients. Cover and cook on low for 6 to 8 hours.

Yield: 8 servings

ASIAN PORK ROAST

This tender and tasty pork roast is perfect with stir-fried vegetables and rice.

3 pounds (1⅓ kg) pork loin roast
½ cup (120 ml) soy sauce
½ cup (120 ml) sherry
½ teaspoon minced garlic
1 tablespoon (9 g) dry mustard
1 teaspoon ground ginger
1 teaspoon thyme

Place the pork roast in a resealable plastic bag; set in a deep bowl.

In a bowl, thoroughly blend together the soy sauce, sherry, garlic, mustard, ginger, and thyme. Pour the marinade over the pork in the bag; close the bag.

Marinate the pork in the fridge for 2 to 3 hours or overnight.

Transfer the pork and marinade to a slow cooker. Cover and cook on high for 3½ to 4 hours.

Lift the roast out onto a cutting board; let stand for 10 minutes before slicing.

Yield: 8 servings

PORK AND SWEET POTATO DINNER
This meal in a pot has just enough sweetener and spice added to give it great flavor without overpowering it.

3 pounds (1⅓ kg) boneless pork loin roast
4 sweet potatoes, peeled
2 medium apples, sliced
¼ cup (60 ml) apple juice or white wine
2 tablespoons (30 g) brown sugar
½ teaspoon apple pie spice

Cube the pork and the sweet potatoes into bite-size pieces.

In a skillet, brown the pork cubes.

In a slow cooker, place the apple, then the potatoes, and then the pork.

In a bowl, combine the juice, sugar, and apple pie spice. Pour the mixture over the pork in the slow cooker. Cover and cook on low for 8 to 12 hours.

Yield: 6 servings

SLOW COOKER SHREDDED PORK
Shredded pork requires slow cooking. If you have a smoker, you can use that. If not, the slow cooker does a great job.

4 pounds (1.8 kg) pork shoulder roast
1½ teaspoons minced garlic
1 cup (160 g) finely chopped onion
4 ounces (115 g) diced green chilies
1 cup (235 ml) cider vinegar

In a slow cooker, place the roast.

In a bowl, combine the remaining ingredients. Pour the mixture over the roast in the slow cooker. Cover and cook on low for 8 to 10 hours.

Remove the pork to a cutting board. Using two forks, shred the pork, discarding the fat and bones.

Yield: 8 servings

▶*Serving Suggestion*
Serve on plain hamburger buns with coleslaw.

EASY MAPLE BARBECUE PULLED PORK SHOULDER
Pulled pork is a classic Southern barbecue treat. Here, we add a Northern twist with maple syrup.

1 pork shoulder roast (about 5 pounds or 2275 g)
2 cups (500 g) barbecue sauce, divided
½ cup (170 g) maple syrup

In a slow cooker, combine the pork, 1 cup (250 g) of the barbecue sauce, and the syrup. Cover and cook on low for 8 hours.

Remove the pork from the slow cooker and allow to cool enough to handle.

Using two forks, shred the pork, discarding the fat and bones.

Add the shredded meat and the liquid back into the slow cooker along with the remaining 1 cup (250 g) barbecue sauce. Cook for another ½ to 1 hour.

Yield: 8 to 10 servings

▶*Serving Suggestion*
Serve with the red beans and rice, or on a bun as a sandwich

PORK LOIN WITH HONEY MUSTARD
This recipe produces a juicy, tender, and delectable pork roast.

1 pork loin roast, bone-in (about 5 pounds or 2275 g) Salt, to taste
Black pepper, to taste
2 tablespoons (60 ml) olive oil
3 medium onions, cut into ½-inch-thick (1-cm) slices
1 cup (250 g) honey mustard

Season the pork with salt and pepper.

In a large sauté pan, heat the oil over medium-high heat. Sear the pork, fatty side down, until nicely browned.

In a slow cooker, place the onions. Put the pork on top of the onions and smear the honey mustard on the pork. Cover and cook on low for 6 to 7 hours.

Serve the pork with the braised onions from the pan, or use the onions and accumulated juices to make a gravy, if desired.

Yield: 4 to 6 servings

STUFFED PORK CHOPS
The rice and vegetable stuffing practically makes these chops a meal in themselves.

4 (1-inch- or 2.5-cm-thick) pork chops (about 2 pounds or 910 g)
1 (8-ounce or 225-g) package cooked rice with vegetables
Salt, to taste
Black pepper, to taste
Cooking oil
1 cup (235 ml) chicken stock or broth

Cut a pocket in the side of each chop, and stuff each one with some of the rice mixture. Close the pocket by securing with a toothpick. Season the pork with salt and pepper
In a large sauté pan, heat the oil over medium-high heat. Sear the pork and brown on each side, about 5 minutes per side, working in batches, if necessary, to avoid crowding the pan.
Transfer the chops to a slow cooker. Add the stock. Cover and cook on low for 4 to 4½ hours. Reduce the pan juices for a sauce, if desired.

Yield: 4 servings

BARBECUED PORK CHOPS
Succulent and saucy, these pork chops will melt in your mouth. Enjoy with green vegetables and 7-grain bread. If you wish, add ½ cup (28 g) minced onion, 1 teaspoon dried oregano, and 2 minced cloves garlic to the sauce mixture. This recipe also makes delicious barbecued chicken wings. Use 8 to 12 wings instead of the chops.

Four ½-inch (1.9-cm)–thick pork loin chops
One 8-ounce (225-g) can tomato sauce
½ cup (125 g) hickory smoke–flavored barbecue sauce
½ teaspoon black pepper

In a slow cooker, place the pork.
In a medium bowl, combine the tomato sauce, barbecue sauce, and pepper. Pour the mixture over the pork in the slow ccooker. Cover and cook on low for 8 to 10 hours.

Yield: 4 servings

PORK CHOPS AND VEGETABLES IN MUSHROOM GRAVY
Here's a truly smooth and savory one-pot meal. Mushrooms pair well with the vegetables and the pork.

6 cups (720 g) frozen stew vegetables, thawed
6 pork loin chops, trimmed
Salt, to taste
Black pepper, to taste
One 10¾-ounce (305 g) can condensed cream of mushroom soup
¼ cup (60 ml) water

In a slow cooker, place the vegetables.
Lightly season the pork with salt and pepper on both sides. Place the pork on top of the vegetables.
In a small bowl, combine the soup and water. Pour the mixture over the pork in the slow cooker. Cover and cook on low for 7½ to 8½ hours or on high for 3½ to 4½ hours.

Yield: 6 servings

SOUTHERN STUFFED PORK CHOPS
Slow-cooked stuffed pork chops go great with greens and cornbread.

4 pork loin chops, 1-inch (2.5 cm) thick
2 cups (150 g) dry cornbread stuffing mix
2 tablespoons (28 ml) chickenbroth (To make your own, see "Chicken Stock" on page 6.)
⅓ cup (80 ml) orange juice
1 tablespoon (7 g) finely chopped pecans
¼ cup (60 ml) light corn syrup
½ teaspoon grated orange peel

With a sharp knife, cut a horizontal slit in the side of each chop, forming a pocket for stuffing.
In a bowl, combine the remaining ingredients. Fill the pockets with stuffing.
Place on a metal rack in a slow cooker. Cover and cook on low for 6 to 8 hours. Uncover and brush with the sauce. Cook on high for 15 to 20 minutes.

Yield: 4 servings

PORK CHOPS WITH SWEET POTATOES
Pork chops and sweet potatoes just seem to go together, so this recipe is a natural. If you like it sweeter, add a couple of tablespoons of honey or brown sugar. If you want firmer sweet potatoes, add them about halfway through the cooking time.

1 tablespoon (15 ml) olive oil
4 pork loin chops
1 cup (160 g) sliced onions
2 sweet potatoes, peeled and cut into large chunks
1 cup (235 ml) chicken broth (To make your own, see "Chicken Stock" on page 6.)

In a large skillet, heat the oil over medium-high heat. Brown the pork on both sides.
   Spray the crock of a slow cooker with nonstick cooking spray.
   Arrange the onions in the bottom and place the pork on top of the onions. Place the potatoes on top. Pour the broth over everything. Cover and cook on low for 5 to 6 hours.

Yield: 4 servings

▶*Kitchen Tip*
If you want firmer sweet potatoes, add them about halfway through the cooking time.

PORK CHOPS WITH APPLES
Pork loin chops, which are great because they are low in fat, can be tough if you aren't careful cooking them. This slow cooker recipe solves that issue, making sure they are always fork-tender.

4 pork loin chops
1 cup (160 g) sliced onion
2 apples, peeled, cored, and sliced
1 tablespoon (15 g) brown sugar
½ teaspoon nutmeg
¼ teaspoon black pepper

Coat a skillet with nonstick cooking spray.
   Heat the skillet over medium-high heat. Quickly brown the pork on each side.
   In a slow cooker, arrange the onion, then the apples. Sprinkle the sugar, nutmeg, and pepper over the apples. Place the pork on top. Cover and cook on low for 5 to 6 hours.

Yield: 4 servings

PORK CHOPS BRAISED WITH SAUERKRAUT
You'll swear you're in Alsace! Serve this pork with mashed potatoes and warm homemade applesauce for a cozy dinner.

4 center-cut pork chops (about 2 pounds or 910 g)
Salt, to taste
Black pepper, to taste
2 tablespoons (60 ml) olive oil
1 (16-ounce or 455-g) package sauerkraut
1 cup (235 ml) white wine

Season the pork with salt and pepper.
   In a large sauté pan, heat the oil over medium-high heat. Brown the pork on both sides in the oil.
   Transfer the pork to a slow cooker.
   Rinse the sauerkraut for a minute under cold water in a colander and allow to drain. Add the rinsed sauerkraut to the slow cooker. Add the wine. Cover and cook on low for 5 to 6 hours.

Yield: 4 servings

EASIEST RIBS
The unusual blend of flavors in this recipe creates a tasty and memorable main dish. Serve the ribs with buttered corn-on-the-cob and coleslaw.

1 slab pork ribs in a size that fits inside your covered slow cooker
One 12-ounce (340-g) bottle chili sauce
One 10-ounce (280-g) jar currant jelly

In a slow cooker, place the ribs.
   In a medium bowl, combine the chili sauce and currant jelly. Pour the mixture over the ribs. Cover and cook on low for 8 to 9 hours.

Yield: 8 servings

49 Pork Chops with Sweet Potatoes; 50 Pork Chops with Apples; 51 Pork Chops Braised with Sauerkraut; 52 Easiest Ribs; 53 Asian Ribs; 54 Honey Mustard Ribs; 55 Thai Curry Pork; 56 Smoked Ham Hocks with White Beans

57 Ham and Scalloped Potatoes; 58 Orange-Glazed Ham; 59 Ham and Cabbage Casserole; 60 Holiday Ham; 61 Coddled Ham; 62 Green Beans with Smoked Sausage; 63 Sausage with Apples and Onions; 64 Slow-Cooker Sausage and Lima Beans

MAIN DISHES • 101

ASIAN RIBS
Country-style ribs marinate in an Asian sauce and then dry cook in the slow cooker for a marvelous flavor and tenderness.

¼ cup (60 g) brown sugar
1 cup (235 ml) soy sauce
¼ cup (60 ml) sesame oil
2 tablespoons (28 ml) olive oil
2 tablespoons (28 ml) rice vinegar
2 tablespoons (28 ml) lime juice
2 tablespoons (20 g) minced garlic
2 tablespoons (12 g) minced fresh ginger
½ teaspoon hot pepper sauce
3 pounds (1⅓ kg) country-style pork ribs

In a slow cooker, stir the sugar, soy sauce, sesame oil, olive oil, vinegar, juice, garlic, ginger, and hot pepper sauce together. Add the ribs. Cover and refrigerate for 8 hours or overnight.
    Before cooking, drain the marinade and discard. Cover and cook on low for 9 hours.

Yield: 9 servings

HONEY MUSTARD RIBS
The simple pleasure of eating fall-off-the-bone ribs starts with your favorite barbecue sauce. Spice it up with an herb blend and a jar of honey mustard.

3½ pounds (1.6 kg) country style pork ribs
1 cup (250 g) barbecue sauce (To make your own, see "Citrus Rum BBQ Sauce" on page 7.)
½ cup (88 g) honey mustard
2 teaspoons seasoning blend, such as Lawry's brand

In a slow cooker, place the ribs.
    In a small bowl, stir together the barbecue sauce, honey mustard, and seasoning blend. Pour the mixture over the ribs in the slow cooker. Stir to coat. Cover and cook on low for 8 to 10 hours or on high for 4 to 5 hours.
    Transfer the ribs to a serving platter. Strain the sauce into a bowl; skim the fat from the sauce. Drizzle some of the sauce over the ribs and pass the remaining sauce at the table.

Yield: 8 servings

THAI CURRY PORK
This luscious dish is perfect served with steamed jasmine rice. You'll want to spoon the sauce over the rice as well as the ribs. If you want a spicier dish, add more curry paste.

2 pounds (910 g) country-style pork ribs
2 tablespoons (32 g) Thai red curry paste
1 cup (235 ml) coconut milk, divided

In a slow cooker, place the ribs. Rub the curry paste on the ribs. Add ½ cup (120 ml) of the milk. Cover and cook on low for 7 to 8 hours. During the final ½ hour of cooking, add the remaining ½ cup (120 ml) milk.

Yield: 4 servings

SMOKED HAM HOCKS WITH WHITE BEANS
If you're going to cook beans in a slow cooker, you must presoak them. You can do this by soaking the beans in cool water overnight, draining them, and then adding them to the recipe. A faster method is to cover the beans with plenty of water in a saucepan, bring them to a boil, remove them from the heat, keep them covered, and allow them to stand for 1 hour. Drain the beans and proceed with the recipe.

1 pound (455 g) great Northern or other white beans, presoaked
2 pounds (910 g) smoked ham hocks
4 cups (940 ml) chicken stock (To make your own, see "Chicken Stock" on page 6.)
Black pepper, to taste

In a slow cooker, place the beans and ham. Add the stock and enough water so you have about twice as much liquid as beans. Cover and cook on low for 8 to 10 hours, or until the beans are tender and the liquid is absorbed. Check and add liquid during the cooking as needed to keep the beans from going dry.

Yield: 4 servings

▶*Add It !*
Stir in 1 or 2 tablespoons (2.5 to 5 g) chopped fresh thyme to add another flavor dimension.

HAM AND SCALLOPED POTATOES
This makes a big pot of potatoes and ham, but we're willing to bet that you won't have any trouble getting rid of it.

8 medium potatoes, peeled and thinly sliced
½ teaspoon cream of tartar
1 cup (235 ml) water
1 pound (455 g) ham, sliced, divided
2 cups (320 g) thinly sliced onions, divided
1 cup (120 g) grated Cheddar cheese
10 ounces (280 g) cream of mushroom soup (To make your own, see "Cream of Mushroom Soup" on page 7.)
Paprika

In a bowl, toss the potatoes in the cream of tartar and water. Drain.
    In a slow cooker, place half of the ham, potatoes, and onions. Sprinkle with the cheese. Repeat with the remaining half of the ham, potatoes, and onions. Spoon the soup over top. Sprinkle with the paprika. Cover and cook on low for 8 to 10 hours or on high for 4 hours.

Yield: 8 servings

ORANGE-GLAZED HAM
This is an easy way to bake a ham and leave the oven available for the rest of the dinner.

1 semi-boneless ham (about 6 pounds or 2730 g)
1 (12-ounce or 340-g) jar orange marmalade
4 or 5 whole cloves

In a slow cooker, place the ham. Slather the marmalade over the ham. Stick the cloves into the ham. Cover and cook on low for 7 to 8 hours or on high for 3 to 4 hours.

Yield: 8 to 10 servings

HAM AND CABBAGE CASSEROLE
This would be perfect with some noodles or spaetzle on the side for a nice, cozy winter dinner!.

1 small head green cabbage
1 pound (455 g) boneless ham, sliced
1 (10-ounce or 285-ml) can condensed cream of Cheddar soup

Core and shred the cabbage. Place it in alternating layers with the ham in the slow cooker. Pour the soup over all. Cover and cook on low for 6 to 7 hours or on high for 2 to 3 hours.

Yield: 4 to 6 servings

HOLIDAY HAM
This quick-and-easy ham will get raves. Don't let on how little time it really took to prepare!

2½- to 4-pound (1.1- to 1.8-kg) ham, depending on slow cooker size
2 cups (498 g) canned pineapple chunks, undrained
½ cup (161 g) pure maple syrup

In a slow cooker, place the ham. Pour the pineapple over the ham. Drizzle on the syrup. Cover and cook on low for 6 to 8 hours.
    Serve the ham with the pineapple on the side.

Yield: 10 servings

CODDLED HAM
Indulge yourself with this easy-to-prepare ham. With very little effort, you can prepare a wonderful meal and win yourself a day away from the kitchen.

½ cup (120 ml) water
½ cup (120 ml) ham glaze
One 3- to 4-pound (1.4- to 1.8-kg) fully cooked ham, or a size that fits inside a covered slow cooker

Pour the water into the slow cooker. Rub the ham glaze over the ham, wrap and seal the ham in aluminum foil, and place it in the water. Cover and cook on low for 6 to 10 hours or on high for 3 to 5 hours, or until the ham is hot throughout. Don't overcook the ham or it may fall apart when sliced.

Yield: 12 servings

GREEN BEANS WITH SMOKED SAUSAGE
These Southern-style green beans, cooked until very done, are flavored with smoked meat. They go great with boiled potatoes.

1 pound (455 g) turkey smoked sausage, sliced ½–inch (1.3 cm) thick
1 pound (455 g) frozen green beans
½ cup (80 g) chopped onion
¼ cup (60 g) brown sugar

In a slow cooker, place the sausage. Top with the beans and then the onion. Sprinkle with the sugar. Cover and cook on low for 4 to 5 hours.

Yield: 5 servings

SAUSAGE WITH APPLES AND ONIONS
This dish is so adaptable it can be served on nearly any occasion. Serve it with pancakes for a hearty breakfast, or pair it with mashed potatoes for a delicious dinner.

2 pounds (910 g) apples
4 medium onions
2 tablespoons (60 ml) olive oil
Salt, to taste
Black pepper, to taste
1 pound (455 g) breakfast sausage links

Peel and core the apples and cut them into ¼-inch-thick (6-mm-thick) slices.
    Peel the onions and julienne them ¼ inch (6 mm) thick. In a large sauté pan, heat the oil over medium-high heat. Sauté the apples and onions until lightly browned. Season with salt and pepper.
    Transfer the apples and onions to a slow cooker.
    In the same pan, brown the sausage on all sides. Transfer the sausage to the slow cooker. Cover and cook on low for 6 to 8 hours or on high for 2 to 3 hours.

Yield: 4 to 6 servings

SLOW-COOKER SAUSAGE AND LIMA BEANS
The mild flavor of limas and the spicy flavor of sausage are perfect counterparts. Serve this with biscuits and honey butter. Did you know? Lima beans, also called butter beans, are a favorite southern staple. Fordhooks are the large variety and slightly stronger in taste. Baby limas are a smaller, milder variety, not just small Fordhooks.

2 cups (475 ml) hot water
2 beef bouillon cubes
1 to 1½ pounds (455 to 683 g) smoked sausage, sliced into ½-inch (1.3-cm) coins
One 15-ounce (417-g) can baby lima beans, drained
½ teaspoon black pepper

In a slow cooker, combine the water and bouillon. Stir until the bouillon has dissolved. Add the sausage and lima beans. Stir again. Cover and cook on low for 8 to 10 hours.
    Before serving, stir the mixture and season it with the pepper.

Yield: 8 servings

▶*Recipe Tip*
Add ½ cup (60 g) chopped green onion, 1 clove garlic, minced, and hot sauce to taste along with the sausage coins and lima beans.

CHICKEN WITH ROOT VEGETABLES
This is sort of a French Country dish. It's delicious and complete just as it is.

5 pounds (2.3 kg) chicken
1½ tablespoons (23 ml) olive oil
1½ tablespoons (21 g) butter
2 medium turnips, cut into 1/2-inch (13 mm) cubes
2 medium carrots, cut into 1/2-inch (13 mm) slices
1 medium onion, cut into 1/4-inch (6 mm) half-rounds
1 head cabbage
4 cloves garlic, crushed
½ teaspoon dried rosemary
½ teaspoon dried thyme
½ teaspoon dried basil
2 bay leaves, crumbled
Salt, to taste
Black pepper, to taste

In a big, heavy skillet, brown the chicken on both sides in the oil and butter over medium-high heat. Remove the chicken to a plate.
    Pour off all but about 2 tablespoons (28 ml) of the fat from the skillet. Sauté the turnips, carrots, and onion, scraping the brown bits off of the bottom of the skillet as you stir, until they're getting a touch of gold, too.
    Transfer the vegetables to a slow cooker.
    Cut the cabbage into eighths and place it on top of the vegetables in the slow cooker. Arrange the chicken on top of the cabbage. Sprinkle the garlic on top, making sure some gets down to the vegetables. Sprinkle the rosemary, thyme, basil, and bay leaves on top, making sure some gets down into the vegetables. Season with salt and pepper. Cover and cook on low for 6 to 7 hours.

Yield: 8 servings

BAKED WHOLE CHICKEN
A slow-baked chicken makes a nice presentation at the table. The chicken looks festive on the platter, and its appetizing aroma announces that a special dinner is ready.

1 tablespoon (15 ml) olive oil
1 teaspoon adobo seasoning
One 3- to 3½-pound (1.4- to 1.6-kg) whole chicken, rinsed and dried inside and out

In a small bowl, stir the oil and seasoning together. Spread the mixture evenly over the chicken.
    In a slow cooker, place the chicken breast side up. Cover and cook on low for 6 to 8 hours, or until the chicken is tender and the juices run clear.

Using several spatulas or a meat fork, remove the chicken from the slow cooker, taking care to preserve the chicken's shape.

Yield: 6 servings

▶ *Recipe Tips*
- *To make a yummy gravy from the cooking liquid, dissolve 3 tablespoons (24 g) flour in ½ cup (120 ml) water and stir the mixture into the cooking liquid remaining in the slow cooker after the chicken has been removed. With the slow cooker on high, cook and stir the mixture continuously until it thickens. Season the gravy with salt and freshly ground black pepper to taste.*

- *Add ½ teaspoon Hungarian paprika to the olive oil along with the adobo seasoning. For a one-pot meal, put 4 potatoes, peeled and cubed, 1 cup (122 g) baby carrots, and ½ cup (120 ml) water in the bottom of the slow cooker, then place the prepared chicken on top of them. Increase the cooking time by about 1 hour, to ensure that the chicken is done and the vegetables are tender.*

EASIEST LEAN ARTICHOKE CHICKEN BREASTS
Artichokes are like the lobster of the veggie community: You have to really dig to get at the good parts, but in the end it's worth it. This spicy artichoke sauce perfectly complements the breast meat of chicken. The best thing about this recipe is how simple it is to make. Okay, maybe tied for best–that tangy artichoke sauce is a definite plus.

12 ounces (336 g) mini baby carrots
4 small boneless, skinless chicken breasts
1 can (14 ounces, or 392 g) artichoke hearts, drained and halved
1 jar (6 ounces, or 168 g) artichoke hearts marinated in olive oil, undrained
¼ cup (60 ml) dry white wine
Juice and zest of ½ lemon
½ teaspoon salt
½ teaspoon black pepper

In a slow cooker, scatter the carrots. Place the chicken on top. Add the drained artichokes. Pour the marinated artichokes and oil evenly over all. Pour in the wine, squeeze in the lemon, and add the zest. Season with salt and pepper. Cover and cook on low for 3 to 4 hours or on high for 2 to 3 hours, or until the chicken is cooked through.

Yield: 4 to 6 servings
▶ *Health Bite*
Artichokes have a number of active chemicals with health benefits for a wide range of conditions. These include silymarin (the active ingredient in the herb milk thistle), which has a long and distinguished resume as a plant compound that helps protect and nourish the liver.

And artichokes are known for their effects on gastrointestinal upset. One study showed that 85 percent of patients with GI upset who were given extract of artichokes experienced significant relief from nausea, stomach pain, and vomiting.

Chicken breasts are a wonderful source of protein and slightly lower in calories than the dark meat.

LEAN LEMON-APRICOT CHICKEN BREASTS
Chicken and apricots are a match made in taste-combo heaven. Apricots originally hail from China, where they've been grown for more than 4,000 years. They were rumored to be introduced to the West by Alexander the Great. The natural sugars and acids in the juices help keep this divine dish as tender as you'd want it to be.

1 large yellow onion, sliced
1 cup (110 g) grated carrot
6 boneless, skinless chicken breasts (or the equivalent bone-in)
⅓ cup (80 ml) apricot nectar
2 tablespoons (30 ml) tamari
1 tablespoon (15 ml) lemon juice
2 tablespoons (22 g) Dijon mustard
1 tablespoon (6 g) lemon zest
½ cup (65 g) chopped dried apricots

In a slow cooker, scatter the onion and carrot. Place the chicken on top.

In a small bowl, whisk the nectar, tamari, juice, mustard, and zest together. Stir in the apricots. Pour the mixture over the chicken. Cover and cook on low for 3 to 4 hours or on high for 2 to 3 hours, or until the chicken is cooked through but still juicy. Stir to baste before serving.

Yield: 6 servings

▶ *Health Bite*
Health experts recommend eating only unsulfured apricots. Otherwise, sulfur dioxide is used to preserve the color. It's probably safe in tiny amounts, but in large amounts, it's a potential carcinogen. Also, many people are allergic to it.

65 Chicken with Root Vegetables

66 Baked Whole Chicken; 67 Easiest Lean Artichoke Chicken Breasts; 68 Lean Lemon-Apricot Chicken Breasts; 69 In-a-Pinch Pesto Chicken and Mushrooms; 70 Cranberry Chicken Breasts; 71 Santa Fe Chicken

MAIN DISHES • 107

IN-A-PINCH PESTO CHICKEN AND MUSHROOMS

Looking for a dish that you can throw together quickly that still tastes great and provides world-class nourishment? This dish fits the bill. It's a basic five-ingredient mix. Best of all, the prep time for this is the same as it takes to brew a pot of coffee.

8 ounces (225 g) sliced white cremini mushrooms
4 large shallots, quartered
⅓ cup (80 ml) chicken broth (To make your own, see "Chicken Stock" on page 6.)
4 boneless, skinless chicken breasts (or the equivalent bone-in)
1 container (6 ounces, or 168 g) pesto

In a slow cooker, combine the mushrooms and shallots. Pour the broth over all. Place the chicken on top. Spoon the pesto evenly over them. Cook on low for 3 to 4 hours or on high for 2 to 3 hours, or until the chicken is just cooked through.

Yield: 4 servings

CRANBERRY CHICKEN BREASTS

Cranberry Chicken is a refreshing twist on the usual weeknight fare. The sweet cranberry essence is enhanced by the tartness of the dressing. For a more complex flavor, add a 2-ounce (55-g) envelope of onion soup mix to the sauce-and-dressing mixture.

1½ pounds (683 g) skinless, boneless chicken breast halves
One 16-ounce (455-g) can whole-berry or jellied cranberry sauce
1 cup (250 g) French dressing

In a slow cooker, place the chicken.
In a medium bowl, combine the cranberry sauce and French dressing. Pour the mixture over the chicken in the slow cooker. Cover and cook on low for 5 to 7 hours, or until the chicken is thoroughly cooked.

Yield: 6 servings

SANTA FE CHICKEN

This simple version of a favorite southwestern dish goes well with Cuban bread, butter, and a green salad. Serve this colorful dish in bright Fiestaware or earthenware dishes with colorful napkins and placemats. Add some margaritas or Mexican beer such as Dos Equis. Or serve the chicken right from the slow cooker for an easy cleanup.

Two 15-ounce (417-g) cans Mexican corn with red and green peppers
1 15-ounce (417-g) can black beans, rinsed and drained
1 cup (225 g) chunky-style salsa, divided
6 skinless, boneless chicken breast halves
1 cup (115 g) shredded Mexican-blend cheese

In a slow cooker, stir the corn, beans, and ½ cup (113 g) of the salsa together. Place the chicken on top. Pour the remaining salsa over the chicken. Cover and cook on low for 5 to 7 hours or on high for 2½ to 3½ hours, or until the chicken is tender. Sprinkle the cheese on top, cover, and cook on low for an additional 10 minutes, or until the cheese has melted.

Yield: 6 servings

▶*Add It!*
Add a 15-ounce (417-g) can black beans, rinsed and drained, along with the corn.

LEMON, ROSEMARY, AND GARLIC CHICKEN BREASTS

Chicken is so versatile and delicious! But nothing steals the fun from family dinners faster than sitting down to the same old poultry main dish night after night after night–except, perhaps, slaving over a hot stove. Get into a new groove with slow cooker dishes like this one! This scrumptious chicken dish gets its sparkle from a bit o' the bubbly. Serve it over rice, with a crusty loaf of focaccia bread and olive-oil dipping sauce.

2 pounds (910 g) skinless, boneless chicken breasts, cut into chunks of uniform size
¾ cup (175 ml) Emeril Lemon, Rosemary, and Garlic Marinade
¾ cup (175 ml) lemon-lime soda

In a slow cooker, place the chicken.

In a small bowl, combine the marinade and soda. Pour the mixture over the chicken. Cover and cook on low for 5 to 7 hours or on high for 2½ to 3½ hours, or until the chicken is thoroughly cooked.

Yield: 8 servings

▶*Recipe Tip*
If you use frozen chicken breasts for this recipe, partially thaw them in the microwave. When they're a smidgeon away from being completely thawed, cut them into chunks using a sharp knife. You'll be surprised by how much easier it is to cut chicken that's still slightly firm from being frozen. Don't forget to finish thawing the chunks in the microwave or in cold water, if necessary, before placing them in the slow cooker. If you use fresh chicken, place the breasts in the freezer for 10 to 15 minutes to enjoy the same cutting ease.

SWEET AND SOUR CHICKEN BREASTS

This isn't, perhaps, what you typically think of when you hear sweet and sour chicken, but these tasty breasts will be a hit with all.

3 pounds (1⅓ kg) chicken breast halves, skinned
¾ cup (213 g) frozen lemonade concentrate, thawed
3 tablespoons (45 g) packed brown sugar
3 tablespoons (45 g) ketchup (To make your own, see "Homemade Smoky Ketchup" on page 8.)
1 tablespoon (15 ml) vinegar
2 tablespoons (16 g) cornstarch mixed with 2 tablespoons (15 ml) cold water

In a slow cooker, place the chicken.

In a medium bowl, combine the lemonade, sugar, ketchup, and vinegar. Pour the mixture over the chicken in the slow cooker. Cover and cook on low for 6 to 7 hours or on high for 3 to 3½ hours.

Transfer the chicken to a serving platter, cover, and keep warm. Pour the cooking liquid into a medium saucepan. Skim off the fat. Stir the cornstarch slurry into the saucepan. Cook and stir over medium heat until thickened and bubbly. Cook and stir for 2 minutes more.

Spoon the sauce over the chicken.

Yield: 6 servings

MOM'S 1960S CHICKEN REDUX

Back in the 1960s, a popular dish was chicken breasts, wrapped in bacon, laid on a layer of chipped beef, and topped with a sauce made of sour cream and cream of mushroom soup. It tasted far more sophisticated than it sounds. Here we've slow-cooker-ized that old familiar dish.

2¼ ounces (62 g) dried beef slices (aka "chipped beef")
6 slices bacon
2 pounds (900 g) boneless, skinless chicken breasts
1 cup (70 g) sliced mushrooms
1 tablespoon (14 g) butter
1 cup (235 ml) heavy cream
1 teaspoon beef bouillon concentrate
1 pinch onion powder
1 pinch celery salt
¼ teaspoon black pepper
Cornstarch
1 cup (230 g) sour cream
Paprika

In a slow cooker, place the dried beef.

In a glass pie plate or on a microwave bacon rack, microwave the bacon for 3 to 4 minutes on high. Drain the bacon.

Cut the chicken into 6 servings. Wrap each piece of chicken in a slice of bacon and place it in the slow cooker on top of the dried beef.

In a big, heavy skillet, sauté the mushrooms in the butter until they're soft. Add the cream and bouillon. Stir until the bouillon dissolves. Stir in the onion powder, celery salt, and pepper. Thicken the mixture with cornstarch until the mixture reaches a gravy consistency. Stir in the sour cream. Spoon the mixture over the chicken in the slow cooker. Sprinkle with paprika. Cover and cook on low for 5 to 6 hours.

To serve, scoop up some of the dried beef and sauce with each bacon-wrapped piece of chicken.

Yield: 6 servings

MAIN DISHES • **109**

72 *Lemon, Rosemary, and Garlic Chicken Breasts*

73

73 Sweet and Sour Chicken Breasts

SERIOUSLY SIMPLE CHICKEN CHILI
The name says it all!

2 pounds (900 g) boneless, skinless chicken breasts
1 jar (16 ounces, or 455 g) salsa
1 tablespoon (8 g) chili powder
1 teaspoon chicken bouillon concentrate
3 ounces (85 g) shredded Monterey Jack cheese
6 tablespoons (90 g) light sour cream

In a slow cooker, place the chicken.
  In a bowl, stir together the salsa, chili powder, and bouillon, until the bouillon has dissolved. Pour the mixture over the chicken in the slow cooker. Cover and cook on low for 7 to 8 hours.
  Remove the chicken from the slow cooker. Using a fork, shred the chicken.
  Serve the chicken topped with the cheese and sour cream.

Yield: 6 servings

PEANUTTY THAI CHICKEN
Asian food can be really healthy, but unfortunately you might not know it. Many restaurants rely on MSG for the flavor that's missing in the overcooked, overprocessed food they serve, and many use sauces that are made "tasty" not by the richness of the flavors, but by the addition of sugar and wheat starch (think "egg drop soup").

½ cup (130 g) smooth peanut butter
½ cup (120 ml) chicken broth (To make your own, see "Chicken Stock" on page 6.)
¼ cup (60 ml) tamari sauce
Juice of 1 large lime
1 tablespoon (15 ml) rice wine vinegar
4 cloves garlic, crushed
1-inch (2.5 cm) chunk peeled fresh ginger
1 tablespoon (20 g) honey
½ teaspoon red pepper flakes
1 sweet onion, chopped
1 red bell pepper, seeded and chopped
1½ pounds (680 g) boneless, skinless chicken breast or thighs, cut into 1½-inch (3.8 cm) pieces
½ cup (8 g) chopped fresh cilantro

In the bowl of a food processor, process the peanut butter, broth, tamari, juice, vinegar, garlic, ginger, honey, and red pepper until smooth, scraping down the sides as necessary.
  In a slow cooker, combine the onion, bell pepper, and chicken. Pour the sauce evenly over all. Stir gently to coat. Cover and cook on low for 5 to 6 hours or on high for 3 to 4 hours, or until the chicken is cooked through but still juicy. Just before serving, stir in the cilantro.

Yield: 4 servings

CHICK'N MUSHROOM CASSEROLE
This is a comforting retro casserole that you'll wish you had when you were growing up. The Creamy Cashew Sour Cream adds richness to the mushroom sauce, while the pasta and seitan make it hearty and filling. It's a perfect potluck dish, as well as a warming meal on a snowy day.

FOR THE CASHEW SOUR CREAM:
½ cup (73 g) cashews
½ cup (120 ml) water
2 teaspoons lemon juice

FOR THE CASSEROLE:
2 tablespoons (30 ml) olive oil
1 small onion, minced
2 cloves garlic, minced
1 package (10 ounces, or 280 g) sliced mushrooms
1 tablespoon (6 g) chicken-flavored bouillon
4 cups (940 ml) milk
1½ cups (340 g) cubed chicken-flavored seitan (To make your own, see "Chick'N Seitan" on page 18.)
8 ounces (225 g) dried whole wheat pasta shells or rotini
½ teaspoon dried thyme
½ teaspoon dried marjoram
Salt, to taste
Black pepper, to taste
2 tablespoons (16 g) flour, if needed
Bread crumbs

To make the Cashew Sour Cream: In a food processor, process the cashews, water, and juice until smooth and creamy.

To make the casserole: In a skillet, heat the oil over medium heat. Sauté the onion for 3 to 5 minutes, or until translucent. Add the garlic and mushrooms and sauté for 5 to 10 minutes, or until the mushrooms reduce in size and are tender.
  Coat the crock of a slow cooker with nonstick cooking spray.
  In the slow cooker, combine the vegetables, Cashew Sour Cream, bouillon, milk, seitan, pasta, thyme, and marjoram. Season with salt and pepper. Mix thoroughly. Cover and cook on high for 1 to 1½ hours, or until the pasta is al dente.
  If the pasta is ready but the sauce is not thick enough, add the flour and stir to combine and thicken. Top each serving with the bread crumbs.

Yield: 4 servings

▶ *Serving Suggestion*
Get nostalgic and top with your family's favorite casserole topping from your youth. Topping ideas include crushed potato chips or Ritz crackers, canned french fried onions, or just about anything crunchy.

SPINACH, BASIL, AND FETA-STUFFED CHICKEN ROLLS WITH PIGNOLI

Pignoli are another name for pine nuts, those small, white, oval-shaped nuts that are actually the edible seeds of pines and are in demand because of the popularity of pesto. Here they add just a touch of flavor, texture, and visual interest to these delicious feta-stuffed chicken rolls.

6 boneless, skinless chicken breast halves
8 ounces (225 g) feta cheese, crumbled
4 cups (120 g) chopped baby spinach
¼ cup (10 g) chopped fresh basil
¼ cup (25 g) finely chopped pitted Kalamata olives
4 cloves garlic, minced
2 teaspoons olive oil
½ teaspoon salt
½ teaspoon black pepper
1 can (14.5 ounces, or 406 g) diced tomatoes with garlic and basil, undrained
¼ cup (34 g) toasted pine nuts

Coat the crock of a slow cooker with nonstick cooking spray.

Place each chicken breast between two sheets of waxed paper. Using a meat mallet, pound them to about ¼-inch (6 mm) thickness; lay them out flat.

In a medium bowl, combine the feta, spinach, basil, olives, garlic, and oil. Mix well.

Lightly and evenly sprinkle each chicken breast with salt and pepper.

Divide the spinach and feta mixture into 6 portions. Spoon an equal measure onto the wider end of each breast and roll it up. Lay the rolls close together, seam sides down, in the slow cooker insert. Pour the tomatoes evenly over all. Cover and cook on low for 5 to 6 hours or on high for about 4 hours, or until the chicken is cooked through.

Garnish with the pine nuts.

Yield: 6 servings

▶*Kalamata olives are named after the city of Kalamata in Greece. They're known for being jumbo size with a meaty taste. They enjoy PDO status (Protected Designation of Origin), which is a legal framework in the European Union designed to protect the names of regional foods.*

EASY ASIAN SWEET CHILI

In this recipe, you can use dark meat or light meat, although the dark meat stays moister longer in the slow cooker. This dish is easy to prepare, and it has a sweet and satisfying "kicky" bite. This dish makes great leftovers because the flavors continue to deepen over time.

1 sweet onion, chopped
1 red bell pepper, seeded and chopped
1 large summer squash, sliced into ¾-inch (2 cm) half-moons
3 pounds (1,362 g) boneless, skinless chicken pieces, dark or light meat
¾ cup (170 g) Thai sweet chili sauce
Juice of 1 lime
2 tablespoons (30 ml) tamari sauce
2 tablespoons (30 ml) Thai fish sauce
4 cloves garlic, crushed and chopped

In a slow cooker, arrange the onion, bell pepper, and squash. Place the chicken on top.

In a small bowl, whisk together the chili sauce, juice, tamari, fish sauce, and garlic. Pour the mixture evenly over the chicken. Cover and cook on low for 4 to 5 hours or on high for 2½ to 3 hours, or until the chicken is cooked through but still juicy.

Yield: 6 servings

▶*Health Bite*

When buying chicken, consider pastured chicken. Pastured chickens are raised outside in fresh air and sunshine on fresh green growing pasture, in small groups, protected by large, bottomless pens that are moved regularly onto new ground. Grazing freely outdoors is the way chickens are supposed to be raised, and pastured chicken is the kind you should try to use in your cooking.

Pastured chicken is actually preferable to free-range, though it's harder to find. Why? Because "free-range" often means the chickens have access to pasture, maybe only for limited times, and often the chickens don't even take advantage of that access, which sometimes consists of a little gate they can walk through if they like. Pastured chickens don't stand around in their own droppings, which naturally breaks the cycle of parasitic infections.

74 Mom's 1960s Chicken Redux; 75 Seriously Simple Chicken Chili; 76 Peanutty Thai Chicken; 77 Chick'N Mushroom Casserole; 78 Spinach, Basil, and Feta-Stuffed Chicken Rolls with Pignoli; 79 Easy Asian Sweet Chili; 80 Apricot Chicken; 81 Sweet and Saucy Free-Range Chicken Thighs

114 • THE LITTLE SLOW COOKER COOKBOOK

82 Slow Cooker Chicken Mole; 83 Chicken and Dumplings; 84 Chicken Cacciatore; 85 Drumsticks with Hoisin and Honey;
86 Cornish Game Hens and Wild Rice; 87 Turkey and Fruit Sweetened Cranberry Sauce Supper; 88 Savory Slow Cooker Tender
Turkey Drumsticks; 89 Turkey Dinner

MAIN DISHES • 115

APRICOT CHICKEN
Here's a sweet-and-sour chicken recipe in which apricots make all the difference. Serve this with a salad of mixed baby greens and lemon–poppy seed muffins.

8 bone-in chicken thighs, skin removed
One 2-ounce (55-g) envelope onion soup mix (To make your own, see "Onion Soup Mix" on page 7.)
One or two 12-ounce (355-ml) cans apricot nectar

In a slow cooker, place the chicken. Sprinkle the chicken with the soup mix. Pour enough apricot nectar into the slow cooker to cover them. Cover and cook on low for 6 to 8 hours or on high for 3 to 4 hours, or until the chicken is thoroughly cooked.

Yield: 8 servings

SWEET AND SAUCY FREE-RANGE CHICKEN THIGHS
The extra richness of the fat in chicken thighs is just what the chef ordered for the longer cooking times required by the slow cooker. The tangy but sweet sauce in this dish is so good, it'll have your family begging for more.

3 tablespoons (45 ml) tamari sauce
3 tablespoons (45 ml) Worcestershire sauce
1 tablespoon (15 ml) lemon juice
3 tablespoons (45 g) Sucanat
⅓ cup (80 g) ketchup (To make your own, see "Homemade Smoky Ketchup" on page 8.)
2 pounds (908 g) boneless, skinless chicken thighs

In a slow cooker, combine the tamari, Worcestershire, juice, Sucanat, and ketchup. Mix well until thoroughly combined. Add the chicken and toss gently to coat. Cover and cook on low for 4 to 5 hours or on high for 3 to 4 hours, or until the chicken is cooked through but still juicy.

Yield: 6 to 8 servings

▶ *Health Bite*
Chicken thighs get a bad rap, but it's undeserved. Sure, they are slightly higher in calories and fat than breast meat, but they are hardly a distant second choice. First of all, they taste great. Second, a 3.5-ounce (98 g) portion delivers a very respectable 23 grams of protein, and most of the fat in the thighs is of the heart-healthy monounsaturated variety, which is the same kind of fat in olive oil. Surprised?

SLOW COOKER CHICKEN MOLE
Chicken mole is the national dish of Mexico. Here's a slow cooker version.

1 can (14½ ounces, or 410 g) tomatoes with green chiles
½ cup (80 g) chopped onion
¼ cup (28 g) plus 2 tablespoons (14 g) slivered almonds, toasted, divided
3 cloves garlic, crushed
3 tablespoons (18 g) unsweetened cocoa powder
2 tablespoons (18 g) raisins
1 tablespoon (8 g) sesame seeds
1 tablespoon (1.5 g) sugar
¼ teaspoon ground cinnamon
¼ teaspoon ground nutmeg
¼ teaspoon ground coriander
¼ teaspoon salt
3 pounds (1.4 kg) skinless chicken thighs Cornstarch

In a food processor, coarsely purée the tomatoes, onion, ¼ cup (28 g) of the almonds, the garlic, cocoa powder, raisins, sesame seeds, sugar, cinnamon, nutmeg, coriander, and salt.
    In a slow cooker, place the chicken. Pour the sauce over it. Cover and cook on low for 9 to 10 hours.
    Using tongs, remove the chicken from the slow cooker. Add cornstarch to thicken the sauce to taste.
    Serve the sauce over the chicken. Top with the remaining 2 tablespoons (14 g) almonds.

Yield: 8 servings

CHICKEN AND DUMPLINGS
This takes some work, but boy, is it comfort food. You could make this with leftover turkey instead if you prefer. If you do that, put the cubed, cooked turkey in about 5 to 6 hours into the initial cooking time.

2 medium carrots, sliced
1 medium onion, chunked
2 medium turnips, cut into 1/2-inch (13 mm) cubes
1½ cups (186 g) frozen green beans, cross-cut
8 ounces (225 g) sliced mushrooms
1½ pounds (680 g) boneless, skinless chicken thighs, cut into 1-inch (2.5 cm) cubes
1½ cups (355 ml) chicken broth
1 teaspoon poultry seasoning
3 teaspoons (18 g) chicken bouillon concentrate
½ cup (120 ml) heavy cream
Cornstarch
Salt, to taste
Black pepper, to taste
Dumplings (See "Dumplings" on page 21.)

In a slow cooker, combine the carrots, onion, turnips, green beans, mushrooms, and chicken.

In a bowl, mix together the broth, poultry seasoning, and bouillon. Pour the mixture over the chicken and vegetables in the slow cooker. Cover and cook on low for 6 to 7 hours.

Stir in the cream. Add cornstarch to thicken to taste. Season with salt and pepper. Re-cover the slow cooker and turn it to high.

While the slow cooker is heating up (it'll take at least 30 minutes), make the Dumplings, stopping before you add the liquid. Wait until the gravy in the slow cooker is boiling. Then stir the buttermilk into the dry ingredients and drop the biscuit dough by spoonfuls over the surface of the chicken and gravy. Re-cover the slow cooker and let it cook for another 25 to 30 minutes.

Yield: 8 servings

CHICKEN CACCIATORE
Here's a slow cooker version of an old favorite. It's easy, too, what we call a dump-and-go recipe. If you like, you can serve this over rice, spaghetti squash, or pasta, but we'd probably eat it as is.

- 6 skinless chicken leg and side quarters (about 3 lbs or 1.4 kg)
- 2 cups (500 g) spaghetti sauce
- 1 can (8 ounces, or 225 g) whole mushrooms, drained
- 2 teaspoons dried oregano
- ½ cup (80 g) chopped onion
- 1 green bell pepper, diced
- 2 cloves garlic, crushed
- ¼ cup (60 ml) dry red wine
- Cornstarch, optional

In a slow cooker, combine all of the ingredients except for the cornstarch. Stir it to combine. Cover and cook on low for 7 hours.

Using tongs, transfer the chicken to a large serving bowl. Add cornstarch to thicken the sauce to taste. Serve the sauce over the chicken.

Yield: 6 servings

DRUMSTICKS WITH HOISIN AND HONEY
Sweet, sassy, and sticky–that's good chicken, and this is a kid favorite.

- 2 pounds (910 g) chicken drumsticks
- 1 cup (250 g) hoisin sauce
- ½ cup (170 g) honey

Preheat the broiler. Put the drumsticks on a broiler pan and broil for 10 to 12 minutes, or until the skin is crisp and brown.

In a large bowl, mix together the sauce and honey. Add the drumsticks and stir gently to coat. Transfer the drumsticks to a slow cooker. Cover and cook on low for 4 to 5 hours or on high for 2 to 3 hours.

Yield: 4 servings

CORNISH GAME HENS AND WILD RICE
These small hens are succulent and tender, and the wild rice is the perfect complement. Serve them with Marmalade-Glazed Carrots (see page 186) and crusty bread.

- One 6-ounce (168-g) envelope wild rice and long-grain converted rice mix
- 1½ cups (355 ml) water
- 2 Cornish game hens
- ½ teaspoon salt
- ¼ teaspoon black pepper

In a slow cooker, combine the rice mix and water. Stir to combine. Place the hens on top of the rice mixture. Sprinkle the hens with the salt and pepper. Cover and cook on low for 6 to 8 hours, or until the hens are thoroughly cooked and the rice is tender.

Yield: 2 servings

90 Braised Turkey Wings with Mushrooms

91 Barbecued Turkey Thighs; 92 Cranberry Barbecued Turkey; 93 Savory Turkey and Rice; 94 Turkey Tortilla Pie

MAIN DISHES • 119

TURKEY AND FRUIT SWEETENED CRANBERRY SAUCE SUPPER

It's ironic that some of the healthiest things on our holiday menus don't make it into heavy rotation during the year. For example, pumpkin is a fabulous vegetable that few people think of except during Halloween and Thanksgiving. Turkey with cranberry sauce is another perfect example. In this dish, we use fresh and dried fruit plus nut purée to give the cranberry base sweetness and body. It's the perfect complement to lean, moist turkey breast.

2 sweet baking apples, peeled, cored, and chopped
1 navel orange, peeled and quartered
½ cup (60 g) dried, juice-sweetened cranberries
½ cup (65 g) chopped unsulfured dried apples or apricots
½ cup (56 g) raw pecans
12 ounces (336 g) fresh cranberries
1 cup (235 ml) apple cider
⅓ cup (75 g) Sucanat (or ½ cup (120 g) xylitol)
1 tablespoon (15 g) minute tapioca
½ teaspoon ground cinnamon
½ teaspoon ground allspice
2 ½- to 3-pound (1,135 to 1,362 g) turkey breast, bone-in ½ teaspoon salt
½ teaspoon black pepper

In a food processor, process the apples, orange, cranberries, dried apples, and pecans until mostly smooth, forming a paste, scraping down the sides as necessary.
    In a slow cooker, combine the fresh cranberries, cider, Sucanat, tapioca, cinnamon, allspice, and fruit paste. Stir gently to thoroughly combine.
    Place the turkey on top of the mixture. Sprinkle with the salt and pepper. Cover and cook on low for 6 to 7 hours or on high for 3½ to 4 hours, or until the temperature reads 170°F (77°C) on an instant-read thermometer inserted into the thickest part of the breast meat. Take care not to touch bone with the thermometer.
    Remove the turkey. Stir the cranberry sauce well to combine.

Serve the turkey with the sauce drizzled over the top.

Yield: 6 servings

▶*Health Bite*
Studies presented at the 223rd national meeting of the American Chemical Society show that cranberries have some of the most potent antioxidants of any common fruit studied. Plant compounds in cranberries possess anticancer properties, inhibit the growth of common food-borne pathogens, and contain antibacterial properties to aid in the prevention of urinary tract infections.

SAVORY SLOW COOKER TENDER TURKEY DRUMSTICKS

You don't have to wait till the holidays to enjoy these tender turkey drumsticks. This recipe is super easy and super fast. When you use the slow cooker, it cooks to a delicious tenderness in its own juices, with no added fat calories. The fat that's in there–perfectly healthy fat, mind you–replaces the conventional gravy or commercial cream of mushroom soup that generally smothers a dish like this. (Note: A can of commercial cream of mushroom soup has an astonishing 1,995 milligrams of sodium. Need we say more?)

3 turkey drumsticks
1 tablespoon (15 ml) olive oil
Salt, to taste
Black pepper, to taste
1 large Vidalia onion, chopped
3 large carrots, peeled and sliced into thin coins
2 large cloves garlic, minced
½ teaspoon dried sage, crumbled
2 tablespoons (8 g) chopped fresh parsley
1 tablespoon (2.4 g) chopped fresh thyme (or 1 teaspoon dried)
1 lemon, halved

Coat the bottom of a slow cooker and the drumsticks with the oil.
    Season the drumsticks liberally with salt and pepper.
    In the bottom of the slow cooker, place the onion and carrots. Top with the drumsticks.
    In a small bowl, combine the garlic, sage, parsley, and thyme. Sprinkle the mixture evenly over the drumsticks. Gently squeeze the lemon halves to release their juices into the vegetables and nestle them at the bottom of the slow cooker. Cover and cook on low for 8 to 10 hours or on high for 4 to 5 hours, or until the drumsticks are cooked through and the drumsticks and vegetables are very tender.

Yield: 4 servings

▶*Health Bite*
Onions are a rich source of sulfur, so they are good for the skin. Plus, they are one of the best sources of a flavonoid called quercetin, one of the most anti-inflammatory plant compounds on the planet, and one that has been shown to have significant anticancer properties to boot.
    It's worth noting that turkeys are frequently raised under horrific factory-farmed conditions, so if possible, buy the free-range variety. They're better for you, anyway.

TURKEY DINNER
It's so simple and quick to make a one-pot turkey meal. Thicken the gravy, if you wish, and enjoy the gravy with the turkey, vegetables, and biscuits.

4 cups (480 g) frozen stew vegetables, thawed
2 pounds (910 g) bone-in turkey thighs, skin removed
One 10¾-ounce can (305-g) condensed cream of mushroom soup (To make your own, see "Cream of Mushroom Soup" on page 7.)
¼ cup (60 ml) water

In a slow cooker, scatter the vegetables. Place the turkey on top of them.

In a small bowl, combine the soup and water. Pour the mixture over the turkey and vegetables. Cover and cook on low for 8 to 10 hours or on high for 4 to 5 hours, or until the turkey is thoroughly cooked and the vegetables are tender.

Yield: 8 servings

▶*Add It In!*
Add 1 medium onion, chopped, and 2 cloves garlic, minced, to the soup mixture, and substitute sherry for the water.

BRAISED TURKEY WINGS WITH MUSHROOMS
Turkey wings are a fabulous cut of turkey for the slow cooker. They fit in the slow cooker easily, they come in good individual serving sizes, and oh yeah, they taste great.

3¼ pounds (1.5 kg) turkey wings
¼ cup (60 ml) olive oil
½ cup (120 ml) chicken broth (To make your own, see "Chicken Stock" on page 6.)
1 teaspoon chicken bouillon concentrate
1 teaspoon poultry seasoning
1 tablespoon (16 g) tomato paste
1 cup (70 g) sliced mushrooms
½ medium onion, sliced
½ cup (115 g) sour cream

In a big, heavy skillet, brown the turkey all over in the oil over medium-high heat.

Transfer the turkey to a slow cooker.

In a bowl, stir together the broth, bouillon, poultry seasoning, and paste. Pour the mixture over the turkey. Add the mushrooms and onion. Cover and cook on low for 6 to 7 hours, or until the turkey is thoroughly cooked.

When the time's up, using tongs, remove the turkey from the slow cooker. Whisk the sour cream into the sauce.

Serve the sauce over the turkey.

Yield: 3 servings

BARBECUED TURKEY THIGHS
You can serve this as part of a main course or shred the meat and use it for sandwiches. Either way, you won't be disappointed.

3 pounds (11/3 kg) turkey thighs, skin removed
¼ teaspoon black pepper
⅓ cup (113 g) molasses
⅓ cup (80 ml) cider vinegar
½ cup (120 g) ketchup (To make your own, see "Homemade Smoky Ketchup" on page 7.)
3 tablespoons (45 ml) Worcestershire sauce
½ teaspoon liquid smoke
2 tablespoons (20 g) minced onion

In a slow cooker, place the turkey.

In a bowl, combine the pepper, molasses, vinegar, ketchup, Worcestershire, liquid smoke, and onion. Pour the mixture over the turkey. Cover and cook on low for 5 to 7 hours, or until the turkey is thoroughly cooked.

Yield: 6 servings

CRANBERRY BARBECUED TURKEY
This isn't your typical cranberry and turkey recipe. This one adds a barbecue flavor to turkey legs for a sweet and spicy treat.

3 pounds (11/3 kg) turkey legs
1 pound (455 g) jellied cranberry sauce
½ cup (140 g) chili sauce (To make your own, see "Chili Sauce" on page 8.)
2 tablespoons (28 ml) cider vinegar
½ teaspoon cinnamon

In a slow cooker, place the turkey.

In a bowl, combine the cranberry sauce, chili sauce, vinegar, and cinnamon. Pour the mixture over the turkey. Cover and cook on low for 8 to 9 hours or on high for 4 to 5 hours, or until the turkey is thoroughly cooked.

Yield: 6 servings

MAIN DISHES • 121

SAVORY TURKEY AND RICE
One-pot dishes are fabulous for those days when you're pressed for time. A basket of flaky biscuits or crusty bread is all you need to round this out into a lovely meal.

2 cups (350 g) chopped cooked turkey
One 14-ounce (398-g) can diced tomatoes with garlic, oregano, and basil, undrained
1 cup (235 ml) water
¾ cup (139 g) converted rice, uncooked
Salt, to taste
Black pepper, to taste

In a slow cooker, combine the turkey, tomatoes, water, and rice. Stir to combine.
    Cover and cook on low for 6 to 8 hours or on high for 3 to 4 hours, or until the turkey is thoroughly cooked.
    Before serving, stir the turkey mixture and season it with salt and pepper.

Yield: 8 servings

▶ Add It!
Add 1½ cups (340 g) frozen mixed vegetables, ½ cup (120 ml) sherry, and 2 cloves garlic, minced.

TURKEY TORTILLA PIE
This is a great way to use up leftovers from a holiday meal. Because you can also make it with cooked chicken meat, there's no need to wait for a holiday.

4 cups (560 g) cooked, cubed, boneless turkey meat, divided
4 cups (900 g) salsa, divided
12 (8-inch or 20-cm) corn tortillas, divided

In a slow cooker, place 1 cup (140 g) of the turkey. Top the turkey with 1 cup (225 g) of the salsa, then top that with 4 tortillas, arranged to fill the circumference of the slow cooker. Repeat the layers twice more, finishing with the remaining 1 cup (140 g) of the turkey and 1 cup (225 g) of the salsa. Cover and cook on low for 4 hours or on high for 2 hours, or until the turkey is thoroughly cooked.

Yield: 4 servings

▶ Add It!
Add 2 cups (230 g) shredded Monterey Jack or Cheddar cheese, divided among the layers.

TURKEY MEAT LOAF
Lower in fat and calories than beef meat loaf, this turkey loaf will still please you and your family with its great taste.

1½ pounds (680 g) ground turkey
1 cup (160 g) chopped onion
½ cup (120 ml) egg substitute
⅔ cup (53 g) quick-cooking oats
2 tablespoons (15 g) onion soup mix (To make your own, see "Onion Soup Mix" on page 7.)
¼ teaspoon liquid smoke
1 teaspoon dry mustard
1 cup (240 g) ketchup, divided (To make your own see "Homemade Smoky Ketchup" on page 8.)

Coat the crock of a slow cooker with nonstick cooking spray.
    In a bowl, combine the turkey and onion thoroughly. Using your hands, mix in the egg substitute, oats, dry soup mix, liquid smoke, mustard, and all but 2 tablespoons (30 g) of the ketchup. Shape the mixture into a loaf and place it in the slow cooker. Top the meat loaf with the remaining ketchup. Cover and cook on low 8 to 10 hours or on high 4 to 6 hours, or until the turkey is thoroughly cooked but not dried out.

Yield: 8 servings

LEAN AND GREEN STUFFED PEPPERS
Stuffed peppers are typically labor-intensive because you have to cook the peppers, cook the meat, cook the rice, and then cook the final dish. The slow cooker can eliminate all of the intermediary steps and make this dish super easy to prepare. Also, to save time, you can use uncooked, parboiled brown rice in place of the cooked long-grain rice. The rice will cook in the juices from the turkey and salsa. If your peppers are smaller and you have leftover filling, simply add it to the salsa. Did you know that many peppers start out as a green vegetable and change color when they fully mature. Red is the sweetest of the bells, and it's is actually a fully ripened green pepper with a milder flavor.

4 large green or red bell peppers
1 pound (454 g) leanest ground turkey
⅓ cup (38 g) shredded pepper Jack cheese
½ cup (50 g) chopped scallion, white and green parts
1 cup (165 g) cooked long-grain brown rice
½ cup (65 g) frozen corn
1½ teaspoons chili powder
1 teaspoon garlic powder
½ teaspoon ground cumin
½ teaspoon salt
½ teaspoon black pepper
2 jars (16 ounces, or 454 g each) salsa

Slice the tops off of the peppers and remove all of the seeds and membranes.

In a medium bowl, combine the turkey, cheese, scallion, rice, corn, chili powder, garlic powder, cumin, salt, and pepper. Mix well to combine.

Stuff each pepper shell with an equal amount of the turkey mixture. Place the peppers, cut sides up, in a slow cooker.

Pour the salsa evenly over the peppers. Cover and cook on low for 6 to 7 hours, or until the turkey is thoroughly cooked.

Yield: 4 servings

▶ *Health Bite*
Bell peppers are an excellent source of vitamins C and A (beta-carotene) as well as potassium and vitamin K. You can use green or red peppers for this dish.

We stuffed the peppers with lean ground turkey and just a bit of cheese for a high-protein, very low-calorie dish.

DILLED SALMON DIJON
Dill and salmon is a classic combination. Here we've added another flavor layer–Dijon!

4 fillets (4 to 6 ounces, or 112 to 168 g each) skinless wild-caught Alaskan salmon
2 tablespoons (22 g) Dijon mustard
1½ teaspoons honey
8 short sprigs fresh dill (or 1 tablespoon [3 g] dried)
½ sweet onion, thinly sliced into rings

On a clean countertop, lay out two sections of foil in a cross shape. Place the salmon in one layer in the center of the foil cross.

In a small bowl, whisk together the mustard and honey until it's well incorporated. Spread one-fourth of the mustard mixture on top of each piece of salmon in an even layer. Lay 2 dill sprigs over the top of each piece of salmon and cover the dill with even layer of one-fourth of the onion. Fold the foil up and over the sides of the salmon. Pinch or crimp the edges together to make a good seal on the packet.

Using a large spatula, carefully transfer the packet to a dry, 6- or 7-quart (5.7 or 6.6 L) slow cooker. Cover and cook on low for about 2 hours, or until the salmon is tender and flakes easily with a fork.

Yield: 4 servings

▶ *Health Bite*
Wild salmon, unlike its farmed brethren, actually swim in rivers and eat their natural diet of crustaceans such as krill, rather than the grain pellets that farmed salmon are fed in salmon pens. The wild kind come by their red color naturally, by ingesting a powerful antioxidant called astaxanthin, which is found in their food. Farmed salmon get their color from a color wheel of artificial shades. According to the Environmental Working Group, farmed salmon are one of the biggest sources of PCBs in our diet. So we like wild salmon.

Consider buying salmon from Vital Choice, which is a terrific company of third-generation Alaskan fishermen who are all about the environment, sustainable fishing, high-quality product, and careful testing for toxic metals and contaminants. They will ship your salmon right to your door in dry ice, and you'll love every piece of fish you get from them!

LEMON-POACHED SALMON FILLETS
Slow cooking brings out the flavor in Lemon-Poached Salmon. Serve this flaky salmon with garlic mashed potatoes and a green vegetable.

1 cup (235 ml) chicken broth (To make your own, see "Chicken Stock" on page 6.)
1¼ pounds (569 g) salmon fillets of uniform thickness
½ teaspoon salt
¼ teaspoon black pepper
½ lemon, cut into thin slices

Coat the inside of the crock of a slow cooker with nonstick cooking spray.

In the slow cooker, pour the broth. Arrange the salmon skin sides down in one layer in the broth. Sprinkle the salmon with the salt and pepper. Place the lemon on top of the salmon. Cover and cook on low for 3 to 4 hours or on high for 1½ to 2 hours, or until the salmon can easily be flaked with a fork.

Yield: 4 servings

▶ *Add It!*
Substitute white wine for half of the chicken broth, and sprinkle a mixture of ½ cup (65 g) chopped onion, ½ cup (60 g) chopped celery, and 1 clove garlic, minced, around the fillets.

95 Turkey Meat Loaf; 96 Lean and Green Stuffed Peppers; 97 Dilled Salmon Dijon; 98 Lemon-Poached Salmon Fillets; 99 Al Gratin Salmon and Potato Bake; 100 Manhattan Braised Halibut Steaks; 101 Zesty Citrus Catfish Fillets

102 Sweet and Sour Shrimp; 103 Szechuan Shrimp; 104 Shellfish Jambalaya; 105 Mix and Match Jambalaya; 106 Zested and Light Lemon-Garlic Tilapia with Roasted Shiitakes; 107 Thai Curry Tofu and Veggies; 108 Sweet and Sour Smoked Tofu; 109 Tempeh Braised with Figs and Port Wine

MAIN DISHES • 125

AU GRATIN SALMON AND POTATO BAKE
The marriage of salmon and potatoes is comfort food at its best. Serve this easy dish with corn on the cob and whole-wheat rolls.

One 19-ounce (540-g) bag frozen Green Giant Au Gratin Potatoes
One 14½-ounce (419-g) can Alaskan salmon, drained and flaked
One 10¾-ounce (305-g) can condensed cream of celery soup

Coat the inside of the crock of a slow cooker with nonstick cooking spray.

In the slow cooker, spread out the potatoes. Top the potatoes with the salmon. Pour the soup over all. Cover and cook on high for 4½ to 5½ hours, or until the potatoes are fork-tender.

Yield: 5 servings

▶*Health Bite*
Always choose wild Alaskan salmon over farmed salmon. Wild salmon is an important source of heart-healthy omega-3 fats and vitamin E. More important, it's harvested from the pristine waters of Alaska, where it matured untouched by antibiotics, pesticides, growth hormones, and synthetic coloring agents.

MANHATTAN BRAISED HALIBUT STEAKS
The firm texture of halibut makes it a natural for braising in the slow cooker.

4 halibut steaks (about 2 pounds or 910 g)
1 (14-ounce or 355-ml) can Manhattan-style clam chowder
1 tablespoon (8 g) cornstarch

In a slow cooker, place the halibut. Pour the clam chowder over it. Cover and cook on low for 1½ hours, or until the halibut is firm and cooked through.

Using a slotted spoon, remove the halibut from the cooker and keep warm. Increase the slow cooker heat to high.

In a bowl, mix the cornstarch with enough water to make a slurry. Stir the mixture into the pan juices until the sauce clears and thickens a little.

Serve the halibut with the sauce.

Yield: 4 servings

SWORDFISH BRAISED WITH THAI GREEN CURRY
Swordfish is a firm fish that's flavorful enough to take the warmth of a curry. Here, it cooks to perfection in a little over 2 hours.

4 swordfish steaks (about 2 pounds or 910 g)
1 tablespoon (15 g) Thai green curry paste
1 (12-ounce or 355-ml) can coconut milk

In a slow cooker, place the swordfish.

In a small bowl, mix together the green curry paste and milk. Pour the mixture over the swordfish in the slow cooker. Cover and cook on low for about 2 hours, or until the swordfish is cooked through but still tender.

Serve the swordfish with some of the sauce.

Yield: 4 servings

ZESTY CITRUS CATFISH FILLETS
Lime is the twist in this zesty dish. Serve this catfish with parsleyed new potatoes and a salad of spring-mix greens. (See "Health Bite" below.)

1 cup (235 ml) chicken broth (To make your own, see "Chicken Stock" on page 6.)
½ cup (120 ml) Lawry's Tequila Lime Marinade
1½ pounds (683 g) catfish fillets of uniform thickness Salt, to taste
Black pepper, to taste

Coat the crock of a slow cooker with nonstick cooking spray.

In the slow cooker, combine the broth and marinade. Stir to mix thoroughly. Arrange the catfish skin sides down in the broth-marinade mixture. Cover and cook on low for 2 to 3 hours, or until the catfish can easily be flaked with a fork.

Before serving, season the catfish with salt and pepper.

Yield: 6 servings

▶*Health Bite*
Spring mix, which is also called field greens or mesclun, is becoming all the rage for the health-conscious. Originating in France, spring mix consists of tender young leaves from a variety of plants, as well as edible flowers on occasion. The bags of prewashed spring mix found at your local grocer are likely to include endive, radicchio, sorrel, frissee, chervil, and other highly nutritious greens, but probably not the edible flowers.

SWEET AND SOUR SHRIMP

Who can resist Sweet and Sour Shrimp with Asian-blend vegetables over fluffy white rice? Pick your favorite Asian or stir-fry blend of vegetables and your favorite sauce for this recipe.

One 12-ounce (340-g) bag frozen Asian-blend vegetables
¾ cup (188 g) sweet and sour sauce
1 pound (455 g) frozen cooked shrimp, thawed, shelled, and deveined
Salt, to taste
Black pepper, to taste

In a slow cooker, combine the vegetables and sauce. Stir to mix. Cover and cook on low for 2 to 2½ hours, or until the vegetables are tender but not mushy.

Add the shrimp to the slow cooker and stir. Cover and cook for another 15 to 30 minutes, or until the shrimp are thoroughly warmed. Do not overcook the shrimp, or they will become tough.

Before serving, stir the mixture and season with salt and pepper.

Yield: 4 servings

SZECHUAN SHRIMP

Enjoy this hot-and-spicy shrimp dish over hot white rice. The secret to this delicious dish is the rich, spicy flavor of the Szechuan peppercorn in the Szechuan hot-and-spicy sauce. This recipe cooks up quickly, in an hour to an hour and a half.

½ cup (120 ml) water
¼ cup (60 ml) soy sauce
2 tablespoons (31 g) Szechuan hot-and-spicy sauce
1 pound (455 g) frozen cooked shrimp, thawed, shelled, and deveined
Salt, to taste
Black pepper, to taste

In a slow cooker, combine the water, soy sauce, and Szechuan sauce. Stir to combine. Add the shrimp. Stir to coat the shrimp with the sauce. Cover and cook on high for 1 to 1½ hours, or until the sauce and shrimp are thoroughly heated.

Before serving, stir the mixture. Season with salt and pepper.

Yield: 4 servings

▶**Add It!**
Substitute chicken broth for the water, and add 2 teaspoons (7 g) minced garlic to the sauce mixture. Thicken the sauce with 1 tablespoon (8 g) cornstarch, and garnish the dish with chopped green onion.

SHELLFISH JAMBALAYA

Practically everyone loves jambalaya. You can mix and match the proteins to your preference or to use what you have on hand. Here we used Italian sausage and chicken-flavored seitan, but you can use another type of sausage, tempeh, tofu, or even red beans as the center attraction if you want.

1 tablespoon (15 ml) olive oil
1 medium onion, minced
2 cloves garlic, minced
2 or 3 large Italian sausage links, cut into halfmoons, or steamed tempeh cubes
1 to 2 cups (225 to 450 g) cubed chicken-flavored seitan To make your own, see "Chick'N Seitan" on page 18) or cubed firm tofu marinated in 2 tablespoons (12 g) vegan chicken-flavored bouillon
1 green bell pepper, seeded and chopped
1 red or orange bell pepper, seeded and chopped
1 can (14½ ounces, or 406 g) diced tomatoes or 1½ cups (340 g) Preserve-the-Harvest Diced Tomatoes (See page 17.)
1 teaspoon to 1 tablespoon hot pepper sauce
2 teaspoons Cajun seasoning
½ teaspoon liquid smoke or smoked paprika
¼ to 1 teaspoon red pepper flakes or chipotle chile powder
3 cups (705 ml) water, plus more as needed
2 tablespoons (12 g) vegan chicken-flavored bouillon
Salt, to taste
Black pepper, to taste
1½ cups (293 g) rice, uncooked

In a skillet, heat the oil over medium heat. Sauté the onion for 3 to 5 minutes, or until it's translucent. Add the garlic and sauté for 1 minute longer.

In a slow cooker, combine the onion mixture, sausage, seitan or tofu, bell peppers, tomatoes, hot sauce, Cajun seasoning, paprika, red pepper, water, and bouillon. Season with salt and pepper. Cover and cook on low for 6 to 8 hours.

About 1 hour before serving, add the rice. If the mixture looks dry, add 1 to 2 cups (235 to 470 ml) additional water.

Increase the heat of the slow cooker to high. Cook for 45 minutes to 1 hour longer. Check occasionally to make sure it doesn't overcook. Taste and adjust the seasonings.

Yield: 8 servings

ZESTED AND LIGHT LEMON-GARLIC TILAPIA WITH ROASTED SHIITAKES

This shiitake presentation comes from the genius concept of chef and author Myra Kornfeld (www.myrakornfeld.com). You can double the recipe and keep leftovers in the fridge to add later to salads or sandwiches. Or you can use them to top a cup of miso or winter squash soup. If you need to save time, you can omit the shiitakes and serve the tilapia as is. It will still be delicious.

4 fillets (6 ounces, or 168 g each) tilapia
Salt, to taste
Black pepper, to taste
4 small cloves garlic, minced
4 small shallots, peeled and thinly sliced
1 tablespoon (15 ml) plus 2 teaspoons (10 ml) olive oil, divided
Juice and zest of 2 lemons
1 tablespoon (15 ml) tamari
8 ounces (225 g) shiitake mushrooms, stems removed and caps thinly sliced (about ⅓ inch [8 mm])

Preheat the oven to 375°F (190°C, or gas mark 5). Line a baking sheet with parchment paper.

On a clean countertop, lay out two sections of foil in a cross shape. Place the fish in one layer in the center of the foil. Season with salt and pepper. Top each fillet evenly with 1 clove minced garlic and 1 sliced shallot in a single layer. Drizzle 1½ teaspoon oil over each piece of fish. Squeeze 1½ lemon over each piece of fish and top each with the zest from 1½ lemon. Fold the foil up and over the sides of the fish. Pinch or crimp the edges together to make a good seal on the packet.

Using a large spatula, carefully transfer the packet to a dry 6- or 7-quart (5.7 or 6.6 L) slow cooker. Cover and cook on low for about 2 hours, or until the fish is tender and flakes easily.

Meanwhile, in a large bowl, whisk together the remaining 1 tablespoon (15 ml) oil and the tamari. Add the shiitakes and toss to coat.

On the prepared baking sheet, spread the shiitakes out in a single layer. Roast for about 35 minutes, turning after 15 minutes, or until the mushrooms have browned and are starting to crisp but have not scorched.

To serve, carefully remove the fish from the foil. Top each piece of fish with a generous portion of the shiitakes.

Yield: 4 servings

▶*Health Bite*

When it comes to fish, tilapia isn't at the very top of the "must-eat" list. Unlike salmon, for example, it has almost no omega-3s. In fact, it has a shockingly low amount of fat of any kind! But what tilapia does offer is an awful lot of protein for a very small number of calories. If you're counting, roughly 3.5 ounces (98 g) of tilapia provide a whopping 26-plus grams of protein for a measly 128 calories. That's a bargain.

Tilapia also provides a hefty dose of selenium, which is one of the most important cancer-fighting trace minerals, and it's one that most of us don't get nearly enough of.

You get bonus points for cooking with the shallots, which are rich in sulfur compounds that help make your skin look great, and for the shiitake mushrooms, which are one of the greatest medicinal foods of all time.

THAI CURRY TOFU AND VEGGIES

You can buy Thai curry paste in most grocery stores. If you like milder foods, use less curry paste. If you like your food fiery hot, use more.

1 large onion, minced
1 bell pepper, julienned
1 can (8 ounces, or 225 g) bamboo shoots, drained and julienned
½ head cauliflower, cut into florets
1½ packages (15 ounces, or 420 g each) extra-firm tofu, cubed
1 to 2 tablespoons (16 to 32 g) red curry paste
2 cups (470 ml) water
Juice of 1 lime
1 can (14 ounces, or 392 g) light coconut milk
½ head broccoli, cut into florets
Fresh Thai basil
1 lime, sliced

In a slow cooker, combine the onion, bell pepper, bamboo shoots, cauliflower, tofu, curry paste, water, and juice. Cover and cook on low for 6 to 8 hours. About 20 minutes before serving, add the milk and broccoli. Cover and cook for 20 minutes, or until the broccoli is tender. Taste and adjust the seasonings.

Serve topped with the Thai basil and a slice of lime.

Yield: 6 servings

▶*Recipe Tip*

Swap out the veggies depending on the season. Zucchini, acorn squash, green beans, and kale all make tasty additions to this dish.

SWEET AND SOUR SMOKED TOFU

This dish was inspired by a recipe for sweet and sour seitan on Learning Vegan's blog. With this recipe, you can save some money and make your Chinese takeout at home. Plus, you'll know exactly what went in it.

1 can (20 ounces, or 560 g) pineapple in juice
2 tablespoons (30 ml) soy sauce
2 to 3 teaspoons grated fresh ginger

1 medium onion, cut in half and thinly sliced
2 large carrots, sliced
1 package (8 ounces, or 225 g) smoked tofu, cubed, or 1 recipe Tea-Scented Tofu made with Lapsang Souchong black tea (See "Tea-Scented Tofu" on page 20.)
1 large bell pepper, thinly sliced
1 medium head broccoli, cut into bite-size pieces
3 tablespoons (24 g) cornstarch
3 tablespoons (45 ml) cold water

In a small bowl, combine the juice from the pineapple can, the soy sauce, and ginger to make the sauce.
In a slow cooker, combine the sauce, onion, carrots, and tofu. Cover and cook on low for 6 to 8 hours.
About 30 to 45 minutes before serving, increase the heat of the slow cooker to high. Add the pepper, broccoli, and pineapple chunks.
In a small cup, combine the cornstarch and water. Add the mixture to the slow cooker. Continue to cook for a few minutes, or until the sauce has thickened and the broccoli is tender.

Yield: 4 servings

▶ *Recipe Tip*
If you don't have canned pineapple, you can use fresh or frozen instead. You'll just need about 1 cup (235 ml) of juice to substitute for the pineapple juice used in the sauce. You could use apple juice, or orange juice would work, too. After all, you're just using it to put the sweet into the sweet and sour.

TEMPEH BRAISED WITH FIGS AND PORT WINE
Looking for a sophisticated dish? Well, look no further. This recipe combines the complex flavor of port wine with fresh figs and nutty tempeh. Serve it over mashed potatoes with roasted asparagus for a meal that will wow even the toughest critic.

2 tablespoons (30 ml) olive oil
1 small onion, minced
2 cloves garlic, minced
1 package (8 ounces, or 225 g) tempeh, cubed
8 fresh figs, each cut into 6 wedges
½ cup (120 ml) water
1 cup (235 ml) port wine
1 tablespoon (15 ml) balsamic vinegar
1 tablespoon (6 g) vegan chicken-flavored bouillon
1 sprig fresh rosemary
1 sprig fresh thyme
Salt, to taste
Black pepper, to taste

In a skillet, heat the oil over medium heat. Sauté the onion for 3 to 5 minutes, or until it's translucent. Add the garlic and sauté for 1 minute longer.

In a slow cooker, combine all of the ingredients. Cover and cook on low for 6 to 8 hours.

Yield: 4 servings

▶ *Recipe Tip*
You can use dried figs in place of the fresh listed here. The stew will be a bit sweeter. You might want to add another teaspoon of balsamic vinegar to balance the flavors.

FROM-THE-PANTRY POT PIE (PHOTO ON PAGE 4)
This recipe is a great way to use up what you have on hand. You can also incorporate leftover vegetables, sausage, or beans.

FOR THE BISCUITS:
1 cup (120 g) white, whole wheat, or gluten-free flour
½ teaspoon salt
½ teaspoon thyme, optional
1½ teaspoons baking powder
3 tablespoons (45 ml) olive oil
½ cup (120 ml) milk

FOR THE STEW:
1 small onion, minced, optional
2 cloves garlic, minced, optional
1 large stalk celery, minced, optional
1½ cups (340 g) cubed chicken-flavored seitan, crumbled, cooked sausage, diced tofu, beans, or diced potato (To make your own seitan, see "Chick'N Seitan" on page 18.)
1 pound (454 g) frozen mixed green beans, corn, carrots, and peas (You can use fresh or leftovers instead.)
1 cup (235 ml) water, plus more if needed
2 tablespoons (12 g) vegetarian chicken-flavored bouillon
1 teaspoon dried thyme
Salt, to taste
Black pepper, to taste
2 tablespoons (16 g) flour, if needed

To make the biscuits: In a bowl, combine all of the biscuit ingredients. Using your hands, work the mixture until it comes together into a dough.
Turn the mixture out onto a floured cutting board. Roll out the dough about ½ inch (1.3 cm) thick. Using the rim of a glass or round cookie cutter, cut the dough it into circles.

To make the stew: Coat the crock of a slow cooker with nonstick cooking spray.
In the slow cooker, combine all of the stew ingredients except for the flour. If you will cook it for longer than 8 hours, or if your slow cooker runs a little hot, add 1 to 2 cups (235 to 470 ml) additional water. Cover and cook on low for 6 to 8 hours.

MAIN DISHES • 129

About 30 minutes before serving, if the mixture is too thick, add more water. If the mixture is too thin, add the flour. Taste and adjust the seasonings.

Place the biscuits in the slow cooker on top of the filling. Increase the heat of the slow cooker to high. Using the handle of a wooden spoon, prop open the lid of the slow cooker. Or place a clean dishtowel under the lid to prevent condensation from dripping onto the biscuits. Cook for an additional 30 minutes.

Yield: 4 to 6 servings

▶ *Recipe Tip*
You can make the biscuits days ahead and freeze them. You can put the biscuits right into the slow cooker still frozen. It will take about 15 more minutes for them to cook, but you won't have to bother with making them that day. Plus, it never hurts to have ready-to-bake biscuits in the freezer for a last-minute treat.

ATOMIC TOFU PECAN LOAF

This loaf was inspired by Vegan Lunch Box's Magical Loaf Studio website. We combined about four recipes and added a few things on top of that. You can add almost anything you have on hand to this dish, so it's a great way to use up leftovers.

1 cup (235 ml) water
1 cup (96 g) textured vegetable protein (TVP)
3 sundried tomatoes
1 cup (250 g) cubed silken, soft, or firm tofu
½ cup (55 g) pecans
1 cup (110 g) oat bran
¼ cup (24 g) nutritional yeast
1 teaspoon garlic powder
1 teaspoon onion salt or ½ teaspoon plain salt
1 tablespoon (3 g) Italian seasoning
½ teaspoon liquid smoke
½ teaspoon garlic hot pepper sauce, optional
Black pepper, to taste
¼ cup (60 ml) ketchup (To make your own, see "Homemade Smoky Ketchup" on page 8.)
¼ cup (60 ml) A1 steak sauce
2 tablespoons (30 ml) Worcestershire sauce

Coat the crock of a slow cooker with nonstick cooking spray.

In a saucepan, boil the water. Mix in the TVP, remove from the heat, and set aside for about 10 minutes while it reconstitutes.

If the sundried tomatoes were not packed in oil, soften them with the TVP in the hot water.

In a food processor, combine the tofu, pecans, and sundried tomatoes until minced.

In a large bowl, combine the tofu mixture, oat bran, yeast, garlic powder, onion salt, Italian seasoning, liquid smoke, and hot pepper sauce. Season with black pepper. Add the TVP and mix thoroughly.

In a separate small bowl, combine the ketchup, steak sauce, and Worcestershire.

Pat the loaf mixture into the slow cooker. Cover and cook on low for 6 to 8 hours.

About 30 minutes before serving, spread the ketchup mixture over the top of the loaf.

Yield: 6 servings

▶ *Serving Suggestion*
Serve this dish with mashed potatoes and mushroom gravy, green beans cooked with liquid smoke, and carrots.

You can substitute ½ small onion and 2 cloves garlic, minced and sautéed in oil for the garlic powder.

CORN-TASTIC TEX-MEX LOAF

Have you ever ended up with half a package of chorizo and a few corn tortillas? Making a loaf out of the ingredients seems like a great solution. You can add bits and pieces of whatever you have on hand. You get the flavors of the chorizo combined with a cheesy corn taste in one bite. It's perfect to serve with Spanish Quinoa. (See page 137.)

3 corn tortillas
½ package (12 ounces, or 340 g) vegetarian chorizo
½ cup (70 g) cornmeal
½ cup (48 g) nutritional yeast
3 tablespoons (21 g) ground flaxseed mixed with ¼ cup (60 ml) water
1 package (12 ounces, or 340 g) silken, soft, or firm tofu
Juice of 1 lime
¼ to ½ teaspoon hot pepper sauce
½ teaspoon garlic powder
½ teaspoon chili powder
¼ to ½ teaspoon salt

In a food processor, grind the corn tortillas.

Coat the crock of a slow cooker with nonstick cooking spray.

In a large bowl, combine the ground tortillas, chorizo, and cornmeal. Stir to combine.

In a food processor, purée the yeast, flaxseed mixture, tofu, juice, hot sauce, garlic powder, chili powder, and salt. Add the tofu mixture to the chorizo mixture. Stir to combine thoroughly.

Pat the loaf mixture into the slow cooker. Cover and cook on low for 6 to 8 hours. Using a wooden spoon handle, prop open the lid or put a clean dish towel underneath the lid to prevent the condensation from dripping onto the loaf during cooking.

Yield: 6 servings

▶ *Recipe Tip*
You can use more or fewer corn tortillas, depending on what you have an hand. Just adjust the cornmeal accordingly.

CHICK'N CACCIATORE

This is a nice way to dress up chicken-flavored meat substitutes, and it works well for a dinner on the deck or a cozy dinner party.

2 tablespoons (30 ml) olive oil
1 small onion, chopped
2 cloves garlic, minced
1 package (8 ounces, or 225 g) sliced mushrooms
1 package (10½ ounces, or 300 g) chicken-flavored seitan, diced (To make your own, see "Chick'N Seitan" on page 18.)
1 can (14½ ounces, or 406 g) diced tomatoes or 1½ cups (340 g) Preserve-the-Harvest Diced Tomatoes (See page 17.)
½ cup (120 ml) white wine or water
1½ tablespoons (9 g) vegetarian chicken-flavored bouillon
1 tablespoon (16 g) tomato paste
1 teaspoon dried basil
1 teaspoon dried oregano
1 sprig fresh rosemary or ½ teaspoon dried leaves or ground
Salt, to taste
Black pepper, to taste
Cooked pasta
1 teaspoon chopped fresh basil

Coat the crock of a slow cooker with nonstick cooking spray.
    In a skillet, heat the oil over medium heat. Sauté the onion for 3 to 5 minutes, or until it's translucent. Add the garlic and mushrooms. Sauté for about 10 minutes, or until the mushrooms give off their water and begin to brown.
    In the slow cooker, combine the sautéed vegetables, seitan, tomatoes, wine, bouillon, paste, dried basil, oregano, and rosemary. Season with salt and pepper. Cover and cook on low for 6 to 8 hours. Taste and adjust the seasonings.
    Serve the cacciatore over cooked pasta and top with the fresh basil for an extra burst of flavor.

Yield: 4 servings

▶ *Serving Suggestion*
Serve this cacciatore by itself with a side salad and some steamed vegetables.

HOLIDAY TEMPEH AND SAGE LOAF

This loaf reminds us a little of Thanksgiving. Leftovers make great sandwiches with cranberry sauce.

1 packages (8 ounces, or 225 g) tempeh, cubed
1 small onion
2 cloves garlic
2 stalks celery
1 medium carrot
1 cup (70 g) sliced mushrooms
2 tablespoons (30 ml) olive oil
1 cup (115 g) whole wheat bread crumbs
2 tablespoons (14 g) ground flaxseed mixed with 2 tablespoons (30 ml) warm water
2 tablespoons (12 g) vegetarian chicken-flavored bouillon
1 teaspoon dried thyme
1 teaspoon rubbed sage
½ teaspoon dried oregano
½ teaspoon dried rosemary or ¼ teaspoon ground
½ teaspoon salt

Coat the crock of a slow cooker with nonstick cooking spray.
    In a steamer basket, steam the tempeh for 10 minutes to take out some of the bitterness.
    Meanwhile, in a food processor, pulse the onion, garlic, celery, carrot, and mushrooms until you have tiny pieces of veggies, but not so much that it liquefies.
    In a skillet, heat the oil over medium heat. Sauté the vegetables for about 3 minutes, or until the onion is translucent.
    In a large bowl, crumble the tempeh. Add the sautéed vegetables, bread crumbs, flaxseed mixture, bouillon, thyme, sage, oregano, rosemary, and salt.
    Pat the loaf mixture into the slow cooker. Cook on low for 6 to 8 hours. Using a wooden spoon handle, prop open the lid or put a clean dish towel underneath the lid to prevent the condensation from dripping onto the loaf during cooking.

Yield: 6 servings

110 From-the-Pantry Pot Pie; 111 Atomic Tofu Pecan Loaf; 112 Chick'N Cacciatore; 113 Holiday Tempeh and Sage Loaf; 114 Meatless Sausage and Mushroom Ragu; 115 Mushroom Lasagna with Garlic-Tofu Sauce; 116 Pumpkin and White Bean Lasagna; 117 Baked Ziti

118

119

120

118 Three-Cheese Vegetarian Spaghetti; 119 Pasta and Mushrooms; 120 Penne with Broccoli

MAIN DISHES • 133

MEATLESS SAUSAGE AND MUSHROOM RAGU

This is definitely not the ragu from your supermarket shelves! It's a great way to transition hard-core meat eaters to a meatless meal. It also makes the perfect topping for grilled polenta. You can just buy a premade tube of polenta, slice it, and then crisp it in the oven or on a grill. This recipe is designed for a larger slow cooker. Cut this recipe in half if you are using a 3½ quart (3.3 L) slow cooker.

1 teaspoon olive oil
1 medium onion, minced
3 cloves garlic, minced
1 package (14 ounces, or 392 g) vegetarian sausage, sliced into rounds (To make your own, see "Apple Sage Sausage on page 19.)
2 cans (28 ounces, or 784 g each) crushed tomatoes
1 pound (454 g) crimini or button mushrooms, chopped
2 large portobello mushrooms, chopped
1 tablespoon (15 ml) balsamic vinegar
2 to 3 tablespoons (30 to 45 ml) red or port wine
Black pepper, to taste
2 tablespoons (5 g) chopped fresh basil

In a skillet, heat the oil over medium heat. Sauté the onion for 3 to 5 minutes, or until it's translucent. Add the garlic and sauté for 1 minute longer.

Transfer the onion and garlic to a bowl.

In the same skillet that you cooked the onion, cook the sausage for 5 to 10 minutes, or until brown. Using a spatula, break the patties apart to make crumbles.

Transfer the sausage to the same bowl as the onion.

In a slow cooker, combine the sausage mixture, tomatoes, mushrooms, vinegar, and wine. Season with pepper. Cover and cook on low for 6 to 8 hours. About 10 minutes before serving, add water if needed and the basil.

Yield: 12 servings

▶*Recipe Tip*
This recipe makes enough to feed a dinner party and still have leftovers, and it freezes well. Freeze it in ice cube trays. Once the cubes are frozen solid, pop them out into a resealable plastic bag. This way you can defrost exactly the amount you need, even if you want a single-serving size.

MUSHROOM LASAGNA WITH GARLIC-TOFU SAUCE

This is a quick and easy dish that's elegant and perfect for last-minute company. For a special treat, add a layer of chanterelle or lobster mushrooms and use one-third less of the regular mushrooms that are called for in the recipe.

FOR THE BÉCHAMEL SAUCE:
1 package (15 ounces, or 420 g) silken or soft tofu
Juice of ½ lemon
1 cup (235 ml) water
3 cloves garlic or 1 teaspoon dried
½ to 1 teaspoon salt
1½ tablespoons (9 g) chicken-flavored bouillon
¼ cup (24 g) nutritional yeast

FOR THE LASAGNA:
2 tablespoons (30 ml) olive oil
20 ounces (560 g) mushrooms, sliced
2 sprigs rosemary
½ to ¾ package (10 ounces, or 280 g) whole wheat lasagna noodles (the regular kind, not the no boil noodles)

To make the béchamel sauce: In a food processor, purée all of the sauce ingredients until smooth.

To make the lasagna: Coat the crock of a slow cooker with nonstick cooking spray.

In a skillet, heat the oil over medium heat. Sauté the mushrooms with the rosemary for about 10 minutes, or until the mushrooms give off their water and begin to brown. Remove the rosemary sprigs and discard them.

In the slow cooker, spread one-fifth of the sauce on the bottom. Top the sauce with a layer of lasagna noodles. Break off the corners on one side of each noodle so they fit snugly in the slow cooker. You can add the corners in as well. Add a layer of one-third of the mushrooms and top with another one-fifth of the sauce. Repeat the layers two more times, ending with a last layer of lasagna noodles, and then top that with the remaining sauce. Cover and cook on high for 1½ to 2½ hours, or until a fork will easily go through the middle and the pasta is al dente.

Yield: 4 servings

▶*Recipe Tip*
Not fond of mushrooms? Substitute precooked vegetarian beef or sausage crumbles instead.

PUMPKIN AND WHITE BEAN LASAGNA

This is a perfect meatless dish even for meat-eaters. It's much healthier than the traditional, fat-laden lasagna. It's easy to make and hearty. Add a spinach salad with a balsamic vinaigrette, and you're all ready to have friends over for dinner.

FOR THE PUMPKIN-TOFU RICOTTA:
1 tablespoon (15 ml) olive oil
3 sundried tomatoes, rehydrated (Pour boiling water over them and let them sit for 5 minutes.)
1 package (15 ounces, or 420 g) silken, soft, or firm tofu
1 can (15 ounces, or 420 g) cooked pumpkin or 1½ cups (368 g) puréed cooked fresh
¼ cup (24 g) nutritional yeast

1 tablespoon (3 g) Italian seasoning
1 teaspoon onion powder
2 cloves garlic, crushed
Salt, to taste
Black pepper, to taste

FOR THE LASAGNA:
1 jar (24 ounces, or 672 g) marinara sauce (To make your own, see " Easy Pasta Sauce" on page 9.)
About ¾ package (10 ounces, or 280 g) whole wheat lasagna noodles (the regular kind, not the no-boil noodles)
1 can (14½ ounces, or 406 g) white beans, drained

To make the pumpkin–tofu ricotta: In a food processor, blend the oil and the rehydrated sundried tomatoes until a paste forms. There may still be some lumps. Add the remaining ricotta ingredients and blend until creamy. If the mixture is too thick, add a little water. Taste and adjust the seasonings.

To make the lasagna: Coat the crock of a slow cooker with nonstick cooking spray.

In the slow cooker, spread a thin layer of sauce on the bottom. Place a layer of noodles on top of the sauce. Break off the corners on one side of each noodle so they fit snugly in the slow cooker. You can add the corners in as well. Spread one-third of the ricotta mixture over the noodles. Spread another thin layer of sauce over the ricotta and sprinkle one-third of the white beans on top of that. Repeat the layers two more times, ending with a last layer of lasagna noodles, and then top that with more sauce. Cover and cook on low for 3 to 4 hours or on high for 1½ to 2 hours, or until a fork will easily go through the middle and the pasta is al dente.

If you need to have the lasagna cook for an hour or two longer, add ½ cup (120 ml) extra sauce or water.

Yield: 6 servings

BAKED ZITI
This is another of those comforting and homey casseroles.

Salt
1 pound (455 g) ziti
1 (20-ounce or 570-ml) jar four-cheese marinara sauce
1 cup (260 g) basil pesto

Coat the crock of a slow cooker with nonstick cooking spray.

Bring a large pot of salted water to a boil. Add the ziti and cook at a low boil for 8 minutes. Drain the pasta. Rinse it with cold water to cool.

Transfer the ziti to the slow cooker. Add the marinara and pesto sauces. Stir to combine well. Cover and cook on low for 3 to 4 hours or on high for 1½ hours.

Yield: 6 to 8 servings

▶ *Add It!*
If you like a lot of cheese, you can add a top layer of grated Parmesan cheese to this dish.

THREE-CHEESE VEGETARIAN SPAGHETTI
Preparing a delicious, home-cooked spaghetti dinner for your family is a labor of love, or at least it used to be. This delicious one-pot spaghetti dish gives you some labor-free time away from the kitchen.

One 28-ounce (795-g) jar three-cheese-flavored pasta sauce
12 ounces (340 g) imitation ground burger
6 ounces (168 g) dry spaghetti, broken into 4-inch (10cm) pieces

In a slow cooker, combine the pasta sauce and ground burger. Stir to combine. Cover and cook on low for 6 to 8 hours or on high for 3 to 4 hours.

About 1 hour before the dish is done, add the dry spaghetti and stir. Cover and cook on high for 1 more hour, or until the spaghetti is tender but not mushy.

Yield: 4 servings

PASTA AND MUSHROOMS
This quick and very flavorful mushroom sauce cooks in the slow cooker, allowing the flavors to develop fully.

8 ounces (225 g) mushrooms, sliced
½ teaspoon minced garlic
¼ cup (14 g) chopped sundried tomatoes
½ cup (120 ml) dry white wine
½ cup (120 ml) vegetable broth (To make your own, see "Freshest Vegetable Broth" on page 6.)
¼ cup (15 g) chopped Italian parsley
1 pound (455 g) pasta

In a slow cooker, combine all of the ingredients except for the pasta. Cover and cook on for low 4 to 6 hours.

The last few minutes of cooking time, cook the pasta according to the package directions.

Serve the pasta with the sauce.

Yield: 4 servings

▶ *Recipe Tip*
For a more special sauce, substitute porcini or wild mushrooms.

PENNE WITH BROCCOLI

This creamy and delicious recipe works wonderfully as both a side dish and a main dish. It cooks for less than 2 hours on high.

1 (16-ounce or 455-g) package frozen broccoli with cheese sauce
½ pound (230 g) penne pasta
1 cup (80 g) shredded Parmesan cheese

Spray the crock with nonstick cooking spray.
    In the slow cooker, place the frozen broccoli with cheese sauce. Cover and cook on high for 45 minutes.
    Meanwhile, bring a large pot of salted water to a boil. Add the penne and cook at a low boil for 8 minutes. Drain the pasta and add it to the slow cooker. Stir to combine the pasta and the broccoli and sauce. Top with the Parmesan cheese. Cover and cook on low for 2 to 3 hours or on high for 1 hour.

Yield: 4 servings

▶*Add It!*
You can spice up this dish with a few shakes of red pepper flakes, or add a couple of cloves of minced garlic for a pungent kick.

MACARONI AND TWO CHEESES

Everyone likes macaroni and cheese, and the slow cooker does a great job on it. This version gets extra flavor from Parmesan cheese added to the topping.

8 ounces (225 g) elbow macaroni, cooked al dente
13 ounces (365 ml) evaporated milk
1 cup (235 ml) milk
¼ cup (60 ml) egg substitute
4 cups (450 g) shredded Cheddar cheese, divided
½ teaspoon white pepper
¼ cup (25 g) grated parmesan cheese

Coat the crock of a slow cooker with nonstick cooking spray. In the slow cooker, combine the cooked macaronit, evaporated milk, milk, egg substitute, 3 cups (345 g) cheddar cheese, salt, and pepper. Top with the remaining cheddar and parmesan chesses. Cover and cook on low for 3 hours.

Yield: 8 servings

BASIC FUSS-FREE RISOTTO

You can use risotto as a base to show off fresh, sautéed, or steamed seasonal herbs and vegetables. This is a dish that you can make on a weeknight after you come home from work because it only takes 1½ to 2½ hours to cook in the slow cooker. There's almost no stirring, compared with the stove-top version, so you can even relax while it's cooking.

3 cups (705 ml) water
1½ cups (280 g) Arborio rice
2 cloves garlic, minced
2 tablespoons (12 g) chicken-flavored bouillon
Salt, to taste
Black pepper, to taste

In a slow cooker, combine the water, rice, garlic, and bouillon. Cover and cook on high for 1½ to 2½ hours, or until the rice is cooked through but still al dente. Stir every 30 minutes and add extra water if needed. Season with salt and pepper.

Yield: 6 servings

▶*Serving Suggestion*
For a stunning dish, steam some purple and orange cauliflower florets. Serve on top of the risotto for a burst of color. You can also add some rainbow chard. Cut the colorful stems small and sauté them.

KUNG PAO CHICK'N

This spicy meatless seitan dish gets a rich flavor from the mushrooms and rice vinegar as well as a great crunch from the water chestnuts.

FOR THE SAUCE:
3 cloves garlic, minced
1 tablespoon (8 g) grated ginger
1½ cups (355 ml) water
¼ cup (60 ml) soy sauce
¼ cup (60 ml) seasoned rice vinegar or plain rice vinegar mixed with 1 teaspoon sweetener
2 tablespoons (12 g) vegetarian chicken-flavored bouillon
¼ to ½ teaspoon red pepper flakes or sriracha

FOR THE KUNG PAO CHICK'N:
1 bell pepper, seeded and diced
5 ounces (140 g) mushrooms, diced
1 can (8 ounces, or 225 g) water chestnuts, drained and diced
1 package (12 ounces, or 335 g) chicken-flavored seitan, diced (To make your own, see "Chick'N Seitan" on page 18.)
2 to 3 tablespoons (16 to 24 g) cornstarch
2 tablespoons (30 ml) sesame oil
Steamed rice
Chopped peanuts

To make the sauce: In a bowl, combine all of the sauce ingredients.

To make the Kung Pao Chick'N: In a slow cooker, combine the sauce, pepper, mushrooms, water chestnuts, and seitan. Cover and cook on low for 6 to 8 hours.

About 30 minutes before the end of the cooking time, increase the heat of the slow cooker to high.

In a bowl, combine the cornstarch with a little of the cooking water to make a thickener.

Pour the cornstarch mixture into the slow cooker.

Right before serving, stir in the oil.

Serve over steamed rice, and top with peanuts.

Yield: 4 servings

▶*Recipe Tips*
- *Get in some extra veggies by adding diced zucchini, carrots, and celery about 30 minutes before serving.*

- *Make a gluten-free version using tempeh or tofu in place of the seitan. Be sure to use gluten-free soy sauce, too.*

LENTILS AND RICE

Many people are afraid to cook with lentils. This recipe will change your mind.

1½ cups (240 g) sliced onions
2 tablespoons (28 ml) olive oil
6 cups (1.4 L) water
1 cup (192 g) lentils, sorted, washed, and drained
2 cups (380 g) brown rice, washed and drained

In a nonstick skillet, sauté the onions in the oil for 3 to 5 minutes, or until the onions are golden brown. Remove about ½ cup (80 g) of the onions from the skillet and them place on paper towel to drain. Transfer the remaining onions and drippings to a slow cooker. Add the water, lentils, and rice. Cover and cook on low 6 to 8 hours. Garnish with the reserved onions.

Yield: 8 servings

SPANISH QUINOA

Love Spanish rice? This meatless recipe uses quinoa instead of rice. It's a nice change of pace and just as tasty.

2 tablespoons (30 ml) olive oil
1 small onion, chopped
2 cloves garlic, minced
1 bell pepper, seeded and chopped
3 cups (705 g) water
1½ cups (260 g) quinoa
2 tablespoons (12 g) vegetarian chicken-flavored bouillon
2 tablespoons (32 g) tomato paste
1 teaspoon salt
½ teaspoon chili powder

In a skillet, heat the oil over medium heat. Sauté the onion for 3 to 5 minutes, or until it's translucent. Add the garlic and pepper. Sauté for 3 to 5 minutes, or until the pepper is soft.

In a slow cooker, combine the sautéed vegetables, water, quinoa, bouillon, paste, salt, and chili powder. Stir until the paste and bouillon are mixed in the liquid. Cover and cook on high for 1½ to 2 hours, or until the quinoa has unfurled. Taste and adjust the seasonings.

Yield: 8 servings

▶*Recipe Variations*
Add a can of black beans or some chicken-flavored seitan, store-bought or homemade (see Chick'N Seitan on page 18), to make this a complete one-dish meal.

MAIN DISHES • **137**

SEEDED AND STUFFED CARNIVAL SQUASH

Even for a carnivore, a vegetarian dish from time to time is a welcome addition to the menu. A vegetarian offering like this one is high in fiber and nutrients, and it will also save you a little cash, because veggies are always cheaper than meat or fish. Carnival squash is a colorful, small, hardskinned variety of winter squash that tastes somewhat similar to a sweet potato or butternut squash.

⅓ cup (67 g) quick-cooking barley (or 1 cup (157 g) cooked barley)
1 cup (175 g) cooked small red beans (Drained and rinsed if using canned.)
¼ cup (40 g) minced onion
2 cloves garlic, minced
1½ tablespoons (23 ml) tamari
¾ teaspoon dried oregano
¾ teaspoon dried basil
½ teaspoon ground cumin
⅛ teaspoon cayenne pepper
2 tablespoons (18 g) roasted sunflower seeds
2 large carnival squash, halved lengthwise and seeded

½ cup (120 ml) water, vegetable broth, or apple cider Cook the barley according to the package directions.

In a medium bowl, combine the barley, beans, onion, garlic, tamari, oregano, basil, cumin, cayenne pepper, and sunflower seeds. Mix well.

Stuff each squash half with one-fourth of the mixture.

Arrange the filled halves in a slow cooker. Gently pour the liquid into the bottom of the slow cooker. Cover and cook on low for 2 to 3 hours, or until the squash is tender.

Yield: 4 servings

▶*Health Bite*
This dish is especially rich in fiber from the red beans, squash, and barley. And speaking of fiber, a recent study published in the Archives of Internal Medicine *investigated diet and the risk of death among 388,000 men and women who were followed over a nine-year period. Men and women consuming the most fiber in their diet (between 25 and 30 grams per day) were significantly less likely to die from cardiovascular, infectious, or respiratory disease, and were an impressive 22 percent less likely to die from any cause whatsoever.*

The Institute of Medicine recommends between 25 and 38 grams of fiber daily. This recipe is a delicious way to help get you to that target.

PERFECT PIZZA FROM YOUR SLOW COOKER

It's really surprising just how much you can do in the slow cooker. Pizza is great in the slow cooker on those blistering hot summer days, when you can't bear to turn on the oven. It's also a great treat when you go camping. Bring premade dough, prechopped veggies, and mozzarella in a cooler. You'll be greeted with lots of oohs and aahs by your camping buddies.

This is a free-form recipe. Use as little or as much sauce as you would typically put on your pizza. The same goes for toppings. If you use fresh onion and bell pepper, cut into a small dice and add them at the beginning so they will be cooked by the end.

¼ recipe Foolproof Focaccia dough (See page 65.)
¼ to ½ cup (63 to 125 g) tomato sauce
Chopped veggies of choice, such as onion, green pepper, All-Occasion Roasted Garlic (see page 17), Balsamic Onion Marmalade (see page 17)
1¼2 to 1 cup (62 to 115 g) shredded mozzarella cheese

Coat the crock of a slow cooker with nonstick cooking spray. Shape the dough to fit in the slow cooker. Top with the sauce and then the vegetables. Cover and cook on high for 1½ to 2 hours in a large oval slow cooker, or up to 3½ hours in a round 4-quart (3.8 L) slow cooker, propping up the lid with a wooden spoon to allow the condensation to escape.

About 15 minutes before serving, sprinkle with the mozzarella.

Yield: 4 servings

▶*Recipe Tip*
This recipe works best in a larger oval slow cooker because the dough will be thinner and cook faster. In a 4-quart (3.8 L) round one, it will be more of a thick-crust pizza, and it will have a longer cooking time.

MA PO TOFU

This is a favorite Chinese dish. You can make it as mild or spicy as you like it. Silken tofu has a custard-like texture and is the main focus of this dish. If you don't like that silky texture, feel free to use soft or firm tofu instead. You can usually find black bean garlic sauce in the international food aisle of most large grocery stores.

FOR THE SAUCE:
2 tablespoons (30 ml) soy sauce
2 tablespoons (30 ml) rice wine or apple cider vinegar
3 tablespoons (48 g) tomato paste
1½ tablespoons (24 g) black bean garlic sauce
1 to 2 teaspoons sriracha
½ teaspoon red pepper flakes, optional
3 cloves garlic, minced
2 to 3 teaspoons grated fresh ginger
1 teaspoon agave nectar
1 cup (235 ml) water
¼ cup (60 ml) white wine

FOR THE MA PO TOFU:
8 shiitake mushrooms, sliced
2 packages (12 ounces, or 336 g each) silken, soft, or firm tofu, cubed
3 tablespoons (24 g) cornstarch
1 medium head broccoli, cut into bite-size, pieces (You can also use frozen broccoli.)
1 tablespoon (15 ml) sesame oil
Steamed rice

To make the sauce: In a bowl, combine all of the sauce ingredients.

To make the Ma Po Tofu: In a slow cooker, combine the sauce, mushrooms, and tofu. Cover and cook on low for 6 to 8 hours.

About 45 to 60 minutes before serving, increase the heat of the slow cooker to high.

In a small bowl, make a thickener by mixing the cornstarch with some of the sauce from the slow cooker. Transfer the cornstarch mixture to the slow cooker. When the sauce is thickened, add the broccoli and cook until bright green.

Right before serving, stir in the oil. Serve over steamed rice.

Yield: 6 servings

▶*Recipe Note*
If you're planning on taking leftovers for lunch the next day, steam the broccoli separately so it doesn't overcook when you reheat it.

MIX AND MATCH JAMBALAYA

Practically everyone loves jambalaya. It's an easy dish to make for a dinner party, and it's filling to boot. You can mix and match the proteins to your preference or to use what you have on hand. Here we used Italian sausage and chicken-flavored seitan, but you can use another type of sausage, tempeh, tofu, or even red beans as the center attraction if you want. This recipe calls for white jasmine rice, but any rice will work. Brown will require a little more cooking time, but it adds tons of nutrients.

1 tablespoon (15 ml) olive oil
1 medium onion, minced
2 cloves garlic, minced
2 or 3 large Italian sausage links, cut into halfmoons, or steamed tempeh cubes
1 to 2 cups (225 to 450 g) cubed chicken-flavored seitan. To make your own, see "Chick'N Seitan on page 18) or cubed firm tofu marinated in 2 tablespoons (12 g) vegan flavored bouillon
1 green bell pepper, seeded and chopped
1 can (14½ ounces, or 406 g) diced tomatoes or 1½ cups (340 g) Preserve-the-Harvest Diced Tomatoes (See page 17)
1 teaspoon to 1 tablespoon hot pepper sauce
2 teaspoons Cajun seasoning
½ teaspoon liquid smoke or smoked paprika
¼ to 1 teaspoon red pepper flakes or chipotle chile powder
3 cups (705 ml) water, plus more as needed
2 tablespoons (12 g) vegan chicken-flavored bouillon
Salt, to tast
Black pepper, to taste
1½ cups (293 g) rice, uncooked

In a skillet, heat the oil over medium heat. Sauté the onion for 3 to 5 minutes, or until it's translucent. Add the garlic and saute for 1 minute longer.

In a slow cooker, combine the onion mixture, sausage, seitan or tofu, bell peppers, tomatoes, hot sauce, Cajun seasoning, paprika, red pepper, water, and bouillon. Season with salt and pepper.

Cover and cook on low for 6 to 8 hours.

About 1 hour before serving, add the rice. If the mixture looks dry, add 1 to 2 cups (235 to 470 ml) additional water.

Increase the heat of the slow cooker to high. Cook for 45 minutes to 1 hour longer. Check occasionally to make sure it doesn't overcook. Taste and adjust the seasonings.

Yield: 8 servings

121 Macaroni and Two Cheeses; 122 Basic Fuss-Free Risotto; 123 Kung Pao Chick'N; 124 Lentils and Rice; 125 Spanish Quinoa; 126 Seeded and Stuffed Carnival Squash; 127 Perfect Pizza from Your Slow Cooker

128 Ma Po Tofu

SALADS AND SOUPS

See pages 146-147, 150-151, 158-159, 164-165, 168-169 and 174-175 for salad and soup recipe photos.

LEAN AND EASY TACO SALAD

It's hard to beat lean, low-cal ground turkey as a source of high-quality protein. You can substitute turkey meat for all kinds of recipes that call for beef. Turkey's not the only thing this taco salad has going for it, though. Garlic lowers blood pressure and cholesterol and reduces the risk for certain cancers. Kidney beans are an excellent source of fiber, providing more than 11 grams per cup, plus 16 grams of protein and about double the potassium in a banana. And tomatoes and peppers have loads of antioxidants such as vitamin C.

2 teaspoons olive oil
1 pound (454 g) ground turkey
4 cloves garlic, minced
1 yellow onion, chopped
1 red or orange bell pepper, seeded and chopped
1 can (15 ounces, or 420 g) kidney beans, drained and rinsed
1 can (14.5 ounces, or 406 g) fire-roasted diced tomatoes, undrained
1 can (4 ounces, or 112 g) chopped green chiles, undrained
1 package (1 ounce, or 28 g) taco seasoning
2 heads romaine lettuce, chopped
¾ cup (75 g) sliced scallion
1 heirloom tomato, chopped

In a large skillet, heat the oil over medium-high heat. Add the turkey and cook for about 6 minutes, stirring frequently, or until no pink remains. Stir in the garlic and cook for 1 minute. Drain.

In a slow cooker, combine the turkey, onion, pepper, beans, tomatoes, green chiles, and taco seasoning. Stir well to combine. Cover and cook on low for about 6 hours or on high for about 3 hours, or until hot and bubbling.

Make 6 beds of romaine lettuce and mound the turkey mixture on top.

Top with the scallion and tomato.

Yield: 6 servings

▶*Make It Even Healthier*
To make your own taco seasoning mix, combine 1 tablespoon chili powder; 1 ½ teaspoons each onion powder, garlic powder, and cumin; 1 teaspoon each paprika and dried oregano; ¾ teaspoon each arrowroot powder and salt; and ½ teaspoon each Sucanat or xylitol and red pepper flakes.

GERMAN POTATO SALAD

Because German potato salad is supposed to be warm anyway, cook the potatoes in the sauce in a slow cooker so the flavor soaks the whole way through.

2 large potatoes, sliced
½ cup (80 g) chopped onion
½ cup (50 g) sliced celery
¼ cup (38 g) diced green bell pepper
¼ cup (60 ml) vinegar
¼ cup (60 ml) olive oil
2 slices bacon, cooked and crumbled
Chopped parsley

In a slow cooker, combine all of the ingredients except for the bacon and parsley. Stir to mix. Cover and cook on low for 5 to 6 hours. Garnish with the bacon and parsley.

Yield: 3 servings

BEEF BARLEY SOUP

Beef, barley, and vegetables combine for a soup sensation that can't be beat. Serve in large bowls, and accompany with a green salad and crusty bread. Nurturing, soothing, and satisfying: Soup is a comfort food that's been feeding the human soul for centuries. More often than not, we eat comfort foods when we're happy, relaxed, and in a mood to reward ourselves. We feel good about choosing healthful foods such as soups that pass the "Mom test"–foods that bring back happy memories of Mom's cooking and nurturing care. A steaming bowl of healthful soup is quite a reward to your palate, especially when it's so easy to fix in the slow cooker.

2 quarts (1.9 L) water
One 9-ounce (255-g) package vegetable-barley soup mix
2 pounds (910 g) beef chuck roast, cut into cubes
1 small onion, chopped
Salt, to taste
Black pepper, to taste

In a slow cooker, combine the water and soup mix. Stir until the soup mix has dissolved. Add the beef and onion. Season with salt and pepper. Stir again. Cover and cook on low for 5 to 6 hours.

Yield: 10 servings

▶ *Try This!*
To clean your slow cooker, pour soapy water (about the same strength as you use to hand-wash dishes) inside your slow cooker and let it cook on high for at least an hour before rinsing. More proof that slow cooking is super-convenient!

SMOKED TOFU AND STARS SOUP

This is the perfect favorite soup when you or someone you love is sick. It's warm and filling, and it evokes memories of childhood soups with fun-shaped pasta. It's meatless to boot.

2 tablespoons (30 ml) olive oil
1 medium onion, minced
4 cloves garlic, minced
2 carrots, diced
2 stalks celery, diced
1 package (8 ounces, or 225 g) smoked tofu or ¾ recipe Tea-Scented Tofu (See page 20.)
2 tablespoons (12 g) chicken-flavored bouillon
8 cups (1,880 ml) water
3 sprigs fresh thyme or 1 teaspoon dried
½ teaspoon Cajun seasoning, optional
Salt, to taste
Black pepper, to taste
1 cup (100 g) small pasta stars or other tiny pasta

In a skillet, heat the oil over medium heat. Sauté the onion for 3 to 5 minutes, or until it's translucent. Add the garlic and sauté for 1 minute longer.

In a slow cooker, combine the sautéed vegetables, carrots, celery, tofu, bouillon, water, thyme, and Cajun seasoning. Season with salt and pepper. Cover and cook on low for 6 to 8 hours. Taste and adjust the seasonings.

You have two choices for adding the pasta.

If you plan on eating all of it that night, then add the pasta 20 minutes before serving. Cook until the pasta is al dente.

If you will be eating it throughout the week or freezing it, cook the pasta separately on the stove top and add it just before serving. The pasta will get mushy if it stays in the soup too long.

Yield: 6 servings

HOT AND SOUR SOUP

This is the perfect cold and flu season soup. It clears those sinuses right up. You can adjust the amount of spice until it's just right for you.

1 package (10 ounces, or 280 g) sliced mushrooms
8 fresh shiitake mushrooms, stems removed and caps sliced
1 can (8 ounces, or 225 g) bamboo shoots, drained and julienned
4 cloves garlic, minced
1 package (15 ounces, or 420 g) firm or silken tofu, cubed
2 tablespoons (16 g) grated fresh ginger, divided
4 cups (940 ml) water
2 tablespoons (12 g) chicken-flavored bouillon
2 tablespoons (30 ml) soy sauce
1 teaspoon sesame oil, plus extra for drizzling
1 teaspoon chili paste, plus more to taste
2 tablespoons (30 ml) rice wine vinegar or apple cider vinegar, plus more to taste
1½ cups (225 g) fresh or frozen peas

In a slow cooker, combine the mushrooms, bamboo shoots, garlic, tofu, 1 tablespoon (8 g) of the ginger, water, bouillon, soy sauce, 1 teaspoon of the sesame oil, chili paste, and vinegar. Cover and cook on low for 8 hours.

A few minutes before serving, add the peas and the remaining 1 tablespoon (8 g) ginger. Stir to combine. Taste the broth and add more vinegar or chili if needed.

Drizzle a few drops of oil on top of each serving.

If you like it milder and your friends like it hot, serve the chili paste on the side.

Yield: 4 servings

CHICKEN NOODLE SOUP

This one has some additional steps, but the results are all you could want in a chicken soup. It's guaranteed to cure common colds, evening grumps, and general sick-of-winter blues.

1 chicken (about 3 pounds or 1365 g)
Salt, to taste
Black pepper, to taste
10 cups (2350 ml) water
½ pound (225 g) egg noodles
1 (16-ounce or 455-g) bag frozen mixed vegetables

Cut the chicken into 4 pieces, removing the skin. Put the chicken, along with the neck, into the slow cooker. Season with salt and pepper. Add the water. Cover and cook on low for 8 hours.

Remove the chicken from the cooker and allow to cool. Leave the broth in the slow cooker.

Bring a pot of salted water to a boil and cook the

SALADS AND SOUPS • 143

noodles for 6 minutes. Drain the noodles and add them to the slow cooker. Add the vegetables.

When the chicken is cool enough to handle, remove the meat from the bones, discarding the bones. Discard the neck. Shred the chicken meat and return it to the cooker. Cook for another 2 hours on low. Adjust the seasonings.

Yield: 8 to 10 servings

TURKEY NOODLE SOUP
This is a tasty and healthful way to use up leftover turkey and stuffing after the holidays.

1½ quarts (1.4 L) hot water
6 chicken bouillon cubes
2 to 3 pounds (.9 to 1.4 kg) leftover turkey, including meat, skin, bones, and stuffing
Salt, to taste
Black pepper, to taste
1 cup (160 g) fresh or frozen egg noodles

In a slow cooker, combine the water and bouillon. Stir until the bouillon cubes have dissolved. Add the turkey meat, skin, bones, and stuffing. Stir again. Cover and cook on low for 10 to 12 hours.

Turn the heat off and allow the slow cooker to cool enough so that you can handle the ceramic pot safely. Transfer the contents of the slow cooker to a large bowl, then strain off the broth and return it to the ceramic pot. Remove the turkey meat from the bones, chop it into bite-size pieces, and return it to the slow cooker. Stir the mixture and season it with salt and pepper.

Increase the heat of the slow cooker to high. Stir in the noodles. Cover and cook on high for another 15 to 30 minutes, or until the noodles are tender.

Yield: 8 servings

▶*Add It!*
For a more flavorful broth, add 1½ cups (340 g) frozen seasoned vegetables and 2 to 3 fresh broccoli stalks (without the florets) along with the turkey meat, skin, bones, and stuffing.

CHICKEN CORN SOUP
This soup is reminiscent of Amish Chicken Corn Soup, which is often served at volunteer fire company carnivals and fund raisers. This easy version includes potatoes to make it a more hearty full meal.

1 pound (455 g) boneless skinless chicken breast, cubed
1 cup (160 g) chopped onion
½ teaspoon minced garlic
¾ cup (98 g) sliced carrots
½ cup (50 g) chopped celery
2 medium potatoes, cubed
12 ounces (340 g) cream-style corn
12 ounces (340 g) frozen corn
2 cups (475 ml) chicken broth (To make your own, see "Chicken Stock" on page 6.)
¼ teaspoon black pepper

In a slow cooker, combine all of the ingredients. Cover and cook on low for 8 to 9 hours, or until the chicken is tender.

Yield: 6 servings

CHICKEN RICE SOUP
This is classic comfort food: chicken and rice in a nice broth. It's sure to warm you and make you feel like everything is all right.

1 pound (455 g) boneless skinless chicken breast, cut into 1-inch (2.5 cm) pieces
5 cups (1.2 L) chicken broth (To make your own, see "Chicken Stock" on page 6.)
8 ounces (225 g) mushrooms, sliced
¾ cup (75 g) sliced celery
½ cup (65 g) sliced carrots
½ cup (93 g) long-grain rice, uncooked
¼ cup (25 g) chopped scallions
½ teaspoon ground sage
¼ teaspoon black pepper

In a slow cooker, combine all of the ingredients. Cover and cook on low for 7 to 9 hours.

Yield: 6 servings

LEAN DRIED APRICOT, CHICKEN, AND WILD RICE SOUP

Unusual and unexpected juxtapositions are at the heart of interesting fashion, art, and music, and unusual pairings are at the heart of interesting food. If you've never tasted apricots with chicken, know that it's unusual, surprising, and delightful. If your taste buds could smile, they'd be grinning from ear to ear. This terrific pairing makes for a flavorful soup–slightly salty, slightly sweet, and very satisfying. The toothy "bite" from the wild rice adds a nice touch.

1 sweet onion, diced
1 sweet potato, peeled and cubed, or 2 cups (300 g) peeled, seeded, and cubed butternut squash (about ¾-inch [2 cm] dice)
2 large chicken breasts, cut into chunks (about 2-inch [5 cm] dice)
½ cup (80 g) wild rice
6 cups (1,410 ml) chicken broth (To make your own, see "Chicken Stock" on page 6.)
1 teaspoon organic chicken Better Than Bouillon
3 tablespoons (45 ml) mirin or dry sherry
1 teaspoon ground ginger
½ teaspoon ground allspice
½ teaspoon salt
½ teaspoon black pepper
⅓ cup (43 g) coarsely chopped dried unsulfured apricots (See "Health Bite" on page 105.)
1½ cups (195 g) frozen corn

In a slow cooker, combine the onion, sweet potato, chicken, and rice. Pour the broth over all. Stir in the Better Than Bouillon, mirin, ginger, allspice, salt, and pepper. Cover and cook on low for 3 to 4 hours or on high for 2 to 3 hours, or until the squash and rice are tender.

During the last 20 minutes of cooking time, add the apricots and corn.

Yield: 6 servings

▶ *Health Bite*

Lean breast meat has a lot going for it nutritionally, but it tends to not be as moist and juicy as the fatter cuts. But because it's immersed in liquid stock in the slow cooker, it will be as moist and tender when you eat it as you could possibly want it to be.

Apricots are a tasty little bundle of nutrients that come in a sun-colored package, provide lots of vitamin A and beta-carotene, plus contain a special relative of beta-carotene called beta-cryptoxanthin, a powerful antioxidant that's associated with lower risk of both lung and colon cancers.

CHICKEN SOUP WITH WILD RICE

Watching your carb intake? Know that wild rice has more fiber and therefore fewer usable carbs than regular rice, either white or brown. And it adds a cachet to your soup.

2 quarts (1.9 L) chicken broth (To make your own, see "Chicken Stock" on page 6.)
2 carrots, thinly sliced
2 stalks celery, diced
½ cup (80 g) chopped onion
1 pound (455 g) boneless, skinless chicken breast, cut into ½-inch (13 mm) cubes
¼ cup (40 g) wild rice
1 teaspoon poultry seasoning

In a slow cooker, combine all of the ingredients. Cover and cook on low for 6 to 7 hours.

Yield: 6 servings

CHICKEN MINESTRONE

Here's a de-carbed version of the Italian favorite. You'll never miss the pasta!

3 slices bacon, chopped
1 medium onion, chopped
2 medium turnips, cut into ½-inch (13 mm) cubes
1 medium carrot, thinly sliced
2 small zucchini, quartered and sliced
2 stalks celery, thinly sliced
3 tablespoons (45 ml) olive oil
1½ quarts (1.4 L) chicken broth (To make your own, see "Chicken Stock" on page 6.)
1½ pounds (680 g) skinless chicken thighs, boned and cubed
1 tablespoon (6 g) Italian seasoning
1 can (14½ ounces, or 410 g) diced tomatoes, undrained
1 can (15 ounces, or 425 g) black soybeans
Salt, to taste
Black pepper, to taste

Coat a big, heavy skillet with nonstick cooking spray.

Start the bacon frying over medium heat. As some grease cooks out of the bacon, add as many of the vegetables as will fit. Sauté them, in batches if necessary, until they soften just a bit.

Transfer the vegetables to a slow cooker and continue sautéing the rest of the vegetables, adding oil as needed, until all the vegetables are softened a bit and in the slow cooker.

Add the broth, chicken, Italian seasoning, tomatoes, and soybeans to the slow cooker. Season with salt and pepper. Cover and cook on low for 7 to 8 hours.

Yield: 6 servings

SALADS AND SOUPS • 145

1 Lean and Easy Taco Salad

2 German Potato Salad

SPRING MINESTRONE WITH PESTO PARMESAN

Minestrone is a great soup anytime of the year. Serve this with focaccia (see "Foolproof Focaccia" on page 65) and a big green salad for a complete meal.

FOR THE PESTO PARMESAN:
15 leaves fresh basil
2 sprigs fresh oregano
¼ cup (36 g) almonds
1 tablespoon (15 ml) olive oil, optional
Salt, to taste

FOR THE MINESTRONE:
1 tablespoon (15 ml) olive oil
½ large onion, chopped
2 cloves garlic, minced
1-inch (2.5 cm) piece lemon peel
1 large carrot, chopped
1 yellow squash, cut into half-moons
1 bunch Swiss chard or beet greens, torn into small pieces
5 cups (1175 ml) water
2 tablespoons (12 g) chicken-flavored bouillon
1 can (14½ ounces, or 406 g) white beans or chickpeas, drained and rinsed
1 can (14½ ounces, or 406 g) diced tomatoes
2 Italian sausages, chopped
2-inch (5 cm) sprig fresh rosemary
Salt, to taste
Black pepper, to taste
Croutons

To make the Pesto Parmesan: In a food processor, pulse all of the pesto ingredients until it begins to form a grainy paste, but is not smooth. You want the texture to be granular like the grated Parmesan that you buy in a shaker. Store leftovers in an airtight container in the fridge.

To make the minestrone: In a skillet, heat the oil over medium heat. Sauté the onion for 3 to 5 minutes, or until translucent. Add the garlic and sauté for 1 minute longer.

In a slow cooker, combine all of the minestrone ingredients except for the croutons. Cover and cook on low for 6 to 8 hours.

Remove and discard the rosemary sprig.

Top each serving with the Pesto Parmesan and croutons.

Yield: 6 servings

▶*Health Bite*
This is a great recipe if you're eating vegan. Just be sure to use vegan bouillon and sausages. You have to be careful when you are looking for vegan sausages. There are a ton of veggie sausages on the market, but many have eggs or dairy in them.

Be sure to read the ingredients carefully, especially if you are trying a new brand.

MIGHTY MINESTRONE

The wide variety of ingredients in this soup makes the whole thing taste amazing! To save chopping time, use 4 to 5 cups fresh prepared vegetables of your choice, such as corn, broccoli florets, cauliflower florets, colored bell pepper strips, sliced carrots and cut green beans.

6 baby red potatoes, scrubbed, unpeeled, and diced or 1 yam or sweet potato, peeled and chopped
2 carrots, peeled and chopped
2 ribs celery, sliced
1 zucchini, coarsely chopped
½ sweet onion, chopped
1 can (15 ounces, or 420 g) chickpeas, drained and rinsed
1 can (15 ounces, or 420 g) kidney beans, drained and rinsed
4 cups (940 ml) vegetable broth (To make your own, see "Freshest Vegetable Broth" on page 6) or beef broth (To make your own, see "Beef Stock" on page 6.)
2 cans (14.5 ounces, or 406 g each) diced tomatoes with basil, garlic, and oregano, undrained
¼ cup (60 ml) red wine
1 teaspoon dried basil
1 bay leaf
¾ teaspoon dried oregano
1 teaspoon salt
½ teaspoon black pepper
1 package (10 ounces, or 280 g) frozen chopped spinach
1 tablespoon (15 ml) red wine vinegar
¼ cup (25 g) grated Parmesan cheese, optional

In a slow cooker, combine the vegetables, beans, broth, tomatoes, wine, basil, bay leaf, oregano, salt, and pepper. Stir gently to mix. Cover and cook on low for 4 to 5 hours, or until all of the vegetables are tender. Stir in the spinach. Cook for 30 minutes, or until the spinach is hot. Add the red wine vinegar and stir. Stir to incorporate the spinach. Garnish with the Parmesan, if using. Remove the bay leaf.

Yield: 8 to 10 servings

▶*Health Bite*
Soups are all about "nutrient density," and if you're not familiar with that term, let us explain. Nutrient density is how many vitamins, minerals, phytochemicals, and other healthful compounds are found per calorie. Broccoli, for example, has a very high nutrient density (lots of nutrients, small number of calories); chocolate ice cream has the opposite–few nutrients at a very high caloric cost.

Now let's turn to this nutritionally dense soup! For a very small number of calories, you've got a nutritional powerhouse, brimming with fiber (beans), lycopene (tomatoes), beta-carotene (carrots), vitamin K (celery), sulfur compounds (onion), and from the zucchini, a truckload of heart-healthy potassium (okay, okay, 843 mg per large zucchini, if you want to get technical). With a little bit of Purmesan, the fat will help you feel satiated with fewer calories.

CABBAGE SOUP WITH KIELBASA

Rich in vitamin C, cabbage is both good and good for you, as this recipe attests. Try to buy a low-fat sausage for even healthier eating.

1 pound (455 g) kielbasa sausage
½ head green cabbage
1 (64-ounce or 1880-ml) can vegetable juice cocktail, such as V-8

Cut the kielbasa into ½-inch-thick rings and put them into a slow cooker.
 Finely shred the cabbage; you should have about 4 cups (280 g). Add the cabbage to the slow cooker. Pour the vegetable juice over all. Cover and cook on low for 6 to 8 hours.

Yield: 6 to 8 servings

TURKEY MUSHROOM SOUP

Turkey meatballs and mushrooms combine to make this soup a real pleaser.

½ pound (225 g) ground turkey
½ teaspoon garlic powder
½ teaspoon onion powder
½ teaspoon black pepper
¼ cup (60 ml) egg substitute
1 tablespoon (15 ml) olive oil
1 cup (130 g) sliced carrots
½ teaspoon crushed garlic
2 cups (140 g) sliced mushrooms
2 cups (475 ml) beef broth (To make your own, see "Beef Stock" on page 6.)
10 ounces (280 g) cream of mushroom soup (To make your own, see "Cream of Mushroom Soup" on page 7.)
2 tablespoons (32 g) tomato paste

In a small bowl, mix together the turkey, garlic powder, onion powder, and pepper. Add the egg substitute, stirring until well blended. Form the mixture into small meatballs.
 In a skillet, heat the oil. Brown the meatballs and drain well. Transfer the meatballs to a slow cooker. Add the remaining ingredients. Cover and cook on low for 6 to 8 hours or on high for 3 to 4 hours.

Yield: 8 servings

▶*Recipe Tip*
Garnish this dish with Parmesan cheese and parsley.

CREAM OF MUSHROOM SOUP

If you've only ever thought of mushroom soup as gooey stuff that came in cans and was used in casseroles, you need to try this. It has a rich, earthy flavor. Even mushroom-phobic people often like it.

8 ounces (225 g) mushrooms, sliced
¼ cup (40 g) chopped onion
2 tablespoons (28 g) butter
1 quart (950 ml) chicken broth (To make your own, see "Chicken Stock" on page 6.)
½ cup (120 ml) heavy cream
½ cup (115 g) light sour cream
Salt, to taste
Black pepper, to taste
Cornstarch, optional

In a big, heavy skillet, sauté the mushrooms and onion in the butter until the mushrooms soften and change color. Transfer them to a slow cooker. Add the broth. Cover and cook on low for 5 to 6 hours.
 When the time's up, using a slotted spoon, scoop out the vegetables and put them in a blender or food processor. Add enough broth to help them process easily and purée them finely. Pour the puréed vegetables back into the slow cooker. Using a rubber spatula, scrape out every last bit. Stir in the heavy cream and sour cream. Season with salt and pepper. If needed, thicken the sauce a bit with cornstarch.

Yield: 5 servings

SALADS AND SOUPS

3 Beef Barley Soup; 4 Smoked Tofu and Stars Soup; 5 Hot and Sour Soup; 6 Chicken Noodle Soup; 7 Turkey Noodle Soup; 8 Chicken Corn Soup

9 Chicken Rice Soup; 10 Lean Dried Apricot, Chicken, and Wild Rice Soup; 11 Chicken Soup with Wild Rice; 12 Chicken Minestrone; 13 Spring Minestrone with Pesto Parmesan; 14 Mighty Minestrone; 15 Cabbage Soup with Kielbasa; 16 Turkey Mushroom Soup

SALADS AND SOUPS • 151

ONION SOUP

Fragrant, piping-hot onion soup–what a wonderful way to greet a chilly night! This soup is delicious as a first course, or it can be a light meal with a salad and crusty bread.

2 pounds (910 g) yellow or Spanish onions, sliced very thin
3 tablespoons (45 g) butter
1 cup (235 ml) red wine
1 (64-ounce or 1880-ml) can beef broth
Salt, to taste
Black pepper, to taste

In a slow cooker, combine the onions and butter. Cover and cook on low for 4 hours, or until the onions are very soft and a little caramelized. Add the wine and broth. Cover and cook on low for another 4 hours. Season with salt and pepper.

Yield: 6 to 8 servings

▶ *Add It!*
Some cheese melted on top of the soup gives it that French Onion Soup feel.

CREAMY POTATO SOUP

This creamy soup benefits from the essence of the herbs in the soup mix. Ladle it into bowls, garnish with fresh chives, and serve with crusty bread.

1½ quarts (1.4 L) water
One 9.3-ounce (263-g) package Fantastic Foods Creamy Potato Simmer Soup
4 large potatoes, peeled and cut into 1-inch (2.5-cm) cubes
One 12-ounce (355-ml) can evaporated milk
Salt, to taste
Black pepper, to taste

In a slow cooker, combine the water and soup mix. Stir until the soup mix has dissolved. Add the potato and stir again. Cover and cook on high for 4 to 5 hours.

An hour before the soup is done, stir in the milk.

Just before serving, season with salt and pepper. Stir it again.

Yield: 8 servings

▶ *Add It!*
For a richer tasting soup, add 5½ tablespoons (½ cup, or 75 g) butter, melted, along with the evaporated milk.

ROSEMARY POTATO SOUP

This is another great comfort food. It's great when you don't feel well, or if it's just chilly outside. It also makes an excellent base for other creamy soups, so add in some broccoli, spinach, or even carrots for an un-cream soup.

4 medium russet potatoes, peeled and cut into medium-size cubes
1 clove garlic, minced
2 cups (470 ml) water
2 tablespoons (12 g) chicken-flavored bouillon
1 sprig fresh rosemary
Salt, to taste
Black pepper, to taste
1 cup (235 ml) milk

In a slow cooker, combine the potatoes, garlic, water, bouillon, and rosemary. Season with salt and pepper. Cover and cook on low for 6 to 8 hours. Add the milk. Remove and discard the rosemary.

Using an immersion blender, purée the soup or transfer it in batches to a countertop blender, being careful of splatters of hot soup, until smooth.

Taste and adjust the seasonings.

Yield: 4 servings

▶ *Serving Suggestion*
Serve this soup topped with bacon bits, thinly sliced scallions, and some shredded Cheddar cheese.

CREAM OF UNPOTATO SOUP

We never cease to marvel at the versatility of cauliflower. This really does taste like potato soup. You can serve this hot right away or chill it and serve it as vichyssoise.

1 quart (950 ml) chicken broth (To make your own, see "Chicken Stock" on page 6.)
½ head cauliflower, chunked
½ cup (80 g) chopped onion
½ cup (50 g) Ketatoes mix
½ cup (120 ml) heavy cream
½ cup (120 ml) milk
Cornstrach, optional
Salt, to taste
Black pepper, to taste
5 scallions, sliced

In a slow cooker, combine the broth, cauliflower, and onion. Cover and cook on low for 4 to 5 hours.

Using an immersion blender, purée the soup or transfer the vegetables and 1 cup (235 ml) of the broth in batches to a countertop blender, being careful of splatters of hot soup, until smooth.

Blend in the Ketatoes. If you have removed the

cauliflower from the slow cooker to purée, pour the purée back in and whisk it into the remaining broth.

Stir in the cream and milk. If needed, thicken it a bit further with cornstarch. Season with salt and pepper. Stir in the scallions.

Yield: 6 servings

LOADED SPLIT PEA SWEET POTATO SOUP

This version is much healthier than the usual pea soup fare for a number of reasons. Traditional split pea soup is made with ham, which is high in sodium and almost always from factory-farmed animals. We skip the ham, making this suitable for vegetarians. But even if you're not a vegetarian, you won't miss the meat. This version is low fat (if you care about that) but also high in heart-friendly fiber and potassium, and that's something you don't often see in soup, especially soup that tastes this good. The mellow sweetness of the sweet potatoes compensates for the saltiness of the ham. You'll never miss it. Split peas are a great vegetarian source of protein.

2 tablespoons (30 ml) olive oil
1 large Vidalia onion, diced
4 medium carrots, sliced into thin rounds
1 large rib celery, cut into thirds
2 cloves garlic, crushed and chopped
1 large sweet potato, peeled and cut into ½-inch (1.3 cm) cubes
½ teaspoon dried thyme
1 pound (454 g) split peas, sorted, rinsed, and drained
8 cups (1.9 L) vegetable broth (To make your own, see "Freshest Vegetable Broth" on page 6) or chicken broth (To make your own, see "Chicken Stock" on page 6.)
¼ to ½ teaspoon red pepper flakes
1 package (10 ounces, or 280 g) frozen spinach, thawed but not drained
½ teaspoon salt
2 tablespoons (30 ml) cooking sherry

In a large skillet, heat the oil over medium heat. Sauté the onion, carrots, and celery for about 6 minutes. Add the garlic and sauté for 1 minute.

Transfer the contents to a slow cooker. Add the potato, thyme, split peas, broth, and red pepper. Cover and cook on low for 7 to 8 hours or on high for 4 to 5 hours, or until everything is very tender. Remove the celery pieces. Stir in the spinach and salt. Cook, uncovered, for 10 to 20 minutes, or until the spinach is hot. Stir in the sherry.

Remove from the heat. Using an immersion blender or transferring in batches to a countertop blender, purée partially until it reaches the desired consistency.

Yield: 6 servings

▶*Time-Saver Tip*
Omit the sauté step and simply combine all the ingredients except the spinach, salt, and sherry in the slow cooker. Follow the rest of the instructions as written.

SWEET TOOTH-BUSTER SWEET POTATO APPLE SOUP

Did you know that you can trick a sweet tooth? Sure, that sweet tooth is whispering in your ear about how wonderful it would be to dive into a quart of Ben and Jerry's, but you can pull the old bait and switch by feeding it nutritious fare that might tame the beast. Case in point is the delicious pairing here of sweet potatoes and apples.

1 Vidalia onion, chopped
2 ribs celery, halved
2 pounds (908 g) sweet potatoes (about 2 large), peeled and chopped
2 large baking apples, peeled, cored, and chopped (Jonagold or Mutsu work well.)
4 cups (940 ml) vegetable broth (To make your own, see "Freshest Vegetable Broth" on page 6.)
1 clove garlic, minced
2 teaspoons minced fresh ginger
2 teaspoons honey, or to taste
½ teaspoon ground cinnamon
½ teaspoon salt
¼ teaspoon ground chipotle chile or cayenne pepper, optional

In a slow cooker, combine the onion, celery, potatoes, and apples.

In a large bowl, whisk together the broth, garlic, ginger, honey, cinnamon, salt, and chipotle, if using. Pour the mixture over the fruit and vegetables in the slow cooker. Cover and cook on low for 5 to 6 hours or on high for 3 to 4 hours, or until the potatoes are very tender.

Remove and discard the celery.

Using an immersion blender or transferring in batches to a countertop blender, purée the soup. Adjust the seasonings to taste.

Yield: 6 servings

▶*Health Bite*
Sweet potatoes are a tasty nutrient powerhouse and very high in potassium, which helps mitigate the negative impact of all of the sodium hidden in our prepared foods. Sweet potatoes are also very high in fiber and vitamin A.

Apples are the original medicinal food. They're loaded with natural anti-inflammatory agents such as the superstar nutrient quercetin. Plus, they're naturally juicy and sweet, to boot.

NO-CREAM LEEK AND POTATO SOUP

This is a creamy and satisfying leek and potato soup without the cream. When making a puréed soup, it's more typical to peel the potatoes for smoothness, but we encourage you to leave them–and their nutrients–intact for this healthier version. Look for potatoes about the size of golf balls. You can use baby red, new, or baby Yukon gold potatoes.

1½ tablespoons (23 ml) olive oil
3 small leeks, white and tender green parts only, washed well to remove all grit and chopped
4 cloves garlic, minced
1 pound (454 g) small baby red or new potatoes, scrubbed, unpeeled, and quartered
4 cups (940 ml) unsweetened plain soymilk
¾ teaspoon salt
¼ teaspoon white pepper, optional
½ teaspoon black pepper
1 to 2 tablespoons (16 to 32 g) mellow white miso
¼ cup (34 g) toasted pine nuts, optional

In a large skillet, heat the oil over medium heat. Sauté the leeks for 5 to 7 minutes, or until tender. Add the garlic and cook for 1 minute.
 Transfer the leeks and garlic to a slow cooker. Add the potatoes, soymilk, salt, and peppers.
 Cover and cook on low for about 4 hours, or until the potatoes are tender.
 Using an immersion or countertop blender, purée the soup until nearly smooth. Stir in the miso, blending lightly with an immersion wand or spoon to get it to disperse and mix. Adjust the seasonings to taste. Garnish with the pine nuts, if using.

Yield: 4 to 6 servings

▶**Health Bite**
The liver is command central for detoxification in the body. Similar to the engine in your car, the liver needs fuel to run on. That fuel comes in the form of vitamins and other liver-supporting nutrients and phytochemicals, and vegetables are just loaded with them.
 Vegetables such as leeks, for example, are like fuel injectors for the metabolic machinery of the liver, making it run as smoothly as a well-tuned Ferrari. Leeks contain vitamin K, which the liver needs to make factors necessary for proper blood clotting.
 Plus, anything that strains or impairs liver function, such as alcohol, can seriously deplete antioxidants. You'll find a ton of antioxidants in the leeks.

BLACK BEAN SOUP

Eating low-carb? You might miss legume soup, especially black bean soup. This is our de-carbed version.

1 can (28 ounces, or 785 g) black soybeans
1 can (14 ounces, or 390 g) black beans
2 cups (475 ml) chicken broth (To make your own, see "Chicken Stock" on page 6.)
1 medium onion, cut into chunks
4 cloves garlic, crushed
1 medium carrot, shredded
2 medium stalks celery, finely diced
1 teaspoon salt, plus more if needed
½ teaspoon black pepper, plus more if needed
1 tablespoon (15 ml) liquid smoke
2 teaspoons hot sauce
2 cups (300 g) ham cubes

Using a food processor with the S-blade in place, purée the soybeans and black beans.
 Transfer the beans to a slow cooker. Stir in the broth.
 In a food processor, pulse the onion, garlic, carrot, and celery until everything is finely chopped. Pour the mixture over the beans in the slow cooker. Stir in the salt, pepper, liquid smoke, hot sauce, and ham. Cover and cook on low for 9 to 10 hours.
 When the time's up, stir the soup up (it'll have settled out some) and check to see if it needs more salt and pepper. (This will depend on how salty your ham is.)

Yield: 8 servings

LO-CAL CARIBBEAN BLACK BEAN SOUP

A famous reggae singer in Anguilla named Bankie Banx owns a legendary beach joint where they serve island food. This soup reminds us of just the kind of fare you'd expect to be served there, on checkered tablecloths overlooking the gorgeous calm turquoise water of the Caribbean. If you're in a hurry, omit the oil and veggie sautéing step and simply add all of the ingredients directly to the slow cooker.

1 pound (454 g) dried black beans
1½ tablespoons (23 ml) olive oil
1 yellow onion, chopped
2 ribs celery, sliced
1 green or red bell pepper, seeded and chopped
8 cloves garlic, crushed and chopped
8 cups (1,880 ml) vegetable broth (To make your own, see "Freshest Vegetable Broth" on page 6.)
1 teaspoon dried oregano
1 teaspoon dried thyme
¾ teaspoon ground cumin
¾ teaspoon salt
½ teaspoon black pepper
3 tablespoons (45 ml) apple cider vinegar

154 • THE LITTLE SLOW COOKER COOKBOOK

1 tablespoon (15 ml) hot pepper sauce
1 teaspoon Sucanat or xylitol
½ cup (8 g) chopped fresh cilantro or basil

Soak the beans overnight in water to cover by 2 inches (5 cm). Drain and rinse the beans well.
  Transfer the beans to a slow cooker.
  In a large skillet, heat the oil over medium heat. Add the onion, celery, and bell pepper. Cover and cook for about 7 minutes, or until the vegetables are starting to soften. Add the garlic and cook for 1 minute.
  Transfer the onion mixture to the slow cooker. Add the broth, oregano, thyme, cumin, salt, and pepper. Stir well. Cover and cook on low for 7 to 8 hours, or until the beans are tender to the squeeze. Just before serving, stir in the vinegar, hot pepper sauce, Sucanat, and cilantro.

Yield: 8 servings

▶*Health Bite*
Black bean soup might not be the first thing you think of when you think of "diet food," but think again.
Beans are the ultimate high-fiber food, meaning they fill you up and keep you full for a long time. One cup of black beans contains a whopping 15 grams of fiber. Beans have about 227 calories per cup, contain more than 15 grams of satisfying, satiating protein, and feature 611 milligrams of potassium.
  The black beans are just about the only ingredient in this soup that contains any calories to speak of, other than the tiny bit of olive oil.

NORTHERN BEAN SOUP
This vegetarian soup is healthful and delicious. Enjoy with hot buttered cornbread on cold winter days.

Two 15-ounce (417-g) cans Great Northern beans or navy beans, drained and rinsed
Two 10¾-ounce (305-g) cans condensed vegetarian vegetable soup
¾ cup (175 ml) water
3 tablespoons (45 ml) olive oil
Salt, to taste
Black pepper, to taste

In a slow cooker, combine the beans, condensed soup, and water. Stir to mix. Cover and cook on low for 8 to 10 hours or on high for 4 to 6 hours.
  Between 1 and 2 hours before the soup is done, thicken the soup by using a potato mashes to mash the beans. About 30 minutes before the soup is done, add the oil and mix well. Just before serving, stir the soup again and season with salt and pepper.

Yield: 6 servings

▶*Add It!*
Add 10 ounces (280 g) meatless sausage cut into bite-size pieces and 2 teaspoons (10 ml) Worcestershire sauce along with the beans and condensed soup.

SPLIT PEA AND LENTIL SOUP
If you're a vegetarian, or even if you're not, you'll love this warm, nutritious soup.

2 tablespoons (30 ml) olive oil
1 small onion, minced
1 clove garlic
1 cup (200 g) lentils
1 cup (200 g) split peas
6 cups (1410 ml) water
2 tablespoons (12 g) chicken-flavored bouillon
2 bay leaves
1 teaspoon dried tarragon
½ teaspoon dried marjoram
¼ teaspoon ground rosemary or 1 teaspoon dried leaves
Salt, to taste
Black pepper, to taste
6 ounces (170 g) fresh baby spinach, washed

In a skillet, heat the oil over medium heat. Sauté the onion for 3 to 5 minutes, or until it's translucent. Add the garlic and sauté for 1 minute longer.
  In a slow cooker, combine the onion mixture, lentils, peas, water, bouillon, bay leaves, tarragon, marjoram, and rosemary. Season with salt and pepper. Cover and cook on low for 6 to 8 hours.
  About 30 minutes before serving, add the spinach. Taste and adjust the seasonings. Before serving, remove and discard the bay leaves.

Yield: 8 servings

▶*Health Bite*
Split peas and lentils are full of fiber, protein, iron, magnesium, and zinc.

SPLIT PEA AND HAM SOUP
This country classic is always a hit at the dinner table, even with folks who generally eschew anything green.

½ pound (225 g) cooked ham, cut into ¼-inch (6-mm) cubes
1 medium onion, diced into small pieces
1 pound (455 g) split green peas, rinsed, drained, and picked over
8 cups (1880 ml) water
Salt, to taste
Black pepper, to taste

In a slow cooker, combine the ham, onion, peas, and water. Cover and cook on low for 6 to 8 hours, or until the peas are very soft. Stir the soup to break up some of the peas and thicken the soup. Season with salt and pepper.

Yield: 6 to 8 servings

BEAN AND VEGETABLE SOUP
A good bean soup must be one of the most satisfying meals there is. This vegetable blend we spotted has a robust variety of veggies and beans, such as broccoli, carrots, green beans, white beans, garbanzo beans, and kidney beans. All of this adds up to a bowlful of healthy and tasty soup goodness.

½ pound (225 g) bacon, chopped into ½-inch (1-cm) dice
1 (16-ounce or 455-g) package Rancho Fiesta Vegetable Blend
2 quarts (1890 ml) chicken broth (To make your own, see "Chicken Stock" on page 6.)

In a skillet, microwave, or oven, cook the bacon. Drain the fat from the bacon and put the bacon into a slow cooker, along with the vegetable blend and the broth. Cover and cook on low for 6 to 8 hours.

Yield: 6 to 8 servings

▶ Add It!
Sprinkle a little finely grated Parmesan cheese on top of each bowl of soup before serving.

OLD-FASHIONED VEGETABLE SOUP
Maybe it's not just like Grandma made, but this soup is close enough to make you remember.

1½ pounds (680 g) beef round steak, cut in ½-inch (1.3 cm) cubes
7 cups (1.6 L) beef broth (To make your own, see "Beef Stock" on page 6.)
1 cup (130 g) thinly sliced carrots
1 pound (455 g) frozen peas
1 pound (455 g) frozen corn
1 pound (455 g) frozen lima beans
1 bay leaf
½ teaspoon dill weed
1 can (28 ounces, or 785 g) diced tomatoes
1 potato, diced
1 cup (160 g) chopped onion
½ teaspoon dried basil
¼ teaspoon black pepper

In a slow cooker, combine all of the ingredients. Cover and cook on high for 4 hours, or until the vegetables are tender. Before serving, remove the bay leaf.

Yield: 10 servings

WHAT'S IN THE FREEZER VEGGIE SOUP
This is the easiest recipe you'll ever make. Even if you only have 5 minutes to start some dinner in the slow cooker before you rush off to work, you can throw this together. You can make this no matter what vegetables you have on hand. It's a great idea to always keep a few bags of organic frozen veggies in the freezer for this soup, which you can serve chunky or puréed. If you want to make it look like a cream soup, add parsnips, potato, or cauliflower with none of the fat or calories.

6 cups mixed vegetables (The weight will vary, depending on the vegetables.)
2 cloves garlic, minced
5 cups (1,175 ml) water
2 tablespoons (12 g) chicken-flavored bouillon
Your favorite combination of herbs and spices
Salt, to taste
Black pepper, to taste
2 to 4 cups (300 to 600 g) cooked grain or pasta

In a slow cooker, combine any slow-cooking vegetables and the garlic, water, bouillon, dried herbs, and spices. Season with salt and pepper. Cover and cook on low for 6 to 8 hours.

About 30 minutes before serving, add any quick-cooking vegetables, fresh herbs, and grains or pasta. Taste and adjust the seasonings.

Yield: 6 servings

▶ *Recipe Variations*
- *Try a few of these combos: sweet potato and ginger with thyme, curried cauliflower carrot, chunky Mexican chowder with fresh cilantro, and mixed vegetable soup with diced tomatoes and basil.*

- *Make it Asian style with a little soy sauce and fresh grated ginger. You can even top off your creation with some sesame oil before serving.*

- *Not enough vegetables in the freezer? Add canned or frozen beans instead.*

HOT AND SOUR CHINESE VEGETABLE SOUP
This is not the same recipe as the hot and sour soup found in your favorite restaurant, but it's quite tasty in its own right.

1 (64-ounce or 1880-ml) can beef broth
1 (10-ounce or 285-ml) jar Szechuan stir-fry sauce
1 (16-ounce or 455-g) package frozen Szechuan or stirfry vegetables
Salt, to taste
Black pepper, to taste

In a slow cooker, combine the broth and stir-fry sauce. Cover and cook on low for 7 hours. Add the vegetables and cook for an additional hour. Season with salt and pepper.

Yield: 6 to 8 servings

BROCCOLI-CHEESE SOUP
Smooth and satisfying, this soup is a lovely light meal or a delicious accompaniment. Serve it with soft honey wheat rolls.

2 large stalks fresh broccoli, washed and dried
Two 10¾-ounce (305-g) cans condensed cream of celery soup
1 cup (235 ml) water
1 pound (455 g) pasteurized processed cheese food, cut into cubes
Salt, to taste
Black pepper, to taste

Prepare the broccoli by cutting off the florets and setting them aside. Cut off the tough lower ends and discard them. Cut the remaining stems into rounds or chunks of uniform size and set them aside. The florets and stem pieces should total about 2½ cups (175 g).

In a slow cooker, combine the condensed soup and water. Stir to combine.

Add the broccoli stem pieces and cheese, and stir again. Cover and cook on low for 4 to 6 hours, or until the stem pieces are tender but not overcooked.

Increase the heat of the slow cooker to high. Add the broccoli florets, and stir. Cover and cook for another 15 to 30 minutes, or just until the florets are tender. Season with salt and pepper.

Yield: 8 servings

▶ *Recipe Tips*
- *To save time, steam the broccoli florets before adding them to the soup, and keep the heat on low.*

- *For a richer soup, substitute milk for the water.*

TOFU BOUILLABAISSE
This is a fragrant, tomato-based stew cooked with saffron and fresh fennel. The potatoes and tofu make it a hearty meal.

2 tablespoons (30 ml) olive oil
1 medium onion, halved and sliced
3 cloves garlic, minced
½ medium fennel bulb, chopped
3 stalks celery, chopped
2 carrots, cut into half-moons
3 medium potatoes, cut into chunks
1 package (15 ounces, or 420 g) extra-firm tofu, cubed
1 can (28 ounces, or 784 g) diced tomatoes or 3 cups (540 g) chopped fresh
1½ cups (353 ml) water
2 bay leaves
½ teaspoon saffron
Salt, to taste
Black pepper, to taste
Zest and juice of ½ lime

In a skillet, heat the oil over medium heat. Sauté the onion for 3 to 5 minutes, or until it's translucent. Add the garlic and sauté for 3 minutes longer.

In a slow cooker, combine all of the ingredients. Cover and cook on low for 6 to 8 hours. Taste and adjust the seasonings. Before serving, remove the bay leaves.

Yield: 6 servings

17 Cream of Mushroom Soup; 18 Onion Soup; 19 Creamy Potato Soup; 20 Rosemary Potato Soup; 21 Cream of UnPotato Soup; 22 Loaded Split Pea Sweet Potato Soup; 23 Sweet Tooth-Buster Sweet Potato Apple Soup; 24 No-Cream Leek and Potato Soup

25 Black Bean Soup; 26 Lo-Cal Caribbean Black Bean Soup; 27 Northern Bean Soup; 28 Split Pea and Lentil Soup; 29 Split Pea and Ham Soup; 30 Bean and Vegetable Soup

SALADS AND SOUPS • 159

CURRIED COCONUT CREAM OF CAULIFLOWER SOUP

The cardamom in this soup adds a nice finishing touch, a hint of unexpected fresh spice.

2½-pound (1.1 kg) cauliflower, stemmed and chopped, or precut florets
1 tablespoon (15 ml) olive oil
2 large Vidalia onions, chopped
2½ teaspoons curry powder
¾ teaspoon ground turmeric
½ teaspoon ground cardamom
¼ teaspoon ground cloves
¼ teaspoon cayenne pepper
2 cups (470 ml) chicken or vegetable broth (To make your own, see "Chicken Stock" on page 6 or "Freshest Vegetable Broth" on page 6.)
¾ teaspoon salt
1 can (15 ounces, or 420 g) light coconut milk
1½ cups (195 g) frozen peas, optional
½ cup (8 g) chopped fresh cilantro

In a slow cooker, place the cauliflower
In a large skillet, heat the oil over medium heat. Sauté the onions for about 5 minutes, or until just softened. Stir in the curry powder, turmeric, cardamom, cloves, and cayenne pepper. Cook for 1 minute. Add the broth and salt. Stir to incorporate the spices.
Pour the mixture over the cauliflower in the slow cooker, being careful to get everything from the pan. Stir in the milk. Cover and cook on low for about 6 hours or on high for about 3 hours, or until the cauliflower is very tender.
Using an immersion blender or in batches in a countertop blender, purée to the desired consistency.
Reduce the heat of the slow cooker to low. Stir in the peas, if using, adjust the seasonings, if necessary, and cook on low for 10 minutes longer. Just before serving, stir in the cilantro.

Yield: 6 to 8 servings

▶Health Bite

Want a super simple diet plan? Don't eat anything white.
Of course, God is in the details, and there are a few exceptions to the rule, one of which is cauliflower. Another is coconut and coconut milk. A third is chicken and turkey, but hey, let's not be picky. You get the idea.
Cauliflower gets a pass on the "no white stuff" rule because it's a member of the Brassica family of vegetable royalty. These vegetables are loaded with cancer-fighting chemicals called indoles. They're low in calories (ridiculously low, actually, at 29 calories per cup!), high in fiber, and brimming with nutrients such as calcium, potassium, vitamin C, and folate.
Coconut milk is the perfect bath for this wonderful vegetable, especially flavored with the super-spice turmeric.

DELICATA SQUASH AND PEAR SOUP

All winter squashes pair well with something a little sweet. We like mixing them with fresh pears and apples in the winter to liven up a soup or casserole. This combo is unexpected, and it's a welcome change of pace during the colder months.

1 medium delicata or other winter squash
2 medium pears or apples
Lemon juice
1 small onion, chopped
1 clove garlic, chopped
4 cups (940 ml) water, plus more if needed
2 tablespoons (12 g) chicken-flavored bouillon
1 tablespoon (15 ml) port or red wine
1 sprig fresh thyme
1 sprig fresh rosemary
Salt, to taste
Black pepper, to taste
Finely chopped pistachios
Minced fresh thyme

Cut the squash in half. Scrape the seeds out. Using a vegetable peeler, remove the skin. Chop the flesh into cubes.
Peel the pears, core, and chop.
In a small bowl, toss the pears with lemon juice to prevent browning.
In a slow cooker, combine all of the ingredients, except for the pistachios and minced fresh thyme. Cover and cook on low for 6 to 8 hours.
Remove the thyme and rosemary sprigs.
Using an immersion blender or in batches in a countertop blender, purée the soup, being careful of splatters of hot soup, until smooth. Adjust the seasonings to taste, and add more water if needed. Top with pistachios and fresh thyme.

Yield: 6 servings

▶*Recipe Variation*

Our favorite combo for this soup is pear and delicata squash, but you can use any winter squash you happen to have on hand to create your own one-of-a-kind soup.

RICH AND CREAMY SWEET POTATO PEANUT BISQUE

What could make sweet potatoes, one of nature's greatest foods, taste even better? Peanuts. This creamy, rich sweet potato dish will light a gentle fire in your taste buds with its lime bite and red pepper kick. It's warming and satisfying. For a different flavor twist and to save peeling and chopping time, replace the fresh sweet potatoes with 3 cups (735 g) canned or fresh pumpkin purée.

1 tablespoon (15 g) coconut oil
1 large yellow onion, chopped
1 cup (110 g) grated carrot
2 tablespoons (12 g) minced fresh ginger
3 cloves garlic, minced
1 can (14.5 ounces, or 406 g) diced tomatoes, drained
2 pounds (908 g) sweet potatoes or yams, peeled and chopped
6 cups (1,410 ml) vegetable broth (To make your own, see "Freshest Vegetable Broth" on page 6.)
⅓ cup (87 g) peanut butter
1 very ripe mango, peeled, pitted, and chopped (or ½ [120 ml] mango nectar)
Juice of 3 limes, divided
1½ teaspoons ground cumin
1 tablespoon (6 g) ground coriander
¾ teaspoon salt
¾ teaspoon red pepper flakes
1 cup (230 g) puréed soft silken tofu, optional
1 bunch fresh cilantro, chopped
½ cup (50 g) sliced scallion
Hot pepper sauce, to taste

In a large skillet, heat the oil over medium-high heat. Sauté the onion and carrot for 4 minutes, or until the onion begins to soften. Add the ginger and garlic and cook for 1 minute, stirring constantly.

Transfer the onion mixture to a slow cooker. Add the tomatoes, potatoes, broth, peanut butter, mango, juice of 2 limes, cumin, coriander, salt, and red pepper. Stir to combine. Cover and cook on low for 6 to 7 hours or on high for 3 to 4 hours, or until the vegetables are tender.

Using an immersion blender or in batches in a countertop blender, purée the soup.

Return the soup to the slow cooker. Increase the heat of the slow cooker to high. Whisk in the tofu, if using, and cook for 5 minutes. Stir in the cilantro and scallion. Season to taste with the juice of the remaining 1 lime and hot pepper sauce.

Yield: 6 servings

▶ Health Bite
Sweet potatoes are a high-fiber food. One large potato has nearly 6 grams of the stuff. They're rich in plant chemicals known as carotenoids. You've probably heard of the most famous carotenoid—beta-carotene, but there are about 600!

What's more, sweet potatoes are a potassium heavyweight. Potassium is one of the nutrients that most protects the blood vessels and cardiovascular system.

In this soup, silken high-protein tofu replaces calorie-rich conventional cream, enriching this flavorful bisque and adding a nice protein "pop."

Resveratrol, which is the famous anti-aging nutrient found in red wine and the skin of dark grapes, is also found in peanuts.

LIGHT LOUISIANA CREOLE SHRIMP SOUP

Shrimp Creole is a classic Louisiana dish of cooked shrimp in a mixture of tomatoes, celery, and peppers that's traditionally served over boiled or steamed rice. Here, we've taken the basic template and turned it into a light, delicious soup.

1 large yellow onion, chopped
1 red bell pepper, seeded and chopped
1 green bell pepper, seeded and chopped
½ jalapeño pepper, seeded and minced
3 ribs celery, thinly sliced
1 bottle (32 ounces, 940 ml) tomato-based vegetable juice (We like Knudsen's Very Veggie.)
½ cup (120 ml) clam juice
2 tablespoons (30 ml) Worcestershire sauce
1 teaspoon paprika
1 teaspoon dried oregano
¾ teaspoon black pepper
½ teaspoon celery salt
¼ teaspoon cayenne pepper
1 bay leaf
1½ pounds (680 g) medium shrimp, peeled and deveined
½ cup (30 g) chopped fresh parsley
4 to 6 slices lemon, optional

In a slow cooker, combine the onion, bell peppers, jalapeño, celery, juices, Worcestershire, paprika, oregano, black pepper, celery salt, cayenne pepper, and bay leaf. Stir well to mix. Cover and cook on low for 6 to 7 hours or on high for 3 to 4 hours, or until the vegetables are soft.

Increase the heat of the slow cooker to high. Add the shrimp and cook for 15 to 20 minutes, or until they are cooked through but still tender. Just before serving, stir in the parsley. Garnish each bowl with a lemon slice, if using.

Yield: 4 to 6 servings

▶ Health Bite
This dish is a perfect example of a weight loss soup. First, it's low in calories. Second, it's high in volume.

According to Barbara Rolls, Ph.D., of the University of Pennsylvania, "high-volume" foods are those that take up a lot of space in the tummy but are relatively low in calories.

They're also "nutrient dense," which means that there is a lot of nutrition packed into very few calories. That's the opposite of a food that has a ton of calories and not so much nutrition–like most desserts. Rolls's research shows that eating a bowl of low-calorie soup before dinner actually causes people to spontaneously eat fewer calories during the meal. That's an effortless weight-loss strategy if there ever was one.

This soup is meal-worthy. Loaded with nutrients from the vegetables and protein from the shrimp, it's perfect.

VEGGIE GUMBO WITH CHEATER ROUX

In New Orleans, everyone has his or her own variation on gumbo. It started as a way to use leftovers and make a full meal out of a not-so-full pantry. This recipe is unique because it replaces a slow-cooked traditional roux with a simple thickener that takes less time than the slow browning method, but still retains a smoky flavor.

FOR THE GUMBO:
2 tablespoons (30 ml) olive oil
1 small onion, minced
2 cloves garlic, minced
2 stalks celery, minced
12 ounces (340 g) okra, sliced
2 medium bell peppers, seeded and chopped
1½ cups (165 g) chopped vegan Italian sausage, tempeh, or tofu
1 can (14½ ounces, or 406 g) diced tomatoes or 1½ cups (340 g) Preserve-the-Harvest Diced Tomatoes (See page 17.)
4 cups (940 ml) water
3 tablespoons (18 g) chicken-flavored bouillon
1 teaspoon Cajun seasoning
Cooked rice

FOR THE CHEATER ROUX:
6 roasted or smoked almonds
1 cup (225 g) white beans, drained and rinsed
¼ teaspoon liquid smoke
1 to 3 teaspoons water, divided

To make the roux: In a food processor, pulse the almonds until coarse. Add the beans and liquid smoke and process again. Add the water, 1 teaspoon at a time, until the mixture comes together and blends thoroughly.

To make the gumbo: In a skillet, heat the oil over medium heat. Sauté the onion for 3 to 5 minutes, or until it's translucent. Add the garlic and celery and sauté for 3 minutes longer.

In a slow cooker, combine the onion mixture, okra, bell peppers, sausage, tomatoes, water, bouillon, and Cajun seasoning. Cover and cook on low for 6 to 8 hours.

About 20 minutes before serving, stir the roux into the gumbo. Heat through, and then taste and adjust the seasonings.

Ladle the gumbo into bowls, and then add a scoop of rice to each one, like an island in the middle of the bowl.

Yield: 6 servings

PUNGENT, LIGHT, AND CLEAR THAI SEAFOOD STEW

During the 2008 presidential primary, Hillary Clinton told interviewers that she owed her indefatigable energy to eating hot peppers!

1 large red onion, chopped
8 baby red potatoes, scrubbed, unpeeled, and halved
6 stalks lemongrass, trimmed and cut into 1-inch (2.5 cm) pieces
6 cups (1,410 ml) chicken broth (To make your own, see "Chicken Stock" on page 6.)
15 kaffir lime leaves or 2 teaspoons fresh lime zest
⅓ cup (80 ml) Thai fish sauce
Juice of 2 limes, divided
2 teaspoons tamari
3 red chiles, seeded and minced
2 tablespoons (30 g) Sucanat or brown sugar
12 ounces (340 g) medium shrimp, shelled and deveined
8 ounces (225 g) halibut, sliced into 1½-inch (4 cm) pieces
⅓ cup (5 g) chopped fresh cilantro

In a slow cooker, combine the onion, potatoes, and lemongrass. Pour the broth over all. Stir in the lime leaves, fish sauce, juice of 1 lime, tamari, chiles, and Sucanat. Cover and cook on low for 3 to 4 hours or on high for 2 to 3 hours, or until the vegetables are tender. Add the shrimp and halibut. Cover and cook on low for 10 to 15 minutes, or until the seafood is just cooked through. Stir in the cilantro and the remaining juice of 1 lime, to taste.

Yield: 6 servings

▶*Health Bite*
The magic ingredient in this delicious and exotic Thai-inspired seafood stew is capsaicin. Found in hot peppers, capsaicin helps to tone down a compound called substance P, which is associated with inflammatory processes in the joints and contributes mightily to various pain syndromes, such as fibromyalgia, low-back pain, and arthritis.

According to WebMD, capsaicin may even help prevent heart disease by stimulating the cardiovascular system and lowering blood pressure. It also improves digestion.

This light and fresh-tasting seafood stew will clear out your sinuses and may even leave you feeling mildly stimulated.

ADOBO STEW

This stew offers a big payoff for such a small amount of effort. Enjoy this peppery, tender stew with rice and mixed vegetables.

1½-pound (683-g) beef or pork roast, cut into 1-inch (2.5-cm) cubes
½ cup (120 ml) water
½ cup (120 ml) apple cider vinegar
¼ cup (60 ml) soy sauce
¼ teaspoon black pepper, plus more if needed

In a slow cooker, place the roast.
In a small bowl, combine the water, vinegar, soy sauce, and ¼ teaspoon of the pepper. Pour the mixture over the roast in the slow cooker. Cover and cook on low for 6 to 8 hours.
Before serving, stir the stew and season with additional pepper if needed.

Yield: 5 servings

▶*Recipe Variations*
If you like the taste of garlic, substitute garlic-flavored soy sauce for the plain soy sauce. If you don't have this gourmet soy sauce on hand, add 2 minced garlic cloves to the stew along with the plain soy sauce.

For an authentic touch, substitute coconut milk for the water. Throw in a bay leaf for good measure. Remove the bay leaf before serving the stew.

BELGIAN BEEF STEW

This recipe is a riff on Beef Carbonnade, which is a classic Belgian stew that's traditionally served with steamed or boiled, buttered potatoes. Use a bottle of good Belgian ale for a full, rich flavor. This stew is even better cooked a day ahead and then reheated on low for 1 to 2 hours. Like most stew recipes in this book, low and slow is the key. A high temperature results in tough meat.

3 pounds (1365 g) stew meat
2 (12-ounce or 355-ml) jars onion gravy
1 (12-ounce or 355-ml) bottle beer
Salt, to taste
Black pepper, to taste

In a slow cooker, combine the stew meat, gravy, and beer. Cover and cook on low for 7 to 8 hours. Seasoning with salt and pepper.

Yield: 4 to 6 servings

▶*Recipe Variations*
Peel and slice 4 or 5 onions and layer them under the beef. Stir in 1 tablespoon (15 g) strong mustard for a tad more zest.

VEGETABLE-LOADED BEEF AND BARLEY STEW

Ancient Romans used to wear celery around the neck to ward off hangovers. This stew is loaded with celery and other goodness.

1 large sweet onion, chopped
1 green bell pepper, seeded and chopped
2 carrots, peeled and sliced
2 parsnips, peeled and sliced
2 ribs celery, sliced
1½ pounds (680 g) stew beef, cubed
4 cups (940 ml) beef stock (To make your own, see "Beef Stock" on page 6.)
1 can (14.5 ounces, or 406 g) diced tomatoes, undrained ¼ cup (60 ml) Burgundy wine
1 teaspoon sweet paprika
1 teaspoon dried oregano
1 teaspoon dried basil
¾ teaspoon salt
¾ teaspoon black pepper
12 ounces (335 g) fresh green beans, sliced into 1½-inch (4 cm) pieces
¾ cup (150 g) pearl barley

In a slow cooker, combine the onion, bell pepper, carrots, parsnips, celery, and beef. Pour the stock and tomatoes over all. Add the wine, paprika, oregano, basil, salt, and pepper. Cover and cook on low for about 4 hours. Add the green beans and barley. Cover and cook for 2 more hours, or until the beef and barley are cooked through and tender.

Yield: 8 servings

▶*Health Bite*
Barley is an excellent food choice for people concerned about type 2 diabetes or pre-diabetes because the grain contains essential vitamins and minerals. Barley is also an excellent source of dietary fiber, particularly beta-glucan soluble fiber. It's also an extremely low glycemic grain, scoring a mere 20 on the glycemic index and (even better) 8 on the glycemic load. Anything under 10 is low, low, low.

Research shows that barley's beta-glucan soluble fiber promotes healthy blood sugar by slowing the entrance of glucose (sugar) into the bloodstream.

Recent studies have shown that substances in celery called phthalides relax muscle tissue in the artery walls and increase blood flow.

When you combine barley with grass-fed beef and a bunch of nutrient-dense vegetables such as celery, you have something pretty close to a nutritionally perfect meal.

SALADS AND SOUPS

31 Old-Fashioned Vegetable Soup

32

32 What's in the Freezer Veggie Soup

SALADS AND SOUPS • 165

CURRIED MULLIGATAWNY LAMB STEW

This hearty Irish-inspired stew is rich and filling, but low in calories. Try it on a cold day where you long to stay wrapped up on the couch in a warm quilt.

1 tablespoon (15 ml) olive oil
1 sweet or yellow onion, chopped
2 ribs celery, chopped
2 medium carrots, peeled and sliced
1 medium green bell pepper, seeded and chopped
1 medium green apple, peeled, cored, and chopped
3 cloves garlic, minced
6 cups (1,410 ml) chicken stock (To make your own, see "Chicken Stock" on page 6.)
⅓ cup (90 g) tomato paste
2 teaspoons curry powder
¼ teaspoon cayenne pepper
¾ teaspoon salt
½ teaspoon black pepper
1 medium Yukon gold potato, unpeeled and chopped
1 pound (454 g) cubed lamb stew meat
1 can (15 ounces, or 420 g) chickpeas, drained and rinsed
1 tablespoon (15 ml) water, if needed

In a large skillet, heat the oil over medium heat. Cook the onion, celery, carrots, bell pepper, and apple for 6 minutes, stirring often. Add the garlic and cook for 1 minute.

Meanwhile, in a large bowl, whisk together the stock, paste, curry powder, cayenne pepper, salt, and black pepper.

Transfer the onion mixture to a slow cooker. Top with the potatoes and lamb. Pour the stock mixture over all. Cover and cook on low for 6 to 7 hours or on high for 4 to 5 hours, or until the vegetables and lamb are tender.

In a food processor, pulse the chickpeas until nearly smooth, adding the water, if needed.

Transfer the chickpeas to the slow cooker. Stir well to incorporate. Cover and cook for 20 minutes longer.

Yield: 6 to 8 serving

▶ Health Bite

Lamb is a wonderful source of protein that also happens to contain a fair amount of minerals such as calcium, magnesium, phosphorus, and potassium. Also it makes a fabulous stew.

This stew, which is a classically Irish stew, has an Indian flair, largely because of the addition of curry.

We especially love the inclusion of the apple, which is a flavor treat that adds just a touch of unexpected sweetness and crunchiness to this hearty dish.

The low-calorie vegetables add to the volume without packing on many calories, making this a nutritionally dense dish that offers a heck of a lot of nutrition without breaking the caloric budget.

The puréed chickpeas add a generous helping of fiber (12.5 grams per cup) and protein (14.5 grams). The chickpeas also give this delicious stew additional heartiness.

ROSEMARY LAMB STEW

Cooking this stew on low, especially if using mutton, a less tender alternative to lamb, will bring out the best flavor. The distinctive aroma of rosemary will scent the whole house. This stew is great with garlic mashed potatoes and a green salad.

1½ to 2 pounds (683 to 910 g) lean lamb or lamb shanks, cut into 1-inch (2.5-cm) cubes
One 14-ounce (398-g) can diced tomatoes with green pepper and onion, undrained
1½ teaspoons (9 g) salt
½ teaspoon black pepper
1 sprig fresh rosemary

Coat the crock of a slow cooker with nonstick cooking spray.

In the slow cooker, combine the lamb and tomatoes and juice. Add the salt, pepper, and rosemary. Stir to combine. Cover and cook on low for 6 to 8 hours or on high for 4 to 5 hours. Before serving, remove the rosemary sprig.

Yield: 6 servings

▶ Add It!

Add 4 medium potatoes, peeled and cut into 1-inch (2.5-cm) cubes, and ½ cup (61 g) baby carrots along with the lamb. Arrange the vegetables around the sides of the slow cooker to help them cook faster.

SIMPLE VEAL STEW

This recipe is great as is, or it can be embellished in many ways. Try adding diced carrots or some tomato, garlic, or fresh herbs. It's great over pasta, polenta, risotto, or mashed potatoes.

2 pounds (910 g) stew veal
1 cup (235 ml) red wine
1 (12-ounce or 355-ml) can mushroom gravy
Salt, to taste
Black pepper, to taste

In a slow cooker, combine the veal, wine, and gravy. Stir to mix. Season with salt and pepper. Cover and cook on low for 7 to 8 hours.

Yield: 6 servings

CHUNKY GERMAN SAUSAGE AND SAUERKRAUT STEW

This recipe uses lower-calorie chicken sausage for the meat, which blends perfectly with the new potatoes and mushrooms. The nice dose of fiber from the beans adds even more nutrition to this already scrumptious stew.

4 links (4 ounces, or 112 g each) smoked (or spicy) chicken sausage, sliced into thick half-moons
1 small yellow onion, chopped
4 to 6 baby new potatoes, quartered
8 ounces (225 g) cremini mushrooms, sliced
2 ribs celery, thinly sliced
2 small carrots, sliced into thin half-moons
1 can (15 ounces, or 420 g) small white beans, drained and rinsed
24 ounces (680 g) sauerkraut, drained and rinsed
4 cups (940 ml) chicken or vegetable broth (To make your own, see "Chicken Stock" on page 6 or "Freshest Vegetable Broth" on page 6.)
1½ tablespoons (23 ml) white wine vinegar
½ teaspoon salt
½ teaspoon black pepper
¾ teaspoon caraway seeds, optional
1 bay leaf

In a 6-quart (5.7 L) slow cooker, combine all of the ingredients. Stir gently to combine. Cover and cook on high for 4 to 6 hours, or until the vegetables are tender.

Yield: 10 servings

▶*Health Bite*
If all you know about sauerkraut is from ballpark hot dogs, be prepared for a shock. Sauerkraut is actually a naturally fermented food, and that alone earns it a place among the healthiest menu items on the planet. Naturally fermented foods include yogurt, real olives (the kind that sit out in brine in the olive bars, not the kind that are chemically processed in the little jars), tempeh, miso, authentic soy sauce, and the Korean dish kimchi.

When foods are naturally fermented, they are rich in enzymes and the "good bacteria" known as probiotics, which stimulate the immune system and help with digestion and assimilation of nutrients.

SOY CHORIZO BLACK BEAN STEW

The complex flavor of the chorizo is grounded with black beans and sautéed vegetables. Serve this vegan stew with tortillas or chips to dip in the stew.

1 tablespoon (15 ml) olive oil
1 small onion, minced
1 clove garlic, minced
½ bell pepper, minced
½ package (6 ounces, or 170 g) soy chorizo
2 cans (15 ounces, or 420 g each) black beans, drained and rinsed
2 cups (470 ml) water
1½ tablespoons (9 g) vegan chicken-flavored bouillon
¼ teaspoon cumin
¼ teaspoon chipotle or pasilla chile powder
Salt, to taste
Black pepper, to taste
Fresh cilantro, chopped, optional

In a skillet, heat the oil over medium heat. Sauté the onion for 3 to 5 minutes, or until it's translucent. Add the garlic and bell pepper. Sauté for 3 minutes longer.

In a slow cooker, combine all of the ingredients, except for the cilantro. Cover and cook on low for 6 to 8 hours. Taste and adjust the seasonings before serving. Top with cilantro, if using.

Yield: 4 servings

▶*Serving Suggestion*
Use leftovers in tacos or burritos.

HEARTY CHICKEN STEW

This recipe is great served over biscuits, rice, or mashed potatoes.

2 pounds (910 g) boneless, skinless chicken breasts, Cut into 1- to 2-inch (2.5- to 5-cm) pieces
1 (16-ounce or 475-ml) jar chicken gravy
1 (16-ounce or 455-g) bag frozen mixed vegetables

In a slow cooker, combine the chicken, gravy, and vegetables. Cover and cook on low for 5 to 6 hours or on high for 2 to 3 hours. Stir well before serving.

Yield: 4 to 6 servings

33 Hot and Sour Chinese Vegetable Soup; 34 Broccoli-Cheese Soup; 35 Tofu Bouillabaisse; 36 Curried Coconut Cream of Cauliflower Soup; 37 Delicata Squash and Pear Soup; 38 Rich and Creamy Sweet Potato Peanut Bisque; 39 Light Louisiana Creole Shrimp Soup; 40 Veggie Gumbo with Cheater Roux

41 Pungent, Light, and Clear Thai Seafood Stew; 42 Adobo Stew; 43 Belgian Beef Stew; 44 Vegetable-Loaded Beef and Barley Stew; 45 Curried Mulligatawny Lamb Stew; 46 Rosemary Lamb Stew; 47 Simple Veal Stew; 48 Chunky German Sausage and Sauerkraut Stew

SALADS AND SOUPS • 169

SZECHUAN CHICKEN STEW
Spice up a boring weekday with this fabulous stew.

1 (1-pound or 455-g) bag frozen Szechuan vegetable blend
1 cup (235 ml) water
2 pounds (910 g) boneless, skinless chicken breasts, cut into 1- to 2-inch (2.5- to 5-cm) pieces
1 (12-ounce or 355-ml) bottle Szechuan cooking sauce

In a saucepan, heat the vegetables in the water over high heat until boiling. Cook for 2 to 3 minutes and drain well.

Transfer the vegetables to a slow cooker. Add the chicken and sauce. Cover and cook on low for 3 to 4 hours or on high for 2 hours.

Yield: 4 to 6 servings

BRUNSWICK STEW
This is an old favorite, de-carbed and updated for your slow cooker.

1 large onion, sliced
2 pounds (900 g) skinless chicken thighs
1½ cups (225 g) ham cubes, cooked
1 teaspoon dry mustard
1 teaspoon dried thyme
½ teaspoon black pepper
1 cup (180 g) canned diced tomatoes
1 can (14 ounces, or 390 g) chicken broth (To make your own, see "Chicken Stock" on page 6.)
3 cloves garlic, crushed
1 tablespoon (15 ml) Worcestershire sauce
¼ teaspoon hot sauce
1 cup (172 g) canned black soybeans, drained

In a slow cooker, scatter the onion. Add the chicken and ham.

In a bowl, mix together the mustard, thyme, pepper, tomatoes, broth, garlic, Worcestershire, and hot sauce. Pour the mixture over the chicken and ham in the slow cooker. Cover and cook on low for 8 hours.

When the time's up, stir in the soybeans. Cover and cook on low for another 20 minutes or so.

Yield: 6 servings

VEGGIE-RICH ASIAN CHICKEN STEW
Though light on calories, this stew is anything but light on flavor and texture.

1 large white onion, thinly sliced
2 carrots, peeled and thinly sliced on the diagonal
2 ribs celery, sliced on the diagonal
1 small red bell pepper, seeded and julienned
1½ cups (135 g) thinly sliced Napa cabbage
1 can (8 ounces, or 225 g) sliced water chestnuts, drained and rinsed
1 can (8 ounces, or 225 g) bamboo shoots, drained and rinsed
6 cups (1,410 ml) chicken broth (To make your own, see "Chicken Stock" on page 6.)
2 tablespoons (12 g) minced fresh ginger
3 cloves garlic, minced
1½ tablespoons (23 ml) tamari
1 tablespoon (15 ml) mirin
2 boneless, skinless chicken breasts, cut into 1½-inch (3.8 cm) cubes
12 ounces (336 g) extra-firm tofu, cut into ½-inch (1.3 cm) cubes
½ cup (50 g) diagonally sliced scallion
1 tablespoon (8 g) black sesame seeds, optional

In a slow cooker, combine the onion, carrots, celery, bell pepper, cabbage, water chestnuts, bamboo shoots, broth, ginger, garlic, tamari, and mirin. Cover and cook on low for 6 to 7 hours, or until all of the vegetables are tender.

For the last ½ hour of cooking time, add the chicken and tofu. Garnish with the scallions and sesame seeds, if using.

Yield: 6 servings

▶*Health Bite*
If stews were basketball games, this one would be the national all-star team. The list of nutrients found in these ingredients—and all the benefits they provide—could fill a chapter of a nutrition textbook. How is this lean, low-cal veggie stew great for you? Let us count the ways sulfur compounds for your skin (onions), beta-carotene and vitamin A (carrots), vitamin K for heart health and bones (celery), vitamin C (red pepper), and cancer-fighting indoles (cabbage) and allicin (garlic).

WHITE BEAN AND KALE STEW
Do you like your beans New Orleans style–thick and creamy? An easy way to do this is to let some of the beans break down and form their own gravy.

1 teaspoon olive oil
1 onion, chopped
2 cloves garlic, minced
Salt, to taste
Black pepper, to taste
1 tablespoon (15 ml) balsamic vinegar
1 tablespoon (4 g) chopped fresh oregano or 1 teaspoon dried
5 cups (1,175 ml) water
2 cans (14½ ounces, or 406 g each) white beans, drained and rinsed
4 cups (270 g) chopped kale

In a skillet, heat the oil over medium heat. Sauté the onion for 3 to 5 minutes, or until it's translucent. Add the garlic and season with salt and pepper. Sauté for 1 to 2 minutes longer. Add the vinegar and stir to combine.

In a slow cooker, combine the onion mixture, oregano, water, and beans. Cover and cook on low for 6 to 8 hours.

About 30 minutes before serving, add the kale. Cover and cook for 30 minutes longer. Taste and adjust the seasonings before serving.

Yield: 6 servings

▶*Recipe Variation*
If you're not a kale lover, you can substitute any green you happen to like or that's ready to pick in your garden. Start by adding 2 cups (135 g) kale instead of 4 cups (270 g) and work your way up. Greens are a nutritional powerhouse, and they're worth getting used to.

ASIAN-STYLE WINTER STEW
This hearty stew can be made with staples and veggies in your pantry. It's perfect for a snowy day, when you can't (or just don't want to) go to the store. It's a warming root stew flavored with miso, then topped with sesame oil.

2 tablespoons (30 ml) olive oil
1 medium onion, cut in half and sliced
2 cloves garlic, minced
1 tablespoon (8 g) grated ginger
1 small turnip, chopped
3-inch (7.5 cm) piece daikon, chopped
8 baby or fingerling potatoes, halved if large
8 ounces (225 g) baby carrots, halved if large
4 ounces (113 g) mushrooms (Use a packaged blend of baby bella, shiitake, and oyster), cut into large chunks
2 tablespoons (12 g) chicken-flavored bouillon
2 tablespoons (32 g) miso
1 cup (235 ml) water
Salt, to taste
Black pepper, to taste
Sesame oil

In a skillet, heat the olive oil over medium heat. Sauté the onion for 3 to 5 minutes, or until it's translucent. Add the garlic and sauté for 3 minutes longer.

In a slow cooker, combine all of the ingredients, except for the sesame oil. Cover and cook on low for 6 to 8 hours. Taste and adjust the seasonings. Serve drizzled with sesame oil.

Yield: 4 servings

▶*Recipe Variation*
If you like heat, add some chile paste. It's also a great way to warm up after a snowball fight!

HARD CIDER AND CABBAGE STEW
This sausage and veggie stew tastes like fall itself. The hard cider mellows out while cooking and makes for a perfect, savory broth.

2 tablespoons (30 ml) olive oil
1 small onion, chopped
3 cloves garlic, minced
2 medium carrots, sliced into coins
1 small head cabbage (about 14½ ounces, or 406 g), cored and chopped
1 small apple, peeled, cored, and diced
1 package (12 ounces, or 340 g) sausage links, sliced
2 cups (470 ml) hard cider
2 tablespoons (12 g) chicken-flavored bouillon
2 bay leaves
1 sprig rosemary
2 sprigs thyme
Salt, to taste
Black pepper, to taste

In a skillet, heat the oil over medium heat. Sauté the onion for 3 to 5 minutes, or until it's translucent. Add the garlic and sauté for 3 minutes longer.

In a slow cooker, combine all of the ingredients. Cover and cook on low for 6 to 8 hours. Before serving, remove and discard the bay leaves, rosemary sprig, and thyme sprigs. Taste and adjust the seasonings.

Yield: 6 servings

GROUND SIRLOIN BORSCHT

Beets are a perfect accompaniment to ground sirloin, which isn't a typical borscht ingredient, but who said we had to be typical? Original, yes. Boring, no. You'll love this rich, beefy soup.

1 pound (454 g) leanest ground sirloin
1 large yellow onion, chopped
2 cloves garlic, minced
4 large beets, peeled and chopped
4 large carrots, peeled and chopped
2 ribs celery, chopped
2 medium Yukon gold potatoes, unpeeled and chopped
1 cup (90 g) thinly sliced green cabbage
6 cups (1,410 ml) beef broth (To make your own, see "Beef Stock" on page 6.)
¼ cup (65 g) tomato paste
2 teaspoons beef Better Than Bouillon
1 teaspoon caraway seeds
½ teaspoon salt
½ teaspoon black pepper
3 tablespoons (45 ml) red wine vinegar
½ cup (115 g) plain Greek yogurt
¼ cup (16 g) chopped fresh dill

In a large saucepan over medium-high heat, cook the sirloin, onion, and garlic for 5 to 6 minutes, or until cooked through, with no pink remaining.

Remove from the heat, drain any excess fat, and transfer to a slow cooker. Add the beets, carrots, celery, potatoes, cabbage, broth, paste, bouillon, caraway seeds, salt, and pepper. Stir to mix well. Cover and cook on low for 6 to 7 hours, or until the vegetables are tender.

During the last 10 minutes of cooking time, stir in the vinegar.

In a small bowl, combine the yogurt and dill. Chill the mixture in the fridge while the soup is cooking.

Serve the soup in individual bowls with a generous dollop of the dilled yogurt.

Yield: 6 servings

▶Health Bite
Beets are a legendary food for the liver, helping it perform its duties as detoxification central.

BEEF BORSCHT

In this recipe, we take a prepared product and transform it into a hearty meal. Serve with crusty pumpernickel bread and a crisp salad for a warming winter repast.

1 pound (455 g) beef stew meat
1 quart (945 ml) prepared borscht
1 cup (230 g) sour cream

In a slow cooker, combine the beef and borscht. Cover and cook on low for 7 to 8 hours.

Using tongs or a slotted spoon, break up the meat into shreds.

Serve with a dollop of sour cream on top.

Yield: 4 servings

GIFTS FROM THE SEA CHOWDER

This rich seafood chowder features a tomato base to reduce the calories, but you'll never miss the cream. "New potatoes" are immature potatoes that are harvested during the summer or spring.

1 tablespoon (14 g) butter
½ tablespoon (8 ml) olive oil
1 yellow onion, chopped
1 carrot, thinly sliced
2 ribs celery, thinly sliced
6 baby Yukon gold potatoes, scrubbed, unpeeled, and quartered or red new potatoes, about the size of golf balls
1 package (10 ounces, or 280 g) frozen chopped spinach, unthawed
1 can (28 ounces, or 784 g) tomato purée
2 cups (470 ml) chicken or vegetable broth (To make your own, see "Chicken Stock" on page 6 or "Freshest Vegetable Broth" on page 6.)
2 cups (470 ml) clam juice
¾ cup (180 ml) dry white wine
1 tablespoon (2.4 g) chopped fresh thyme or 1 teaspoon dried
¾ teaspoon salt
½ teaspoon black pepper
2 cans (8 ounces, or 225 g each) whole oysters, drained and rinsed
8 ounces (225 g) peeled, frozen shrimp, uncooked, unthawed
12 ounces (336 g) fresh bay scallops
½ cup (30 g) chopped fresh flat-leaf parsley
6 to 8 thin slices lemon

In a large skillet, heat the butter and oil over medium heat. Sauté the onion, carrot, and celery for about 8 minutes, or until they're beginning to soften.

Transfer the contents to a slow cooker. Add the potatoes, spinach, tomato purée, broth, clam juice, wine, thyme, salt, and pepper. Cover and cook on low for 6 to 7 hours, or until the vegetables are tender. Stir well to incorporate the spinach. Add the oysters, shrimp, and scallops. Cover and cook on low for 10 to 15 minutes longer, or until the seafood is cooked through but still tender. Stir in the parsley. Float a lemon slice in each individual bowl to serve.

Yield: 6 to 8 servings

EASY MANHATTAN CLAM CHOWDER

Here's the simplest "red kind" of chowder you'll ever find.

2 pounds (910 g) boiling potatoes, such as Yukon Gold, peeled and cubed
2 (12-ounce or 355-ml) bottles clam juice
2 (14-ounce or 425-ml) cans red clam sauce
3 cups (705 ml) water
Salt, to taste
Black pepper, to taste

In a slow cooker, combine the potatoes, juice, sauce, and water. Cover and cook on low for 6 to 8 hours, or until the potatoes are soft. Season with salt and pepper.

Yield: 4 to 6 servings

▶Add ¼ cup (50 g) chopped celery into the mix.

CORN CHOWDER WITH CRAB

This is an elegant sort of soup that you could serve to company. But why wait? It's easy to make just for your family.

6 slices bacon, diced
¼ cup (40 g) chopped onion
2 potatoes, peeled and diced
1 pound (455 g) frozen corn
1 tablespoon (13 g) sugar 1 teaspoon Worcestershire sauce
¼ teaspoon black pepper
½ cup (120 ml) water
1 cup (235 ml) milk
6 ounces (170 g) crab meat

In a skillet, brown the bacon until crisp. Using a slotted spoon, remove the bacon to a plate, reserving the drippings. Add the onion and potatoes to the skillet. Sauté for 5 minutes. Drain.
　In a slow cooker, combine all of the ingredients, except for the milk and crab. Mix well. Cover and cook on low 6 to 7 hours.
　During the last 30 minutes of cooking, stir in the milk and crab.

Yield: 4 servings

SHRIMP CHOWDER

This rich chowder with bacon and shrimp is sure to become a favorite.

3 slices bacon, diced
1 cup (160 g) chopped onion
3 medium red potatoes, unpeeled, diced
1 pound (455 g) frozen corn
1 teaspoon Worcestershire sauce
½ teaspoon paprika
½ teaspoon black pepper
12 ounces (340 g) shrimp
2 cups (475 ml) water
12 ounces (355 ml) evaporated milk
¼ cup (12 g) chives

In a nonstick skillet, brown the bacon until lightly crisp. Add the onion. Sauté until transparent.
　Using a slotted spoon, transfer the bacon and onion to a slow cooker. Add the remaining
　ingredients to the slow cooker, except for the milk and chives. Cover and cook on low for 3 to 4 hours.
　During the last 30 minutes of cooking time, add the milk and chives.

Yield: 6 servings

TOMATO SALMON BISQUE

This rich and delicious soup is so easy to make. Try to find a really good quality tomato soup to use as a base for the recipe. We recommend those soups that come in cardboard cartons, generally found in the natural foods section of the grocery store.

1 quart (945 ml) tomato soup (not condensed)
1 (12-ounce or 340-g) can salmon
2 cups (225 g) shredded Cheddar cheese
Salt, to taste
Black pepper, to taste

In a slow cooker, combine the soup and salmon. Cover and cook on low for 3 to 4 hours.
　Using an immersion blender or in batches in a countertop blender, blend the soup. Stir in the cheese until it has melted and the soup is smooth. Season with salt and pepper.

Yield: 4 to 6 servings

49 Soy Chorizo Black Bean Stew; 50 Hearty Chicken Stew; 51 Szechuan Chicken Stew; 52 Brunswick Stew; 53 Veggie-Rich Asian Chicken Stew; 54 White Bean and Kale Stew; 55 Asian-Style Winter Stew; 56 Hard Cider and Cabbage Stew

57 Beef Borscht; 58 Ground Sirloin Borscht; 59 Gifts from the Sea Chowder; 60 Easy Manhattan Clam Chowder; 61 Corn Chowder with Crab; 62 Shrimp Chowder; 63 Tomato Salmon Bisque

SALADS AND SOUPS • 175

SIDE DISHES

See pages 178-179, 182-183, 188-189, 192-193, 196-197, 202-203 and 207-209 for side dish recipe photos.

CREAMY CORN

This recipe makes corn-on-the-cob goodness plus cheese in your slow cooker–without the cob.

One 16-ounce (455-g) bag frozen corn, partially thawed
One 3-ounce (85-g) package cream cheese, softened
2 tablespoons (28 g) butter
½ teaspoon salt

Coat the crock of a slow cooker with nonstick cooking spray.
In the slow cooker, combine the corn, cream cheese, butter, and salt. Stir to mix. Cover and cook on low for 1½ to 3½ hours, or until the corn is thoroughly heated and the cream cheese has melted.

Yield: 4 servings

▶Recipe Variation
Try this dish with sliced frozen carrots or frozen lima beans instead of the corn.

CORN WITH PEPPERS AND ONION

The colors in this dish are pretty, and the taste delights.

1 pound (455 g) frozen corn
1 medium onion, diced
1 red or orange bell pepper, seeded and diced
2 to 3 tablespoons (28 to 42 g) butter
Salt, to taste
Black pepper, to taste

In a slow cooker, combine the corn, onion, and bell pepper. Stir to mix. Top with the butter and season with salt and pepper to taste. Cover and cook on low for 3 to 4 hours or on high for 1½ hours.

Yield: 4 to 6 servings

▶Add It!
To create a bright trifecta of color, sprinkle a handful of chopped fresh cilantro over the corn before serving.

CORN PUDDING

This is a favorite side dish for family get-togethers, which is fine with us because it's so easy to make ahead.

2 pounds (900 g) frozen corn, thawed
½ cup (120 ml) egg substitute
1 cup (235 ml) milk
¼ teaspoon black pepper
2 tablespoons (26 g) sugar
3 tablespoons (24 g) all-purpose flour

Coat the crock of a slow cooker with nonstick cooking spray.
In the bowl, combine all of the ingredients.
Pour the mixture into the slow cooker. Cover and cook on high for 3 hours.

Yield: 8 servings

FRESH CHILI LIME COB CORN

Is there anyone who doesn't love corn on the cob at the peak of the season? The heat and tang of chili lime are the perfect complement to corn's natural sweetness.

4 teaspoons (20 ml) olive oil or melted butter
½ teaspoon cayenne pepper
½ teaspoon garlic salt
1 teaspoon lime zest
3 tablespoons (3 g) minced fresh cilantro, divided
4 ears freshest corn, husks and silks removed
Juice of ½ lime

In a small bowl, whisk together the oil, cayenne, garlic salt, zest, and 1½ tablespoons (1.5 g) of the cilantro.
In a large bowl, place the corn. Pour the oil mixture over the corn, rubbing gently to thoroughly coat.
Wrap each ear of corn tightly in a piece of aluminum foil and lay them all horizontally in a slow cooker. Add water to about ½ inch (1.3 cm). Cover and cook on low for 4 to 5 hours or on high for 2 hours, or until cooked through.
Carefully unwrap the packs, squeeze the lime over top, and sprinkle with the remaining 1½ tablespoons (1.5 g) minced cilantro.

Yield: 4 servings

▶Health Bite
Real fresh corn right off the cob is a wonderful vegetable, especially if you don't eat a ton of it every day. Each ear of corn has a couple grams of fiber, some potassium and vitamin A, and a good amount of lutein and zeaxanthin.

STEWED TOMATOES

Here's an easy way to preserve extra tomatoes from the garden. You can serve this as a side dish or freeze it in portions for soups or other recipes.

4 large tomatoes
1 cup (160 g) chopped onion
¾ cup (75 g) chopped celery
½ cup (75 g) chopped green bell pepper
3 tablespoons (39 g) sugar
1 bay leaf
⅛ teaspoon black pepper

Core the tomatoes. Place them in boiling water for about 15 to 20 seconds, and then plunge them into ice water to cool quickly; peel. Cut tomatoes in wedges.

In a slow cooker, combine the tomatoes and the remaining ingredients. Cover and cook on low for 8 to 9 hours.

Before serving, remove the bay leaf.

Yield: 6 servings

SUMMER STEWED TOMATOES

This recipe is another great way to use the bounty of your (or your local farmer's) harvest.

3 pounds (1365 g) ripe tomatoes
2 tablespoons (20 g) minced garlic
½ cup (20 g) shredded fresh basil
Salt, to taste
Black pepper, to taste

Core the tomatoes and cut them into wedges.

In a slow cooker, combine the tomatoes, garlic, and basil. Season with salt and pepper.

Stir gently. Cover and cook on low for 6 to 7 hours or on high for 3 hours.

Yield: 4 to 6 servings

▶*Serving Suggestion*
Cook up a pot of pasta and toss this on as a delicious summer sauce.

TANGY BEANS

Even people who don't like green beans will love this interesting take on them.

4 cups (496 g) frozen green beans, unthawed
¼ cup (40 g) chopped onion
¼ cup (38 g) chopped green bell pepper
¼ cup (60 ml) cider vinegar
2 tablespoons (3 g) sugar
⅛ teaspoon black pepper
Butter
Salt, to taste

In a slow cooker, combine all of the ingredients except for the butter and salt. Stir to distribute evenly. Cover and cook on low for 5 hours.

Serve with a pat of butter and a little salt.

Yield: 4 servings

NOT YOUR GRANDMA'S GREEN BEANS

A lot of people call green beans "string beans" because of the fibrous string running through the length of the pod seam that had to be removed from each bean before cooking. As you can imagine, this doesn't exactly make them a breeze to prepare. Today's green beans, however, have been conveniently bred to be stringless, which is a boon to cooks everywhere.

1 pound (454 g) fresh green beans, trimmed
Juice and zest of ½ lemon
2 tablespoons (30 ml) water
2 teaspoons tamari
2 cloves garlic, minced
2 anchovy fillets, minced
1 tablespoon (15 ml) olive oil
2 tablespoons (10 g) grated Parmesan cheese
¼ cup (30 g) toasted, chopped walnuts

In a slow cooker, combine the green beans, juice, zest, water, tamari, and garlic. Toss to coat. Cover and cook on low for 1½ hours, or until the green beans are tender.

In a serving bowl, whisk together the anchovies and oil. Add the green beans and Parmesan. Toss to coat. Garnish with the walnuts.

Yield: 4 servings

▶*Health Bite*
Green beans aren't at the top of the list of superstar vegetables. They still have small but decent amounts of a lot of nutrients, including folate, calcium, potassium, manganese, vitamin A, and half the daily requirement of heart-healthy bone-building vitamin K. They also contain about 4 grams of fiber per cup.

1 Creamy Corn

2 Corn with Peppers and Onion

GREEN BEAN CASSEROLE
Here's an updated version of the classic holiday dish.

28 ounces (785 g) frozen green beans, unthawed
1 cup (70 g) chopped mushrooms
¼ cup (45 g) roasted red pepper, diced
¼ cup (40 g) chopped onion
2 teaspoons dried sage
1 teaspoon salt
1 teaspoon black pepper
½ teaspoon ground nutmeg
1 cup (235 ml) beef broth (To make your own, see "Beef Stock" on page 6.)
1 teaspoon beef bouillon concentrate
½ cup (120 ml) heavy cream
Cornstarch
¾ cup (83 g) slivered almonds
1 tablespoon (14 g) butter

In a slow cooker, combine the green beans, mushrooms, red pepper, and onion.
 In a bowl, mix together the sage, salt, black pepper, nutmeg, broth, and bouillon.
 Pour the mixture over the vegetables. Stir to combine. Cover and cook on low for 5 to 6 hours.
 When the time's up, stir in the cream and thicken the sauce a bit with cornstarch. Re-cover the slow cooker to keep it warm.
 In a skillet, sauté the almonds in the butter until golden. Stir the almonds into the green beans.

Yield: 8 servings

SOUTHERN BEANS
Have you ever tasted the Southerners dish of green beans slowly cooked with bacon? If not, you're in for a treat.

4 cups (496 g) frozen green beans, unthawed
⅓ cup (53 g) diced onion
¼ cup (30 g) diced celery
4 slices bacon, cooked and crumbled
1 tablespoon (15 g) bacon grease
½ cup (120 ml) water

In a slow cooker, combine all of the ingredients. Cover and cook on low for 4 hours.

Yield: 6 servings

ASPARAGUS SIDE DISH
A delicious side dish without comparison, serve this tempting fare with any Italian entrée for a real treat.

1½ pounds (683 g) asparagus, sliced diagonally into 1-inch (2.5-cm) pieces
One 10¾-ounce (305-g) can condensed cream of celery soup
¾ cup (86 g) coarsely crushed saltine crackers

Coat the crock of a slow cooker with nonstick cooking spray.
 Place the asparagus in the slow cooker, pour the condensed soup over it, and sprinkle it with the cracker crumbs. Cover and cook on low for 4 to 6 hours.

Yield: 6 servings

▶*Add It!*
When the asparagus has finished cooking, add 1 cup (120 g) grated cheddar cheese. Cover and cook on low for another 15 to 30 minutes, or until the cheese has melted. Stir the mixture before serving it.

BALSAMIC BRUSSELS SPROUTS
This is an easy side dish that you can throw in a 1- to 1½-quart (0.9 to 1.4 L) slow cooker while you're making dinner, or better yet, while you relax before dinner!

Note: This recipe uses a 1- to 1½-quart (0.9 to 1.4 L) slow cooker or a small ovenproof dish in a larger slow cooker.

8 ounces (225 g) Brussels sprouts, cut into quarters
1 tablespoon (14 ml) balsamic vinegar
2 tablespoons (30 ml) red wine or an extra 1 tablespoon (15 ml) balsamic
4 sprigs fresh thyme or 1 teaspoon dried
½ teaspoon agave nectar or maple syrup
½ cup (120 ml) water
Salt, to taste
Black pepper, to taste

In a slow cooker, combine all of the ingredients. Cover and cook on high for 2 hours.
 Remove and discard the thyme sprigs. Taste and adjust the seasonings.

Yield: 4 servings

▶*Serving Suggestions*
Try eating the leftovers straight from the fridge, or in a chilled pasta salad.

SHALLOT APPLE BRUSSELS SPROUTS

This dish features the juxtaposition of the sprouts with sweetness from the apple cider and a mild bite from the Dijon. It's like a taste trifecta. Just a bit of butter provides a nice richness to finish it off perfectly.

1 pound (454 g) Brussels sprouts, trimmed
6 shallots, peeled and sliced
¼ cup (60 ml) apple cider
1½ tablespoons (21 g) butter, melted
2 teaspoons Dijon mustard
½ teaspoon salt
½ teaspoon black pepper

In a 2-quart (1.9 L) slow cooker, combine the Brussels sprouts and shallots.
   In a small bowl, whisk together the cider, butter, mustard, salt, and pepper. Pour the mixture evenly over the vegetables. Stir gently to coat. Cover and cook on low for 4 to 5 hours or on high for 2 to 3 hours, or until the Brussels sprouts reach the desired tenderness.

Yield: 4 to 6 servings

▶ *Health Bite*
Brussels sprouts are members of the cruciferous vegetable family. They have many of the same nutritional benefits of other cabbages, namely cancer-fighting nutrients that are so powerful the American Cancer Society recommends consumption of cruciferous vegetables on a regular basis. Brussels sprouts contain a special chemical called sinigrin, which actually suppresses the development of precancerous cells. They are also high in a particularly powerful antioxidant called sulforaphane, which has the added benefit of helping to neutralize potentially carcinogenic toxins.

ASIAN BROCCOLI

This is a great Asian-flavored side dish. Serve over brown rice.

2 pounds (900 g) broccoli, trimmed and chopped into bite-size piece
½ teaspoon minced garlic
½ cup (75 g) thinly sliced red bell pepper
¾ cup (120 g) sliced onion
¼ cup (60 ml) soy sauce
Dash black pepper
1 tablespoon (8 g) sesame seeds

In a slow cooker, combine all of the ingredients except for the sesame seeds. Cover and cook on low for 6 hours. Top with the sesame seeds.

Yield: 8 servings

BROCCOLI CASSEROLE

Broccoli cooks in a cheesy sauce while a crispy topping forms in this popular side dish recipe.

20 ounces (560 g) frozen broccoli spears
1 can (10 ounces, or 280 g) cream of celery soup
1¼ cups (150 g) grated Cheddar cheese, divided
¼ cup (25 g) minced scallions
12 saltine crackers, crushed

Coat the crock of a slow cooker with nonstick cooking spray.
   In a large bowl, combine the broccoli, soup, 1 cup (115 g) of the cheese, and the scallions. Pour the mixture into the slow cooker. Sprinkle with the crackers and the remaining cheese. Cover and slip a wooden toothpick between the lid and slow cooker to vent. Cover and cook on for low 5 to 6 hours or on high for 2 to 3 hours.

Yield: 6 servings

BROCCOLI RICE CASSEROLE

A hearty side dish of broccoli and rice in a creamy, cheesy sauce, this recipe only needs a piece of meat to make a complete meal.

1 pound (455 g) frozen broccoli, cooked and drained
10 ounces (280 g) cream of mushroom soup (To make your own, see "Cream of Mushroom Soup" on page 7.)
⅓ cup (53 g) chopped onion
10 ounces (280 g) Swiss cheese, shredded, divided
½ cup (120 ml) milk
1½ cups (248 g) cooked rice

In a bowl, mix everything together, reserving enough cheese to sprinkle over the top.
   Transfer the mixture to a slow cooker. Top with the reserved cheese. Cover and cook on low for 2 hours.

Yield: 4 servings

3 Corn Pudding; 4 Fresh Chili Lime Cob Corn; 5 Stewed Tomatoes; 6 Summer Stewed Tomatoes; 7 Tangy Beans; 8 Not Your Grandma's Green Beans

9 Green Bean Casserole; 10 Southern Beans; 11 Asparagus Side Dish; 12 Balsamic Brussels Sprouts; 13 Shallot Apple Brussels Sprouts; 14 Asian Broccoli

SIDE DISHES • 183

BROCCOLI AND BACON WITH PINE NUTS
This is quite special. Don't cook the broccoli any longer than 2 hours.

1 pound (455 g) frozen broccoli, unthawed
1 clove garlic, crushed
3 slices cooked bacon, crumbled
1 tablespoon (28 g) butter
1 tablespoon (15 ml) olive oil
2 tablespoons (18 g) pine nuts, toasted

In a slow cooker, combine the broccoli, garlic, and bacon. Cover and cook on low for 2 hours.

Before serving, stir in the butter and oil and top with the pine nuts.

Yield: 3 servings

CURRIED CAULIFLOWER
To make this dish sing, use a good-quality curry powder.

1 head cauliflower
Salt, to taste
Black pepper, to taste
½ cup (120 ml) water
1 medium onion, diced
1 tablespoon (7 g) curry powder

Remove the outer leaves and the core from the cauliflower and cut it into florets. Place the florets in a slow cooker. Season with salt and pepper to taste. Add the water, onion, and curry powder. Stir to combine. Cover and cook on low for 5 to 6 hours or on high for 2 hours, or until the cauliflower is tender.

Yield: 4 to 6 servings

SPINACH PARMESAN CASSEROLE

This is a lot like creamed spinach, only less—well, creamy.

20 ounces (560 g) frozen chopped spinach, thawed and drained (See "Recipe Note" at above right.)
⅓ cup (80 ml) heavy cream
½ cup (40 g) shredded Parmesan cheese
1 clove garlic, crushed
2 tablespoons (20 g) minced onion
1 egg
½ teaspoon salt

Coat a 6-cup (1.4 L) glass casserole dish with nonstick cooking spray.

In a bowl, stir together all of the ingredients. Transfer the mixture to the prepared dish, smoothing the top.

Place the casserole dish in a slow cooker. Carefully pour water around it up to 1 inch (2.5 cm) of the rim. Cover the slow cooker, set it to low, and let it cook for 4 hours.

At least 30 minutes before serving time, uncover the slow cooker and turn it off so the water cools enough that you can remove the dish without scalding yourself.

Yield: 6 servings

▶*Recipe Note*
Make sure that the spinach is very well drained. It's best to put it in a colander and press it as hard as you can, turning it several times.

BRAISED RED CABBAGE
This savory dish is great with sausages, pot roast, and roast pork.

1 head red cabbage (about 2 pounds or 910 g)
½ cup (120 ml) red wine vinegar
2 tablespoons (13 g) caraway seeds
Salt, to taste
Black pepper, to taste

Core the cabbage and shred it. Place the cabbage in a slow cooker. Pour the vinegar over the cabbage and sprinkle with the caraway seeds. Season with salt and pepper. Cover and cook on low for 6 to 7 hours or on high for 3 hours, or until the cabbage is soft. Stir before serving.

Yield: 6 to 8 servings

BAVARIAN CABBAGE
This is great with almost any pork dish.

1 head red cabbage
1 medium onion, chopped
1 medium Granny Smith apple, chopped
6 slices cooked bacon, crumbled
2 teaspoons salt
1 cup (235 ml) water
3 tablespoons (4.5 g) sugar
⅔ cup (160 ml) cider vinegar
3 tablespoons (45 ml) gin

Cut the head of cabbage in quarters and remove the core. Then cut it into large chunks.

In a large bowl, combine the cabbage, onion, apple, and bacon. Toss everything together. Transfer the mixture to a slow cooker. (This will fill a 3-quart (2.8 l) slow cooker just about to overflowing!)

In a bowl, mix together the salt, water, sugar, vinegar, and gin. Pour the mixture over the cabbage in the slow cooker. Cover and cook on low for 6 to 8 hours.

Yield: 6 servings

CAYENNE CARAMELIZED ONIONS

Slow cooking allows you to caramelize the onions using the barest minimum of added sugar, and it draws out the natural sweetness of the Vidalias, which are the perfect counterpoint to the bite of cayenne pepper.

9 Vidalia onions (about 3 pounds [1.4 kg]), thinly sliced
2½ tablespoons (35 g) butter, melted
1½ tablespoons (23 g) sugar
1 teaspoon cayenne pepper

Scatter the onions in an even layer in a slow cooker.
    In a bowl, whisk the butter, sugar, and cayenne together. Drizzle it evenly over the onions in the slow cooker. Toss to coat. Cover and cook on low for 8 to 9 hours.
    For the last half hour, remove the cover and increase the temperature of the slow cooker to high to reduce any remaining moisture.

Yield: about 3 cups (735 g)

▶*Health Bite*
Onions are such a fixture on the menu of fast food joints and large chain restaurants that it's easy to overlook the fact that they're one of the world's healthiest foods. In Vidalia, Georgia, where the Vidalia onion comes from and where onions are consumed in large quantities, the death rate from stomach cancer is about 50 percent lower than the national mortality rate from that same disease. One theory: Onions contain diallyl sulfide, which increases the body's production of an important cancer-fighting enzyme. Onions also benefit your bones and contain powerful antioxidants as well as compounds that are anti-inflammatory, antibiotic, and antiviral. Best of all, they're a great source of a superstar flavonoid known as quercetin, which has been shown to have anticancer activity as well as being a powerful anti-inflammatory.

BRAISED LEEKS WITH VINAIGRETTE

Hailing originally from the Mediterranean region, leeks have been prized for centuries–sometimes for the belief that they gave strength (sixth-century Wales) and sometimes just because their subtle, mild flavor is delicious (rest of the world). This dish can be served hot or cold, and it's sure to delight either way. As always, make sure you thoroughly wash these buggers, as they hide bits of dirt.

1 bunch leeks (usually 3 per bunch)
½ cup (120 ml) water
Salt, to taste
Black pepper, to taste
½ cup (120 ml) Italian vinaigrette
¼ cup (30 g) chopped flat-leaf parsley

Trim the root ends of the leeks and cut off the tough upper dark green parts.
    You can shave away some of the dark green to get to the tender light green part underneath. Split the leeks in half, lengthwise, and soak them in lots of cold water for several minutes. It is important to soak leeks well to get out the grit between the layers of the vegetable.
    In a slow cooker, place the leeks. Add the water. Season with salt and pepper. Cover and cook on low for 5 to 6 hours or on high for 2 hours, or until the leeks are very tender.
    Remove the leeks carefully from the slow cooker and put them on a serving plate to serve hot, or refrigerate if serving cold.
    When ready to serve, drizzle the leeks with the vinaigrette and top with the parsley.

Yield: 4 servings

CANDIED CARROTS AND PECANS

Flavored syrup gives this carrot dish a nutty taste. This side dish is delicious with pork and wild rice.

Two 16-ounce (455-g) packages frozen sliced carrots
¾ cup (242 g) butter pecan–flavored syrup
½ cup (113 g) brown sugar, packed

In a slow cooker, combine the carrots, syrup, and sugar. Stir to mix. Cover and cook on low for 6 to 8 hours or on high for 3 to 4 hours.

Yield: 8 servings

▶*Add It!*

Add 1 cup (109 g) chopped pecans, and cook the dish on high for 5½ to 6½ hours. If you add the nuts, don't cook this dish on low.

MARMALADE-GLAZED CARROTS

This medley of tangy-sweet orange marmalade and inherently sweet carrots is divine. You can almost eat this one for dessert.

4 cups (488 g) diagonally sliced carrots
2½ cups (588 ml) water
½ teaspoon salt
4 tablespoons (55 g) butter or margarine
½ cup (75 g) orange marmalade

In a slow cooker, combine the carrots, water, and salt. Stir to mix. Cover and cook on high for 2 to 4 hours, or until the carrot slices are tender.

Turn the heat off and allow the slow cooker to cool enough so that you can handle the ceramic pot safely. Drain the carrots well, add the butter and orange marmalade, and stir the mixture. Cover and cook on high for 20 to 30 minutes.

Yield: 8 servings

▶*Add It!*
Add ½ cup (30 g) chopped walnuts along with the butter and marmalade.

VODKA AND DILL-GLAZED BABY CARROTS

Sometimes you need a side dish with a little zip. The vodka, bouillon, and dill cook down into a tasty sauce that isn't plain or overpowering. It's just right.

1 pound (454 g) baby carrots
½ cup (120 ml) water
2 tablespoons (30 ml) vodka
2 tablespoons (12 g) chicken-flavored bouillon
2 teaspoons dill
Salt, to taste
Black pepper, to taste

Coat the crock of a 1½- to 2-quart (1.4 to 1.9 L) slow cooker or a small ovenproof dish in a larger slow cooker with nonstick cooking spray. (You can double or triple the recipe and use a larger slow cooker.)

In the crock or dish, combine all of the ingredients. Cover and cook on low for 6 to 8 hours. Taste and adjust the seasonings.

Yield: 4 servings

▶*Health Bite*
Carrots are the reigning queen of vitamin A. Just ½ cup (60 g) of cooked carrots provides almost three times the daily recommended amount.

GLAZED ROOT VEGETABLES

These cook up similar to roasted vegetables with the easy fixing afforded by the slow cooker.

2 parsnips, sliced
2 cups (260 g) sliced carrot
1 turnip, cut in 1-inch (2.5 cm) cubes
1 cup (235 ml) water
½ cup (100 g) sugar
3 tablespoons (42 g) butter

In a large pot, boil the vegetables in water for 10 minutes. Drain, reserving ½ cup (120 ml) of the liquid.

Transfer the vegetables to a slow cooker. Pour the reserved liquid over the top. Add the sugar and butter. Cover and cook on low for 3 hours.

Yield: 6 servings

PARSNIP AND CARROT MEDLEY

If you've ever had parsnips that have stayed in the ground beyond the first frost, you know how sweet this delightful root can be. Here we capitalize on that sweetness, to the delight of parsnip fans everywhere.

1 pound (455 g) carrots, peeled and cut into 1-inch-long (2.5-cm) pieces
1 pound (455 g) parsnips, peeled and cut into 1-inch-long (2.5-cm) pieces
1 teaspoon (2.2 g) nutmeg
Salt, to taste
Black pepper, to taste
½ cup (120 ml) water
3 tablespoons (42 g) butter

In a slow cooker, place the vegetables. Stir in the nutmeg. Season with salt and pepper. Add the water and dot with the butter. Cover and cook on low for 5 to 6 hours or on high for 2 hours, or until the vegetables are tender.

Yield: 4 to 6 servings

FRESH SWEET 'N SOUR BEETS
These slow-cooked beets are tangy and sweet with a citrus-y bite.

1 pound (454 g) fresh, young beets, peeled and halved
¼ cup (60 g) sugar
1 tablespoon (8 g) enriched wheat flour
2 tablespoons (30 ml) apple cider vinegar
2 tablespoons (30 ml) lemon juice

In a slow cooker, place the beets.
    In a small bowl, whisk together the sugar and flour. Add the vinegar and juice and whisk to combine. Pour the sauce over the beets in the slow cooker. Cover and cook on low for 2 to 3 hours, or until the beets are tender. Baste the beets before serving.

Yield: 4 servings

▶*Health Bite*
Beets are not exactly nutritional lightweights. They're an important dietary source of betaine, which is a nutrient known for its role in bringing down high levels of a toxic inflammatory compound in our bodies known as homocysteine. (High homocysteine levels are a risk factor for heart disease and stroke.) Beets are also loaded with potassium, a vitally important mineral for heart health.

BEETS WITH GINGER AND ORANGE
The sweet earthiness of beets is one of our favorites. Here it sparkles with the infusion of ginger and orange.

3 pounds (1365 g) beets
Salt, to taste
Black pepper, to taste
1 tablespoon (6 g) minced fresh ginger
1 cup (235 ml) orange juice
2 to 3 tablespoons (28 to 42 g) butter, cut into small pieces

Wash and peel the beets and slice them ½ inch (1 cm) thick.
    In a slow cooker, place the beets. Season with salt and pepper. Sprinkle the ginger over the beets and pour the juice on top. Top with the butter. Cover and cook on low for 6 to 7 hours or on high for 3 hours, or until the beets are tender.

Yield: 6 to 8 servings

ORANGE BEETS WITH WALNUTS
In this dish, the walnuts provide a nice textural balance to the beets. The sherry and orange lend a light, complementary flavor note and blend beautifully with the sweet beets.

½ cup (120 ml) freshly squeezed orange juice
2 tablespoons (30 ml) sherry vinegar
2 pounds (908 g) whole beets, unpeeled, stemmed
¼ cup (30 g) roasted chopped walnuts, optional

In a small bowl, whisk together the orange juice and sherry. Place the whole beets in the slow cooker and pour the juice mixture over all. Cover and cook on low for about 3 hours, or to the desired tenderness. Stir well and remove the beets to cool. When cool enough to handle, slip the skins off with your fingers (or use a paper towel to protect your hands from the staining juices).
    Quarter the beets and top with the walnuts, if using.

Yield: 8 servings

▶*Health Bite*
Have you often wondered why beets are red? The red color comes from a plant compound in beets called betacyanin, which researchers believe could protect against the development of cancerous cells and might even play a role in reducing the inflammation that's a big part of heart disease–as well as every other degenerative disease. Beets also contain fiber, potassium, and a decent amount of folate.
    The walnuts provide heart-healthy monounsaturated fat along with fiber and minerals.
    A study from the Journal of Applied Physiology *found that athletes drinking organic beet juice for six consecutive days were able to cycle for 92 seconds longer than athletes given a placebo to drink. This translates into approximately a 2 percent reduction in the time needed to cover a set distance.*

15 Broccoli Casserole

16 Broccoli Rice Casserole

SIDE DISHES • 189

GARLIC SPINACH WITH ROASTED REDS

The vibrant colors of this dish give a clue to its extraordinary taste–and healthful properties too.

2 teaspoons olive oil
1 sweet onion, chopped
4 cloves garlic, minced
½ teaspoon ground cumin
½ teaspoon salt
½ teaspoon black pepper
2 roasted red peppers, chopped
1 can (14 ounces, or 392 g) fire-roasted diced tomatoes, drained
4 or 5 dashes hot pepper sauce
3 packages (10 ounces, or 280 g) frozen chopped spinach, unthawed

FOR THE OPTIONAL GARNISH:
¼ cup (60 g) plain low-fat Greek yogurt
1 tablespoon (15 ml) lemon juice
1 clove garlic, minced
¼ teaspoon salt

In a large skillet, heat the oil over medium heat. Add the onion and cook for 5 to 6 minutes, or until starting to soften. Add the garlic and cook for 30 seconds, stirring constantly. Remove from the heat and stir in the cumin, salt, pepper, peppers, tomatoes, and hot pepper sauce.

In the bottom of a slow cooker, place the spinach. Pour the onion mixture evenly over the top. Cover and cook on low for 4 to 5 hours, or until heated through.

To make the garnish: In a small bowl, combine the yogurt, juice, garlic, and salt. Whisk thoroughly. Chill in the fridge to let the flavors combine.

To serve, stir the spinach gently to mix, adjust the seasonings to taste, and top with the garnish, if using.

Yield: 6 servings

▶*Health Bite*

The ingredients list in this recipe is kind of like an "all-star" team of superfoods. There's not a lightweight in the bunch.

Spinach is one of the great vegetables of all time, providing vitamin A, manganese, folic acid, magnesium, iron, vitamin C, and a powerful anti-inflammatory called quercetin. What's more, spinach is a great source of calcium, and one of the best sources of the important heart-protective, bone-supporting nutrient, vitamin K.

Garlic, one of the oldest medicinal foods on the planet, is a powerful antioxidant that is also antimicrobial and antiviral. Plus, compounds in garlic have been shown in many lab studies to be chemoprotective (anticancer).

Roasted red peppers have a high vitamin C content, and tomatoes contain the cancer-fighting antioxidant lycopene.

High-protein Greek yogurt rounds out the superstar team of fabulous foods in this scrumptious recipe.

FRESH AND LIGHT SUMMER MEDLEY WITH FETA

This vegetable dish is slow cooked to tender perfection and topped with tangy feta. What's not to like?

4 medium zucchini, sliced
1 large Vidalia onion, thinly sliced into rings
1 large red bell pepper, julienned
1 can (14.5 ounces, or 406 g) roasted diced tomatoes, undrained
1 teaspoon dried basil
1 teaspoon dried thyme
3 cloves garlic, minced
¾ teaspoon salt
½ teaspoon black pepper
½ cup (75 g) crumbled feta cheese

In the bottom of a slow cooker, layer the zucchini, onion, and bell pepper.

In a small bowl, combine the tomatoes, basil, thyme, garlic, salt, and black pepper. Stir to mix. Pour the tomato mixture evenly over the vegetables in the slow cooker. Cover and cook on low for 1 to 2 hours, or until the veggies are tender. Before serving, sprinkle individual servings with the feta.

Yield: 6 servings

EASIEST VEGETABLE-SURPRISE DISH

The surprise is that this dish is so quick and easy. While you run to the gym, you can be cooking a healthful veggie side dish.

Two 16-ounce (455-g) bags frozen mixed vegetables, partially thawed
One 10¾-ounce (305-g) can condensed cream of mushroom or cream of celery soup
1 small onion, chopped
½ teaspoon salt

In a slow cooker, combine the vegetables, soup, onion, and salt. Stir to mix. Cover and cook on low for 1½ to 2½ hours or on high for 45 to 75 minutes.

Yield: 8 servings

VEGETABLE MEDLEY

This is a perfect summer side dish when fresh vegetables are abundant. Feel free to substitute ingredients based on taste and availability. It's excellent with ham or fish.

¾ cup (120 g) sliced onion
1 cup (100 g) celery, cut in 2-inch (5 cm) strips
1 cup (130 g) carrots, cut in 2-inch (5 cm) strips
1 cup (100 g) green beans
½ cup (75 g) diced green bell pepper
1 large tomato, sliced
¼ cup (55 g) butter
⅛ teaspoon black pepper
1 tablespoon (13 g) sugar
3 tablespoons (25 g) tapioca

In a slow cooker, combine all of the ingredients. Cover and cook on low for 3 to 4 hours.

Yield: 6 servings

RED CABBAGE, GREEN APPLE, AND SWEET ONION

The sweetness of the apples and onions together mellows the edgy taste of the cabbage, creating a simply perfect side dish for any meal.

1 small Vidalia onion, halved and sliced into ¼-inch (6 mm) slices
1 head red cabbage, cored, quartered, and sliced into ¼-inch (6 mm) strips
2 green apples, unpeeled, cored, and chopped
¾ teaspoon salt
Black pepper, to taste
1 teaspoon caraway seeds, optional
3 cups (705 ml) chicken or vegetable broth (To make your own, see "Chicken Stock" on page 6 or "Freshest Vegetable Broth" on page 6.)
1 tablespoon (15 ml) apple cider vinegar

In a slow cooker, place the onion. Top with the cabbage, and then the apples. Sprinkle with the salt, pepper, and caraway seeds, if using. Pour the broth and vinegar over all. Cover and cook on low for 3 to 4 hours or on high for about 2 hours, or until the cabbage and onion are tender.

Yield: 8 servings

SQUASH CASSEROLE

This version is anything but plain squash. It has loads of color and flavor.

4 cups (480 g) thinly sliced yellow squash
½ cup (80 g) chopped onion
1 cup (130 g) shredded carrot
1 can (10 ounces, or 280 g) cream of chicken soup
1 cup (230 g) sour cream
¼ cup (31 g) all-purpose flour
8 ounces (225 g) stuffing mix, crumbled
½ cup (112 g) butter, melted

In large bowl, combine the squash, onion, carrot, and soup. In a separate bowl, mix the sour cream and flour together. Stir the mixture into the vegetables.

In a separate bowl, toss the stuffing with butter and place half of it in a slow cooker. Add the vegetable mixture and top with the remaining stuffing crumbs. Cover and cook on low for 7 to 9 hours.

Yield: 6 servings

ACORN SQUASH

This is just too simple! Pair Acorn Squash with your favorite entrée for a delicious meal.

1½- to 2-pound (683- to 910-g) whole acorn squash, rinsed well
2 teaspoons (12 g) salt
½ teaspoon black pepper
6 tablespoons (84 g) butter, melted
2 tablespoons (28 g) brown sugar, packed

Using a fork, pierce the acorn squash in several places. Place it in a slow cooker. Cover and cook on low for 8 to 10 hours, or until the squash is fork-tender.

Remove the squash from the slow cooker and allow it to cool enough to be handled safely. Cut the squash in half, and then cut each half in half. Scoop out and discard the seeds, place each squash quarter pulp side up on a plate, and season each squash quarter with one-fourth of the salt and pepper.

In a small bowl, combine the butter and sugar. Pour one-fourth of the mixture over each squash quarter.

Yield: 4 servings

▶*Recipe Tip*
Place the cooked, seasoned squash quarters on a baking sheet, and then fill them with the butter–brown sugar mixture. Warm the squash quarters in a 350°F (180°C) oven for 10 minutes, or until the sugar has melted.

17 Broccoli and Bacon with Pine Nuts; 18 Curried Cauliflower; 19 Spinach Parmesan Casserole; 20 Braised Red Cabbage; 21 Bavarian Cabbage; 22 Cayenne Caramelized Onions; 23 Braised Leeks with Vinaigrette; 24 Candied Carrots and Pecans

25 Marmalade-Glazed Carrots; 26 Vodka and Dill-Glazed Baby Carrots; 27 Glazed Root Vegetables; 28 Parsnip and Carrot Medley; 29 Fresh Sweet 'n Sour Beets; 30 Beets with Ginger and Orange; 31 Orange Beets with Walnuts; 32 Garlic Spinach with Roasted Reds

SIDE DISHES • 193

FRUIT-STUFFED ACORN SQUASH
The sweet and crunchy mix of apples, raisins, and pecans form the absolutely pitch-perfect accompaniment to acorn squash, which is a naturally sweet vegetable.

2 acorn squash halved
2 teaspoons sugar
1 teaspoon ground cinnamon
½ teaspoon ground nutmeg
½ teaspoon ground cardamom
¼ teaspoon salt
1 sweet apple, such as Jonagold, unpeeled, finely chopped
½ cup (75 g) raisins
¼ cup (26 g) chopped pecans
4 teaspoons (18 g) butter or coconut oil, melted
½ cup (120 ml) apple cider or water

Using a heavy chef's knife or a cleaver, halve the squash. Using a heavy spoon, remove the seeds.

In a medium bowl, mix together the sugar, cinnamon, nutmeg, cardamom, and salt. Add the apple, raisins, and pecans. Toss to coat thoroughly. Stuff each half of the squash with one-fourth of the mixture and drizzle 1 teaspoon of butter over the top of each. Pour the cider into a slow cooker.

If you have a large cooker (6 or 7 quarts [5.7 or 6.6 L]), place the squash halves side by side, cut sides up, in the cooker, cover, and cook. If you have to stack them, wrap each half tightly in foil before stacking (to keep the contents inside) and cook with water, not cider. Cover and cook on low for 8 hours or on high for 4 hours, or until the squash is very tender.

Yield: 4 servings

▶*Health Bite*
Acorn squash is literally a fiber heavyweight, delivering a sizeable 9 grams of fiber per cup, plus 896 milligrams of potassium (twice that of a banana) and almost 2 milligrams of iron.

In addition to keeping the proverbial doctor away, apples are a great source of a little-known mineral called boron, which is increasingly being seen by scientists as essential for bone health. In animal studies, low boron intake is associated with abnormal bone growth and development. In humans, patients affected with arthritic joints show lower levels of boron in their bones than those without arthritis.

ACORN SQUASH STUFFED WITH CRANBERRY-PECAN RICE
By using your slow cooker instead of an oven, you'll have a dish ready to serve as soon as you get home. Use the recipe below as a jumping-off point. You can use any leftover grains, beans, or chopped stale bread (think Thanksgiving stuffing) to make a filling. Because the acorn squash is a little sweet, you might want to add some dried fruit, as well as savory herbs. It's a perfect place to use up that last bit of cooked sausage or crumbled baked tofu.

1 medium acorn squash
Olive oil, for rubbing
1 cup (165 g) cooked brown rice or other precooked grain
1 can (15 ounces, or 420 g) lentils, white beans, or kidney beans, drained and rinsed
1 tablespoon (8 g) chopped dried cranberries
1 tablespoon (7 g) chopped pecans
1 clove garlic, minced
2 sprigs fresh thyme, minced
1 teaspoon chopped fresh rosemary
Salt, to taste
Black pepper, to taste
Water or broth, as needed

Using a heavy chef's knife or a cleaver, cut the acorn squash in half. Using a heavy spoon, remove the seeds. Lightly rub the exposed flesh with a little oil.

In a bowl, combine the rice, lentils, cranberries, pecans, garlic, thyme, and rosemary. Season with salt and pepper. Stir to mix. If the mixture is too dry, add some water or broth.

Pour about ½ inch (1.3 cm) water in the bottom of a slow cooker. Crumple up some aluminum foil and place it under the squash halves to keep them from turning over and spilling out the stuffing. No aluminum foil? Cut a little off the bottom side of the squash half to get it to sit straight. Fill the squash with the stuffing and round it over the flesh, if possible. Cover and cook on low for 6 to 8 hours, or until the squash is tender when pierced with a fork.

Yield: 2 servings

▶*Recipe Tip*
If you have a large, oval slow cooker, you can double this recipe and make 4 servings instead of 2.

BUTTERNUT SQUASH PUREE
It doesn't get any easier than this slow-cooker method to make this fall classic. To make this dish even easier, buy the squash already peeled.

1 butternut squash (about 3 pounds or 1365 g)
Salt, to taste
Black pepper, to taste
½ cup (120 ml) water
½ cup (115 g) light brown sugar
1 teaspoon (2.3 g) ground cinnamon
3 tablespoons (42 g) butter

Peel the squash. Using a heavy chef's knife or a cleaver, cut it in half lengthwise. Using a heavy spoon, scoop out and discard the seeds and any pulp in the seed cavity. Cut the squash into 2- or 3-inch (5- or 7.5-cm) chunks.

Place the squash in a slow cooker. Season with salt and pepper. Add the water, sugar, and cinnamon. Cover and cook on low for 4 to 5 hours on high for 2 hours, or until the squash is quite soft. Add the butter. Using a potato masher, mash the squash well.

Yield: 6 to 8 servings

SPICE-RUBBED SPAGHETTI SQUASH
Spaghetti squash is a tiny bit bland. The pungent spice rub in this dish really kicks the taste quotient up a few notches. This filling, low-carb winter squash is both delicious and incredibly easy to make.

1 teaspoon paprika
1 teaspoon garlic powder
1 teaspoon onion powder
½ teaspoon dried oregano
½ teaspoon dried thyme
½ teaspoon cayenne pepper
½ teaspoon black pepper
½ teaspoon salt
1 medium spaghetti squash
½ cup (120 ml) vegetable broth or water (To make your own broth, see "Freshest Vegetable Broth" on page 6.)
1 tablespoon (15 ml) olive oil or butter, diced

In a small bowl, mix the spices together.

Using a heavy chef's knife or a cleaver, slice the squash in half lengthwise. Using a heavy spoon, scrape out all the seeds and connective threads and discard.

Pour the broth into a slow cooker. Lay the squash halves on a counter surface, cut sides up, and drizzle half of the oil into each squash half. Gently rub the oil with your fingers to evenly coat all the cut flesh. (If you're using butter, distribute the chopped pieces evenly into the "bowls" of each half.) Sprinkle each half evenly with the rub mixture.

You may have some rub left over. Arrange the squash in the slow cooker so the cut sides are up. Cover and cook on low for 7 to 8 hours or on high for 3½ to 4 hours, or until the squash is fork-tender.

Spoon the flesh out of the skins (discarding the skins) and/or pull the individual strands apart, if desired, to serve.

Yield: 4 to 6 servings

▶*Health Bite*
Feel free to butter your vegetables and season them well. If the price of an extra hundred or so calories from the butter is going to get you to eat a whole plate of broccoli, it's a nutritional bargain. It's kind of the same deal here.

Spaghetti squash isn't a great nutritional heavyweight, but it's incredibly low in calories. It provides 2.2 grams of fiber (plus about half the potassium in a banana) for a single 42-calorie 1-cup (225 g) serving.

CREAMY ZUCCHINI CASSEROLE
This casserole is easy to put together, and it tastes great. Serve it with chicken or fish.

3 cups (360 g) thinly sliced zucchini
1 cup (160 g) diced onion
1 cup (130 g) shredded carrot
10 ounces (280 g) cream of mushroom soup (To make your own, see "Cream of Mushroom Soup" on page 6.)
10 ounces (280 g) cream of chicken soup

Coat the crock of a slow cooker with nonstick cooking spray.

In the slow cooker, combine the zucchini, onion, carrot, and soups together gently. Cover and cook on for high 4 to 6 hours, or until the vegetables are as crunchy or as soft as you like.

Yield: 6 servings

33 Fresh and Light Summer Medley with Feta

34 Easiest Vegetable-Surprise Dish; 35 Vegetable Medley; 36 Red Cabbage, Green Apple, and Sweet Onion; 37 Squash Casserole; 38 Acorn Squash; 39 Fruit-Stuffed Acorn Squash; 40 Acorn Squash Stuffed with Cranberry-Pecan Rice; 41 Butternut Squash Purée

SIDE DISHES • 197

ITALIAN ZUCCHINI
These zucchini cooked in an Italian seasoned tomato sauce can be used as a side dish for meat or pasta, or they can be used as a pasta sauce itself.

½ cup (80 g) chopped onion
½ cup (75 g) chopped green bell pepper
¼ cup (55 g) butter
1 can (6 ounces, or 170 g) tomato paste
4 ounces (115 g) mushrooms, sliced
2 tablespoons (12 g) Italian seasoning
1 cup (235 ml) water
2½ pounds (1.1 kg) zucchini, cut in ⅜-inch (0.9 cm) slices
4 ounces (115 g) shredded mozzarella cheese

In a saucepan, cook the onion and green pepper in the butter until they're tender but not brown. Transfer the onion and green pepper to a slow cooker. Stir in the paste, mushrooms, Italian seasoning, and water. Add the zucchini, stirring gently to coat. Cover and cook on low for 8 hours.
　To serve, top individual bowls of the zucchini with the mozzarella.

Yield: 8 servings

EGGPLANT CURRY
When eggplant cooks down, it gets an almost creamy consistency. Add extra chipotle chile powder to make it spicier, or use a different type of chili to omit the smokiness.

2 tablespoons (30 ml) olive oil
1 small onion, minced
2 cloves garlic, minced
2 teaspoons grated ginger
4½ cups (about 1 pound, or 454 g) chopped eggplant
1 cup (235 ml) water
Salt, to taste
½ teaspoon garam masala
1 teaspoon cumin
½ teaspoon turmeric
Pinch of chipotle chile powder

In a skillet, heat the oil over medium heat. Sauté the onion for 3 to 5 minutes, or until translucent. Add the garlic and sauté for 2 minutes longer.
　In a slow cooker, combine all of the ingredients. Cover and cook on low for 6 to 8 hours. Taste and adjust the seasonings.

Yield: 6 servings

MIXED SQUASH CASSEROLE
This squash casserole makes a great side dish for just about any kind of meal.

1½ cups (180 g) sliced zucchini, divided
1½ cups (180 g) sliced yellow squash, divided
1 cup (180 g) peeled and chopped tomatoes, divided
¼ cup (25 g) sliced scallions, divided
½ cup (75 g) chopped green bell pepper, divided
¼ cup (60 ml) chicken broth (To make your own, see "Chicken Stock" on page 6.)
¼ cup (30 g) bread crumbs

In a slow cooker, layer half the zucchini, squash, tomatoes, scallions, and green pepper. Repeat the layers. Pour the broth over the vegetables. Sprinkle the bread crumbs over top. Cover and cook on low for 4 to 6 hours.

Yield: 8 servings

BAKED BEANS
This is a simple, but good, baked bean recipe. There are only a few ingredients, but the long, slow cooking makes the most of them.

2½ cups (538 g) dried navy beans, rinsed
6 tablespoons (120 g) molasses
¼ cup (60 g) brown sugar
¼ pound (115 g) bacon
¼ teaspoon black pepper

Boil the beans for 30 minutes to soften.
　Transfer the beans to a slow cooker. Add the remaining ingredients. Cover and cook on low for 10 hours, stirring every 3 hours or so.

Yield: 6 servings

VEGETARIAN BAKED BEANS
In this tasty bean recipe without meat, the beans are precooked to shorten the cooking time.

1 pound (455 g) navy beans, dried/rinsed
6 cups (1.4 L) water
¾ cup (120 g) chopped onion
¼ cup (60 g) ketchup (To make your own, see "Homemade Smoky Ketchup" on page 8.)
½ cup (115 g) brown sugar
¾ cup (180 ml) water
1 teaspoon dry mustard
3 tablespoons (60 g) molasses

In a large soup kettle, soak the beans in the water overnight. The next morning, cook the beans in the water for about 1½ hours, or until they're soft. Drain, discarding cooking liquid.

In a slow cooker, combine the beans and the other ingredients. Stir to mix well. Cover and cook on low for 5 to 8 hours, or until the beans are well-flavored but not breaking down.

Yield: 8 servings

LIMA BEANS

You could make a whole meal of this recipe. But it also makes a great side dish.

1 pound (455 g) dried lima beans, washed
1½ cups (240 g) chopped onion
½ cup (50 g) chopped celery
2 large potatoes, peeled and diced
1 cup (130 g) sliced carrots

In a slow cooker, combine all of the ingredients. Add enough water to cover the vegetables. Cover and cook on low for at least 10 hours.

Yield: 6 servings

FANTASTIC MEXI BEANS

These beans have a clean, fresh flavor with subtle hints of Mexican spice–completely different from the canned version.

1 piece dried kombu (about 1 by 2 inches [2.5 by 5 cm]), optional
1½ tablespoons (23 ml) olive oil
1 large yellow onion
1 jalapeño pepper, seeded and finely chopped, optional
4 cloves garlic, minced
2 teaspoons ground cumin
1 teaspoon dried oregano
½ teaspoon chili powder
½ teaspoon hot paprika
1 pound (454 g) dried black beans, rinsed and picked through
6 cups (1.4 L) vegetable broth or water (To make your own vegetable broth, see "Freshest Vegetable Broth" on page 6.)
2 tablespoons (30 ml) apple cider vinegar
Salt, to taste
Black pepper, to taste
¼ cup (4 g) chopped fresh cilantro or chives, optional
Lime slices, optional

In a small bowl of water, soak the kombu, if using, for 5 to 10 minutes, or until tender. Chop finely.

In a large Dutch oven or soup pot, heat the oil over medium heat. Sauté the onion for about 6 minutes, or until tender. Add the jalapeño, if using, and the garlic, cumin, oregano, chili powder, and paprika. Cook for about 30 seconds, stirring constantly. Add the beans and broth. Stir to combine, and increase the heat to bring the mixture to a boil.

When the mixture reaches a full boil, remove the pot from the heat. Carefully transfer the contents to a slow cooker. Stir in the prepared kombu, if using. Cover and cook on high for 3 to 5 hours, or until the beans are tender to the squeeze.

Stir in the vinegar. Season with salt and pepper. Cover and cook for about 15 minutes longer. Garnish with the cilantro and lime slices, if using.

Yield: about 8 cups (2 kg) (½ cup [125 g] per serving)

▶ *Recipe Tip*
Hippocrates, the father of modern medicine, once said: "Passing gas is necessary to well-being." Enter kombu, a kind of edible kelp that's widely eaten in Japan and Asia. Kombu happens to do a fine job of decreasing the flatulence factor.

CARIBBEAN MANGO BLACK BEANS

Sometimes you need something easy to make that's good enough for company. These beans have a hint of sweetness from the mango with a layer of spiciness underneath. You can halve this recipe if you aren't serving a crowd, or you can freeze the leftovers for another night. Serve the beans as a side dish or make them a meal over rice or in a burrito.

3 cloves garlic
2 mangoes
4 cans (15 ounces, or 420 g each) black beans, drained and rinsed
1 cup (235 ml) water
2 tablespoons (12 g) chicken-flavored bouillon
3 tablespoons (24 g) grated fresh ginger
1½ teaspoons paprika
2 teaspoons thyme
¼ teaspoon nutmeg
⅛ teaspoon ground cloves
⅛ teaspoon allspice
⅛ to ½ teaspoon ground hot pepper
Salt, to taste
Black pepper, to taste

Mince the garlic. Cut along both sides of the mango pit to remove 2 cheeks. Using a knife, cut lengthwise into the mango just to the skin. Do the same across widthwise, so

SIDE DISHES • 199

that you have a checkerboard. Take the piece in hand and open the crisscross section so it bows out. Now take the knife and run it under the flesh. The fruit will easily fall off into chunks. Repeat with the remaining mango cheek.

Coat the crock of a slow cooker with nonstick cooking spray.

In the slow cooker, combine all the ingredients. Cover and cook on low for 6 to 8 hours. Taste and adjust the seasonings.

Yield: 8 servings

CHANA SAAG

You can use any combinations of greens here, such as spinach, Swiss chard, turnip greens, and collards, or anything that's plentiful where you live.

2 tablespoons (30 ml) olive oil
1 small onion, minced
2 cloves garlic, minced
1 tablespoon (8 g) grated fresh ginger
1 pound (454 g) assorted greens, washed, torn into bite-size pieces, and spun dry (You can also buy a prewashed mix in a bag.)
1 teaspoon cumin powder
½ teaspoon turmeric
½ teaspoon ground coriander
½ teaspoon garam masala
1½ cups (353 ml) water
2 tablespoons (12 g) chicken-flavored bouillon
1 can (15 ounces, or 420 g) chickpeas, drained and rinsed
½ to 1 cup (120 to 235 ml) milk
Zest of ½ lime
Salt, to taste
Rice

Coat the crock of a slow cooker with nonstick cooking spray.

In a skillet, heat the oil over medium heat. Sauté the onion for 3 to 5 minutes, or until it's translucent. Add the garlic and sauté for 2 minutes longer.

In the slow cooker, combine the onion and garlic, ginger, greens, spices, water, and bouillon. Cover and cook on low for 6 to 8 hours.

About 30 minutes before serving, using an immersion blender or in batches in a countertop blender, purée the soup until smooth, being careful of splatters of hot soup. Add the chickpeas, milk, and zest. Season with salt. Cover and cook on high for 30 more minutes, or until the beans are heated through. Taste and adjust the seasonings.

Serve over rice.

Yield: 6 servings

▶*Recipe Variations*
• *Add 1 or 2 chopped mild chiles during the last 30 minutes of cooking to give it more heat.*

• *Don't like chickpeas? Substitute ½ package (15 ounces, or 420 g) soft, firm, or extra-firm tofu, pressed and then cut into cubes. It will mimic a popular dish called saag paneer.*

SMOKY MAC AND CHEESE

Eating vegan? Veganized comfort food is a beautiful thing. The liquid smoke and Cajun seasoning dress this dish up a little, but go ahead and leave them out if you're craving the kind of mac and cheese that you grew up on. This one is extra creamy, and leftovers reheat well.

4 cups (940 ml) nondairy milk
2 tablespoons (12 g) vegan chicken-flavored bouillon
8 ounces (225 g) dried whole wheat macaroni
2 cups (230 g) shredded vegan Cheddar cheese
1 cup (115 g) shredded vegan mozzarella cheese
¼ to ½ teaspoon liquid smoke, optional
½ teaspoon Cajun seasoning, optional
Salt, to taste
Black pepper, to taste

Coat the crock of a slow cooker with nonstick cooking spray.

In the slow cooker, combine all of the ingredients. Stir to mix. Cover and cook on high for 1 to 1½ hours, or until the pasta is al dente, stirring the mixture every 20 to 30 minutes.

If you don't use whole wheat pasta, it will cook faster, so check it around 45 minutes. It's important to check this one frequently or you will end up with mushy pasta.

Yield: 4 servings

▶*Recipe Tip*
This is a great dish to sneak in a few veggies. During the last 30 minutes of cooking, add leftover precooked vegetables to the slow cooker.

SIMPLE WHITE RICE
No peeking allowed! This rice cooks itself to perfection, as long as you don't lift the lid.

2¼ cups (529 ml) water
1 cup (185 g) long-grain converted rice, uncooked
3 tablespoons (42 g) margarine
½ to 1 tablespoon (2 to 4 g) dried or minced fresh parsley
1 teaspoon salt

Coat the crock of a slow cooker with nonstick cooking spray.
 In the slow cooker, combine the water, rice, margarine, parsley, and salt. Stir to mix. Cover and cook on low for 6 to 8 hours, or just until the rice is tender.

Yield: 6 servings

▶Add It!
- Add ¼ teaspoon freshly ground black pepper.

- Substitute chopped fresh chives or mint for the parsley for a refreshingly different taste.

BARLEY RISOTTO
Okay this isn't really risotto, but the creamy texture of this side dish will remind you of risotto, and it's a lot easier to make.

2 cups (400 g) pearl barley
1¾ cups (410 ml) chicken broth (To make your own, see "Chicken Stock" on page 6.)
½ cup (65 g) shredded carrot
1 tablespoon (15 ml) lemon juice
1 teaspoon thyme
½ teaspoon minced garlic
½ teaspoon black pepper
½ cup (55 g) shredded Swiss cheese
1 cup (130 g) frozen peas
½ cup (120 ml) milk
2 tablespoons (28 g) butter

In a slow cooker, combine the barley, broth, carrot, juice, thyme, garlic, and pepper. Cover and cook on low for 5 to 5½ hours. Stir in the cheese, peas, milk, and butter. Cover and let for stand 10 minutes.

Yield: 6 servings

CREAMY BUTTERNUT SQUASH RISOTTO
Butternut squash makes the perfect fall risotto. You can use a combination of herbs in this dish, or you can just use one if you'd prefer. You can switch out any winter squash for the butternut, depending on what you have on hand.

2½ cups (588 ml) water, plus more if needed
1½ cups (280 g) Arborio rice
1 can (15 ounces, or 420 g) cooked butternut squash or 1½ cups (368) puréed cooked fresh
½ cup (48 g) nutritional yeast
1 teaspoon thyme
¼ teaspoon rubbed sage
⅛ teaspoon dried rosemary
Salt, to taste
Black pepper, to taste

In a slow cooker, combine the 2½ cups (588 ml) water, rice, squash, yeast, thyme, sage, and rosemary. Cover and cook on high for 1½ to 2½ hours, or until the rice is cooked through but still al dente. Stir every 20 to 30 minutes, adding extra water if needed. Season with salt and pepper. Taste and adjust the herbs.

Yield: 6 servings

▶Recipe Tip
You can precook the squash in your slow cooker following the directions in Perfect Pumpkin Purée on page 16.

CHEESY BROCCOLI RICE
Cheesy rice grows up here with the addition of broccoli. If you're in a hurry, you can defrost the broccoli in the fridge the night before.

3 cups (705 ml) water, plus more if needed
1½ cups (280 g) long-grain brown rice
3 tablespoons (18 g) chicken-flavored bouillon
½ cup (48 g) nutritional yeast
1 pound (454 g) fresh or frozen broccoli
Salt, to taste
Black pepper, to taste
1 cup (115 g) shredded Cheddar cheese, optional

In a slow cooker, combine the 3 cups (705 ml) water, rice, bouillon, and yeast. Cover and cook on high for 1½ hours. Stir in the broccoli. Check every 10 to 15 minutes, adding more water if needed. Stir the mixture until the rice and broccoli are tender when pierced with a fork, 15 to 40 minutes, depending on whether you use fresh or frozen broccoli.
 Once the rice is ready, season with salt and pepper. Stir in the cheese.

Yield: 6 servings

42 Spice-Rubbed Spaghetti Squash; 43 Creamy Zucchini Casserole; 44 Italian Zucchini; 45 Eggplant Curry; 46 Mixed Squash Casserole; 47 Baked Beans; 48 Vegetarian Baked Beans; 49 Lima Beans

50 Vegan Fantastic Mexi Beans; 51 Caribbean Mango Black Beans; 52 Chana Saag; 53 Vegan Smoky Mac and Cheese; 54 Simple White RIce; 55 Barley Risotto; 56 Creamy Butternut Squash Risotto; 57 Cheesy Broccoli Rice

SIDE DISHES • 203

CURRIED COUSCOUS
This side dish has it all: the flavor of fresh vegetables, the heat of curry powder and jalapeño, the sweetness of raisins, and the crunch of almonds. What's not to like?

1 medium onion, cut in thin wedges
2 cups (240 g) coarsely chopped yellow squash
1 can (28 ounces, or 785 g) diced tomatoes, undrained
4 ounces (115 g) chopped jalapeño chilies
2 cups (475 ml) water
2 tablespoons (12.6 g) curry powder
11 ounces (310 g) couscous
1 cup (110 g) slivered almonds
½ cup (75 g) raisins
Fresh cilantro sprigs, optional

In a slow cooker, combine the onion, squash, tomatoes with juice, jalapeños, water, and curry powder. Cover and cook on low for 4 to 6 hours or on high for 2 to 3 hours. Stir in the couscous. Turn off the heat of the slow cooker. Cover and let stand for 5 minutes. Using a fork, fluff the couscous mixture.

To serve, sprinkle each serving with almonds and raisins. Garnish with cilantro sprigs, if using.

Yield: 8 servings

BAKED POTATOES
If you had known that baking potatoes in your slow cooker was so easy, wouldn't you have tried it before?

6 baking potatoes, unpeeled, scrubbed
Olive oil
Salt

Rub each potato with oil and sprinkle it with salt. Wrap each potato in foil. Place all of the potatoes in a slow cooker. Cover and cook on low for 6 to 8 hours or on high for 3 to 4 hours, or until the potatoes are fork-tender.

Yield: 6 servings

▶*Did You Know?*
You can cook as few or as many potatoes as you wish in the slow cooker. Just make sure the potatoes fit in one layer on the bottom of the slow cooker, and adjust the cooking time accordingly.

SAUCY CREAM CHEESE POTATOES
These are creamy, tender potatoes with just a hint of garlic. They're perfect as a side dish or as a lunchtime meal, especially with a scallion garnish.

6 large potatoes, unpeeled, scrubbed, and thinly sliced, divided
One 8-ounce (225-g) package cream cheese, cut into cubes, divided
1 teaspoon (6 g) garlic salt, divided
½ teaspoon black pepper, divided

Coat the crock of a slow cooker with nonstick cooking spray.

Put one-third of the potato slices in the slow cooker and spread them out evenly. Top them with half of the cream cheese and sprinkle them with half of the garlic salt and pepper. Layer on another third of the potato slices and the rest of the cream cheese, and sprinkle the mixture with the remainder of the garlic salt and pepper. Spread the rest of the potato slices over the top.

Cover and cook on low for 6 to 8 hours or on high for 3 to 4 hours, or until the potato slices are tender.

Before serving, stir the mixture well.

Yield: 6 servings

▶*Try This!*
For extra color, flavor, and protein, top this dish with shredded Swiss or white Cheddar cheese and a sprinkling of paprika just before serving; serve bubbly hot as soon as the cheese melts.

EASY CHEESY POTATO CASSEROLE
Home-style good! The creamy potato flavor and tasty hash browns are enhanced by the melted Cheddar.

One 24-ounce (680-g) bag frozen Southern-style chunky hash brown potatoes, partially thawed
One 10¾-ounce (305-g) can condensed cream of potato soup
Salt, to taste
Black pepper, to taste
1 cup (113 g) grated Cheddar cheese

In a slow cooker, combine the hash browns and soup. Stir to mix. Cover and cook on low for 6 to 8 hours or on high for 3 to 4 hours. Stir the mixture. Season with salt and pepper. Sprinkle it with the cheese. Cover and cook for another 15 to 30 minutes, or until the cheese has melted.

Yield: 10 servings

AUTUMNAL RICH-ROOTS MEDLEY POTATOES

This recipe is a warming, cold-weather medley that deliciously accompanies any roasted meat dish.

2 sweet potatoes, peeled and chopped into ½-inch (1.3 cm) dice
3 parsnips, peeled and chopped into ½-inch (1.3 cm) dice 1 small celery root, peeled and chopped into ½-inch (1.3 cm) dice
2 red cooking apples, peeled, cored, and sliced
1½ cups (353 ml) vegetable or chicken broth (To make your own, see "Freshest Vegetable Stock" on page 6 or "Chicken Stock" on page 6.)
½ cup (120 ml) apple cider
½ teaspoon ground nutmeg
½ teaspoon salt

In a slow cooker, combine the potatoes, parsnips, celery root, and apples.

In a small bowl, whisk together the broth, cider, nutmeg, and salt. Pour the mixture over the potatoes in the slow cooker. Cover and cook on low for 6 to 7 hours on high for 4 to 5 hours, or until the vegetables are tender. The celery root will be firmer than the other veggies, but it should not be crunchy.

Using an immersion blender, partially purée the mixture. Adjust the seasonings to taste.

Yield: 8 to 10 servings

▶*Health Bite*

Parsnips are one of the most underappreciated vegetables, and when you taste them in this recipe you'll instantly know why. They're as sweet as sugar, beautifully complement the flavor and texture of celery and apples, and happen to be extraordinarily low in calories while providing a nice blend of fiber (2.8 grams per 1½2 cup [112 g]), potassium (286 mg), and folate (45 mcg). Sweet potatoes are the best the potato family has to offer, rich in the carotenoids such as beta-carotene that give it that deep orange-red color, fairly high in fiber (slightly less than 6 grams per large potato), and with almost twice the potassium of a banana.

AU GRATIN POTATOES

Here's another successful pairing of hash browns and cheesy goodness. Enjoy it with breakfast, lunch, or dinner.

Two 10¾-ounce (305-g) cans condensed Cheddar cheese soup
One 13-ounce (390-ml) can evaporated milk
One 32-ounce (905-g) bag frozen hash brown potatoes, partially thawed
Salt, to taste
Black pepper, to taste

Coat the crock of a slow cooker with nonstick cooking spray.

In the slow cooker, combine the soup and milk. Add the hash browns and stir again. Cover and cook on low for 7 to 9 hours or on high for 3½ to 4½ hours.

Before serving, stir the mixture and season it with salt and pepper.

Yield: 10 servings

▶*Add It In!*

- *Garnish the dish with canned french-fried onion rings just before serving it.*

- *If you wish, you can substitute 10 thinly sliced or cubed baking potatoes for the hash browns in this recipe.*

HOLIDAY SWEET POTATO CASSEROLE

Every family seems to have a special recipe for sweet potato casserole. This one is less sweet than most. It skips the caramel and marshmallow that are sometimes included. Any day is a holiday when you get to eat sweet potato casserole!

FOR THE TOPPING:
2 tablespoons (28 g) butter
3 tablespoons (45 ml) olive oil
¾ cup (170 g) packed brown sugar
¼ cup (30 g) whole wheat flour
3 tablespoons (45 ml) milk or water

FOR THE POTATOES:
8 large sweet potatoes, peeled and cut into chunks
1½ cups (355 ml) water
¼ to ½ teaspoon cinnamon
¼ teaspoon grated nutmeg
⅛ teaspoon allspice
Pinch of ground cloves
¼ to ½ cup (60 to 120 ml) milk, divided
½ cup (55 g) chopped pecans

To make the topping: In a large bowl, combine all of the topping ingredients. Mix thoroughly.

To make the potatoes: Coat the crock of a slow cooker with nonstick cooking spray.

Add the sweet potatoes and water. Cover and cook on low for 6 to 8 hours.

About 30 to 45 minutes before serving, increase the slow cooker heat to high.

SIDE DISHES • 205

Using a potato masher, mash the sweet potatoes in the crock. Add the cinnamon, nutmeg, allspice, cloves, and ¼ cup (60 ml) of the milk. Stir to combine.

If the potatoes are too stiff, add the remaining ¼ cup (60 ml) milk, but leave it out if they are runny.

Drop spoonfuls of the topping onto the sweet potatoes. As the topping begins to melt, spread it evenly with the back of a spoon. Sprinkle on the nuts. Serve once the topping is melted and heated throughout.

Yield: 8 servings

WARM APPLESAUCE
This homey favorite is terrific as a side dish or as a dessert served over ice cream or pound cake.

6 large cooking apples, such as Cortland
¾ cup (150 g) sugar
1 tablespoon (7 g) apple pie spice, or more to taste
¼ cup (60 ml) water

Peel and core the apples, then cut them into small chunks. In a slow cooker, combine the apples, sugar, spice, and water, stirring to combine. Cover and cook on low for 4 to 6 hours.

Yield: 6 servings

CHUNKY APPLESAUCE
It's fun and easy to make your own mouth-watering applesauce. Serve it warm, or chill it first.

6 large cooking apples, peeled, cored, and cut into chunks of uniform size
½ to ¾ cup (95 to 142 g) cinnamon sugar (To make your own, see below.)
½ teaspoon ground nutmeg
¼ cup (60 ml) water

In a slow cooker, combine the apples, cinnamon sugar, nutmeg, and water. Stir to mix.

Cover and cook on low for 4 to 6 hours.
Before serving, stir the applesauce and add more cinnamon sugar to taste.

Yield: 6 servings

▶*Cinnamon Sugar*
½ cup (100 g) granulated sugar
2 tablespoons (14 g) ground cinnamon

Put the sugar and cinnamon in a small bowl and stir to combine. Store the mixture in an airtight container in a cool place.

CRANBERRY APPLESAUCE
It's very easy to make applesauce in the slow cooker. This version has cranberries added for even more flavor. Serve this warm or refrigerate and serve chilled.

6 apples, peeled or unpeeled, cut into 1-inch (2.5 cm) cubes
½ cup (120 ml) apple juice
½ cup (55 g) fresh cranberries
¼ cup (50 g) sugar
¼ teaspoon cinnamon

In a slow cooker, combine all of the ingredients. Cover and cook on low for 3 to 4 hours, or until the apples are as soft as you like them.

Yield: 6 servings

STEWED APPLES
In this dish, dried apples are cooked in sweetened orange juice to produce a real treat.

9 ounces (225 g) dried apples
1 cup (235 ml) orange juice
1 cup (235 ml) water
½ cup (120 ml) maple syrup
1 tablespoon (15 ml) lemon juice

In a slow cooker, place the apples.

In a bowl, combine the orange juice, water, syrup, and lemon juice. Pour the mixture over the apples in the slow cooker. Cover and cook on low for 8 hours.

Yield: 6 servings

▶*Recipe Tip*
These apples are great warm, right out of the slow cooker, but they're also very good cold.

58 Curried Couscous

59 Baked Potatoes; 60 Saucy Cream Cheese Potatoes; 61 Easy Cheesy Potato Casserole; 62 Autumnal Rich-Roots Medley Potatoes; 63 Au Gratin Potatoes; 64 Holiday Sweet Potato Casserole; 65 Warm Applesauce; 66 Chunky Applesauce

67 Cranberry Applesauce; 68 Stewed Apples

SIDE DISHES • 209

DESSERTS

See pages 212-213, 216-217, 224-225, 230-231, 238-239 and 243-245 for desserts recipe photos.

CARAMEL APPLES

Here's an eternal favorite that evokes memories of fall carnivals and fairs. You can easily halve this recipe, but you'd end up with just half the fun.

8 wooden sticks
8 medium apples, washed and dried
2 pounds (910 g) caramel candies
¼ cup (60 ml) water

Insert a stick into the stem end of each apple. Line the counter with enough waxed paper to hold all the apples.

In a slow cooker, combine the caramels and water. Cover and cook on high for 1 to 1½ hours, stirring frequently.

Reduce the heat of the slow cooker to low. When the slow cooker has cooled enough to allow you to work without burning yourself, dip an apple into the hot caramel, turning the apple to coat it all the way around. Try to dip the apple up to the stick, but be careful not to burn yourself on the edge of the slow cooker. Let the excess caramel drip back into the slow cooker, then set the apple down to cool on the waxed paper. Repeat with the remaining apples.

Yield: 8 servings

SLIGHTLY DRUNKEN APPLES

This recipe uses a 1½- to 2-quart (1.4 to 1.9 L) slow cooker or a small ovenproof dish in a larger slow cooker. You can double or triple the recipe and use a larger slow cooker if you like.

4 apples, peeled if not organic, cored, and sliced
1 tablespoon (15 g) brown sugar
Juice of 2 or 3 tangerines
Juice of ½ lime or lemon
3 tablespoons (45 ml) rum, optional
1½ tablespoons (23 ml) Navan, Amaretto, or Triple Sec, optional
½ teaspoon ground ginger
½ teaspoon dried marjoram or basil (or 1 teaspoon fresh added right before serving)

In a slow cooker, place the apples.

In a bowl, combine the sugar, tangerine juice, lime juices, rum if using, Navan if using, ginger, and marjoram. Pour the mixture over the apples in the slow cooker. Cover and cook on low for 6 to 8 hours.

Yield: 4 servings

BAKED APPLES WITH RAISINS

Serve these apples warm or chilled, along with a selection of cheeses.

6 baking apples, cored
½ cup (73 g) raisins
1 cup (189 g) cinnamon sugar (To make your own, see "Cinnamon Sugar" on page 206.)
1 cup (235 ml) hot water

In a slow cooker, place the apples upright. Fill the center of each apple with one-sixth of the raisins.

In a small bowl, combine the cinnamon sugar and water. Pour the mixture over the apples. Cover and cook on low for 3 to 5 hours.

Yield: 6 servings

▶*Add It!*
Add 2 tablespoons (28 g) butter, melted, and ½ teaspoon apple pie spice to the Cinnamon Sugar-hot water mixture.

HOMEY BAKED APPLES

We like the tartness that dried cranberries bring to the mix, but you can substitute any of your favorite dried fruits here.

6 large cooking apples, such as Cortland, cored
½ cup (120 ml) water
1½ (180 g) cups dried cranberries
1 cup (340 g) maple syrup

In a slow cooker, place the apples upright. Pour the water into the bottom of the cooker. Fill the center of each apple with the cranberries. Drizzle the syrup over the apples. Cover and cook on low for 3 to 5 hours, or until the apples are soft but not mushy.

Yield: 6 servings

SPICED CANDIED APPLES AND YAMS WITH RAW CHOCOLATE DRIZZLE

Here's an example of unusual combinations of ingredients used in a way that makes you think, "Why didn't someone think of this before?" The tang of the apples in this dish creates a perfect harmony with the soft sweetness of the yams, made even more perfect by the visual harmony of the rich red and orange. An unexpected flavor delight is added by the dark chocolate. This sweet-as-pie dessert has a minimum of added sugar. It's just not needed because of the inherent sweetness of the cooked yams and apples. Fun fact, courtesy of Alan Gaby, M.D., nutritional medicine specialist: Cinnamon is an ancient herbal medicine mentioned in Chinese texts as long ago as 4,000 years. Did we mention that this dessert is ridiculously delish?

FOR THE APPLES AND YAMS:
¾ cup (180 ml) apple cider
⅓ cup (106 g) honey
2 cinnamon sticks
4 whole cloves
4 allspice berries
1 yam or sweet potato, peeled and cut into 1¼2-inch (1.3 cm) dice
3 Granny Smith apples, unpeeled, cored, and halved

FOR THE CHOCOLATE DRIZZLE:
2 tablespoons (14 g) dark cocoa powder, such as Callebaut Extra Brute
2 tablespoons (14 g) raw cacao powder or more cocoa powder
2 tablespoons (40 g) brown rice syrup
2 tablespoons (30 ml) unsweetened vanilla almond milk
1 teaspoon melted coconut oil
½ teaspoon vanilla stevia
Pinch of salt

To make the apples and yams: In a slow cooker, combine the cider and honey. Whisk to mix. Add the cinnamon sticks, cloves, allspice, and yam. Toss to coat. Stir the mixture gently, add the apples, cut sides up, and baste the apples with the liquid. Cover and cook on high for 2 hours, or until the apples and yams are tender, basting one or two times at the end of cooking time. When the fruit is tender, make the Chocolate Drizzle.

To make the chocolate dizzle: In a small bowl, whisk together the cocoa and cacao powders, syrup, milk, oil, stevia, and salt until very smooth.

To serve, remove the apples and place one half on each plate. Spoon an equal amount of yams into the halves, and drizzle them lightly with the Chocolate Drizzle.

Yield: 6 servings

SPICED APPLES

With the slow cooker, it's easy to make these delicious spicy apples. And the flavor is better than anything you can get out of a jar or can.

4 pounds (1.8 kg) apples, pealed, cored, and sliced
½ cup (100 g) sugar
½ teaspoon sugar
1 cup (235 ml) water
1 tablespoon (15 ml) lemon juice

In a slow cooker, combine the sugar and cinnamon. Mix with the apples. Blend in the water and juice. COver and cook on low for 5 to 7 hours or on high for 2½ to 3½ hours.

Yield: 8 servings

EARL GREY POACHED PEARS

Poached pears are the ultimate grown-up dessert. Peeled and left whole, they add a bit of drama to a dinner party. Chopped up, they make a perfect topping for vanilla ice cream.

These pears are poached in Earl Grey tea sweetened with brown sugar. The flavor is reminiscent of a floral caramel. In fact, you could use the leftover poaching liquid and reduce it on the stove until it's thicker. Add it to coffee or tea, or top some other dessert with it.

4 pears, peeled, left whole or cored and chopped
1 cup (235 ml) Earl Grey tea (steep 1 tablespoon [4 g] tea in 1 cup (235 ml) hot water for 4 minutes)
½ cup (115 g) brown sugar
½ vanilla bean, scraped, or 1 teaspoon vanilla extract
Pinch of salt

In a slow cooker, place the pears.

In a bowl, combine the tea, sugar, vanilla, and salt. Pour the mixture over the pears in the slow cooker. Cover and cook on high for 11¼2 to 21¼2 hours.

If you're using whole pears, place them on their sides and turn them every 30 minutes.

Yield: 4 servings

1 Caramel Apples

2 Slightly Drunken Apples

POACHED PEARS IN RED WINE

This dish is simple and elegant as a stand-alone dessert, or you can use these pears in tarts or napoleons.

6 pears
2 cups (400 g) sugar
4 cups (940 ml) red wine

Peel the pears, leaving the stems intact. Put the pears into a slow cooker.

In a small bowl, combine the sugar and wine. Pour the mixture over the pears in the slow cooker. Cover and cook on low for 4 hours, or until the pears are soft but not mushy.

Using a slotted spoon, remove the pears from the poaching liquid.

Serve the pears warm or cold.

To make a syrup to accompany the pears, boil the poaching liquid in a saucepan over high heat until it thickens.

Yield: 6 servings

▶*Add It!*

For added flavor, add 2 tablespoons (14 g) ground cinnamon to the sugar-wine mixture.

FRESH PINEAPPLE WITH COCONUT LIME RUM SAUCE

Who doesn't love pineapple? This rich, juicy fruit conjures up thoughts of tropical paradises and mixed drinks with parasols on the beach. Hot pineapple is a unique taste treat, and slow cooking really brings out the natural sweetness of the fruit.

2 tablespoons (30 ml) coconut rum
1 fresh pineapple, peeled and quartered lengthwise, 1 tablespoon (15 ml) juice reserved
Juice and zest of 1 lime
½ to 1 teaspoon vanilla stevia or 1 to 2 teaspoons Sucanat or xylitol
4 teaspoons (7 g) coconut flakes

In a small bowl, whisk together the rum, pineapple juice, lime juice and zest, and stevia.

In a slow cooker, lay the pineapple. Pour the sauce over all. Cover and cook on low for 3 to 4 hours, or until very tender. Garnish with the coconut.

Yield: 8 servings

▶*Health Bite*

Fresh pineapple doesn't ripen after picking, so choose a ripe one. How can you tell? The leaves should be green and look fresh, and the "eyes" on the skin should be plump. The pineapple should be firm and give off a strong, sweet smell of pineapple.

To prepare a fresh pineapple, twist the crown from the pineapple, slice it in half the long way, and then quarter it. You can then cut out the core and cut off the rind.

Along with all the lovely beach-y associations, pineapple is a nutritious gem. Its main claim to fame is an amazing substance called bromelain, which is a rich source of enzymes with many health benefits, including aiding digestion, speeding wound healing, and reducing inflammation.

It's also a natural blood thinner, preventing excessive blood platelet stickiness.

On top of that, pineapple has almost 100 percent of the Daily Value for manganese, which is an essential trace mineral needed for healthy skin, bone, and cartilage formation.

GINGERED HONEY PEARS WITH CINNAMON STICKS

Pear juice never causes bad or allergic reactions or problems with digestion, is tolerated by just about everyone, and tastes great. Really ripe delicious Anjou pears are just heaven to bite into. Here the sublime is made even more sublime by seasoning with ginger, honey, and cinnamon. The names of those three spices together sounds almost as good as they taste. The sweetness comes from the fruit and the mineral-rich honey, but the base is pure fruit–one of the healthiest desserts you can choose.

6 Anjou pears, peeled
1½ cups (353 ml) pear nectar
1 cup (235 ml) water
½ cup (160 g) honey
½ cup (120 ml) ginger brandy or Poire William
6 thick slices fresh ginger, about the size of quarters
3 cinnamon sticks
2 tablespoons (16 g) minced candied ginger, optional

In a slow cooker, arrange the pears in a single layer.

In a medium saucepan, heat the nectar, water, honey, brandy, fresh ginger, and cinnamon sticks over mediumhigh heat. Bring to a boil, stirring frequently. Let the mixture boil for 30 seconds, and then pour the mixture evenly over the pears. Cover and cook on low for 4 to 5 hours or on high for 2 to 3 hours, or until the pears are soft, removing the lid and basting the pears for the last half hour of cooking time.

Before serving, remove the cinnamon sticks and ginger

coins. Serve warm with a little sauce poured over the top. Garnish with the candied ginger crumbles, if using.

Yield: 6 servings

PEACHES WITH BUTTERSCOTCH SAUCE
These are delectable. You can serve them as is, with a little heavy cream, with whipped topping, or with a scoop of vanilla ice cream.

1 pound (455 g) frozen, unsweetened, sliced peaches
2 teaspoons lemon juice
⅓ cup (8 g) sugar
2 tablespoons (42 g) honey
½ teaspoon blackstrap molasses
2 tablespoons (28 ml) heavy cream
¼ teaspoon cinnamon
2 tablespoons (28 g) butter, melted
Cornstarch

In a slow cooker, place the peaches.
    In a bowl, stir together the juice, sugar, honey, molasses, cream, cinnamon, and butter. Pour the mixture over the peaches. Cover and cook on low for 6 hours.
    Thicken the sauce to a creamy consistency with a little cornstarch and serve hot.

Yield: 6 servings

PEACHES WITH DUMPLINGS
This is a great dessert on those summer days when the peaches are at their ripest.

3 pounds (1365 g) peaches
1¾ cups (350 g) sugar, divided
2 cups (250 g) self-rising flour
¾ cup (170 g) shortening, such as Crisco
1 cup (235 ml) water

Bring a large pot of water to a boil and drop the peaches in for 30 seconds.
    Drain and run under cold water to cool. Peel the peaches and cut the flesh from the pits (stones) and into wedges.
    In a slow cooker, combine the peaches and 1 cup (200 g) of the sugar. Stir to mix.
    In a mixing bowl, combine the flour and the remaining ¾ cup (150 g) sugar. Stir. Add the shortening.
    Using a pastry cutter or your fingers, cut the shortening into the dry ingredients. Stir the water into the dry ingredients just enough to make a batter.
    Drop the batter by spoonfuls onto the peaches in the slow cooker. Cover and cook on high for 2 hours, or until the biscuit batter is cooked through and the peaches are bubbling.

Yield: 4 to 6 servings

▶*Add It!*
Adding 1 teaspoon (2.2 g) nutmeg or 2 teaspoons (4.6 g) cinnamon to the peaches makes a nice spice accent. Feel free to serve with ice cream or whipped cream.

GLORIOUS GLAZED BANANAS
Here we've taken the simple and healthy banana and made its natural sweetness the centerpiece of this dessert. One tablespoon of butter or coconut oil adds only about 100 or so calories, all good fat (yes, you heard that right), and the only additional sweetener comes from noncaloric (or virtually noncaloric) xylitol or Sucanat plus stevia. The rum adds a flavor that perfectly complements the vanilla overtones of the stevia and the freshly squeezed lime juice.

1 tablespoon (14 g) butter or coconut oil, softened
4 large bananas (ripe but not soft), peeled and halved lengthwise
2 tablespoons (30 g) Sucanat or xylitol
2 tablespoons (30 ml) lime juice
2 tablespoons (30 ml) coconut rum
½ teaspoon vanilla stevia (We like NuNaturals.)

Smear the butter evenly over the bottom of a slow cooker insert. Lay the bananas, cut sides down, in one layer on the bottom. You may have to cut them in half widthwise to get them to fit.
    In a small bowl, whisk together the Sucanat, juice, rum, and stevia. Drizzle the mixture evenly over the bananas. Cover and cook for on low for about 2 hours, or until the bananas are hot and tender.

Yield: 8 servings

3 Baked Apples with Raisins; 4 Homey Baked Apples; 5 Spiced Candied Apples and Yams with Raw Chocolate Drizzle; 6 Earl Grey Poached Pears; 7 Poached Pears in Red Wine

8 Fresh Pineapple with Coconut Lime Rum Sauce; 9 Gingered Honey Pears with Cinnamon Sticks; 10 Peaches with Butterscotch Sauce; 11 Peaches with Dumplings; 12 Glorious Glazed Bananas; 13 Run Raisin Bananas; 14 Hot Spiced Pears; 15 Rhubarb Flummery

DESSERTS • 217

RUM RAISIN BANANAS

It doesn't get any sweeter than this. These bananas are perfect by themselves, but they're also good over vanilla ice cream.

3 tablespoons (45 ml) dark rum, divided
¼ cup (35 g) raisins
3 tablespoons (42 g) butter
¼ cup (60 g) brown sugar
4 bananas
¼ teaspoon nutmeg
¼ teaspoon cinnamon

In a bowl, pour 2 tablespoons (30 ml) of the rum over the raisins.

In a slow cooker, place the butter, sugar, and the remaining 1 tablespoon (15 ml) rum. Cover and cook on high until the butter and sugar have melted.

Peel the bananas and cut them in half lengthwise. Place the bananas in the slow cooker. Cover and cook on high for 30 minutes, turning halfway through the time. Pour the reserved rum and raisins over the bananas and cook for 10 minutes longer.

In a bowl, combine the nutmeg and cinnamon. Sprinkle the mixture over the bananas before serving.

Yield: 4 servings

HOT SPICED PEARS

For centuries, people have enjoyed the spicy goodness of baked pears. This luscious dessert is flavorful enough to stand alone, but it's also fabulous served over waffles, pancakes, pound cake, or ice cream.

8 pears, peeled, cored, and sliced
One 8-ounce (225-g) can pineapple chunks, undrained
1 tablespoon (7 g) apple pie spice

In a slow cooker, combine the pear, pineapple and juice, and apple pie spice. Stir to mix. Cover and cook on low for 8 to 10 hours.

Stir the mixture again and serve it warm or cold.

Yield: 8 servings

▶*Try This!*
Add ¼ cup (36 g) raisins, and substitute apples or peaches for half of the pears. Top with whipped cream or ice cream.

RHUBARB FLUMMERY

This is a simple, old-fashioned dessert. It's great with a little heavy cream or whipped topping.

1 pound (455 g) frozen rhubarb
½ cup (12 g) sugar
½ cup (120 ml) water
⅛ teaspoon orange extract
Cornstarch

In a slow cooker, combine the rhubarb, sugar, water, and orange extract. Cover and cook on low for 5 to 6 hours.

When the time's up, the rhubarb will be very soft. Using a fork, mash it to a rough pulp.

Thicken the sauce to a soft pudding consistency with cornstarch. Serve hot or cold.

Yield: 6 servings

HOT SPICED FRUIT

This is great for Thanksgiving or during the winter. It's best served the next day to allow the spices to blend with the fruit. You can also add apricots, Queen Anne cherries, or any other fruit you like.

1 pound (455 g) peaches canned in water, undrained
1 pound (455 g) pears canned in water, undrained
1 pound (455 g) pineapple canned in water, undrained
1 cup (250 g) stewed prunes
½ cup (160 g) orange marmalade
2 tablespoons (28 g) butter
1 stick cinnamon
⅛ teaspoon nutmeg
⅛ teaspoon ground cloves

Drain the liquid from all fruit, reserving 1½ cups (355 ml) to make the syrup.

In a saucepan, combine the marmalade, butter, cinnamon stick, nutmeg, cloves, and reserved liquid. Bring the mixture to a boil, and then simmer it for 3 to 4 minutes.

Cut the fruit into chunks and gently add to saucepan.

Transfer to a slow cooker and cover and cook on low for at least 4 hours.

Yield: 12 servings

BRANDIED FRUIT

This makes a marvelous topping for ice cream or pound cake. Or you could just attack it with a spoon.

20 ounces (560 g) pineapple chunks, undrained
4 plums, pitted and cut into pieces
2 apples, cored and cubed
2 pears, cored and cubed
½ cup (65 g) dried apricots
⅓ cup (75 g) brown sugar
¼ cup (55 g) butter, melted
¼ cup (60 ml) brandy
2 tablespoons (19 g) pearl tapioca, crushed

In a slow cooker, combine the fruit.
    In a small bowl, combine the sugar, butter, brandy, and tapioca. Pour the mixture over the fruit in the slow cooker. Stir to mix. Cover and cook on low for 3½ to 4 hours.

Yield: 12 servings

JUICE-SWEETENED TROPICAL FRUIT COMPOTE

Compotes originated in France in the 1600s. They were made by immersing fruit in water with sugar and spices and simmering over gentle heat. But compotes are perfectly suited for slow cookers, which simmer and mix the flavors perfectly. The added kick from the coconut-lime combo puts this dish over the taste top.

2 cups (330 g) chopped fresh pineapple, ¾ cup (180 ml) juice reserved
2 ripe mangoes, peeled, pitted, and chopped
4 ripe kiwis, peeled and chopped
2 cups (340 g) chopped ripe honeydew melon
2 ripe bananas, peeled and sliced
1 tablespoon (15 ml) lime juice
2 teaspoons lime zest
¼ cup (20 g) shaved coconut
1½ tablespoons (16 g) quick-cooking tapioca

In a slow cooker, combine all of the ingredients. Stir gently to mix. Cover and cook on low for 4 to 5 hours or on high for 2 to 3 hours, or until the fruit is very tender. Stir well before serving.

Yield: 8 to 10 servings

▶*Recipe Notes*
- *This unique version of the classic compote features tropical fruits, all of which are high in water and nutrient dense—meaning that, for not too many calories, you get a whole lot of nutrition. That's the opposite, of, say, cheesecake or ice cream, which are high in calories and not so high in nutrients.*

- *There's a load of vitamin C here (from the kiwi, melons, pineapple, and mangoes), beta-carotene from the mangoes, and the digestive enzyme bromelain from the pineapple.*

- *This compote is excellent chilled and stirred into Greek yogurt for a light dessert, or served warm over pancakes or waffles for a filling snack or dessert.*

GOLDEN FRUIT COMPOTE

This compote is as delightfully fruity as it is pretty when served cold with white cake, pound cake, or vanilla ice cream. It's also wonderful served warm as an alternative to cranberry sauce.

Two 20-ounce (570-g) cans pineapple chunks, undrained
One 15-ounce (417-g) package golden raisins or dried mixed apples, peaches, and apricots
1 cup (120 ml) water
½ teaspoon apple pie spice

In a slow cooker, combine the pineapple, raisins, water, and apple pie spice. Stir to mix. Cover and cook on low for 8 to 10 hours, or until the flavors have melded and the mixture has become very thick, stirring every 2 hours and adding water as needed.

Yield: 10 servings

▶*Add It!*
Substitute apple juice for the water.

TAPIOCA PUDDING

Yes, you can cook tapioca in a slow cooker. This makes great, custard-flavored tapioca.

8 cups (1.9 L) milk
1¼ cups (250 g) sugar
1 cup (125 g) tapioca
1 cup (120 ml) egg substitute
1 teaspoon vanilla extract

In a slow cooker, combine the milk and sugar, stirring until the sugar is dissolved as well as possible. Stir in the tapioca. Cover and cook on high for 3 hours.
    In a small bowl, beat the egg substitute slightly. Beat in the vanilla and about 1 cup (235 ml) of the hot milk from slow cooker. When well mixed, stir the egg mixture into the slow cooker. Cover and cook on high for 20 more minutes.
    Transfer the mixture to a container. Chill in the fridge for several hours.

Yield: 10 servings

TAPIOCA PUDDING FOR TWO

Sometimes you don't want to have leftover dessert to tempt you. This makes just the right amount for two people. Make it the night before to have dessert after dinner the next night.

This recipe uses a 1½- to 2-quart (1.4 to 1.9 L) slow cooker. You can double or triple the recipe and use a larger slow cooker if you like.

2 cups (470 ml) milk
¼ cup (38 g) tapioca pearls (not soaked)
¼ cup (50 g) sugar
1 teaspoon vanilla extract
Pinch of salt

Coat the crock of a slow cooker with nonstick cooking spray.
In the slow cooker, combine all of the ingredients. Cover and cook on low for 3 hours or on high for 1½ hours. Stir and transfer to a container to cool for 1 hour, and then chill in the fridge overnight. The pudding will still seem very runny, but it will set up in the fridge.

Yield: 2 large servings

▶ *Recipe Variations*

You don't need to have "Plain Jane" tapioca just because you're showing some restraint. Try adding in a few drops of almond extract or orange flower water in place of the vanilla. Of course, you can always add dried fruit, applesauce, or even a few chocolate chips.

FRUITED TAPIOCA

This tapioca variation uses pineapple, but you could substitute other fruits as well.

2¼ cups (535 ml) water
2½ cups (570 ml) pineapple juice
½ cup (63 g) tapioca pudding mix
1 cup (200 g) sugar
15 ounces (420 g) crushed pineapple, undrained

In a slow cooker, combine the water, juice, tapioca, and sugar. Mix them together. Cover and cook on high for 3 hours. Stir in the pineapple. Chill for several hours.

Yield: 6 servings

TURKISH DELIGHT TAPIOCA PUDDING

Turkish delight is a gel candy from the Middle East. Although it comes in many flavors, our favorite is rosewater. This pudding has that wonderful sweet floral flavor in a pudding that's textured with tapioca pearls.

4 cups (940 ml) milk
½ cup (75 g) tapioca pearls (not soaked)
½ cup (100 g) sugar
Pinch of salt
1 teaspoon rosewater (Make sure it's labeled food grade.)

Coat the crock of a slow cooker with nonstick cooking spray.
In the slow cooker, combine the milk, tapioca, sugar, and salt. Cover and cook on low for 3½ hours or on high for 2 hours. Stir in the rosewater.
Transfer the mixture to a container to cool for 1 hour, then chill in the fridge overnight. The pudding will still seem very runny, but it will set up in the fridge.

Yield: 6 servings

▶ *Recipe Note*
This recipe works fine in a 4-quart (3.8 L) slow cooker; however, you should double it if you are using a 6 quart (5.7 L).

LOW-CAL COCOA TAPIOCA

This recipe is the easiest way to whip up a rich, creamy tapioca dessert with virtually no fuss.

2 cans (12 ounces, or 353 ml each) evaporated skim milk
2 eggs
¼ cup (28 g) dark cocoa powder (such as Cacao Barry Extra Brute)
¼ cup (60 g) xylitol or erythritol
3 tablespoons (45 g) Sucanat (Or substitute more xylitol or erythritol for a no-added sugar option.)
1 teaspoon vanilla stevia
½ teaspoon ground cinnamon
¼ teaspoon salt
⅓ cup (58 g) small pearl tapioca

In a medium bowl, whisk together the evaporated milk and eggs until smooth and well incorporated. Whisk in the cocoa powder, xylitol, Sucanat, stevia, cinnamon, salt, and tapioca.
Transfer the contents to a slow cooker. Cover and cook on low for 2 hours, whisking well at 1 hour. Whisk well at the end of cooking time to break up the bottom layer and incorporate the lumps before serving.

Yield: 6 servings

▶Health Bite
Real cocoa is a rich treasure trove of plant chemicals called flavanols, which have been found to have a huge number of health benefits. A study in Circulation, *the prestigious journal of the American Heart Association, found that women who ate a small amount of chocolate every week had lower risks of heart disease. This comes on the heels of a ton of research showing that cocoa flavanols lower blood pressure and improve blood flow, making blood platelets less sticky. The key to getting these benefits is to use high-cocoa chocolate. There are no flavanols in white or milk chocolate, so you should always choose a dark chocolate that has no less than 60 percent cocoa.*

The evaporated skim milk in this recipe is low-cal, and using xylitol as a sweetener keeps the calorie count down and blunts the impact on your blood sugar. Just for good measure we threw in a couple of eggs both for creaminess and for extra protein.

CHOCOLATE PUDDING

This is really more of a cake than a pudding, but it's good no matter what you call it.

⅓ cup (67 g) sugar
2 tablespoons (28 g) butter
¼ cup (60 ml) egg substitute
1 ounce (28 g) unsweetened chocolate, melted and cooled
1¼ cups (156 g) flour
1 teaspoon baking soda
½ cup (120 ml) buttermilk
½ teaspoon vanilla extract
½ cup (120 ml) warm water

Coat two 1-pound (455 g) vegetable can with nonstick cooking spray.

In a bowl, using an electric mixer, cream the sugar and butter together. Add the egg substitute and mix well. Beat in the chocolate.

In a separate bowl, stir together the flour and baking soda. Add to the sugar mixture alternately with buttermilk and vanilla; beat well.

Divide the mixture into the prepared cans. Cover tightly with foil.

Place the cans in a slow cooker. Pour the water around the cans. Cover and cook on high for 1½ hours. Carefully remove the cans from the slow cooker. Cool for 10 minutes; unmold.

Yield: 8 servings

PUMPKIN PUDDING

Like pumpkin pie without the crust, this is sure to become a favorite.

1 can (15 ounces, or 420 g) unsweetened pumpkin
1½ cups (355 ml) evaporated milk
¼ cup (50 g) sugar
¼ cup (31 g) Heart-Healthy Baking Mix (see below)
½ cup (120 ml) egg substitute
2 teaspoons pumpkin pie spice
1 teaspoon lemon peel

Coat the crock of a slow cooker with nonstick cooking spray.

In the slow cooker, combine all of the ingredients. Stir until all of the lumps disappear. Cover and cook on low for 3 hours. Serve warm or cold.

Yield: 8 servings

▶Heart-Healthy Baking Mix
This makes a mix similar to Reduced Fat Bisquick but even lower in fat. Use it in any recipes that call for baking mix. You can also reduce the sodium if you buy sodium-free baking powder. For unrefrigerated storage, use trans fat-free shortening.

6 cups (750 g) flour
3 tablespoons (41 g) baking powder
⅓ cup (75 g) unsalted butter

Stir the flour and baking powder together. Cut in the butter with pastry blender or 2 knives until the mixture resembles coarse crumbs. Store in a container with a tight-fitting lid in the refrigerator.

Yield: 12 servings

PUMPKIN PIE PUDDING

This tastes just like pumpkin pie. It's perfect for those times you have a gluten-intolerant guest (or a crust hater) over for dinner.

9½ ounces (270 g) firm tofu (about ½ package)
2½ cups (613 g) pumpkin purée, (To make your own, see "Perfect Pumpkin Purée on page 16.)
½ cup (120 ml) maple syrup
2 tablespoons (30 g) packed brown sugar
1 teaspoon cinnamon
½ teaspoon allspice
⅛ teaspoon ground ginger
⅛ teaspoon ground cloves

Coat the crock of a slow cooker with nonstick cooking spray.

In a blender, purée all of the ingredients until smooth. Pour into the slow cooker. Cover and cook on low for 5 to 6 hours or on high for 2½ to 3 hours, or until the top stops being jiggly and cracks a bit, just like a baked pumpkin pie.

Serve warm or chilled.

Yield: 6 servings

▶*Serving Suggestion*
Make a topping bar by using small bowls on a tray to bring to the table when you serve this pudding. Offer granola, chopped nuts, marshmallows, or even candied cranberries.

ANTIOXIDANT-RICH SWEET POTATO CARROT PUDDING
Vegetables for dessert? Why not!

2 cups (220 g) grated sweet potato
2 cups (220 g) grated carrot
1 small baking apple, such as McIntosh, peeled, cored, and grated
1 cup (235 ml) heavy cream
1 egg
3 tablespoons (45 g) Sucanat or xylitol
1 teaspoon vanilla extract
1½ teaspoons ground cinnamon
½ teaspoon ground cardamom
¼ teaspoon ground cloves
½ teaspoon salt

In a slow cooker, combine the potato, carrot, and apple.

In a bowl, using an electric mixer, beat together the cream, egg, Sucanat, vanilla, cinnamon, cardamom, cloves, and salt. Pour the mixture over the potato mixer in the slow cooker. Cover and cook on low for 4 to 6 hours or on high for 2 to 3 hours, or until the vegetables are tender. Using an immersion blender or in batches in a countertop blender, purée the mixture until it's mostly smooth.

Yield: 8 servings

▶*Health Bite*
Here's a little nutrition trivia for you: When vegetables or fruits are orange or yellow, it means they're filled with beta-carotene and other members of the carotenoid family. They're also rich in vitamin A. One cup (130 g) of carrots contains more than 21,000 IUs of vitamin A, 10,000 micrograms of beta-carotene, and 4,000 micrograms of its relative, alpha-carotene, and that's not counting the fiber, calcium, and potassium.

One medium sweet potato has almost 4 grams of fiber, a whopping 542 milligrams of potassium, 13,000 micrograms of beta-carotene, and almost 22,000 IUs of vitamin A.

CARROT PUDDING
This tempting pudding, cooked in a fluted mold, is great for your holiday meal. But you don't have to wait for a holiday.

1¼ cups (156 g) flour
1 teaspoon baking powder
½ teaspoon baking soda
½ teaspoon cinnamon
½ teaspoon ground nutmeg
½ cup (120 ml) egg substitute
¾ cup (170 g) packed brown sugar
½ cup (112 g) butter
1 cup (130 g) sliced carrots
1 apple, peeled, cored, and cut in eighths
1 medium potato, peeled and cut in pieces
¾ cup (110 g) raisins

Grease and flour a 6-cup (1.4 L) mold.

In a bowl, stir together the flour, baking powder, baking soda, cinnamon, and nutmeg.

In a blender, combine the egg substitute, sugar, and butter until smooth. Add the carrot to the blender; blend until chopped. Add the apple; blend until chopped. Add potato; blend until finely chopped. Stir the carrot mixture and raisins into the dry ingredients; mix well.

Turn the mixture into the prepared mold; cover tightly with foil. Place in a slow cooker. Cover and cook on high for 4 hours. Remove from the cooker. Cool for 10 minutes; unmold.

Yield: 8 servings

STEAMY, CREAMY, HIGH-CALCIUM CHAI PUDDING
Chai has achieved a well-deserved popularity.

2 cans (12 ounces, or 353 ml) evaporated skim milk
⅓ cup (80 g) small pearl tapioca
½ cup (120 g) Sucanat (Or substitute xylitol or erythritol for part or all of the Sucanat for less sugar.)
¾ teaspoon ground cinnamon
¾ teaspoon ground cardamom
¾ teaspoon ground ginger
½ teaspoon ground mace
¼ teaspoon ground cloves
¼ teaspoon black pepper
Pinch of salt
1 egg, beaten

In a slow cooker, combine the milk, tapioca, Sucanat, cinnamon, cardamom, ginger, mace, cloves, pepper, and salt. Cover and cook on low for 90 minutes. Remove the cover and whisk in the egg until well incorporated. Cover and cook on low for 30 minutes more. Whisk well before serving.

Yield: 9 servings

▶ *Health Bite*
Replacing cream or even whole-fat milk with evaporated skim does a lot to lighten the caloric load of cheesecake, ice cream, and puddings, and best of all, it boosts the nutrition substantially. Did you know, for example, that 1 cup (235 ml) of evaporated skim milk has 742 mg of calcium, nearly 50 percent more than a similar amount of regular skim milk? Evaporated skim is also loaded with potassium (850 milligram versus the 422 in a medium-size banana) and phosphorus (499 milligram), an important constituent of bones. It's also high in protein (19 grams per cup of evaporated milk), making this a high-protein dessert as well as an utterly delectable one.

FLAN
This is a rich slow cooker flan.

2 tablespoons (42 g) honey
1 teaspoon blackstrap molasses
1 cup (235 ml) milk
1 cup (235 ml) heavy cream
6 eggs
⅔ cup (16 g) sugar
1 teaspoon vanilla extract
1 pinch nutmeg
1 pinch salt

Coat a 6-cup (1.4 L) glass casserole dish with nonstick cooking spray.

In a bowl, mix together the honey and molasses. Pour the mixture in the bottom of the prepared dish.

In a mixing bowl, preferably one with a pouring lip, combine the milk, cream, eggs, sugar, vanilla, nutmeg, and salt. Whisk everything together well. Pour the mixture into the casserole dish.

Carefully lower the casserole dish into a slow cooker. Pour water around the casserole dish to within 1 inch (2.5 cm) of the rim. Cover and cook on low for 3 to 3½ hours.

Yield: 6 servings

RICE PUDDING
Making rice pudding doesn't have to be a production. With three ingredients commonly found in the kitchen, you can have a warm and comforting dessert.

2½ cups (413 g) cooked rice
One 14-ounce (398-g) can sweetened condensed milk
3 eggs, well beaten

Coat the crock of a slow cooker with nonstick cooking spray.

In the slow cooker, combine the rice, milk, and eggs. Stir well to mix. Cover and cook on low for 4 to 6 hours, stirring only once, after 1 hour.

Serve the pudding warm or cold.

Yield: 6 servings

▶ *Try This!*
For a richer, more traditional pudding, add ¾ cup (109 g) raisins; 2 tablespoons (28 g) butter, melted; 1 teaspoon vanilla extract (5 ml); and ⅛ teaspoon ground nutmeg.

BROWN SUGAR RICE PUDDING
Who can resist rice pudding, warm from the slow cooker. Not us, that's for sure.

2½ cups (413 g) cooked rice
3 tablespoons (42 g) butter
2 teaspoons vanilla
¾ cup (175 ml) egg substitute
1½ cup (355 ml) evaporated milk
⅔ cup (150 g) brown sugar
½ teaspoon nutmeg
1 cup (145 g) raisins

Coat the crock of a slow cooker with nonstick cooking spray.

In a bowl, combine all of the ingredients. Pour the mixture into the slow cooker. Cover and cook on low for 4 to 6 hours or on high for 2 hours. Stir after the first hour.

Yield: 6 servings

16 Hot Spiced Fruit; 17 Brandied Fruit; 18 Juice-Sweetened Tropical Fruit Compote; 19 Golden Fruit Compote; 20 Tapioca pudding; 21 Tapioca Pudding for Two; 22 Fruited Tapioca; 23 Turkish Delight Tapioca Pudding

224 • THE LITTLE SLOW COOKER COOKBOOK

24 Low-Cal Cocoa Tapioca; 25 Chocolate Pudding; 26 Pumpkin Pudding; 27 Pumpkin Pie Pudding; 28 Antioxidant-Rich Sweet Potato Carrot Pudding; 29 Carrot Pudding; 30 Steamy, Creamy, High-Calcium Chai Pudding; 31 Flan

DESSERTS • 225

LOW-SUGAR COCO-NUTTY RICE PUDDING

Sweet, satisfying, and filling, this treat really hits the spot. It's perfect for dessert. Or try it as a breakfast, either alone or as an accompaniment to a couple of eggs.

2 cans (12 ounces, or 353 ml each) evaporated skim milk
½ cup (120 g) xylitol or Sucanat
⅓ cup (106 g) honey or rice syrup
¼ cup (28 g) cocoa powder (or use 1⅓ cup [37 g] raw cacao powder)
¾ cup (143 g) long-grain brown or brown basmati rice
½ cup (55 g) sliced almonds
1 teaspoon vanilla extract
1 teaspoon ground cinnamon
¼ teaspoon ground cardamom or cloves, optional

In a slow cooker, combine all of the ingredients. Mix gently. Cover and cook on low for about 5 hours, or until the rice is tender and the pudding reaches the desired thickness. Stir well before serving.

Yield: 8 servings

▶*Health Bite*
Rice pudding is usually made with white rice and whole-fat homogenized milk, not to mention a ton of added sugar. This recipe requires very little sweetener, and if you choose xylitol you'll cut down on the sugar load even more.

Cocoa is a rich source of plant chemicals called flavanols, which can lower blood pressure and protect the heart.

MANGO COCONUT RICE PUDDING

This recipe is reminiscent of mango sticky rice. Coconut milk adds creaminess while mango adds a burst of fruit flavor to the mix. We like to use light coconut milk, but regular will work fine, too.

2 mangoes, peeled and diced
1½ cups (280 g) Arborio rice
1 can (14 ounces, or 392 g) light coconut milk
1½ cups (355 ml) milk, plus more as needed
½ cup (100 g) sugar or (120 ml) maple syrup or agave nectar
1 teaspoon vanilla extract

Coat the crock of a slow cooker with nonstick cooking spray.
In the slow cooker, combine all of the ingredients. Cover and cook on high for 1½ to 2 hours.
If the mixture is not wet or creamy enough, add a little more milk.

Yield: 8 servings

▶*Serving Suggestions*
- *This is a perfect dessert for a dinner party. Prep the ingredients ahead of time. Start cooking when you sit down to dinner, and dessert will be ready by the time you are!*

- *To show off, top with more fresh mango slices and some shredded coconut.*

LOWER-SUGAR RAISIN-ORANGE PUMPKIN PIE PUDDING

This light pudding also makes a great breakfast. Seriously. Canned pumpkin is one of the few exceptions to the "don't buy vegetables in the can" rule. But if you can find it, get organic.

5 eggs
1 can (28 ounces, or 784 g) pumpkin purée (To make your own, see "Perfect Pumpkin Purée" on page 16.)
1 can (12 ounces, or 353 g) evaporated milk
½ cup (160 g) maple syrup, or more, to taste
2 teaspoons orange zest
1 teaspoon orange extract or vanilla extract
1 teaspoon ground cinnamon
½ teaspoon ground cloves
½ cup (75 g) raisins

Coat the crock of a slow cooker with nonstick cooking spray.
In a bowl, using an electric mixer, beat the eggs. Add the pumpkin, milk, syrup, zest, extract, cinnamon, and cloves and beat until well combined. Stir in the raisins. Pour the mixture into the slow cooker. Cover and cook on high for 4 to 4½ hours, or until set.

Yield: 6 servings

▶*Health Bite*
What's so great about pumpkin? "P" stands for pumpkin and also potassium. While most of us tend to think of bananas when it comes to potassium, pumpkin leaves them in the dust, providing about 33 percent more potassium per cup than a medium-size banana. And why should you care? Because several large studies suggest that increased potassium intake is associated with decreased risk of stroke as well as a generally healthier heart and lower blood pressure. Pumpkin's also ridiculously low in calories, very low in sugar, and high in fiber.

CINNAMON EGGNOG BREAD PUDDING

Smooth, creamy, and soothing, a good bread pudding is a fine ending to any meal. You can serve this one hot or cold.

1 (1-pound or 455-g) loaf cinnamon swirl bread, cut into 2-inch (5-cm) cubes
3 cups (705 ml) eggnog
3 eggs

In a slow cooker, place the bread. Press it down lightly to flatten.

In a bowl, whisk together the eggnog and eggs. Pour the mixture over the bread in the slow cooker. Using a spoon, press the bread down so that it's all soaked in the egg mixture. Cover and cook on low for 4 to 5 hours.

Serve hot or cold.

Yield: 4 to 6 servings

CHOCOLATE BREAD PUDDING

Chocolate bread pudding is decadent and cozy—all in all, it's a mouthwatering dessert. Serve this hot or cold.

5 or 6 chocolate muffins, cut into 2-inch (5-cm) cubes
3 cups (705 ml) light cream
3 eggs

In a slow cooker, place the muffins. Press them down lightly to flatten.

In a bowl, whisk together the cream and eggs. Pour the mixture over the muffins in the slow cooker. Using a spoon, press the muffin cubes down so that they are all soaked in the egg mixture. Cover and cook on low for 4 to 5 hours.

Serve hot or cold.

Yield: 4 to 6 servings

▶*Add It!*
Top this yummy offering with whipped cream and a handful of fresh raspberries.

CARAMEL BREAD PUDDING

You could eat this for breakfast, but to us, it's more of a dessert recipe.

12 ounces (340 g) sweet bread, such as challah or Hawaiian, cubed
4 cups (950 ml) milk
½ cup (100 g) sugar
¾ cup (175 ml) egg substitute
1 teaspoon vanilla extract
1 cup (225 g) caramel ice cream topping

In a slow cooker, place the bread.

In a bowl, whisk together the milk, sugar, egg substitute, and vanilla. Pour the mixture over the bread in the slow cooker. Using a spoon, press the bread down into the egg substitute mixture. Cover and chill in the fridge for at least 4 hours.

Cover and cook on low 7 to 8 hours. Before serving, drizzle the topping on top.

Yield: 12 servings

STRAWBERRY BREAD PUDDING

This is a delightful variation on bread pudding, with strawberries lifting it above the ordinary.

5 cups (250 g) cubed French bread
2½ cups (570 ml) milk, scalded
2 egg yolks
1 cup (200 g) sugar
1 teaspoon vanilla extract
2 tablespoons (28 g) butter, melted
12 ounces (340 g) strawberries, at room temperature

In a slow cooker, place the bread.

In a bowl, whisk together the milk, egg yolks, sugar, vanilla, and butter. Stir in the berries. Pour the mixture over the bread in the slow cooker. Using a spoon, gently press the bread down into the liquid (do not stir). Cover and cook on low for 4 to 6 hours.

Yield: 6 servings

INDIAN PUDDING

This is a traditional New England dessert.

6 cups (1.4 L) milk, heated, divided
1 cup (140 g) cornmeal
1 cup (340 g) dark molasses
¼ cup (50 g) sugar
¼ cup (55 g) butter
¼ teaspoon baking soda
½ cup (120 ml) egg substitute

In a saucepan, mix half of the milk with the rest of the ingredients over medium heat. Bring to a boil. Add the rest of the milk.

Transfer the mixture to a slow cooker. Cover and cook for 6 hours on low.

Yield: 6 servings

SLOW COOKER CUSTARD

This may seem like a bit of work at first glance, but it really only takes about 10 minutes. And the feeling of being transported back in time you'll get with the first taste makes it all worthwhile.

2 cups (475 ml) milk
¾ cup (175 ml) egg substitute
⅓ cup (67 g) sugar
1 teaspoon vanilla extract
¼ teaspoon cinnamon
½ teaspoon brown sugar

Coat a 1-quart (950 ml) baking dish that will fit into your slow cooker or baking insert designed for your slow cooker with nonstick cooking spray.

In a small saucepan, heat the milk until a skin forms on top. Remove from the heat and let it cool slightly.

Meanwhile, in a large bowl combine the egg substitute, sugar, and vanilla. Slowly stir the cooled milk into the egg-sugar mixture. Pour into the prepared dish.

In a small bowl, mix the cinnamon and sugar. Sprinkle over the custard mixture. Cover the baking dish or insert with foil. Set the container on a metal rack, trivet, or crumpled foil in the slow cooker. Pour hot water around dish to a depth of 1 inch (2.5 cm). Cover and cook on high for 2 to 3 hours, or until the custard is set and the blade of a knife inserted in center of the custard comes out clean. Serve warm from the baking dish or insert.

Yield: 6 servings

LOW-SUGAR LEMON HONEY CUSTARD

Simple, basic ingredients combine to make a luscious, rich custard that's high in protein and low in sugar and still tastes great.

3 cups (705 ml) milk
5 eggs
½ cup (120 g) honey
2 teaspoons vanilla extract
2 teaspoons lemon zest
Pinch of salt

Place a 6-cup (1.4 L) shallow glass baking dish into the center of a 6-quart (5.7 L) slow cooker. Using a spouted container, slowly add water to the cooker until the level reaches halfway up the empty baking dish.

In a medium saucepan, heat the milk over medium heat until steaming hot, but not boiling.

Meanwhile, in a large bowl, whisk together the eggs, honey, vanilla, zest, and salt. When the milk is ready, slowly add ¼ cup (60 ml) of the milk to the egg mixture, whisking it in to coddle the eggs. Slowly pour the remaining milk into the eggs, whisking constantly.

Gently pour the custard mix into the prepared baking dish in the slow cooker. Cover and cook on high for 2 to 4 hours, until almost set (the center will not be fully set). Remove the cover, turn off the heat, and let cool until you're able to handle the baking dish enough to remove. Serve soft and hot or chill for a couple of hours to fully set.

Yield: 4 to 6 servings

▶*Recipe Tip*
There's a trick for retrieving dishes from the hot insert or hot water baths in slow cookers:

Make temporary handles out of aluminum foil. Working with 18- to 24-inch (46 to 61 cm) lengths of foil, fold the sheets vertically until they're 2 to 3 inches (5 to 7.5 cm) wide and several layers thick. You'll need at least 4 strips. Arrange them in the bottom of the cool, dry slow cooker insert like the spokes of a wheel (good for round dishes) or parallel–2 running lengthwise and 2 running widthwise–evenly spaced (good for rectangular or square dishes), and set the filled dish on top. Bring the ends of the foil strips together in the center and fold them together tightly to make a handle that will lift and support the dish. Add your water and cook, and then you can remove the dish at the end of cooking time without waiting for it to cool.

▶*Health Bite*
Real whole foods such as eggs contribute nutrients like choline for the brain and lutein and zeaxanthin for the eyes; the protein comes from the eggs and the milk.

We go light on the sweetener, keeping glycemic impact low. Highly recommended is raw, cold-pressed honey for its richer array of enzymes and nutrients.

If possible, buy organic milk, and don't try to save on calories by going nonfat. Recent research shows that there's a compound in milk fat called trans-palmitoleic acid that boosts heart health and helps regulate blood sugar.

CHOCOLATE FUDGE CUSTARD
This really is dense and fudgy. It's intensely chocolatey, too.

1 cup (235 ml) milk
3 ounces (85 g) unsweetened baking chocolate
²/₃ cup (16 g) sugar
1 cup (235 ml) heavy cream
½ teaspoon vanilla extract
1 pinch salt
6 eggs

Coat a 6-cup (1.4 L) glass casserole dish with nonstick cooking spray.

In a saucepan, over the lowest possible heat (use a double boiler or heat diffuser if you have one), warm the milk with the chocolate. When the chocolate melts, whisk the two together and then whisk in the sugar. Pour in the cream. Whisk in the vanilla and salt. Add the eggs, one at a time, whisking each in well before adding the next one.

Put the prepared casserole dish in a slow cooker and pour water around it up to 1 inch (2.5 cm) of the top rim. Cover and cook on low for 4 hours.

Turn the heat off of the slow cooker, remove the lid, and let the water cool enough so it won't scald you before removing the casserole dish. Chill the custard well before serving.

Yield: 6 servings

SOUTHEAST ASIAN COCONUT CUSTARD
This custard has a wonderful Latino feel to it. Look for shredded unsweetened coconut in Asian markets and health food stores.

¼ cup (84 g) honey
½ teaspoon blackstrap molasses
1½ teaspoons grated ginger root, divided
1 tablespoon (15 ml) lime juice
1 can (14 ounces, or 390 ml) coconut milk
²/₃ cup (16 g) sugar
¼ teaspoon ground cardamom
½ cup (120 ml) milk
½ cup (120 ml) heavy cream
½ teaspoon vanilla extract
4 eggs
½ cup (40 g) shredded unsweetened coconut

Coat a 6-cup (1.4 L) glass casserole dish with nonstick cooking spray.

In the prepared dish, combine the honey and molasses. Cover the casserole dish with plastic wrap or a plate and microwave on high for 2 minutes. Add the 1½ teaspoons ginger and lime juice. Stir to mix.

In a mixing bowl, combine the coconut milk, sugar, cardamom, the remaining ginger, milk, cream, vanilla, and eggs. Whisk until well combined. Pour into the casserole dish. Cover the casserole dish with foil and secure it with a rubber band.

Place the casserole dish in a slow cooker and pour water around it to within 1 inch (2.3 cm) of the rim. Cover the slow cooker and cook on low for 3 to 4 hours.

Turn off the slow cooker, uncover, and let it cool till you can lift out the casserole dish without risk of scalding your fingers. Chill overnight.

Before serving, in a dry skillet, stir the coconut over medium heat until it's golden.

Remove the custard from the fridge and run a knife carefully around the edge. Put a plate on top and carefully invert the custard onto the plate. Sprinkle the coconut on top.

Yield: 8 servings

MAPLE CUSTARD
This is for all you maple fans out there, and we know that you are legion!

1½ cups (355 ml) milk
½ cup (120 ml) heavy cream
⅓ cup (107 ml) maple syrup
⅓ cup (8 g) sugar
3 eggs
1 pinch salt
1 teaspoon vanilla extract
½ teaspoon maple extract

Coat a 6-cup (1.4 L) glass casserole dish with nonstick cooking spray.

In a bowl, whisk all of the ingredients together. Pour the mixture into the prepared casserole dish.

Place the casserole dish in a slow cooker. Pour water around it to within 1 inch (2.5 cm) of the rim. Cover the slow cooker and cook on low for 4 hours.

When the time's up, turn off the slow cooker, remove the lid, and let it sit until the water is cool enough so that you can remove the casserole dish without risk of scalding your fingers. Chill well before serving.

Yield: 6 servings

32 Rice Pudding; 33 Brown Sugar Rice Pudding; 34 Low-Sugar Coco-Nutty Rice Pudding; 35 Mango Coconut Rice Pudding; 36 Lower-Sugar Raisin-Orange Pumpkin Pie Pudding; 37 Cinnamon Eggnog Bread Pudding; 38 Chocolate Bread Pudding; 39 Caramel Bread Pudding

40 Strawberry Bread Pudding; 41 Indian Pudding; 42 Slow Cooker Custard; 43 Chocolate Fudge Custard; 44 Southeast Asian Cocount Custard; 45 Low-sugar Lemon Honey Custard; 46 Maple Custard; 47 Maple Pumpkin Custard

MAPLE PUMPKIN CUSTARD

This is very much like the filling of a pumpkin pie, without the crust. The pecans add a little textural contrast.

1 can (15 ounces, or 425 g) canned pumpkin purée
1 cup (235 ml) milk beverage
½ cup (120 ml) heavy cream
⅓ cup (107 ml) maple syrup
⅓ cup (8 g) sugar
½ teaspoon maple flavoring
3 eggs
1 pinch salt
1 tablespoon (6 g) pumpkin pie spice
⅓ cup (37 g) chopped pecans
1½ teaspoons butter
Whipped topping

Coat a 6-cup (1.4 L) glass casserole dish with nonstick cooking spray.

In a bowl, preferably one with a pouring lip, whisk together the pumpkin, milk, cream, syrup, sugar, maple flavoring, eggs, salt, and pumpkin pie spice.

Pour the custard mixture into the prepared dish. Place it in a slow cooker. Carefully fill the space around the casserole with water up to 1 inch (2.5 cm) from the rim. Cover the slow cooker and cook on low for 3 to 4 hours.

Remove the lid, turn off the slow cooker, and let it cool till you can remove the casserole dish without risk of scalding your fingers. Chill the custard for at least several hours.

Before serving, in a heavy skillet, heat the pecans and butter over medium heat for about 5 minutes, stirring.

Serve the custard with a dollop of whipped topping and 1 tablespoon (7 g) of toasted pecans on each serving.

Yield: 6 servings

APRICOT CUSTARD

Like apricots? You'll love this yummy dessert.

⅓ cup (107 g) apricot preserves
2 tablespoons (28 ml) lemon juice
2 teaspoons plus ⅔ cup (16 g) sugar, divided
1½ cups (355 ml) milk
½ cup (120 ml) heavy cream
4 eggs
½ teaspoon almond extract
1 pinch salt

Coat a 6-cup (1.4 L) glass casserole dish with nonstick cooking spray.

In a bowl, whisk together the preserves, juice, and the 2 teaspoons of sugar. Spread the mixture over the bottom of the prepared dish.

In a separate bowl, whisk together the milk, cream, eggs, ⅔ cup (16 g) of sugar, almond extract, and salt. Pour into the prepared casserole gently, so as not to mix in the apricot preserves.

Place the casserole dish in a slow cooker. Pour water around the casserole to within 1 inch (2.5 cm) of the rim. Cover the slow cooker and cook on low for 4 hours.

When the time's up, turn off the slow cooker, uncover it, and let it cool until you can remove the casserole dish without risk of scalding your fingers. Chill well before serving.

Yield: 6 servings

CHOCOLATE FONDUE

You can use angel food cake to dip into the fondue. This is also delicious served with a variety of fruits, such as strawberries, kiwi, pineapple, and pears.

1 pound (455 g) good-quality semisweet chocolate bar or chips
1 cup (235 ml) half-and-half
1 store-bought angel food cake

If the chocolate is a solid piece, cut it into small pieces and put it into a slow cooker. If you use chips, just put them into the cooker. Pour the half-and-half over the chocolate. Cover and cook on low for 2 hours. Stir until the mixture is smooth. Cut the cake into cubes and dip it into the fondue.

Yield: 6 to 8 servings

▶*Recipe Note*

You can make this ahead and hold it on warm for an extended period while serving.

CHERRY COBBLER

This cobbler is super simple, so you may find yourself preparing it frequently. Or will that be because it's simply delicious?

One 21-ounce (595-g) can cherry pie filling
One 18½-ounce (511-g) box yellow cake mix
4 tablespoons (55 g) butter, melted

In a slow cooker, spread the pie filling out evenly.

In a medium bowl, stir the cake mix and melted butter until a crumbly mixture forms, and then sprinkle the mixture over the pie filling. Cover and cook on low for 3 to 4 hours or on high for 1½ to 2 hours.

Yield: 8 servings

APPLE COBBLER

In this cobbler, apples and granola bake together to a slow cooker perfection.

2 cups (220 g) peeled and sliced apples
2 cups (250 g) granola
1 teaspoon cinnamon
¼ cup (85 g) honey
2 tablespoons (28 g) butter, melted

Coat the crock of a 3- to 4-quart (2.9 to 3.8 L) slow cooker with nonstick cooking spray.
   In the slow cooker, combine the apples, granola, and cinnamon. Stir to mix well.
   In a bowl, stir together the honey and butter. Drizzle the mixture over the apple mixture in the slow cooker. Mix gently. Cover and cook on low for 5 to 7 hours, or until the apples are tender.

Yield: 4 servings

▶*Serving Suggestion*
Serve this slow cooker cobbler with fruit yogurt, if desired.

PEACH COBBLER

Warm and sweet, this is an old-fashioned kind of dessert. You can use either fresh or canned peaches.

4 cups fresh (680 g), or canned (888 g) sliced peaches
¼ cup (20 g) rolled oats
⅓ cup (42 g) Heart-Healthy Baking Mix (See page xxx.)
½ cup (100 g) sugar
½ cup (115 g) brown sugar
¼ teaspoon cinnamon
½ cup (120 ml) water, or reserved peach juice if using canned peaches

Coat the crock of a slow cooker with nonstick cooking spray.
   Place the peaches in the slow cooker.
   In a bowl, mix together the oats, baking mix, sugar, brown sugar, and cinnamon. When blended, stir in the water or juice until well mixed. Spoon batter into the slow cooker and stir into the peaches, just until blended. Cover and cook on low for 4 to 5 hours.

Yield: 6 servings

▶*Serving Suggestion*
Serve warm with vanilla ice cream or frozen yogurt.

ANTIOXIDANT-BURST RASPBERRY PEACH COBBLER

Peaches and raspberries are two good-looking fruits that are relatively low in sugar, are high in fiber (a whopping 8 grams per cup for raspberries), and extremely delicious. And they're surprisingly perfect for the slow cooker, which brings out the fruits' natural sweetness.

1 pint (250 g) fresh raspberries or 1 bag (10 ounces, or 280 g) frozen, thawed and drained
2½ pounds (1.1 kg) fresh, ripe peaches, unpeeled, pitted, and sliced, or 2 bags (16 ounces, or 454 g each) frozen, thawed and drained
¼ cup (71 g) frozen orange juice concentrate, thawed
1½ tablespoons (12 g) kudzu or quick-cooking tapioca
2 teaspoons orange zest
¼ cup (60 g) plus 2 tablespoons (30 g) Sucanat or xylitol, divided
2 teaspoons ground cinnamon, divided
½ teaspoon ground cloves
1 teaspoon vanilla stevia
⅓ cup (27 g) rolled oats
⅓ cup (37 g) toasted sliced almonds
¼ cup (30 g) oat flour or whole wheat pastry flour
4 tablespoons (56 g) butter, chopped, or coconut oil, softened
Pinch of salt

Coat the inside crock of a slow cooker with nonstick cooking spray.
   In the slow cooker, combine the raspberries and peaches.
   In a small cup, combine the melted juice concentrate and kudzu, mixing well to blend. Pour the mixture over the fruit in the slow cooker. Sprinkle in the zest, ¼ cup (60 g) of the Sucanat, 1 teaspoon of the cinnamon, the cloves, and vanilla stevia. Stir gently to evenly coat.
   In a small bowl, combine the oats, almonds, flour, the remaining 2 tablespoons (30 g) Sucanat, butter, the remaining 1 teaspoon cinnamon, and salt. Work them together until the mixture forms large crumbs. Sprinkle the mixture evenly over the fruit. Cover and cook on high for 2 hours.

Yield: 6 servings

▶*Health Bite*
Classic cobblers are made from sugar, butter, flour, and milk. Our version is a lot lower in sugar and overall carbs, and a lot higher in fiber from the oats and almonds. The stevia plus the xylitol or Sucanat give this cobbler all the extra sweetness you could possibly want.

BERRYLICIOUS BISCUIT-TOPPED FRUIT COBBLER

For this cobbler, you can use any fresh or frozen fruit you have on hand. It's easy to make and a real crowd-pleaser. You can use agave nectar or maple syrup instead of white sugar, if you prefer.

FOR THE STEWED FRUIT:
1 pint (340 g) berries (blueberries, strawberries, raspberries, or blackberries), washed, stemmed, hulled if strawberries, and chopped if large
5 large apples, peeled and cored
1 tablespoon (15 ml) lemon juice
1 teaspoon lemon zest
½ cup (100 g) sugar
1 tablespoon (8 g) cornstarch, plus more if needed
Pinch of salt

FOR THE BISCUITS:
1½ cups (180 g) flour
½ cup (50 g) oat bran
⅓ cup (67 g) sugar
1½ teaspoons baking powder
Pinch of salt
3 tablespoons (45 ml) olive oil
½ cup (120 ml) milk
1 teaspoon vanilla extract

To make the stewed fruit: Coat the crock of a slow cooker with nonstick cooking spray. Combine all of the ingredients in the slow cooker.

If you'll cook it longer than 8 hours or if your slow cooker runs very hot, add ½ cup (120 ml) water. Cover and cook on low for 6 to 8 hours.

About 30 minutes before serving, if the mixture is too thick, add a little water. If the mixture is too thin, add an additional ½ teaspoon cornstarch.

To make the biscuits: In a bowl, combine the flour, oat bran, sugar, baking powder, and salt.

In a separate bowl, combine the oil, milk, and vanilla. Add the dry ingredients to the wet. Using a wooden spoon, stir to combine.

Turn the mixture out onto a floured cutting board. Roll out about ½ inch (1.3 cm) thick. Using a glass, cut it into circles.

Place the dough in the slow cooker on top of the filling. Increase the heat of the slow cooker to high. Prop the lid open with a wooden spoon to allow the condensation to evaporate. Cook for 30 minutes longer.

Yield: 4 to 6 servings

▶*Recipe Variations*
You can substitute any in-season fruit and make this any day of the year. Try peach and raspberry, or pear and apple. Jazz up the cobbler by mixing minced mint, thyme, or rosemary into the biscuit dough.

APPLE CRISP

The recipe for apple crisp is made even easier by using canned pie filling. But it tastes just as good as if you made it all by hand.

4 cups (1 kg) apple pie filling
¾ cup (60 g) quick cooking oats
½ cup (115 g) brown sugar
½ cup (63 g) flour
¼ cup (55 g) butter, at room temperature

Place the pie filling in a slow cooker.

In a bowl, combine the remaining ingredients until crumbly. Sprinkle the mixture over the apple filling. Cover and cook on low for 2 to 3 hours.

Yield: 8 servings

GRANOLA APPLE CRISP

Slow cookers are not known for their browning and crisping abilities, but by using granola as our topping, you can build that quality in, and the result is a great dessert. It's a bit more on the chewy side than an oven-baked crisp, but you'll love it anyway.

3 pounds (1365 g) apples, such as Granny Smith, peeled, cored, and cut into wedges
1 cup (200 g) sugar
2 cups (300 g) granola

In a large bowl, place the apples.

In a small bowl, stir together the sugar and cinnamon. Toss with the apples.

Transfer the mixture to a slow cooker. Top with the granola. Cover and cook on low for 4 to 5 hours or on high for 2 to 3 hours, or until the apples are soft and bubbling.

Yield: 6 to 8 servings

▶*Add it!*
We generally consider vanilla ice cream de rigueur as an accompaniment to any crisp.

TEA "THYME" LEMON BLONDIES
These are super moist and full of lemony goodness. If you're not a fan of thyme, you can leave it out. If you're feeling adventurous, try it with rosemary.

¾ cup (150 g) sugar
2 cups (240 g) whole wheat pastry flour
1 teaspoon dried thyme
1 teaspoon baking powder
½ teaspoon baking soda
½ teaspoon salt
¾ cup (355 ml) milk mixed with ½ teaspoon vanilla extract
Zest of 1 lemon
Juice of 2 lemons
3 tablespoons (45 ml) olive oil
1 tablespoon (15 ml) almond-flavored liqueur or ½ teaspoon almond extract
1 teaspoon lemon or orange extract

Coat a pan that fits in a slow cooker with nonstick cooking spray. If you have a round slow cooker, you can use a round dish (about 1-quart [0.9 L] size) or a loaf pan. Or you can coat the crock of the slow cooker

In a bowl, combine the sugar, flour, thyme, baking powder, baking soda, and salt.

In a separate bowl, combine the milk mixture, zest, juice, oil, liqueur, and extract.

Add the wet mixture to the dry. Using a wooden spoon, stir until just combined.

Pour the mixture into the prepared pan. Prop the lid open with a wooden spoon to allow the condensation to evaporate. Cook on high for 1½ to 2½ hours, or until a knife inserted into the center comes out almost clean.

Yield: 1 loaf

▶*Recipe Note*
If you cook this directly in the crock, rotate the crock two or three times during cooking. This way, if your slow cooker has a side that cooks hotter, your blondies will cook more evenly.

CHILE BLACK BEAN BROWNIES
These healthy brownies are extremely fudgey and moist. Lining your baking dishes with parchment paper will help you pull the entire cooked contents out of the slow cooker and pan. It will be very hard, maybe impossible, to get the brownies out of the dish in one piece if you skip this step.

½ cup (40 g) rolled oats or instant oatmeal
½ cup (60 g) chopped walnuts
1 can (15 ounces, or 420 g) black beans, drained and rinsed
2 ripe bananas
3 tablespoons (45 g) applesauce
¼ cup (60 ml) agave nectar or maple syrup
½ cup (60 g) unsweetened cocoa powder
¼ teaspoon chile powder
½ teaspoon cinnamon
1 teaspoon vanilla extract

Line two baking dishes that fit in your slow cooker with parchment paper, cut long enough to hang over the edge of the pan. You could use a 6-quart (5.7 L) oval slow cooker and two small 3-cup (705 ml) rectangular Pyrex dishes. You can use different sizes, but make sure the dishes you plan to use fit in your slow cooker before you start making the batter.

In a food processor, process the oats to a flourlike consistency.

Transfer the oats to a large bowl with the walnuts.

In the food processor, pulse the beans, bananas, applesauce, agave, cocoa, chile powder, cinnamon, and vanilla until smooth.

Add this mixture to the bowl with the oats. Stir to combine.

Spoon the brownie mixture into the prepared pans. You will need to push it into the corners or your brownies won't have the shape you're expecting.

Roll up some aluminum foil, make a ring with it, and place it in the bottom of the slow cooker. Put the baking dishes on top of the foil ring. (You can put one dish crisscrossed over the other on top of the aluminum foil ring.) Place a clean dish towel underneath the lid to catch the condensation. Cover the slow cooker and cook on low for 6 to 8 hours.

Yield: 12 pieces

▶*Recipe Tip*
If you're making this for kids, leave out the chile powder and add a few more tablespoons (30 to 45 ml) agave nectar to make them sweeter. You can also leave out the cinnamon and add some mint extract instead.

HAVE-IT-YOUR-WAY BROWNIES
Make this recipe and embellish it with all your favorites, such as chocolate chips, nuts, and other goodies.

1 cup (120 g) whole wheat pastry flour
1 cup (120 g) unsweetened cocoa powder
½ teaspoon baking powder
¼ teaspoon salt

FOR THE WET INGREDIENTS:
½ cup (112 g) butter
½ cup (115 g) packed brown sugar
2 tablespoons (14 g) ground flaxseed mixed with 2 tablespoons (30 ml) warm water

DESSERTS • 235

1 cup (235 ml) milk
1 teaspoon vanilla extract

Coat two casserole dishes that will fit into your slow cooker with nonstick cooking spray, for example, a 6-quart (5.7 L) oval slow cooker and two small 3-cup (705 ml) rectangular Pyrex dishes. You can use different sizes, but make sure the dishes you plan to use fit in your slow cooker before you start making the batter.

In a bowl, combine the flour, cocoa powder, baking powder, and salt.

In a separate bowl, cream the butter with the sugar. Add the flaxseed mixture, milk, and vanilla. Mix until combined, and then add half of the dry mixture and combine. Add the last of the dry mixture, combine well, and spread into the prepared dishes.

Take a piece of aluminum foil, roll it up, make a ring with it, and place on the bottom of the slow cooker. Put the baking dishes on top of the foil ring. You can arrange one dish crisscrossed over the other on top of the aluminum foil ring.) Place a clean dish towel underneath the lid to catch the condensation. Cover and cook on high for 4 to 5 hours, or until a knife inserted into the center comes out almost clean.

Yield: 12 pieces

APPLE CAKE
This is a simple cake, but it's very moist and with great flavor.

1 cup (125 g) flour
¾ cup (150 g) sugar
2 teaspoons baking powder
1 teaspoon cinnamon
4 apples, chopped
¼ cup (60 ml) egg substitute
2 teaspoons vanilla

Coat the crock of a slow cooker with nonstick cooking spray.

In a bowl, combine the flour, sugar, baking powder, and cinnamon. Add the apples, stirring lightly to coat.

In a separate bowl, combine the egg substitute and vanilla. Add to the apple mixture. Stir until just moistened.

Spoon the batter into the slow cooker. Cover and cook on high for 2½ to 3 hours. Serve warm.

Yield: 8 servings

CARROT CAKE
This carrot cake is marvelous.

½ cup (120 ml) canola oil
½ cup (120 ml) egg substitute
1 tablespoon (15 ml) hot water
½ cup (65 g) grated carrots
¾ cup plus 2 tablespoons (110 g) flour, divided
¾ cup (150 g) sugar
½ teaspoon baking powder
¼ teaspoon allspice
½ teaspoon cinnamon
¼ teaspoon cloves
½ cup (55 g) chopped pecans
½ cup (75 g) raisins

Grease and flour a 3-pound (1⅓ kg) shortening can or slow cooker baking insert.

In a large bowl, beat the oil, egg substitute, and water for 1 minute. Add the carrots. Mix well.

In a separate bowl, stir together ¾ cup (94 g) of the flour, the sugar, baking powder, allspice, cinnamon, and cloves. Add the mixture to the carrot mixture.

In a separate bowl, toss the nuts and raisins with the remaining 2 tablespoons (16 g) flour. Add to the batter and mix well. Pour into the prepared can or slow cooker baking insert.

Place the can or baking insert in the slow cooker. If using a can, cover it with 3 paper towels, folded down over the edge of the slow cooker to absorb moisture. If using a baking insert, cover with its lid. Cover the slow cooker and cook on high for 3 to 4 hours.

Yield: 8 servings

SLOW COOKER CHOCOLATE CAKE
If you know someone who doesn't believe that you can make cakes and desserts in the slow cooker, this is the one to use to convince them. It's an incredibly rich cake, made directly in the slow cooker.

1¼ cups (285 g) brown sugar, divided
1 cup (125 g) flour
½ cup (45 g) unsweetened cocoa powder, divided
1½ teaspoons baking powder
½ cup (120 ml) milk
2 tablespoons (28 g) butter, melted
½ teaspoon vanilla extract
1¾ cups (410 ml) boiling water

Coat the crock of a slow cooker with nonstick baking spray.

In a mixing bowl, mix together 1 cup (225 g) of the sugar, the flour, ¼ cup (22 g) of the cocoa, and the baking powder. Stir in the milk, butter, and vanilla. Pour the mixture into the slow cooker.

In a separate bowl, mix together the remaining ¼ cup (60 g) sugar and ¼ cup (22 g) cocoa. Sprinkle the mixture over the batter in the slow cooker. Do not stir. Pour the boiling water over the mixture. Do not stir. Cover and cook on high for 1½ to 1¾ hours, or until a toothpick inserted into cake comes out clean.

Yield: 8 servings

VANILLA UPSIDE-DOWN CAKE

Oopsie daisy! We got turned upside down–upside down about everything except the yummy quotient of this cake, served with ice cream or a drizzle of chocolate syrup.

1 cup (120 g) all-purpose baking mix
1 cup (200 g) Vanilla Sugar, divided (see below)
½ cup (120 ml) milk
1⅔ cups (392 ml) hot water
Whipped cream, chocolate sauce, or ice cream

Coat the crock of a slow cooker with nonstick cooking spray.
In a medium bowl, combine the baking mix, ½ cup (100 g) of the Vanilla Sugar, and the milk. Stir to mix well. Spoon the batter evenly into the slow cooker.
In a separate bowl, mix the remaining ½ cup (100 g) of the Vanilla Sugar and the hot water. Pour the mixture over the batter in the slow cooker. Cover and cook on high for 2 to 3 hours, or until the center of the cake springs back when pressed.
Scoop the cake out of the slow cooker and serve it with whipped cream, chocolate sauce, or ice cream.

Yield: 8 servings

▶*Try This!*
To make a Chocolate Upside-Down Cake, mix 3 tablespoons (15 g) unsweetened cocoa into the baking mix and 1/3 cup (27 g) cocoa into the Vanilla Sugar-hot water mixture.

▶*Vanilla Sugar*
2 cups (100 g, or 50 g) granulated or powdered sugar
1 vanilla bean

Put the sugar in an airtight container, then push the vanilla bean down into the sugar until it's completely submerged. Let the sugar with the vanilla bean sit undisturbed for 1 to 2 weeks, then remove the bean. Store the mixture in an airtight container in a cool place.

WHITE FRUIT CAKE

Yes, you can bake your fruitcake in the slow cooker. Some years ago, slow cookers came with a steaming pan that had a vented lid. You're not likely to have one, so you can also use something like a coffee can covered with foil that has vent holes punched in it.

½ cup (112 g) butter, softened
1 cup (200 g) sugar
4 eggs, separated
1½ cups (189 g) flour, plus more for coating fruit
1½ teaspoons (7 g) baking powder
1 cup (225 g) unsweetened crushed pineapple, well drained and juice reserved
⅔ cup (160 ml) pineapple juice, drained from crushed pineapple
1½ cups (220 g) golden raisins
4 ounces (115 g) mixed candied fruit
4 ounces (115 g) candied cherries, halved
1 cup (110 g) slivered almonds
½ teaspoon vanilla extract
½ teaspoon almond extract
½ cup (120 ml) water

Grease and flour a cake pan that will fit into your slow cooker.
In a bowl, using an electric mixer, cream the butter and sugar. Add the egg yolks and beat well.
In a separate bowl, combine the flour and baking powder. Add it alternately with the pineapple juice to the butter mixture.
In a separate bowl, sprinkle the extra flour the over the raisins and candied fruit and toss to coat. Stir the raisins, candied fruit, crushed pineapple, vanilla, and almond extract into the batter, blending thoroughly.
Beat the egg whites until stiff but not dry; fold into the batter.
Pour the batter into the prepared pan and cover; place in a slow cooker. Pour the water around the cake pan in the slow cooker. Cover and steam the fruitcake on high for 3 to 5 hours. After baking, allow the cake to rest in the pan for 10 to 15 minutes before removing.
Let cool thoroughly before slicing.

For mellowing, wrap the cake in plastic wrap when cool.

Yield: 12 servings

48 Apricot Custard; 49 Chocolate Fondue; 50 Cherry Cobbler; 51 Apple Cobbler; 52 Peach Cobbler; 53 Antioxidant-Burst Raspberry Peach Cobbler; 54 Berrylicious Biscuit-Topped Fruit Cobbler; 55 Apple Crisp

56 Granola Apple Crisp; 57 Tea "Thyme" Lemon Blondies; 58 Chile-Chipotle Black Bean Brownies; 59 Have-It-Your-Way Brownies; 60 Apple Cake; 61 Carrot Cake; 62 Slow Cooker Chocolate Cake; 63 Vanilla Upside-Down Cake

DESSERTS • 239

CINNAMON-SWIRL CHERRY DELIGHT CAKE
Cherry and cinnamon are delightful together. This is a wonderful change-of-pace dessert that's served best in a bowl, with vanilla ice cream.

One 21-ounce (595-g) can cherry pie filling
Half of a 21-ounce (595-g) box cinnamon swirl cake mix
4 tablespoons (55 g) butter, melted

Coat the crock of a slow cooker with nonstick cooking spray.
Put the pie filling in the slow cooker and spread it out evenly.
In a medium bowl, stir the cake mix and butter until a crumbly mixture forms. Sprinkle the mixture over the pie filling in the slow cooker. Cover and cook on low for 2 to 3 hours.
Serve the cake at room temperature.

Yield: 5 servings

▶*Add It!*
Sprinkle ¼ cup (31 g) slivered almonds over the crumb mixture before cooking the cake.

STRAWBERRY CHOCOLATE CRUMBLE
Who doesn't go straight for the strawberry and chocolate on the dessert tray? This scrumptious dessert satisfies both cravings, particularly when served with Neapolitan ice cream.

One 18-ounce (510-g) can strawberry pie filling
One 21-ounce (595-g) box chocolate cake mix
8 tablespoons (1 stick, or 112 g) butter, melted

Coat the crock of a slow cooker with nonstick cooking spray.
Put the pie filling in the slow cooker and spread it out evenly.
In a medium bowl, stir the cake mix and butter until a crumbly mixture forms. Sprinkle the mixture over the pie filling. Cover and cook on low for 3 to 4 hours or on high for 1½ to 2 hours.
Serve the cake at room temperature.

Yield: 8 servings

▶*Add It!*
Garnish the cake with chocolate curls.

CRUST-FREE CHEESECAKE
This cheesecake has no crust to compete with its delicious flavor. Whether you introduce whipped cream or fruit glaze to the debate is up to you.

12 ounces (340 g) cream cheese, softened
½ cup (50 g) Vanilla Sugar (See page 217.)
1 whole egg plus 1 egg white

Coat the interior of a slow cooker's baking unit with cooking spray, and position the slow cooker's rack on the floor of the machine. If your slow cooker did not come with this equipment, use any baking pan and rack that fit inside the machine.
In a large bowl, using an electric mixer, beat the cream cheese, Vanilla Sugar, whole egg, and egg white until well blended; do not overbeat the batter.
Pour the batter into the pan and place the pan on the rack in the slow cooker. Cover and cook on high for 3 to 5 hours, or until the sides of the cheesecake look dry and just a little cracked, and its center is firm but still jiggles a bit when shaken.
Turn the heat off and allow the slow cooker to cool for 20 minutes, or until you can remove the pan without burning yourself. Run a knife around the edges of the pan to release the cake and to prevent cracks from forming.
Allow it to cool completely, and cover it and chill it in the fridge for at least 3 hours.
To serve the cheesecake, cover the pan with a plate, then carefully invert the pan and let the cheesecake release onto the plate. Place another plate over the cheesecake and invert the cake again, so that the cheesecake is right side up.

Yield: 10 servings

▶*Try This!*
Pour the batter into a graham cracker pie shell in a pie pan, and bake it as directed above.

NEW YORK STYLE CHEESECAKE
You can top this with fruit if you like, but it's mighty good just as it is.

"Graham" Cracker Crust (see at right)
1 pound (455 g) light cream cheese or Neufchâtel cheese, softened
½ cup (115 g) light sour cream
2 eggs
½ cup (12 g) sugar
2 teaspoons vanilla extract
1 pinch salt

Prepare the crust
In a bowl, using an electric mixer, beat the cream

cheese, sour cream, and eggs until they're very smooth, scraping down the sides of the bowl at least a few times. Beat in the sugar, vanilla, and salt. Pour into the crust. Cover the pan tightly with foil, squeezing it in around the rim.

Take a big sheet of foil, at least 18 inches (45 cm) long, and roll it into a loose cylinder.

Bend it into a circle and place it in the bottom of the slow cooker to make a rack to put the pan on. Pour ¼ inch of water into the slow cooker and then put the pan on the donut of foil. Cover the slow cooker and cook on high for 3 to 4 hours.

Turn off the slow cooker, uncover, and let cool for at least 20 to 30 minutes before you try to remove the pan from the slow cooker. Chill well before serving.

Yield: 12 servings

▶*Graham Cracker Crust*
1¼ cups (181 g) almonds
2 tablespoons (14 g) wheat germ
2 tablespoons (14 g) wheat bran
3 tablespoons (4.5 g) Splenda
1 pinch salt
6 tablespoons (85 g) butter, melted

Preheat the oven to 325°F (170°C, or gas mark 3).

Put the almonds in a food processor with the S-blade in place. Run it until they're ground to about the texture of corn meal. Add the wheat germ, wheat bran, Splenda, and salt and pulse to combine. Now turn on the processor and pour in the butter, running the processor until everything's well combined. (You may need to stop the processor and run a knife around the bottom edge to make sure all the dry ingredients come in contact with the butter.)

Turn this mixture out into an 8-inch (20 cm) springform pan you've sprayed with nonstick cooking spray. Press firmly into place. Bake for 10 to 12 minutes, or until just turning gold around the edges. Cool before filling.

Yield: 12 servings

PEANUT BUTTER CHEESECAKE
You can certainly eat this plain, or you could top it with some chocolate sauce.

Crisp Chocolate Crust (see page 242.) or "Graham" Cracker Crust (See above)
16 ounces (455 g) light cream cheese or Neufchâtel cheese, softened
½ cup (115 g) light sour cream
1 egg
¾ cup (195 g) peanut butter
⅔ cup (16 g) sugar
½ teaspoons blackstrap molasses

Prepare the crust.

In a bowl, using an electric mixer, beat the cheese, sour cream, and egg until they're very smooth, scraping down the sides of the bowl several times. Beat in the peanut butter, sugar, and molasses.

When the mixture is very smooth and well blended, pour it into the crust. Cover the pan tightly with foil, squeezing it in around the rim.

Take a big sheet of foil, at least 18 inches (45 cm) long, and roll it into a loose cylinder.

Bend it into a circle and place it in the bottom of the slow cooker. (You're making a rack to put the pan on.) Pour ¼ inch of water into the slow cooker and then put the pan on the donut of foil. Cover the slow cooker and cook on high for 3 to 4 hours.

Turn off the slow cooker, uncover, and let cool for at least 20 to 30 minutes before you try to remove the pan from the slow cooker. Chill well before serving.

Yield: 12 serving

MOCHACCHINO CHEESECAKE
This cheesecake is extraordinary, as good as any dessert you'd get in a restaurant.

Crisp Chocolate Crust (see page 242.)
16 ounces (455 g) light cream cheese or Neufchâtel cheese, softened
1 egg
¼ cup (60 ml) heavy cream
½ cup (45 g) + 2 tablespoons (12 g) unsweetened cocoa powder
½ cup (12 g) sugar
¼ cup (60 ml) Mockahlua (see page 262)
2 tablespoons (28 ml) brewed coffee

Prepare the crust.

In a bowl, using an electric mixer, beat the cream cheese, egg, and cream until quite smooth, scraping down the sides of the bowl several times. Beat in the cocoa powder, sugar, Mockahlua, and coffee until well blended and very smooth. Pour the mixture into the crust. Cover the springform pan tightly with foil, squeezing it in around the rim.

Take a big sheet of foil, at least 18 inches (45 cm) long, and roll it into a loose cylinder. Bend it into a circle and place it in the bottom of a slow cooker. (You're making a rack to put the pan on.) Pour ¼ inch of water in the bottom of the slow cooker and then put the pan on the donut of foil. Cover the slow cooker, set it to high, and let it cook for 3 to 4 hours.

Turn off the slow cooker, uncover, and let cool for at least 20 to 30 minutes before you try to remove the pan from the slow cooker. Chill well before serving.

Yield: 12 servings

▶*Crisp Chocolate Crust*
1½ cups (218 g) almonds
¼ cup (6 g) Splenda
2 squares bitter chocolate, melted
3 tablespoons (45 g) butter, melted
2 tablespoons (20 g) vanilla whey protein powder

Preheat the oven to 325°F (170°C, or gas mark 3).

Using the S-blade of your food processor, grind the almonds until they're the texture of corn meal. Add the Splenda and pulse to combine. Pour in the chocolate and butter and run processor till evenly distributed. (You may need to stop the processor and run the tip of a knife blade around the outer edge to get everything to combine properly.)

Then add the protein powder and pulse again to combine.

Turn the mixture into an 8-inch (20 cm) springform pan you've coated with nonstick cooking spray. Press firmly and evenly into place. Bake for 10 to 12 minutes. Cool before filling.

Yield: 12 servings

LAYERED CREPE DESSERT

This rich dessert features the classic flavor combination of raspberries and chocolate.

20 premade dessert crêpes
4 cups (700 g) good-quality semisweet chocolate chips, divided
4 cups (440 g) red raspberries, divided

Coat the crock of a slow cooker with nonstick cooking spray.

Arrange 4 crêpes to cover the bottom of the cooker and top with 1 cup (175 g) chocolate and 1 cup (110 g) raspberries. Repeat the layers, ending with crêpes. Cover and cook on low for 4 to 5 hours. Then turn off the slow cooker and allow the dessert to sit for 30 minutes.

Cut into wedges.

Yield: 6 to 8 servings

▶*Add It!*
A whipped cream topping would be perfect, or add a dollop of crème fraîche if you want to gussy it up a little.

STRAWBERRY-LIME GRANITA (PHOTO PAGE 4)

Granita is a tasty and easy summertime treat that doesn't require any special equipment, goes together like a dream, and has basically two ingredients.

1½ pounds (680 g) fresh strawberries, stemmed and halved
1 cup (235 ml) water
3 tablespoons (45 g) erythritol or Sucanat
3 tablespoons (45 ml) lime juice
½ to 1 teaspoon vanilla stevia, to taste
1 teaspoon lime zest

In a 3-quart (2.8 L) slow cooker, combine the strawberries, water, and erythritol, and stir well. Cover and cook on high for 2 to 3 hours, until the strawberries have mostly broken down.

Cool slightly and transfer the contents to a blender or food processor and process until very smooth. Strain the mixture through a fine-mesh sieve into a 9 x 11-inch (23 x 28 cm) baking pan, pressing well to extract all the juices, then discard the pulp and seeds. Stir in the lime juice, vanilla stevia, and zest.

Cover with a rubber top (if using Pyrex) or plastic wrap and place in the freezer. Freeze for 3 to 4 hours, stirring at least once an hour to break up the ice chunks. If freezing overnight, break into pieces and process briefly in the food processor just before serving.

Yield: 6 servings

64 White Fruit Cake

65 Cinnamon-Swirl Cherry Delight Cake; 66 Strawberry Chocolate Crumble; 67 Crust-Free Cheesecake; 68 New York Style Cheesecake; 69 Peanut Butter Cheesecake; 70 Mochacchino Cheesecake

244 • THE LITTLE SLOW COOKER COOKBOOK

71 Layered Crêpe Dessert

DESSERTS • 245

BEVERAGES

See pages 248-249, 252-253, 258-259 and 263-265 for beverage recipe photos.

HABANERO-SPIKED "RED HOT" CIDER

A favorite candy came to mind when we tried this spicy drink–those little "red hots" that burned your tongue but felt so good in your mouth. This is spicy, cinnamon-y, with just enough of an overtone of peppery fire to make your eyes water.

1 gallon (3.8 L) cider
1 or 2 habanero or jalapeño peppers, seeded and sliced
6 cinnamon sticks

In a slow cooker, combine the cider, jalapeños, and cinnamon. Cover and cook on low for 2 to 3 hours or on high for 1 to 2 hours, or until the desired spiciness is reached. After the first hour, taste test for heat at half-hour intervals.

Strain out and discard all solids. Serve the cider warm or cold.

Yield: 1 gallon (3.8 L)

▶ **Health Bite**
This cider is loaded with capsaicin, courtesy of the habanero chile peppers. Among other things, capsaicin helps turn off pain signals in the body, and is a potential treatment for arthritis and neuropathy. Good stuff!

▶ **Recipe Tips**
• For the best flavor and richest nutrients, look for unpasteurized cider that's been treated with UV light to prevent bacterial growth.

• Take care when slicing chile peppers. It's best to use rubber gloves to protect your skin fromthe hot oils, and never, ever rub your eyes.

HOT APPLE CIDER

This apple cider has a little bit of spice and a nice citrus touch this is popular with kids and adults alike.

7 cups (1.6 L) apple cider
2 cups (475 ml) orange juice
½ cup (120 ml) honey
6 whole cloves
1 apple, peeled
1 orange, sliced

In a Dutch over or large kettle, combine the cider, juice, and honey.

Insert the cloves into the apple. Add the apple and orange to the juice mixture. Bring to a boil. Reduce the heat and simmer for 5 minutes.

Transfer the mixture to a slow cooker. Cover and cook on low for 2 hours. Keep warm in the cooker for serving.

Yield: 14 servings

SPICED CIDER

Cinnamon candies help to provide the spice for this apple cider.

½ gallon (1.9 L) apple cider, divided
¼ cup (56 g) red hots candies
¼ cups brown sugar
1 teaspoon cloves
1 teaspoon allspice

In a microwave-safe bowl, combine 2 cups (475 ml) of the cider, the red hots, and sugar. Microwave on medium power for 7 to 8 minutes. Add the cloves and allspice. Add the remaining cider.

Transfer the mixture to a slow cooker. Cover and cook on low for at least 1 hour, or until flavor is well developed.

Yield: 8 servings

MAPLE CIDER

Maple syrup adds a little different kind of sweetness to this spiced cider.

½ gallon (1.9 L) apple cider
4 cinnamon sticks
2 teaspoons whole cloves
2 teaspoons whole allspice berries
2 tablespoons (36 g) orange juice concentrate
2 tablespoons (40 g) maple syrup

In a slow cooker, combine all of the ingredients. Cover and cook on low for 2 hours. Serve warm.

Yield: 10 servings

CRANBERRY ORANGE CIDER
This is a fruity cider, with a hint of cinnamon if desired.

4 cups (950 ml) apple cider
2 cups (475 ml) cranberry juice
1 cup (235 ml) orange juice
1½ cups (355 ml) apricot nectar
4 cinnamon sticks, optional

In a slow cooker, combine all of the ingredients. Cover and cook on low for 4 to 10 hours. Serve warm from the cooker.

Yield: 10 servings

CITRUS CIDER
This is a warm fruity punch, good for both children and adults.

1 cup (200 g) sugar
2 cinnamon sticks
1 teaspoon nutmeg
2 cups (475 ml) apple cider
3 cups (700 ml) orange juice
1 orange, sliced thinly

In a slow cooker, combine all of the ingredients, except for the orange. Cover and cook on low for 4 to 10 hours or on high 2 to 3 hours. Before serving, float the orange in the slow cooker.

Yield: 12 servings

HOT VITAMIN C-POP CRANBERRY CIDER
This cider is a delicious way to add cranberries to your diet. It's great hot or cold.

1 gallon (3.8 L) cider
12 ounces (336 g) fresh cranberries or frozen, thawed
4 cinnamon sticks
2 tablespoons (13.2 g) ground cloves
4 to 6 thin slices fresh lemon, sliced around the "equator"

In a slow cooker, combine the cider, cranberries, cinnamon, and cloves. Float the lemon on top. Cover and cook on low for 4 to 5 hours or on high for 3 to 4 hours.
Strain and serve hot or cold.

Yield: 1 gallon (3.8 L)

▶*Health Bite*
Cranberries have one of the highest antioxidant ratings, which is called the ORAC score. They're loaded with phenols, which are plant chemicals that are known to be highly protective against a wide range of health problems. Research shows that several bioactive compounds in cranberries are toxic to a variety of cancer tumor cells. And of course, there's the well-established ability of cranberries and cranberry juice to prevent urinary tract infections.
This tangy cider is rich in vitamin C, lightly sweet, and it's mellowed by the warming spices. It's great either hot or cold.
For the best flavor and richest nutrients, look for unpasteurized cider that has been treated with UV light to prevent bacterial growth.

▶*Time-Saver Tip*
Combine the cider, cranberries, cinnamon, and cloves in a large soup pot and bring to a boil over medium-high heat. Carefully transfer the contents to the slow cooker, add the lemon slices, and cook on high for 1 hour.

HOT, SPIKED, AND BUTTERED SPICED CIDER
There's no need to choose between spiced cider and hot buttered rum when you can have it all in one mug. Make it to your liking by leaving out the rum or butter, or use apple juice instead of cider.

4 cups (940 ml) apple cider
2 cinnamon sticks, plus extra for serving
4 cardamom pods
3 allspice berries
4 whole cloves
4 teaspoons (20 g) butter
½ to ¾ cup (120 to 180 ml) rum

In a slow cooker, combine all of the ingredients. If not everyone can have the rum, you can wait to add the rum to individual servings. Cover and cook on low for 2 to 4 hours.
Strain out the cinnamon, cardamom, allspice, and cloves.
Stir well before serving in mugs garnished with extra cinnamon sticks.

Yield: 4 servings

▶*Recipe Tip*
You can halve this recipe for 2 servings and cook it in a 1½-quart (1.4 L) slow cooker.

1 Habernero-Spiked "Red Hot" Cider

2 Hot Apple Cider

MULLED GRAPE CIDER

This warm, spicy cider fills your home with the tantalizing aroma of grapes. It looks pretty when served from the slow cooker garnished with lemon and orange slices.

1 quart (.95 L) grape juice
2 cinnamon sticks
1 lemon slice

In a slow cooker, combine the juice, cinnamon sticks, and lemon. Cover and cook on high for 2 to 3 hours, tasting the cider after 1 hour, then every 30 minutes thereafter.

When the cinnamon flavor is just right, using a slotted spoon, remove the cinnamon sticks and discard them. Remove the lemon slice or keep it as a garnish. Serve the cider warm.

Yield: 8 servings

CLEAN CLASSIC WASSAIL

Wassail refers to an ancient tradition called "wassailing," which was done in the cider-producing countries in England. The purpose of the traditional wassailing ritual was to "awaken" the cider trees and scare away evil spirits to better guarantee a good harvest of autumn fruit. The word "wassail" actually comes from the salute "waes hail," a contraction of the Middle English phrase waes heil, meaning "good health" or "be healthy." Meanwhile, wassail the beverage is a hot, spicy punch or mulled cider, traditionally made with sugar, ginger, cinnamon, and nutmeg. (Mouthwatering, right?). This version uses the slow cooker to great effect, allowing the apples to cook slowly (duh!) in a bit of ale and sherry. Drink enough of this and you can carol all snowy-night long.

3 McIntosh or Winesap apples, peeled, cored, and coarsely chopped
1/3 cup (80 g) Sucanat (or 1 1/3 cup (80 g) sugar and 1 teaspoon blackstrap molasses)
1 quart (946 ml) nut brown ale, divided
1 1/2 cups (353 ml) dry sherry, divided
3/4 teaspoon ground cinnamon
1/2 teaspoon ground nutmeg
1/4 teaspoon ground cloves
1/4 teaspoon ground allspice
1/4 cup (32 g) grated fresh ginger
6 thin slices fresh lemon, sliced around the equator

In a slow cooker place the apples. Sprinkle the apples evenly with the Sucanat. Gently pour 2/3 cup (160 ml) of the ale and 1/4 cup (60 ml) of the sherry over the apples. Cover and cook on high for 1 to 2 hours, or until the apples are soft.

Using an immersion blender or in batches in a countertop blender, purée the cooked apples to the consistency of applesauce.

Return the apples to the slow cooker. Reduce the heat of the slow cooker to low. Add the remaining 3 1/3 cups (786 ml) ale, the remaining 1 1/4 cups (293 ml) sherry, cinnamon, nutmeg, cloves, and allspice. Using your hand, squeeze the juice out of the grated ginger into the ale mixture. Mix gently to combine well.

Float the lemon slices. Cover and cook on low for 15 to 30 minutes, or until the mixture is hot. Do not let it boil.

Yield: 10 to 12 servings

▶ *Health Bite*
Any drink made from apples can't be bad. Loaded with vitamins, nutrients, and a great source of the anti-inflammatory flavonoid quercetin, the apple blends beautifully with the spices, creating a drink that's warming and delicious.

MULLED NON-WINE FRESHGRAPE DELIGHT

This clean distillation of pure grape juice is a sweet treat sure to delight the taste buds. Word to the wise: This drink is also terrific cold!

4 pounds (1.8 kg) fresh Concord grapes
7 cups (1.6 L) water, divided
1/2 to 2/3 cup (120 to 160 g) honey, to taste
Juice and zest of 1/2 lemon

In a large soup pot, bring the grapes and 2 cups (470 ml) of the water to a boil over high heat, stirring frequently. Boil for 1 minute, stirring constantly, and then remove from the heat.

Strain the contents of the pot through a double-mesh sieve into a slow cooker, pressing hard on the fruit to extract all juices. Discard the pulp, skin, and seeds. Stir in the remaining 5 cups (1.2 L) water, the honey, and juice and zest. Cover and cook on low for 3 hours. Serve hot or chilled.

Yield: 9 cups (2.1 L)

▶ *Health Bite*
The search for the fountain of youth has been going on for thousands of years, with legends and reports of such a fountain dating back to the writings of the Greek Herodotus in the fifth century BCE. More recently, scientists discovered that we can extend life span (at least in animals) by restricting calories. This has worked in every species tested, from yeast cells to fruit flies to, more recently, monkeys. Researchers found that calorie restriction appears to activate certain longevity genes known as the SIRT genes. Unfortunately, restricting calories isn't a hugely popular strategy among humans!

Fortunately, these same scientists have also discovered

a substance in food that can "turn on" the longevity genes almost as well as a Spartan, calorie-restricted diet. The substance is a plant chemical called resveratrol, and it's the ingredient in red wine that makes red wine such a healthy drink (in moderation, of course). Resveratrol is found in the skins of darkly colored grapes (there's none to speak of in white wine).

You don't actually have to drink wine to get resveratrol; you can get it from grapes. And you should! It's great for you. In addition to showing tremendous potential as an anti-aging compound, resveratrol from grapes (or wine) is a powerful antioxidant, helping to protect your cells and DNA from damage.

DOUBLE BLACKBERRY BRANDY WINE
Enjoy the unforgettable flavor of blackberries with a hint of apple. Serve very hot in small cups garnished with raisins and slivered almonds.

1 bottle (750 ml) blackberry wine
1½ pints (710 ml) apple juice
1 cup (235 ml) blackberry brandy or liqueur

In a slow cooker, combine the wine, juice, and brandy. Cover and cook on low for 3 to 4 hours.
   Serve the brandy-wine hot.

Yield: 10 servings

▶ *Add It!*
For a spicy treat, add a cinnamon stick to the mixture as it's heating. Using a slotted spoon, remove the cinnamon stick and discard it before serving the brandy-wine.

SPICED APPLE WINE
We've got spiced cider and spiced wine, so why not spiced cider wine? It just makes sense.

5 cups (1.2 L) apple cider
3 cups (700 ml) dry red wine
¼ cup (60 g) brown sugar
½ teaspoon whole cloves
¼ teaspoon whole allspice berries
1 cinnamon stick

In a slow cooker, combine all of the ingredients. Cover and cook on low for 3 to 4 hours. Before serving, using a slotted spoon, remove the cloves, allspice, and cinnamon stick.

Yield: 9 servings

MULLED WINE
This is a fairly traditional mulled wine, of the kind that has been around since colonial days.

½ teaspoon whole cloves
½ teaspoon whole allspice berries
8 cups (1.9 L) dry red wine
2 cinnamon sticks
1 teaspoon nutmeg

Place the cloves and allspice in cheesecloth bag or tea ball.
   In a slow cooker, combine the spice bag, wine, cinnamon sticks, and nutmeg. Cover and cook on high for 1 hour. Reduce the slow cooker heat to low and simmer for 2 to 3 hours.

Yield: 10 servings

▶ *Serving Suggestion*
Garnish individual servings with orange slices or cinnamon sticks.

CIDER TEA PUNCH
This spicy apple and tea combination is a perfect warmer for those cold winter nights.

½ gallon (1.9 L) apple cider
½ gallon (1.9 L) tea
1 lemon, sliced
1 orange, sliced
3 cinnamon sticks
1 tablespoon (6 g) whole cloves
1 tablespoon (6 g) whole allspice berries
¼ cup (60 g) brown sugar

In a slow cooker, combine all of the ingredients. Cover and cook on low for 2 hours.

Yield: 16 servings

3 Spiced Cider; 4 Maple Cider; 5 Cranberry Orange Cider; 6 Citrus Cider; 7 Hot Vitamin C-Pop Cranberry Cider; 8 Hot, Spiked, and Buttered Spiced Cider

9 Mulled Grape Cider; 10 Clean Classic Wassail; 11 Mulled Non-Wine Fresh Grape Delight;
12 Double Blackberry Brandy Wine; 13 Spiced Apple Wine; 14 Mulled Wine; 15 Cider Tea Punch; 16 Wassail

BEVERAGES • 253

WASSAIL

This is another hot drink based on cider but with more orange juice and a little different combination of spices.

1 cup (200 g) sugar
½ teaspoon ground ginger
1½ cinnamon sticks
½ teaspoon allspice
1 cup (235 ml) water
4 cups (950 ml) orange juice
2½ quarts (2.4 L) apple cider or juice
1½ cups (355 ml) lemon juice

In a saucepan, combine the sugar, ginger, cinnamon sticks, and allspice. Stir in the water and simmer until the sugar dissolves, stirring constantly. Add the orange juice, cider, and lemon juice.

Transfer the mixture to a slow cooker. Cover and cook on low for 2 hours. Serve warm or chill in the fridge and serve cool.

Yield: 12 servings

WASSAIL RUM PUNCH

This recipe is a variation of one that has been popular since the days of colonial America. Maybe it's the rum that gives it its popularity.

1 gallon (3.8 L) apple juice
4 apples
4 oranges
1 cup (145 g) raisins
1 tablespoon (15 ml) rum extract
½ cup (120 ml) rum
2 tablespoons (12 g) allspice
4 cups (950 ml) brewed tea
Sugar, to taste
Cinnamon sticks

The night before you'd like to serve the punch, slice the oranges and cut apples into quarters.

In a bowl, combine the oranges, apples, and raisins. Add the rum extract, rum, and allspice. Blend together. Cover and chill in the fridge overnight.

The next day, at least 1 hour before serving, transfer the mixture to a slow cooker. Add the tea and sugar to taste. Add the cinnamon sticks. Serve piping hot.

Yield: 24 servings

HOT BUTTERED RUM

This is a traditional grog for warming up a cold night.

½ cup (112 g) butter
3 cinnamon sticks
6 whole cloves
½ teaspoon nutmeg
8 cups (1.9 L) hot water
2 cups (475 ml) rum

In a slow cooker, combine all of the ingredients. Stir well. Cover and cook on high for 2 hours. Reduce the heat of the slow cooker to low. Cover and cook on low for 3 to 10 hours. Serve from the slow cooker.

Yield: 15 servings

HOT RUM AND FRUIT PUNCH

If you like cold fruity rum drinks, it's a pretty good bet you'll like this warm one too.

8 cups (1.9 L) apple cider
2 cups (475 ml) cranberry juice
1¼ cups (250 g) sugar
1 cinnamon stick
1 teaspoon whole allspice berries
1 orange, studded with whole cloves
1 cup (235 ml) rum

In a slow cooker, combine all of the ingredients. Cover and cook on high for 1 hour. Reduce the heat of the slow cooker to low. Cover and cook on low for 4 to 8 hours.

Serve warm from the slow cooker.

Yield: 12 servings

SPICED RASPBERRY PUNCH

Raspberries, cranberries, and orange blend together.

4 cups (950 ml) cranberry juice
3 cups (700 ml) water
¾ cup (213 g) frozen orange juice concentrate, thawed
10 ounces (280 g) frozen raspberries, thawed
2 oranges, sliced
6 cinnamon sticks
12 whole allspice berries

In a slow cooker, combine all of the ingredients. Cover and cook on high for 1 hour, or until the punch is hot. Before serving, reduce the heat of the slow cooker to low.

Yield: 10 servings

THANKSGIVING PUNCH
We've made this several times for holiday meals. The pineapple juice cuts the tartness of the cranberry, and the spices are just enough.

2 pounds (900 g) cranberry sauce, mashed
4 cups (950 ml) water
4 cups (950 ml) pineapple juice
¼ cup (60 g) brown sugar
¼ teaspoon nutmeg
¼ teaspoon cloves
¼ teaspoon allspice
12 cinnamon sticks

In a slow cooker, combine all of the ingredients, except for the cinnamon sticks. Cover and cook on low 4 hours.
    Serve with cinnamon stick stirrers.

Yield: 12 servings

CRANBERRY PUNCH
This is sort of warm cranberry sangria, or just cranberry punch.

8 whole cardamom pods
2 cinnamon sticks
12 whole cloves
4 cups (950 ml) dry red wine
1½ cups (426 g) frozen cranberry concentrate, thawed
2½ cups (570 ml) water
½ cup (170 g) honey
1 orange, sliced into 8 thin crescents

To make a spice packet, pinch open cardamom pods to release the seeds. Place them on a piece of cheesecloth or paper coffee filter. Add cinnamon sticks and cloves. Tie with a string to make a bag.
    In a slow cooker, combine the wine, cranberry concentrate, water, and honey. Cover and cook on low. Submerge the spice packet in the liquid and heat but do not boil. Let the punch steep on low for up to 4 hours.
    Before serving, remove and discard the spice bag. Float an orange slice in each cup. Serve warm.

Yield: 8 servings

TROPICAL TEA
Enjoy a little slice of tropical paradise any day. Serve this tea in a tall glass, with an orange wedge as a garnish.

2 quarts (1.9 L) boiling water
8 black teabags
1½ pints (710 ml) pineapple-orange juice
1 cinnamon stick

In a slow cooker, pour the boiling water and add the teabags. Let the teabags steep for 5 minutes, and then remove and discard them.
    Add the pineapple-orange juice and cinnamon stick, and stir to combine.
    Cover and cook on low for 2 to 3 hours, sampling the tea after 1 hour, and then every 30 minutes thereafter.
    When the cinnamon flavor is just right, using a slotted spoon, remove the cinnamon stick and discard it. Serve the tea immediately or keep it warm in the slow cooker.

Yield: 10 servings

▶*Recipe Variation*

Substitute orange-flavored tea or herb tea for the black tea.

FRUIT TEA
Here's a citrus-flavored tea to warm you up and make you think of the islands on a cold night.

6 cups (1.4 L) boiling water
6 teabags
⅓ cup (67 g) sugar
2 tablespoons (40 g) honey
1½ cups (355 ml) orange juice
1½ cups (355 ml) pineapple juice
1 orange, sliced

In a slow cooker, pour the boiling water over the teabags. Cover. Let the tea steep for 5 minutes. Add the remaining ingredients. Cover and cook on low for 2 to 3 hours.

Yield: 9 servings

RASPBERRY ICED TEA

Yes, this is an iced tea recipe made in a slow cooker. You will need to make this ahead so that you have time to chill the beverage before serving.

8 black teabags, or 1 cup (115 g) loose black tea
2 cups (500 g) frozen raspberries, plus some fresh ones for garnish
1 cup (200 g) sugar
8 cups (1880 ml) water
Ice

In a slow cooker, combine the tea, 2 cups (500 g) of the raspberries, the sugar, and water. Stir to mix. Cover and cook on high for 1½ hours.

Strain the tea, pushing down on the solids in the strainer. Discard the tea and raspberries. Chill the brewed tea. Serve over ice with additional raspberries for garnish.

Yield: 6 to 8 servings

LEMON MINT TEA

This blend of lemon, chamomile, and mint refreshes and soothes at the same time. It's delicious sweetened with honey.

1½ quarts (1.4 L) cold water
6 black tea with lemon-flavor teabags
3 chamomile teabags
6 sprigs fresh mint

In a slow cooker, pour the water and add the teabags and mint. Cover and cook on high for 1 to 2 hours, or until the water begins to simmer.

Before serving, remove and discard the teabags and mint. Serve the tea immediately or keep it warm in the slow cooker.

Yield: 6 servings

▶*Health Bite*
This flavorful herb tea is delicious, and it's ideal for settling an upset stomach or as a finishing touch to a big meal.

RUSSIAN TEA

Russian tea is a spiced and fruited tea that is a perfect recipe for the slow cooker.

1 gallon (3.8 L) water
2 teaspoons ground cinnamon
3 cloves
3 teabags
1½ cups (300 g) sugar
¾ cup (213 g) frozen orange juice, thawed
¾ cup (213 g) frozen lemonade, thawed

In a saucepan, combine the water, cinnamon, cloves, and teabags over high heat. Bring to a boil and boil for 2 to 3 minutes.

Using a slotted spoon, remove the teabags and cloves. Add the juices.

Transfer the tea to a slow cooker. Cover and cook on low for 1 hour, or until the flavors are blended.

Yield: 16 servings

SPICED TEA

This lets you mix up a big batch of spiced tea powder and then make it in whatever quantities you want in the slow cooker.

1 cup (32 g) instant tea
2 cups (416 g) instant orange drink mix
1 cup (200 g) sugar
2 tablespoons (28 g) lemonade mix
1 tablespoon (6.6 g) ground cloves
1 tablespoon (7 g) ground cinnamon

In an airtight container, combine all of the ingredients.

To use: Add ¼ cup (50 g) of the mix for each quart (960 ml) of water to a slow cooker. Cover and cook on low until warm, stirring occasionally to make sure the powder is dissolved.

Yield: 48 servings

DO-IT-YOURSELF CHAI CONCENTRATE

Chai is lovely, but it's getting pricey at coffee shops. It's well worth stocking up on a few spices to make your own, and it's super easy, too. Feel free to add more or less of some spices until it resembles your favorite. If you like a licorice flavor, add one star anise. It creates a big flavor.

6 cups (1,410 ml) water
5 slices fresh ginger
7 whole cinnamon sticks
10 whole cloves
10 whole peppercorns
8 whole allspice berries
¼ teaspoon cardamom seeds
10 teabags (black, green, or roobios)
½ to 1 cup (120 to 235 ml) agave nectar or maple syrup, optional

In a slow cooker, combine the water and spices. Cover and cook on low for 8 to 10 hours. Add the teabags. Increase the heat of the slow cooker to high. Let steep for 5 to 10 minutes, depending on how concentrated you want the flavor to be.

Before serving, using a slotted spoon remove the teabags and cinnamon sticks. Add the agave. Pour into a pitcher while straining out the spices through a piece of cheesecloth placed in a funnel.

Store in the fridge for 1 to 2 weeks.

Yield: About 6 cup (1,410 ml)

▶*Serving Suggestion*
Add ½ to 1 cup (120 to 235 ml) of the concentrate to an equal amount of milk. It's great hot or iced!

▶*Recipe Note*
You can put the spices in a muslin, reusable teabag, if you have one, and you won't have to strain it later.

CHAI TEA
Traditionally served piping hot in little clay cups that are discarded after use, chai tea is fun to sip with a meal or dessert. Enjoy it with whipped cream and a sprinkle of ground cinnamon or cocoa.

4½ cups (1.1 L) cold water
6 chai teabags
½ cup plus 2 tablespoons (125 g) orange or clover honey
4½ cups (1.1 L) milk

In a slow cooker, pour the water and add the teabags. Cover and cook on high for 1 to 2 hours, or until the water begins to simmer.

Using a slotted spoon, remove the teabags.

Reduce the heat of the slow cooker to low. Add the honey and stir until it has dissolved.

Add the milk and stir again. Serve the tea immediately or keep it warm in the slow cooker.

Yield: 12 servings

▶*Add It!*
Crush a large knob of fresh ginger and add it to the cold water along with the teabags. Remove when you remove the teabags.

LOWER-CAL VANILLA BEAN CHAI
This tastes as good as the expensive cup you can buy at you-know-where.

8 orange pekoe teabags
¼ cup (60 g) xylitol or erythritol
½ cup (64 g) grated fresh ginger
6 cinnamon sticks
2 tablespoons (8 g) lightly crushed whole cardamom pods
2 teaspoons whole cloves
½ teaspoon whole black peppercorns
2 star anise, optional
1 whole vanilla bean
8 cups (1.9 L) water
1 teaspoon vanilla stevia
2 cups (470 ml) unsweetened vanilla almond milk

In a 4-quart (3.8 L) slow cooker, combine the teabags, xylitol, ginger, cinnamon sticks, cardamom pods, cloves, peppercorns, and star anise, if using,

Carefully slice the vanilla bean lengthwise to open it. Using the point of a knife, scrape out all of the seeds and add them to the tea and spices. Gently pour the water over all. Cover and cook on high for 2 to 3 hours, or to the desired strength.

Strain the mixture through a double-mesh sieve and discard the spices. Return the liquid to the slow cooker and stir in the vanilla stevia and almond milk. Cover and cook for 10 minutes, or until heated through.

Yield: 8 servings

▶*Health Bite*
Even though green tea gets the lion's share of the press on health benefits, black tea is no also-ran. One review article in the medical journal Stroke *reported that individuals consuming 3 or more cups (705 ml) of black tea a day had a 21 percent lower risk of stroke than those consuming less than 1 cup (235 ml) a day. And black tea is loaded with health-giving polyphenols and antioxidants. The second thing you need to know is that there's quite a controversy about the effect of milk on the antioxidant power of tea (black or any other kind).*

Most data indicate that adding milk neutralizes many of the health-giving properties of compounds found in tea (like those antioxidants and polyphenols). However, research from Germany published in the European Heart Journal *found that it's the proteins in milk, called casein, that cancel out the positive effects. This wonderful chai recipe, uses unsweetened almond milk, which should have no negative impact on all those good things in the tea, because there's no casein in almond milk. And if that weren't enough, this version uses a healthy sweetener (xylitol or erythritol), which has virtually no impact on your blood sugar.*

BEVERAGES • 257

17 Wassail Rum Punch; 18 Hot Buttered Rum; 19 Hot Rum and Fruit Punch; 20 Spiced Raspberry Punch; 21 Thanksgiving Punch; 22 Cranberry Punch; 23 Tropical Tea; 24 Fruit Tea

258 • THE LITTLE SLOW COOKER COOKBOOK

25 Raspberry Iced Tea; 26 Lemon Mint Tea; 27 Russian Tea; 28 Spiced Tea; 29 Do-It-Yourself Chai Concentrate; 30 Chai Tea; 31 Lower-Cal Vanilla Bean Chai; 32 Maple-Sweetened Pumpkin-Spiced Latte

BEVERAGES • 259

MAPLE-SWEETENED PUMPKIN-SPICED LATTE

Fall comes around and hot drinks start seeming better, or at least as good as, the iced ones.

Wake up, throw all the ingredients into the slow cooker, and in 1½ to 2 hours you have piping hot lattes. Because you made this yourself, you can walk around in your comfy sweater, and feel slightly smug as you watch the leaves fall. This recipe uses a 1½- to 2-quart (1.4 to 1.9 L) slow cooker. You can double or triple the recipe and use a larger slow cooker if you like.

1 to 2 cups (235 to 470 ml) brewed coffee or espresso (Use more if you like stronger coffee flavor.)
2 cups (470 ml) vanilla-flavored almond milk or nondairy milk mixed with 1 teaspoon vanilla extract
2 to 4 tablespoons (30 to 60 ml) maple syrup
3 tablespoons (46 g) pumpkin purée (To make your own, see "Perfect Pumpkin Purée" on page 16.)
1 teaspoon cinnamon
¼ teaspoon ground cloves
¼ teaspoon allspice
⅛ teaspoon nutmeg

In a slow cooker, combine all of the ingredients. Whisk to combine. Cover and cook on low for 3 hours or on high for 1½ to 2 hours. Before serving, stir well because the pumpkin tends to settle at the bottom.

Yield: 4 servings

▶*Serving Suggestions*
- Serve with whole cinnamon sticks for stirring. The pumpkin tends to sink to the bottom, so this a stylish way to stir it back together.

- If you have the time, purée the pumpkin with the nondairy milk in a blender. This will keep it from separating as much.

CINNAMON SPIKED COFFEE

This zesty coffee has a whiff of cinnamon and a whisper of brown sugar. Garnish it with whipped cream and a cinnamon stick.

1 quart (.95 L) strong coffee
¼ cup (56 g) brown sugar, packed
1 cinnamon stick
Half-and-half, optional

In a slow cooker, combine the coffee, sugar, and cinnamon stick. Cover and cook on low for 2 to 3 hours, sampling the coffee after 1 hour, then every 30 minutes thereafter.

When the cinnamon flavor is just right, using a slotted spoon, remove the cinnamon stick and discard it. Serve the coffee black or with a generous helping of half-and-half, if using.

Yield: 4 servings

RASPBERRY CAPPUCCINO

Perfect for a shower or bachelorette party—a raspberry-flavored explosion in a mug! It looks and tastes festive in an Irish coffee mug.

4½ cups (1.1 L) strong coffee
2 cups (.47 L) half-and-half
1 cup (.24 L) raspberry liqueur
Whipped cream

In a slow cooker, combine all of the ingredients. Stir to mix well. Cover and cook on low for 30 to 60 minutes, or until the flavors have melded.

Warm 10 mugs in the oven or microwave. Divide the espresso mixture among the warm mugs, then fill the mugs the rest of the way with whipped cream. Serve the cappuccino immediately.

Yield: 10 servings

▶*Add It!*
Top the whipped cream with chocolate curls, dust it with ground cinnamon or cocoa powder, or drizzle it with raspberry sauce.

MOCHA

This is chocolate and coffee, with a little cinnamon flavor, topped by whipped cream. This is every bit as good—and a whole lot cheaper–than what you'll get at your local coffee shop.

2 cups (475 ml) brewed coffee
6 heaping tablespoons (45 g) instant hot chocolate mix
1 cinnamon stick, broken into large pieces
1 cup (235 ml) whipping cream
1 tablespoon (8 g) powdered sugar

In a slow cooker, combine the coffee, hot chocolate mix, and cinnamon sticks. Stir to mix. Cover and cook on high for 1 to 2 hours, or until very hot.

Using a slotted spoon, remove and discard the cinnamon stick pieces.

Just before serving, pour the whipping cream into a chilled mixer bowl. Beat the cream on high speed until soft peaks form. Fold the sugar into whipped cream. Beat again on high speed until stiff peaks form.

Ladle the hot chocolate coffee into small cups. Top each with a dollop of whipped cream.

Yield: 6 servings

HOT CINNAMON MOCHA

Assemble this in your slow cooker before going skating, caroling, or to a football game and have a winter party waiting when you get home. If it's a grown-up party, put a bottle of Mockahlua on the side for spiking. (See page 262.)

½ gallon (1.9 L) chocolate milk
2 cinnamon sticks
3 tablespoons (18 g) instant coffee granules
1½ teaspoons vanilla extract

In a slow cooker, combine all of the ingredients. Stir to mix. Cover and cook on high for 3 hours. Reduce the heat of the slow cooker to low. Serve from the slow cooker.

Yield: 10 servings

HOT COCOA

This is hot cocoa just like the good old days, but without having to stand over the stove stirring.

½ cup (100 g) sugar
½ cup (45 g) unsweetened cocoa powder
2 cups (475 ml) boiling water
3½ cups (448 g) dry milk powder
6 cups (1.4 L) water
1 teaspoon vanilla extract

In a slow cooker, combine the sugar and cocoa powder. Add the boiling water. Stir well to dissolve. Add the dry milk powder, water, and vanilla. Stir well to dissolve. Cover and cook on low for 4 hours or on high for 1 to 1½ hours.

Before serving, beat with rotary beater to make frothy. Ladle into mugs.

Yield: 9 servings

▶*Serving Suggestion*

Top with marshmallows and sprinkle with cinnamon.

PEPPERMINT HOT COCOA

This recipe is great for large groups.

1 gallon (3.8 L) cold milk
1 to 2 cups (235 to 470 ml) chocolate-flavored syrup
½ to 1 cup (120 to 235 ml) peppermint-flavored syrup
Whipped cream
Crushed mint candies

Pour the cold milk into the slow cooker. Cover and cook on low for 30 minutes, or until the milk is warm enough to dissolve the syrups. Add the chocolate- and peppermint-flavored syrups and gently stir until the syrups have dissolved. Cover and cook on low for another 1½ to 2½ hours, or until the mixture is hot; do not let it simmer.

Serve the cocoa warm in mugs topped with whipped cream and crushed mint candies.

Yield: 18 servings

▶*Recipe Variation*

Instead of peppermint, try substituting raspberry or hazelnut syrup.

HOT WHITE COCOA

For something a little different, make hot chocolate using white chocolate.

3 cups (700 ml) milk
3 cups (700 ml) evaporated milk
1½ cups (255 g) white chocolate chips
2 teaspoons vanilla extract

In a slow cooker, combine all of the ingredients. Cover and cook on low for 3 to 4 hours or on high for 1 to 2 hours.

Yield: 8 servings

EXOTIC CARDAMOM HOT CHOCOLATE

Who needs cake or cookies when all you have to do is ladle yourself a warm mug of extra-thick, sweetly spiced hot chocolate from the slow cooker? Throw this together before dinner and you'll have a sweet treat before you go to bed. You can halve this recipe for 2 or 3 servings and cook it in a 1½-quart (1.4 L) slow cooker.

4 cups (940 ml) unsweetened vanilla almond milk or plain almond milk mixed with 1 teaspoon vanilla extract
3 ounces (84 g) semisweet chocolate disks or bars, coarsely chopped
¼ to ½ cup (50 to 100 g) sugar
12 whole cardamom pods
2 cinnamon sticks, optional
4 to 6 marshmallows, optional

In a slow cooker, combine the milk, chocolate, sugar, cardamom, and cinnamon. Cover and cook on low for 2 to 3 hours, whisking every 30 minutes, or until all the chocolate is melted. Strain out the cardamom and cinnamon. Stir well before serving in mugs, topped with marshmallow, if using.

Yield: 4 to 6 servings

▶ *Recipe Variations*
- *I f you are avoiding refined sugar, use unsweetened chocolate instead of the semisweet, and replace the sugar with a natural sweetener of your choice, such as stevia, agave nectar, or maple syrup.*

- *Omit the spices for a traditional hot chocolate. Or add some mint extract or 2 herbal peppermint teabags for a peppermint chocolate treat.*

COQUITO EGGNOG (PHOTO PAGE 4)

It's good to create a new holiday tradition. Chilled coconut eggnog is a delicious tradition in Puerto Rico. Try it and see why.

2 quarts (1.9 L) eggnog
1 pint (475 ml) coconut milk
½ teaspoon ground nutmeg

In a slow cooker, combine the eggnog and milk. Stir gently to mix. Cover and cook on low for 1 to 2 hours, or until the mixture is hot; do not let it simmer.

Ladle the eggnog into mugs, dust it with nutmeg, and serve it warm. To be traditional, refrigerate it for several hours and serve it chilled.

Yield: 10 servings

▶ *Health Bite*
Coconut oil has been touted as the new weight-loss miracle food. Try cooking with coconut oil instead of your current cooking oil—unlike coconut milk and flesh, the oil won't add a coconut flavor to your food.

MOCKAHLUA

This recipe makes quite a lot, but don't worry about that; 100-proof vodka's a darned good preservative. Your Moackahlua will keep indefinitely.

2½ cups (570 ml) water
3 cups (75 g) Splenda
3 tablespoons (18 g) instant coffee granules
1 teaspoon vanilla extract
1 bottle (750 milliliters) 100-proof vodka (Use the cheap stuff)

In a large pitcher or measuring cup, combine the water, Splenda, coffee granules, and vanilla extract. Stir until the coffee and Splenda are completely dissolved.

Pour the mixture through a funnel into a 1.5 or 2 liter bottle. (A clean 1.5 liter wine bottle works fine, so long as you've saved the cork.) Pour in the vodka. Cork and shake well.

Yield: 32 servings or 1½ ounces (42 ml)–a standard "shot"

33 Cinnamon Spiced Coffee

34 Rasberry Cappuccino; 35 Mocha; 36 Hot Cinnamon Mocha; 37 Hot Cocoa; 38 Peppermint Hot Cocoa; 39 Hot White Cocoa

264 • THE LITTLE SLOW COOKER COOKBOOK

40 Exotic Cardamon Hot Chocolate

CREDITS

With thanks to recipe authors:

Jeannette Bessinger, CHHC

Suzanne Bonet

Jonny Bowden, PhD, CNS

Dana Carpender

Kathy Hester

Carol Hildebrand

Robert Hildebrand

INDEX

A

Acorn squash
    Acorn Squash, 191, 197
    Acorn Squash Stuffed with Cranberry-Pecan Rice, 194, 197
    Fruit-Stuffed Acorn Squash, 194, 197
    health benefits of, 194
Adobo Stew, 163, 169
All-Occasion Roasted Garlic, 17, 22
Almond meal
    Peach Almond Breakfast Polenta, 41, 43
Almonds
    Curried Almonds, 28, 32
    Fruit 'n Nutty Overnight Breakfast Groats, 41, 42–43
    health benefits of, 28
    Low-Sugar Coco-Nutty Rice Pudding, 226, 230
    Mixed Berry and Almond Granola, 38, 40
    Sweet and Spicy Nuts, 25, 32
Anchovies
    health benefits of, 12
    Mega Omega Piquant Artichoke, Olive, and Anchovy Sauce, 12, 15
Antioxidant-Burst Raspberry Peach Cobbler, 233, 238
Antioxidant-Rich Sweet Potato Carrot Pudding, 222, 225
Appetizers
    Asian Chicken Wings, 30, 33
    Cheesy Spoonbread, 24
    Cinnamon Walnuts, 25, 32
    Clean and Tasty Pizza Fondue, 35, 37
    Cranberry Meatballs, 29, 33
    Curried Almonds, 28, 32
    Dark Chocolate Trail Mix for a Crowd, 25, 32
    Gourmet Mushrooms, 34, 37
    Honey Chicken Wings, 30, 33
    Low-Carb Sesame Turkey Meatballs, 29–30, 33
    Mediterranean Stuffed Grape Leaves, 34, 37
    Mexican Dip, 31, 37
    Party Meatballs, 28, 33
    Pimiento Cheese Fondue, 35, 37
    Queso Dip, 31, 36
    Spiced Nuts, 28, 32
    Spinach Artichoke Dip, 29, 33
    Spinach Dip, 31, 36
    Subtly Spicy Peanut Fondue, 4, 35
    Sugared Pecans, 28, 32
    Sweet and Sour Chicken Wings, 30, 33
    Sweet and Sour Hot Dog Bites, 30, 33
    Sweet and Spicy Nuts, 25, 32
    Taco Dip, 31, 37
    Whole-Grain Crunchy Party Mix, 24, 26–27
    Wine-Braised Artichokes, 34, 37
Apple Butter, 16, 22
Apple Cake, 236, 239
Apple cider
    Cider Tea Punch, 251, 253
    Citrus Cider, 245, 252
    Cranberry Orange Cider, 245, 252
    Hot, Spiked, and Buttered Spiced Cider, 247, 252
    Hot Apple Cider, 246, 249
    Hot Rum and Fruit Punch, 254, 258
    Maple Cider, 244, 252
    Shallot Apple Brussels Sprouts, 181, 183
    Spiced Apple Wine, 251, 253
    Spiced Cider, 244, 252
    Wassail, 253, 254
Apples
    Apple Butter, 16, 22
    Apple Cake, 236, 239
    Apple Cobbler, 233, 238
    Apple Cranberry Pork Roast, 94, 96
    Apple Crisp, 234, 238
    Apple Oatmeal Breakfast Pudding, 39, 40
    Apple Sage Sausage, 19–20, 23
    Baked Apples with Raisins, 210, 216
    Berrylicious Biscuit-Topped Fruit Cobbler, 234, 238
    Brandied Fruit, 219, 224
    Breakfast Apple Crunch, 39, 40
    Breakfast Cobbler, 51, 53
    Caramel Apples, 210, 212
    Chunky Applesauce, 206, 208
    Clean Classic Wassail, 250, 253
    Cranberry Applesauce, 206, 209
    Fall Harvest Fruit Butter, 16, 22
    Fruit-Stuffed Acorn Squash, 194, 197
    Granola Apple Crisp, 234, 239
    health benefits of, 153, 194, 250
    Homey Baked Apples, 210, 216
    Hot Apple Cider, 246, 249
    Lightly Sweetened Autumnal Fruit Butter, 13, 22
    Pork Chops with Apples, 99, 100
    Red Cabbage, Green Apple, and Sweet Onion, 191, 197
    Sausage with Apples and Onions, 101, 104
    Slightly Drunken Apples, 210, 213
    Spiced Apples, 211, 216
    Spiced Candied Apples and Yams with Raw Chocolate Drizzle, 211, 216
    Stewed Apples, 206, 209
    Sweet Tooth–Buster Sweet Potato Apple Soup, 153, 158
    Turkey and Fruit Sweetened Cranberry Sauce Supper, 115, 120
    Warm Applesauce, 206, 208
    Wassail Rum Punch, 254, 258
Apricots
    Apricot Chicken, 114, 116
    Apricot Custard, 232, 238
    Brandied Fruit, 219, 224
    Lean Dried Apricot, Chicken, and Wild Rice Soup, 145, 151
    Lean Lemon-Apricot Chicken Breasts, 105, 107
    nutrients in, 145
    unsulfured, 105
Artichokes
    Easiest Lean Artichoke Chicken Breasts, 105, 107
    health benefits of, 105

Mega Omega Piquant Artichoke, Olive, and Anchovy Sauce, 12, 15
Spinach Artichoke Dip, 29, 33
Wine-Braised Artichokes, 34, 37
Asian Broccoli, 181, 183
Asian Chicken Wings, 30, 33
Asian Pork Roast, 94, 96–97
Asian Ribs, 100, 102
Asian-Style Winter Stew, 171, 174
Asian Tempeh Lettuce Wraps, 69–70, 74
Asparagus
  Asparagus Side Dish, 180, 183
  Steak Rollups with Asparagus, 79, 81
Atomic Tofu Pecan Loaf, 130, 132
Au Gratin Potatoes, 205, 208
Au Gratin Salmon and Potato Bake, 124, 126
Autumnal Rich-Roots Medley Potatoes, 205, 208

B

Bacon
  Broccoli and Bacon with Pine Nuts, 184, 192
  Broccoli-Bacon-Colby Quiche, 51, 53
Baked Apples with Raisins, 210, 216
Baked Beans, 198, 202
Baked Potatoes, 204, 208
Baked Whole Chicken, 104–5, 107
Baked Ziti, 132, 135
Baking Mix, Heart-Healthy, 221
Balsamic vinegar
  Balsamic Brussels Sprouts, 180, 183
  Balsamic Onion Marmalade, 17, 22
  Blueberry-Balsamic Meatball Sauce with Rosemary, 8, 15
Bamboo shoots
  Thai Curry Tofu and Veggies, 125, 128
Bananas
  Banana Bread, 59, 66
  Glorious Glazed Bananas, 215, 217
  Juice-Sweetened Tropical Fruit Compote, 219, 224
  Rum Raisin Bananas, 217, 218
  Wholesome Chocolate Chip Banana Bread, 59, 66
Barbecue sauce
  Barbecued Pork Chops, 95, 98
  Barbecued Short Ribs, 79, 82
  Barbecued Turkey Thighs, 119, 121
  Citrus Rum BBQ Sauce, 7, 14
  Cranberry Barbecued Turkey, 119, 121
  Easy Maple Barbecue Pulled Pork Shoulder, 95, 97
Barley
  Barley Risotto, 201, 203
  Beef Barley Soup, 142, 150
  Breakfast Grains, 39, 40
  health benefits of, 163
  Seeded and Stuffed Carnival Squash, 138, 140
  Vegetable-Loaded Beef and Barley Stew, 163, 169
Basic Fuss-Free Risotto, 136, 140
Basic Granola, 38, 40
Basil
  Pesto, 12, 15
  Spinach, Basil, and Feta-Stuffed Chicken Rolls with Pignoli, 113, 114
Bavarian Cabbage, 184–85, 192
Beans. See also Lima Beans
  Baked Beans, 198, 202
  Bean and Vegetable Soup, 156, 159

Black Bean Soup, 154, 159
Caribbean Mango Black Beans, 199–200, 203
Chana Saag, 200, 203
Chile Black Bean Brownies, 235, 239
Dry Beans from Scratch, 18, 22
Fantastic Mexi Beans, 199, 203
fiber in, 155
Firehouse Chili, 84, 86
Lean and Easy Taco Salad, 142, 146
Lo-Cal Caribbean Black Bean Soup, 154–55, 159
Northern Bean Soup, 155, 159
Pumpkin and White Bean Lasagna, 132, 134–35
Santa Fe Chicken, 107, 108
Seeded and Stuffed Carnival Squash, 138, 140
Slow-Cooked Shepherd's Pie, 84, 87
Smoked Ham Hocks with White Beans, 100, 102
Soy Chorizo Black Bean Stew, 167, 174
Vegetarian Baked Beans, 198–99, 202
White Bean and Kale Stew, 171, 174
Beef. See also Corned beef
  Adobo Stew, 163, 169
  Barbecued Short Ribs, 79, 82
  Beef Barley Soup, 142, 150
  Beef Biryani, 78, 80
  Beef Borscht, 172, 175
  Beef Burgundy in Hunter Sauce, 77, 78
  Beef Stock, 6, 10
  Beef with Butternut Squash and Cherries, 77, 78
  Beef with Gravy, 79, 82
  Belgian Beef Stew, 163, 169
  Braised Beef in Red Wine, 78, 80
  choosing, for stews, 76
  Comfort Food Casserole, 84, 86
  Fajitas, 65, 73
  Firehouse Chili, 84, 86
  French Dip, 65, 74
  grass-fed, 76, 77
  Greek Sandwich Filling, 68, 74
  Ground Sirloin Borscht, 172, 175
  Hamburger Casserole, 83, 84
  Loaded Sloppy Joe with a Kick, 69, 74
  Mexican Dip, 31, 37
  Mushroom Pot Roast, 77, 78
  nutrients in, 76
  Orange Onion Pot Roast, 78, 80
  Quick Stroganoff, 79, 82
  Real Deal Beef Stew with Orange and Clove, 76, 78
  salting, as preservative, 90
  Savory Slow-Cooked Meat Loaf, 79, 81
  Short Ribs, 79, 83
  Shredded Beef, 68, 74
  Simplest Beefy Tacos, 68, 74
  Smothered Steak, 79, 82
  Steak Rollups with Asparagus, 79, 81
  Stuffed Peppers with Beef and Corn, 83, 84
  Swiss Steak, 79, 81
  Taco Dip, 31, 37
  Tangy Tomato Grass-Fed Pot Roast, 76–77, 78
  Three-Alarm Chili, 84, 86
  Vegetable-Loaded Beef and Barley Stew, 163, 169
Beefy Seitan, 19, 23
Beets
  Beets with Ginger and Orange, 187, 193
  Fresh Sweet 'n Sour Beets, 187, 193

INDEX • 269

Ground Sirloin Borscht, 172, 175
health benefits of, 172, 187
Orange Beets with Walnuts, 187, 193
Belgian Beef Stew, 163, 169
Berries. See also specific berries
    Berrylicious Biscuit-Topped Fruit Cobbler, 234, 238
    Fruit 'n Nutty Overnight Breakfast Groats, 41, 42–43
    Mixed Berry and Almond Granola, 38, 40
Beverages
    Chai Tea, 257, 259
    Cider Tea Punch, 251, 253
    Cinnamon Spiked Coffee, 260, 263
    Citrus Cider, 247, 252
    Clean Classic Wassail, 250, 253
    Coquito Eggnog, 4, 262
    Cranberry Orange Cider, 247, 252
    Cranberry Punch, 255, 258
    Do-It-Yourself Chai Concentrate, 256–57, 259
    Double Blackberry Brandy Wine, 251, 253
    Exotic Cardamom Hot Chocolate, 262, 265
    Fruit Tea, 255, 258
    Habanero-Spiked "Red Hot" Cider, 246, 248
    Hot, Spiked, and Buttered Spiced Cider, 247, 252
    Hot Apple Cider, 246, 249
    Hot Buttered Rum, 254, 258
    Hot Cinnamon Mocha, 261, 264
    Hot Cocoa, 261, 264
    Hot Rum and Fruit Punch, 254, 258
    Hot Vitamin C-Pop Cranberry Cider, 247, 252
    Hot White Cocoa, 262, 264
    Lemon Mint Tea, 256, 259
    Lower-Cal Vanilla Bean Chai, 257, 259
    Maple Cider, 246, 252
    Maple-Sweetened Pumpkin-Spiced Latte, 259, 260
    Mocha, 261, 264
    Mockahlua, 262
    Mulled Grape Cider, 250, 253
    Mulled Non-Wine, 250, 253
    Mulled Wine, 251, 253
    Peppermint Hot Cocoa, 261, 264
    Raspberry Cappuccino, 260, 264
    Raspberry Iced Tea, 256, 259
    Russian Tea, 256, 259
    Spiced Apple Wine, 251, 253
    Spiced Cider, 246, 252
    Spiced Raspberry Punch, 254, 258
    Spiced Tea, 256, 259
    Thanksgiving Punch, 255, 258
    Tropical Tea, 255, 258
    Wassail, 253, 254
    Wassail Rum Punch, 254, 258
Big Pot of Grits, 45
Big Pot of Oatmeal, 41, 44
Biscuit-Topped Fruit Cobbler, Berrylicious, 234, 238
Black Bean Soup, 154, 159
Blackberry Brandy Wine, Double, 251, 253
Blondies, Tea "Thyme" Lemon, 235, 239
Blueberries
    Blueberry-Balsamic Meatball Sauce with Rosemary, 8, 15
    health benefits of, 12
    Memorable Gingered Peaches and Blues Sauce, 12, 15
Borscht
    Beef Borscht, 172, 175
    Ground Sirloin Borscht, 172, 175

Boston Brown Bread, 62, 67
Bouillabaisse, Tofu, 157, 168
Braised Beef in Red Wine, 78, 80
Braised Leeks with Vinaigrette, 185, 192
Braised Red Cabbage, 184, 192
Braised Turkey Wings with Mushrooms, 118, 121
Bran cereal
    Oat Bran Bread, 55, 56
Brandy
    Brandied Fruit, 219, 224
    Double Blackberry Brandy Wine, 251, 253
Bread puddings
    Caramel Bread Pudding, 227, 230
    Chocolate Bread Pudding, 227, 230
    Eggy Spicy Whole-Grain Breakfast Bread Pudding, 39, 40
    Strawberry Bread Pudding, 227, 231
    Strawberry Sourdough Bread Pudding, 40, 42
Breads
    Banana Bread, 59, 66
    Boston Brown Bread, 62, 67
    Carrot Bread, 58, 60
    Cheesy Spoonbread, 24
    Chock-Full-of-Veggies Cornbread, 63, 67
    Citrusy Rosemary Breakfast Bread, 62, 67
    Coconut Bread, 58, 66
    Cornbread, 63, 67
    Cranberry Bread, 62, 66
    Cranberry Orange Nut Bread, 58, 61
    Eggy Spicy Whole-Grain Breakfast Bread Pudding, 39, 40
    Foolproof Focaccia, 65, 67
    Granola Bread, 55, 56
    health effects from, 42
    Honey Wheat Bread, 56, 64
    Italian Quick Bread, 54, 56
    Lemon Bread, 59, 66
    Oat Bran Bread, 55, 56
    Pear and Cardamom French Toast Casserole, 47, 48
    Savory Cheddar Sausage Bread, 64, 67
    Scrumptious Strawberry Cornbread, 63, 67
    Strawberry Sourdough Bread Pudding, 40, 42
    Tomato-Herb Bread, 55, 57
    White Bread, 54, 56
    Whole Grain Bread, 54–55, 56
    Wholesome Chocolate Chip Banana Bread, 59, 66
    Whole Wheat Bread, 54, 56
    Whole Wheat Pumpkin Gingerbread, 64, 67
    Zucchini Bread, 58–59, 66
Breakfast Apple Crunch, 39, 40
Breakfast Burritos, 50, 53
Breakfast Casserole, 47, 48
Breakfast Cobbler, 51, 53
Breakfast Grains, 39, 40
Breakfast Risotto, 41, 43
Breakfasts
egg-based
    Breakfast Burritos, 50, 53
    Broccoli-Bacon-Colby Quiche, 51, 53
    Broccoli Egg Casserole, 47, 48
    Eggs Florentine, 50, 53
    Eggy Spicy Whole-Grain Breakfast Bread Pudding, 39, 40
    Mexican Egg Scramble, 47, 49
    Slow Cooker Poached Eggs, 50, 53
    Western Omelet, 49, 52
French toast

Pear and Cardamom French Toast Casserole, 47, 48
grain-based
    Apple Oatmeal Breakfast Pudding, 39, 40
    Basic Granola, 38, 40
    Big Pot of Grits, 45
    Big Pot of Oatmeal, 41, 44
    Breakfast Apple Crunch, 39, 40
    Breakfast Cobbler, 51, 53
    Breakfast Grains, 39, 40
    Breakfast Risotto, 41, 43
    Carrot Cake and Zucchini Bread Oatmeal, 41, 44–45
    Cranberry Vanilla Quinoa, 41, 44
    Eggy Spicy Whole-Grain Breakfast Bread Pudding, 39, 40
    Fruit 'n Nutty Overnight Breakfast Groats, 41, 42–43
    Maple Pecan Granola, 38, 40
    Mixed Berry and Almond Granola, 38, 40
    Peach Almond Breakfast Polenta, 41, 43
    Pick-Your-Pleasure Breakfast Rice Pudding, 41, 42
    Pumpkin Pie Oatmeal, 41, 45
    Raspberry Yogurt Oatmeal, 45, 46
    Strawberry Sourdough Bread Pudding, 40, 42
hash brown–based
    Breakfast Casserole, 47, 48
    Spicy Hash Browns, 51, 53
    Weekend Tofu and Hash Brown Breakfast Casserole, 47, 49
    Western Omelet, 49, 52
tofu-based
    Scrambled Tofu with Peppers, 49
    Weekend Tofu and Hash Brown Breakfast Casserole, 47, 49
Broccoli
    Asian Broccoli, 181, 183
    Broccoli and Bacon with Pine Nuts, 184, 192
    Broccoli-Bacon-Colby Quiche, 51, 53
    Broccoli Casserole, 181, 188
    Broccoli-Cheese Soup, 157, 168
    Broccoli Egg Casserole, 47, 48
    Broccoli Rice Casserole, 181, 189
    Cheesy Broccoli Rice, 201, 203
    Ma Po Tofu, 139, 141
    Penne with Broccoli, 133, 136
Broth. See also Stocks
    Freshest Vegetable Broth, 6–7, 14
    stock vs., 7
Brownies
    Chile Black Bean Brownies, 235, 239
    Have-It-Your-Way Brownies, 235–36, 239
Brown Sugar Rice Pudding, 223, 230
Brunswick Stew, 170, 174
Brussels sprouts
    Balsamic Brussels Sprouts, 180, 183
    health benefits of, 181
    Shallot Apple Brussels Sprouts, 181, 183
Bulgur
    Breakfast Grains, 39, 40
Burritos
    Breakfast Burritos, 50, 53
    Mashed Potato and Edamame Burrito Filling, 72, 75
Burst of Flavor Butternut Squash and Pesto Panini Filling, 72, 75
Butter Chick'n, 18, 23
Butternut squash
    Beef with Butternut Squash and Cherries, 77, 78
    Burst of Flavor Butternut Squash and Pesto Panini Filling, 72, 75
    Butternut Squash Puree, 195, 197
    Creamy Butternut Squash Risotto, 201, 203
    Fall Harvest Fruit Butter, 16, 22
Butterscotch Sauce, Peaches with, 215, 217

C

Cabbage
    Bavarian Cabbage, 184–85, 192
    Braised Red Cabbage, 184, 192
    Cabbage Soup with Kielbasa, 149, 151
    Corned Beef and Cabbage, 85, 91
    Ham and Cabbage Casserole, 101, 103
    Hard Cider and Cabbage Stew, 171, 174
    health benefits of, 90
    Maple Glazed Corned Beef with Vegetables, 85, 90–91
    New England Corned Beef and Cabbage, 84, 90
    Red Cabbage, Green Apple, and Sweet Onion, 191, 197
Cakes
    Apple Cake, 236, 239
    Carrot Cake, 236, 239
    Cinnamon-Swirl Cherry Delight Cake, 240, 244
    Crust-Free Cheesecake, 240, 244
    Mochaccino Cheesecake, 241, 244
    New York Style Cheesecake, 240–41, 244
    Peanut Butter Cheesecake, 241, 244
    Slow Cooker Chocolate Cake, 236–37, 239
    Strawberry Chocolate Crumble, 240, 244
    Vanilla Upside-Down Cake, 237, 239
    White Fruit Cake, 237, 243
Calorie restriction, benefits of, 250–51
Candied Carrots and Pecans, 185, 192
Cappuccino, Raspberry, 260, 264
Capsaicin, health benefits of, 162, 246
Caramel Apples, 210, 212
Caramel Bread Pudding, 227, 230
Cardamom
    Exotic Cardamom Hot Chocolate, 262, 265
    Pear and Cardamom French Toast Casserole, 47, 48
Caribbean Mango Black Beans, 199–200, 203
Caribbean Slow Cooker Lamb, 89, 93
Carnival Squash, Seeded and Stuffed, 138, 140
Carrots
    Antioxidant-Rich Sweet Potato Carrot Pudding, 222, 225
    Asian-Style Winter Stew, 171, 174
    Candied Carrots and Pecans, 185, 192
    Carrot Bread, 58, 60
    Carrot Cake, 236, 239
    Carrot Cake and Zucchini Bread Oatmeal, 41, 44–45
    Carrot Pudding, 222, 225
    Chicken with Root Vegetables, 104, 106
    health benefits of, 186, 222
    Maple Glazed Corned Beef with Vegetables, 85, 90–91
    Marmalade-Glazed Carrots, 186, 193
    Old-Fashioned Vegetable Soup, 156, 164
    Parsnip and Carrot Medley, 186, 193
    Vegetable Medley, 191, 197
    Vodka and Dill-Glazed Baby Carrots, 186, 193
Cashews
    Spiced Nuts, 28, 32
    Sweet and Spicy Nuts, 25, 32
Cassoulet, Lamb, 85, 92
Catfish Fillets, Zesty Citrus, 124, 126
Cauliflower

Cream of Unpotato Soup, 152–53, 158
Curried Cauliflower, 184, 192
Curried Coconut Cream of Cauliflower Soup, 160, 168
health benefits of, 160
Thai Curry Tofu and Veggies, 125, 128
Cayenne Caramelized Onions, 185, 192
Celery
health benefits of, 163
Vegetable Medley, 191, 197
Celiac disease, 24
Cereal
hot (see Oats)
Whole-Grain Crunchy Party Mix, 24, 26–27
Chai
Chai Tea, 257, 259
Do-It-Yourself Chai Concentrate, 256–57, 259
Lower-Cal Vanilla Bean Chai, 257, 259
Steamy, Creamy, High-Calcium Chai Pudding, 222, 225
Chana Saag, 200, 203
Cheese. See also Cream cheese
Broccoli-Bacon-Colby Quiche, 51, 53
Broccoli-Cheese Soup, 157, 168
Cheesy Broccoli Rice, 201, 203
Cheesy Spoonbread, 24
Clean and Tasty Pizza Fondue, 35, 37
Fresh and Light Summer Medley with Feta, 190, 196
Macaroni and Two Cheeses, 136, 140
Philadelphia-Style Cheesy Portobello Sandwich, 70, 75
Pimiento Cheese Fondue, 35, 37
Queso Dip, 31, 36
Savory Cheddar Sausage Bread, 64, 67
Smoky Mac and Cheese, 200, 203
Spinach, Basil, and Feta-Stuffed Chicken Rolls with Pignoli, 113, 114
Spinach Parmesan Casserole, 184, 192
Spring Minestrone with Pesto Parmesan, 148, 151
Three-Cheese Vegetarian Spaghetti, 133, 135
Cheesecakes
Crust-Free Cheesecake, 240, 244
Mochaccino Cheesecake, 241, 244
New York Style Cheesecake, 240–41, 244
Peanut Butter Cheesecake, 241, 244
Cheesy Broccoli Rice, 201, 203
Cheesy Spoonbread, 24
Cherries
Beef with Butternut Squash and Cherries, 77, 78
Cherry Cobbler, 232, 238
Cinnamon-Swirl Cherry Delight Cake, 240, 244
Chicken
Apricot Chicken, 114, 116
Asian Chicken Wings, 30, 33
Baked Whole Chicken, 104–5, 107
Brunswick Stew, 170, 174
Chicken and Dumplings, 115, 116–17
Chicken Cacciatore, 115, 117
Chicken Corn Soup, 144, 150
Chicken Minestrone, 145, 151
Chicken Noodle Soup, 143–44, 150
Chicken Rice Soup, 144, 151
Chicken Soup with Wild Rice, 145, 151
Chicken Stock, 6, 11
Chicken with Root Vegetables, 104, 106
Cranberry Chicken Breasts, 107, 108
Drumsticks with Hoisin and Honey, 115, 117
Easiest Lean Artichoke Chicken Breasts, 105, 107
Easy Asian Sweet Chili, 113, 114
Hearty Chicken Stew, 167, 174
Honey Chicken Wings, 30, 33
In-a-Pinch Pesto Chicken and Mushrooms, 107, 108
lean breast of, 145
Lean Dried Apricot, Chicken, and Wild Rice Soup, 145, 151
Lean Lemon-Apricot Chicken Breasts, 105, 107
Lemon, Rosemary, and Garlic Chicken Breasts, 109, 110
Mom's 1960s Chicken Redux, 109, 114
pastured vs. free-range, 113
Peanutty Thai Chicken, 112, 114
as protein source, 105
Quick Sesame Teriyaki Lettuce Wraps, 69, 74
Santa Fe Chicken, 107, 108
Seriously Simple Chicken Chili, 112, 114
Slow Cooker Chicken Mole, 115, 116
Spinach, Basil, and Feta-Stuffed Chicken Rolls with Pignoli, 113, 114
Sweet and Saucy Free-Range Chicken Thighs, 114, 116
Sweet and Sour Chicken Breasts, 109, 111
Sweet and Sour Chicken Wings, 30, 33
Szechuan Chicken Stew, 170, 174
thighs, 116
Veggie-Rich Asian Chicken Stew, 170, 174
Versatile Lean and Easy Chicken Base, 21, 23
Chick'n Cacciatore, 131, 132
Chick'n Mushroom Casserole, 112, 114
Chick'n Seitan, 18–19, 23
Chickpeas
Chana Saag, 200, 203
Chile Black Bean Brownies, 235, 239
Chili
Easy Asian Sweet Chili, 113, 114
Firehouse Chili, 84, 86
Pineapple Pepper Chili, 84, 87
Seriously Simple Chicken Chili, 112, 114
Three-Alarm Chili, 84, 86
Chili Sauce, 8, 14
Chock-Full-of-Veggies Cornbread, 63, 67
Chocolate. See also Cocoa
Chocolate Bread Pudding, 227, 230
Chocolate Fondue, 232, 238
Chocolate Fudge Custard, 229, 231
Chocolate Pudding, 221, 225
Crisp Chocolate Crust, 242
Dark Chocolate Trail Mix for a Crowd, 25, 32
Exotic Cardamom Hot Chocolate, 262, 265
health benefits of, 221
Hot Cinnamon Mocha, 261, 264
Hot White Cocoa, 262, 264
Layered Crepe Dessert, 242, 245
Mocha, 261, 264
Peppermint Hot Cocoa, 261, 264
Slow Cooker Chocolate Cake, 236–37, 239
Spiced Candied Apples and Yams with Raw Chocolate Drizzle, 211, 216
Strawberry Chocolate Crumble, 240, 244
Wholesome Chocolate Chip Banana Bread, 59, 66
Chorizo
Corn-Tastic Tex-Mex Loaf, 130
Soy Chorizo Black Bean Stew, 167, 174
Chowders. See Soups
Chunky Applesauce, 206, 208

Chunky German Sausage and Sauerkraut Stew, 167, 169
Cider. See also Wassail
    Cider Tea Punch, 251, 253
    Citrus Cider, 247, 252
    Cranberry Orange Cider, 247, 252
    Habanero-Spiked "Red Hot" Cider, 246, 248
    Hard Cider and Cabbage Stew, 171, 174
    Hot, Spiked, and Buttered Spiced Cider, 247, 252
    Hot Apple Cider, 246, 249
    Hot Vitamin C–Pop Cranberry Cider, 247, 252
    Maple Cider, 246, 252
    Mulled Grape Cider, 250, 253
    Shallot Apple Brussels Sprouts, 181, 183
    Spiced Cider, 246, 252
Cinnamon
    Cinnamon Eggnog Bread Pudding, 227, 230
    Cinnamon Spiked Coffee, 260, 263
    Cinnamon Sugar, 206
    Cinnamon-Swirl Cherry Delight Cake, 240, 244
    Cinnamon Walnuts, 25, 32
    Gingered Honey Pears with Cinnamon Sticks, 214–15, 217
    Hot Cinnamon Mocha, 261, 264
Citrus Cider, 247, 252
Citrus Rum BBQ Sauce, 7, 14
Citrusy Rosemary Breakfast Bread, 62, 67
Clam Chowder, Easy Manhattan, 173, 175
Clean and Tasty Pizza Fondue, 35, 37
Clean Classic Wassail, 250, 253
Cleaning method, for slow cooker, 143
Cloves
    Real Deal Beef Stew with Orange and Clove, 76, 78
Cobblers
    Antioxidant-Burst Raspberry Peach Cobbler, 233, 238
    Apple Cobbler, 233, 238
    Berrylicious Biscuit-Topped Fruit Cobbler, 234, 238
    Breakfast Cobbler, 51, 53
    Cherry Cobbler, 232, 238
    Peach Cobbler, 233, 238
Cocoa. See also Chocolate
    Have-It-Your-Way Brownies, 235–36, 239
    health benefits of, 221, 226
    Hot Cocoa, 261, 264
    Hot White Cocoa, 262, 264
    Low-Cal Cocoa Tapioca, 220, 225
    Low-Sugar Coco-Nutty Rice Pudding, 226, 230
    Mochacchino Cheesecake, 241, 244
    Peppermint Hot Cocoa, 261, 264
Coconut
    Coconut Bread, 58, 66
    Coconut Lemon Curd, 15
    Southeast Asian Coconut Custard, 229, 231
Coconut milk
    Coquito Eggnog, 4, 262
    Curried Coconut Cream of Cauliflower Soup, 160, 168
    Mango Coconut Rice Pudding, 226, 230
    Southeast Asian Coconut Custard, 229, 231
Coconut oil
    benefits of, 13
    Coconut Lemon Curd, 13
Coddled Ham, 101, 103
Coffee
    Cinnamon Spiked Coffee, 260, 263
    Hot Cinnamon Mocha, 261, 264
    Maple-Sweetened Pumpkin-Spiced Latte, 259, 260
    Mocha, 261, 264
    Mochacchino Cheesecake, 241, 244
    Mockahlua, 262
    Raspberry Cappuccino, 260, 264
Comfort Food Casserole, 84, 86
Condensed Cream of Mushroom Soup, 7, 14
Coquito Eggnog, 4, 262
Corn
    Cheesy Spoonbread, 24
    Chicken Corn Soup, 144, 150
    Chock-Full-of-Veggies Cornbread, 63, 67
    Corn Chowder with Crab, 173, 175
    Corn Pudding, 176, 182
    Corn with Peppers and Onions, 176, 179
    Creamy Corn, 176, 178
    Fresh Chili Lime Cob Corn, 176, 182
    health benefits of, 176
    Old-Fashioned Vegetable Soup, 156, 164
    Santa Fe Chicken, 107, 108
    Stuffed Peppers with Beef and Corn, 83, 84
Cornbread, 63, 67
    Cheesy Spoonbread, 24
    Chock-Full-of-Veggies Cornbread, 63, 67
    Scrumptious Strawberry Cornbread, 63, 67
Corned beef
    Corned Beef and Cabbage, 85, 91
    Maple Glazed Corned Beef with Vegetables, 85, 90–91
    New England Boiled Dinner, 85, 90
    New England Corned Beef and Cabbage, 84, 90
Cornish Game Hens and Wild Rice, 115, 117
Corn Pudding, 176, 182
Corn-Tastic Tex-Mex Loaf, 130
Corn with Peppers and Onions, 176, 179
Couscous, Curried, 204, 207
Crab, Corn Chowder with, 173, 175
Cranberries
    Acorn Squash Stuffed with Cranberry-Pecan Rice, 194, 197
    Apple Cranberry Pork Roast, 94, 96
    Cranberry Applesauce, 206, 209
    Cranberry Barbecued Turkey, 119, 121
    Cranberry Bread, 62, 66
    Cranberry Chicken Breasts, 107, 108
    Cranberry Orange Nut Bread, 58, 61
    Cranberry Vanilla Quinoa, 41, 44
    health benefits of, 120, 247
    Hot Vitamin C–Pop Cranberry Cider, 247, 252
    Turkey and Fruit Sweetened Cranberry Sauce Supper, 115, 120
Cranberry juice
    Cranberry Orange Cider, 247, 252
    Cranberry Punch, 255, 258
    Spiced Raspberry Punch, 254, 258
Cranberry sauce
    Cranberry Meatballs, 29, 33
    Thanksgiving Punch, 255, 258
Cream, replacement for, 223
Cream cheese
    Crust-Free Cheesecake, 240, 244
    Mochacchino Cheesecake, 241, 244
    New York Style Cheesecake, 240–41, 244
    Peanut Butter Cheesecake, 241, 244
    Saucy Cream Cheese Potatoes, 204, 208
Cream of Mushroom Soup, 149, 158

INDEX • **273**

Cream of Unpotato Soup, 152–53, 158
Creamy Butternut Squash Risotto, 201, 203
Creamy Corn, 176, 178
Creamy Potato Soup, 152, 158
Creamy Zucchini Casserole, 195, 202
Crepe Dessert, Layered, 242, 244
Crisp Chocolate Crust, for cheesecake, 242
Crisps
    Apple Crisp, 234, 238
    Granola Apple Crisp, 234, 239
Crust-Free Cheesecake, 240, 244
Crusts
    Crisp Chocolate Crust, 242
    Graham Cracker Crust, 241
Curd, Coconut Lemon, 13, 15
Curry
    Curried Almonds, 28, 32
    Curried Cauliflower, 184, 192
    Curried Coconut Cream of Cauliflower Soup, 160, 168
    Curried Couscous, 204, 207
    Curried Mulligatawny Lamb Stew, 166, 169
    Eggplant Curry, 198, 202
    Swordfish Braised with Thai Green Curry, 124, 126
    Thai Curry Pork, 100, 102
    Thai Curry Tofu and Veggies, 125, 128
Custards
    Apricot Custard, 232, 238
    Chocolate Fudge Custard, 229, 231
    Flan, 223, 225
    Low-Sugar Lemon Honey Custard, 228, 231
    Maple Custard, 229, 231
    Maple Pumpkin Custard, 231, 232
    Slow Cooker Custard, 228, 231
    Southeast Asian Coconut Custard, 229, 231

D

Dark Chocolate Trail Mix for a Crowd, 25, 32
Delicata Squash and Pear Soup, 160, 168
Desserts
    baking mix
        Heart-Healthy Baking Mix, 221
    brownies and blondies
        Chile Black Bean Brownies, 235, 239
        Have-It-Your-Way Brownies, 235–36, 239
        Tea "Thyme" Lemon Blondies, 235, 239
    cakes
        Apple Cake, 236, 239
        Carrot Cake, 236, 239
        Cinnamon-Swirl Cherry Delight Cake, 240. 244
        Crisp Chocolate Crust, 242
        Crust-Free Cheesecake, 240, 244
        Mochacchino Cheesecake, 241, 244
        New York Style Cheesecake, 240–41, 244
        Peanut Butter Cheesecake, 241, 244
        Slow Cooker Chocolate Cake, 236–37, 239
        Strawberry Chocolate Crumble, 240, 244
        Vanilla Upside-Down Cake, 237, 239
        White Fruit Cake, 237, 243
    cobblers and crisps
        Antioxidant-Burst Raspberry Peach Cobbler, 233, 238
        Apple Cobbler, 233, 238
        Apple Crisp, 234, 238
        Berrylicious Biscuit-Topped Fruit Cobbler, 234, 238
        Cherry Cobbler, 232, 238
        Granola Apple Crisp, 234, 239
        Peach Cobbler, 233, 238
    crusts
        Crisp Chocolate Crust, 242
        Graham Cracker Crust, 241
    fondue
        Chocolate Fondue, 232, 238
    fruit-based
        Baked Apples with Raisins, 210, 216
        Brandied Fruit, 219, 224
        Caramel Apples, 210, 212
        Earl Grey Poached Pears, 211, 216
        Fresh Pineapple with Coconut Lime Rum Sauce, 214, 217
        Gingered Honey Pears with Cinnamon Sticks, 214–15, 217
        Glorious Glazed Bananas, 215, 217
        Golden Fruit Compote, 219, 224
        Homey Baked Apples, 210, 216
        Hot Spiced Fruit, 218, 224
        Hot Spiced Pears, 217, 218
        Juice-Sweetened Tropical Fruit Compote, 219, 224
        Layered Crepe Dessert, 242, 245
        Peaches with Butterscotch Sauce, 215, 217
        Peaches with Dumplings, 215, 217
        Poached Pears in Red Wine, 214, 216
        Rhubarb Flummery, 217, 218
        Rum Raisin Bananas, 217, 218
        Slightly Drunken Apples, 210, 213
        Spiced Apples, 211, 216
        Spiced Candied Apples and Yams with Raw Chocolate Drizzle, 211, 216
        Strawberry-Lime Granita, 4, 242
    puddings and custards
        Antioxidant-Rich Sweet Potato Carrot Pudding, 222, 225
        Apricot Custard, 232, 238
        Brown Sugar Rice Pudding, 223, 230
        Caramel Bread Pudding, 227, 230
        Carrot Pudding, 222, 225
        Chocolate Bread Pudding, 227, 230
        Chocolate Fudge Custard, 229, 231
        Chocolate Pudding, 221, 225
        Cinnamon Eggnog Bread Pudding, 227, 230
        Flan, 223, 225
        Fruited Tapioca, 220, 224
        Indian Pudding, 227, 231
        Low-Cal Cocoa Tapioca, 220, 225
        Lower-Sugar Raisin-Orange Pumpkin Pie Pudding, 226, 230
        Low-Sugar Coco-Nutty Rice Pudding, 226, 230
        Low-Sugar Lemon Honey Custard, 228, 231
        Mango Coconut Rice Pudding, 226, 230
        Maple Custard, 229, 231
        Maple Pumpkin Custard, 231, 232
        Pumpkin Pie Pudding, 221–22, 225
        Pumpkin Pudding, 221, 225
        Rice Pudding, 223, 230
        Slow Cooker Custard, 228, 231
        Southeast Asian Coconut Custard, 229, 231
        Steamy, Creamy, High-Calcium Chai Pudding, 222, 225
        Strawberry Bread Pudding, 227, 231
        Tapioca Pudding, 219, 224
        Tapioca Pudding for Two, 220, 224
        Turkish Delight Tapioca Pudding, 220, 224
Dijon mustard
    Dilled Salmon Dijon, 123, 124

Dill
- Dilled Salmon Dijon, 123, 124
- Vodka and Dill-Glazed Baby Carrots, 186, 193

Dips. See also Fondues
- Mexican Dip, 31, 37
- Queso Dip, 31, 36
- Spinach Artichoke Dip, 29, 33
- Spinach Dip, 31, 36
- Taco Dip, 31, 37

Do-It-Yourself Chai Concentrate, 256–57, 259
Double Blackberry Brandy Wine, 251, 253
Drumsticks with Hoisin and Honey, 115, 117
Dry Beans from Scratch, 18, 22
Dumplings, 21, 23
- Chicken and Dumplings, 115, 116–17
- Peaches with Dumplings, 215, 217

E

Earl Grey Poached Pears, 211, 216
Easiest Lean Artichoke Chicken Breasts, 105, 107
Easiest Ribs, 99, 100
Easiest Vegetable-Surprise Dish, 190, 197
Easy Asian Sweet Chili, 113, 114
Easy Cheesy Potato Casserole, 204, 208
Easy Manhattan Clam Chowder, 173, 175
Easy Maple Barbecue Pulled Pork Shoulder, 95, 97
Easy Pasta Sauce, 9, 15
Easy Pork Roast, 94, 96
Edamame Burrito Filling, Mashed Potato and, 72, 75
Eggnog
- Cinnamon Eggnog Bread Pudding, 227, 230
- Coquito Eggnog, 4, 262

Eggplant
- Eggplant Curry, 198, 202
- Vegetarian Spaghetti Sauce, 9, 15

Eggs
- Breakfast Burritos, 50, 53
- Broccoli-Bacon-Colby Quiche, 51, 53
- Broccoli Egg Casserole, 47, 48
- Eggs Florentine, 50, 53
- Eggy Spicy Whole-Grain Breakfast Bread Pudding, 39, 40
- health benefits of, 228
- Mexican Egg Scramble, 47, 49
- Slow Cooker Poached Eggs, 50, 53
- Western Omelet, 49, 52

Evaporated skim milk, health benefits of, 223
Exotic Cardamom Hot Chocolate, 262, 265

F

Fajitas, 65, 73
Fall Harvest Fruit Butter, 16, 22
Fantastic Mexi Beans, 199, 203
Fermented foods, naturally, 167
Fiber
- health benefits of, 138
- sources of, 155, 163, 194

Figs and Port Wine, Tempeh Braised with, 125, 129
Firehouse Chili, 84, 86
Fish. See also Shellfish
- Au Gratin Salmon and Potato Bake, 124, 126
- Dilled Salmon Dijon, 123, 124
- Lemon-Poached Salmon Fillets, 123, 124
- Manhattan Braised Halibut Steaks, 124, 126
- Pungent, Light, and Clear Thai Seafood Stew, 162, 169
- Swordfish Braised with Thai Green Curry, 124, 126
- Tomato Salmon Bisque, 173, 175
- Zesty Citrus Catfish Fillets, 124, 126

Flan, 223, 225
Focaccia, Foolproof, 65, 67
Fondues
- Chocolate Fondue, 232, 238
- Clean and Tasty Pizza Fondue, 35, 37
- Pimiento Cheese Fondue, 35, 37
- Subtly Spicy Peanut Fondue, 4, 35

Foolproof Focaccia, 65, 67
French Dip, 65, 74
French Toast Casserole, Pear and Cardamom, 47, 48
Fresh and Light Summer Medley with Feta, 190, 196
Fresh Chili Lime Cob Corn, 176, 182
Freshest Vegetable Broth, 6–7, 14
Fresh Pineapple with Coconut Lime Rum Sauce, 214, 217
Fresh Sweet 'n Sour Beets, 187, 193
From-the-Pantry Pot Pie, 4, 129–30, 132
Fruit butters
- Apple Butter, 16, 22
- Fall Harvest Fruit Butter, 16, 22
- Lightly Sweetened Autumnal Fruit Butter, 13, 22

Fruits. See also specific fruits
- Berrylicious Biscuit-Topped Fruit Cobbler, 234, 238
- Brandied Fruit, 219, 224
- Fruited Tapioca, 220, 224
- Fruit 'n Nutty Overnight Breakfast Groats, 41, 42–43
- Fruit-Stuffed Acorn Squash, 194, 197
- Fruit Tea, 255, 258
- Golden Fruit Compote, 219, 224
- Hot Rum and Fruit Punch, 254, 258
- Hot Spiced Fruit, 218, 224
- Juice-Sweetened Tropical Fruit Compote, 219, 224
- Turkey and Fruit Sweetened Cranberry Sauce Supper, 115, 120
- White Fruit Cake, 237, 243

G

Garlic
- All-Occasion Roasted Garlic, 17, 22
- Garlic Spinach with Roasted Reds, 190, 193
- health benefits of, 190
- Mushroom Lasagna with Garlic-Tofu Sauce, 132, 134
- Zested and Light Lemon-Garlic Tilapia with Roasted Shiitakes, 125, 128

German Potato Salad, 142, 147
Gifts from the Sea Chowder, 172, 175
Ginger
- Beets with Ginger and Orange, 187, 193
- Gingered Honey Pears with Cinnamon Sticks, 214–15, 217
- Memorable Gingered Peaches and Blues Sauce, 12, 15
- Whole Wheat Pumpkin Gingerbread, 64, 67

Glazed Root Vegetables, 186, 193
Glorious Glazed Bananas, 215, 217
Gluten-free foods, 24
Gluten sensitivity or intolerance, 24
Golden Fruit Compote, 219, 224
Gourmet Mushrooms, 34, 37
Graham Cracker Crust, for cheesecake, 241
Grains, Breakfast, 39, 40
Granita, Strawberry-Lime, 4, 242
Granola
- Basic Granola, 38, 40

INDEX • 275

Breakfast Apple Crunch, 39, 40
Breakfast Cobbler, 51, 53
Granola Apple Crisp, 234, 239
Granola Bread, 55, 56
Maple Pecan Granola, 38, 40
Mixed Berry and Almond Granola, 38, 40
Grape Cider, Mulled, 250, 253
Grape Leaves, Mediterranean Stuffed, 34, 37
Grapes
    Mulled Non-Wine, 250, 253
    resveratrol in, 251
Grass-fed meats, 76, 77
Gravy, Beef with, 79, 82
Greek Sandwich Filling, 68, 74
Green beans
    Green Bean Casserole, 180, 183
    Green Beans with Smoked Sausage, 101, 103
    health benefits of, 177
    Not Your Grandma's Green Beans, 177, 182
    Southern Beans, 180, 183
    Tangy Beans, 177, 182
    Vegetable Medley, 191, 197
Greens
    Chana Saag, 200, 203
Grits, Big Pot of, 45
Groats, Fruit 'n Nutty Overnight Breakfast, 41, 42–43
Ground Sirloin Borscht, 172, 175
Gumbo, Veggie, with Cheater Roux, 162, 168

H

Habanero-Spiked "Red Hot" Cider, 246, 248
Halibut
    Manhattan Braised Halibut Steaks, 124, 126
    Pungent, Light, and Clear Thai Seafood Stew, 162, 169
Ham
    Brunswick Stew, 170, 174
    Coddled Ham, 101, 103
    Ham and Cabbage Casserole, 101, 103
    Ham and Scalloped Potatoes, 101, 103
    Holiday Ham, 101, 103
    Orange-Glazed Ham, 101, 103
    Smoked Ham Hocks with White Beans, 100, 102
    Split Pea and Ham Soup, 156, 159
Hamburger Casserole, 83, 84
Hard Cider and Cabbage Stew, 171, 174
Hash browns
    Au Gratin Potatoes, 205, 208
    Breakfast Casserole, 47, 48
    Easy Cheesy Potato Casserole, 204, 208
    Spicy Hash Browns, 51, 53
    Weekend Tofu and Hash Brown Breakfast Casserole, 47, 49
    Western Omelet, 49, 52
Have-It-Your-Way Brownies, 235–36, 239
Hawaiian Pork Roast, 94, 96
Heart-Healthy Baking Mix, 221
Hearty Chicken Stew, 167, 174
Herbs, Tomato-Herb Bread, 55, 57
High-volume foods, 161–62
Hoisin and Honey, Drumsticks with, 115, 117
Holiday Ham, 101, 103
Holiday Sweet Potato Casserole, 205–6, 208
Holiday Tempeh and Sage Loaf, 131, 132
Homemade Smoky Ketchup, 8, 14

Homey Baked Apples, 210, 216
Honey
    Drumsticks with Hoisin and Honey, 115, 117
    Gingered Honey Pears with Cinnamon Sticks, 214–15, 217
    Honey Chicken Wings, 30, 33
    Honey Wheat Bread, 56, 64
    Low-Sugar Lemon Honey Custard, 228, 231
Honeydew melon
    Juice-Sweetened Tropical Fruit Compote, 219, 224
Honey mustard
    Honey Mustard Ribs, 100, 102
    Pork Loin with Honey Mustard, 95, 97
Honey Wheat Bread, 46, 64
Hot, Spiked, and Buttered Spiced Cider, 247, 252
Hot and Sour Chinese Vegetable Soup, 157, 168
Hot and Sour Soup, 143, 150
Hot Apple Cider, 246, 249
Hot Buttered Rum, 254, 258
Hot Cinnamon Mocha, 261, 264
Hot Cocoa, 261, 264
Hot dogs
    Sweet and Sour Hot Dog Bites, 30, 33
Hot Rum and Fruit Punch, 254, 258
Hot Spiced Fruit, 218, 224
Hot Spiced Pears, 217, 218
Hot Vitamin C–Pop Cranberry Cider, 247, 252
Hot White Cocoa, 262, 264
Hunter Sauce, Beef Burgundy in, 77, 78

I

In-a-Pinch Pesto Chicken and Mushrooms, 107, 108
Indian Pudding, 227, 231
Italian Quick Bread, 54, 56
Italian Zucchini, 198, 202

J

Jambalaya
    Mix and Match Jambalaya, 125, 139
    Shellfish Jambalaya, 125, 127
Juice-Sweetened Tropical Fruit Compote, 219, 224

K

Kalamata olives, facts about, 113
Kale Stew, White Bean and, 171, 174
Ketchup, Homemade Smoky, 8, 14
Kielbasa, Cabbage Soup with, 149, 151
Kiwis
    Juice-Sweetened Tropical Fruit Compote, 219, 224
Kung Pao Chick'n, 137, 140

L

Lamb
    Caribbean Slow Cooker Lamb, 89, 93
    Curried Mulligatawny Lamb Stew, 166, 169
    health benefits of, 91, 166
    Lamb Cassoulet, 85, 92
    Lamb Shanks with Lentils, 85, 92
    Lemon Lamb Shanks, 88, 93
    Luscious, Leanest Lamb Chops, 85, 91
    Mediterranean Stuffed Grape Leaves, 34, 37
    Moroccan Braised Lamb Shanks in Fresh Tomatoes and Red Wine, 85, 91–92
    Pomegranate Lamb, 85, 92
    Rosemary Lamb Stew, 166, 169

Slow-Cooked Shepherd's Pie, 84, 87
Lasagna
    Mushroom Lasagna with Garlic-Tofu Sauce, 132, 134
    Pumpkin and White Bean Lasagna, 132, 134–35
Latte, Maple-Sweetened Pumpkin-Spiced, 259, 260
Layered Crepe Dessert, 242, 245
Lean and Easy Taco Salad, 142, 146
Lean and Green Stuffed Peppers, 122–23, 124
Lean Dried Apricot, Chicken, and Wild Rice Soup, 145, 151
Lean Lemon-Apricot Chicken Breasts, 105, 107
Leeks
    Braised Leeks with Vinaigrette, 185, 192
    health benefits of, 154
    No-Cream Leek and Potato Soup, 154, 158
Lemons
    Citrusy Rosemary Breakfast Bread, 62, 67
    Coconut Lemon Curd, 13, 15
    health benefits of, 13
    Hot Vitamin C–Pop Cranberry Cider, 247, 252
    Lean Lemon-Apricot Chicken Breasts, 105, 107
    Lemon, Rosemary, and Garlic Chicken Breasts, 109, 110
    Lemon Bread, 59, 66
    Lemon Lamb Shanks, 88, 93
    Lemon-Poached Salmon Fillets, 123, 124
    Low-Sugar Lemon Honey Custard, 228, 231
    Tea "Thyme" Lemon Blondies, 235, 239
    Zested and Light Lemon-Garlic Tilapia with Roasted Shiitakes, 125, 128
Lentils
    Lamb Shanks with Lentils, 85, 92
    Lentils and Rice, 137, 140
    nutrients in, 155
    Split Pea and Lentil Soup, 155, 159
Lettuce
    Asian Tempeh Lettuce Wraps, 69–70, 74
    Quick Sesame Teriyaki Lettuce Wraps, 69, 74
Light Louisiana Creole Shrimp Soup, 161–62, 168
Lightly Sweetened Autumnal Fruit Butter, 13
Lima Beans, 199, 202
    Old-Fashioned Vegetable Soup, 156, 164
    Slow Cooker Sausage and Lima Beans, 101, 104
Limes
    Fresh Chili Lime Cob Corn, 176, 182
    Fresh Pineapple with Coconut Lime Rum Sauce, 214, 217
    Strawberry-Lime Granita, 4, 242
    Zesty Citrus Catfish Fillets, 124, 126
Liver function, foods benefiting, 154, 172
Loaded Sloppy Joe with a Kick, 69, 74
Loaded Split Pea Sweet Potato Soup, 153, 158
Loaves. See also Meat loaf
    Atomic Tofu Pecan Loaf, 130, 132
    Corn-Tastic Tex-Mex Loaf, 130
    Holiday Tempeh and Sage Loaf, 131, 132
Lo-Cal Caribbean Black Bean Soup, 154–55, 159
Low-Cal Cocoa Tapioca, 220, 225
Low-Carb Sesame Turkey Meatballs, 29–30, 33
Lower-Cal Vanilla Bean Chai, 257, 259
Lower-Sugar Raisin-Orange Pumpkin Pie Pudding, 226, 230
Low-Sugar Coco-Nutty Rice Pudding, 226, 230
Low-Sugar Lemon Honey Custard, 228, 231
Luscious, Leanest Lamb Chops, 85, 91

M
Macaroni

Macaroni and Two Cheeses, 136, 140
Smoky Mac and Cheese, 200, 203
Main dishes
    beef
        Barbecued Short Ribs, 79, 82
        Beef Biryani, 78, 80
        Beef Burgundy in Hunter Sauce, 77, 78
        Beef with Butternut Squash and Cherries, 77, 78
        Beef with Gravy, 79, 82
        Braised Beef in Red Wine, 78, 80
        Comfort Food Casserole, 84, 86
        Corned Beef and Cabbage, 85, 91
        Firehouse Chili, 84, 86
        Hamburger Casserole, 83, 84
        Maple Glazed Corned Beef with Vegetables, 85, 90–91
        Mushroom Pot Roast, 77, 78
        New England Boiled Dinner, 85, 90
        New England Corned Beef and Cabbage, 84, 90
        Orange Onion Pot Roast, 78, 80
        Quick Stroganoff, 79, 82
        Real Deal Beef Stew with Orange and Clove, 76, 78
        Savory Slow-Cooked Meat Loaf, 79, 81
        Short Ribs, 79, 83
        Smothered Steak, 79, 82
        Steak Rollups with Asparagus, 79, 81
        Stuffed Peppers with Beef and Corn, 83, 84
        Swiss Steak, 79, 81
        Tangy Tomato Grass-Fed Pot Roast, 76–77, 78
        Three-Alarm Chili, 84, 86
    fish and shellfish
        Au Gratin Salmon and Potato Bake, 124, 126
        Dilled Salmon Dijon, 123, 124
        Lemon-Poached Salmon Fillets, 123, 124
        Manhattan Braised Halibut Steaks, 124, 126
        Sweet and Sour Shrimp, 125, 127
        Swordfish Braised with Thai Green Curry, 124, 126
        Szechuan Shrimp, 125, 127
        Zested and Light Lemon-Garlic Tilapia with Roasted Shiitakes, 125, 128
        Zesty Citrus Catfish Fillets, 124, 126
    lamb
        Caribbean Slow Cooker Lamb, 89, 93
        Lamb Cassoulet, 85, 92
        Lamb Shanks with Lentils, 85, 92
        Lemon Lamb Shanks, 88, 93
        Luscious, Leanest Lamb Chops, 85, 91
        Moroccan Braised Lamb Shanks in Fresh Tomatoes and Red Wine, 85, 91–92
        Pomegranate Lamb, 85, 92
        Slow-Cooked Shepherd's Pie, 84, 87
    meatless
        Atomic Tofu Pecan Loaf, 130, 132
        Baked Ziti, 132, 135
        Basic Fuss-Free Risotto, 136, 140
        Chick'n Cacciatore, 131, 132
        Chick'n Mushroom Casserole, 112, 114
        Corn-Tastic Tex-Mex Loaf, 130
        From-the-Pantry Pot Pie, 4, 129–30, 132
        Holiday Tempeh and Sage Loaf, 131, 132
        Kung Pao Chick'n, 137, 140
        Lentils and Rice, 137, 140
        Macaroni and Two Cheeses, 136, 140

Ma Po Tofu, 139, 141
Meatless Sausage and Mushroom Ragu, 132, 134
Mix and Match Jambalaya, 125, 139
Mushroom Lasagna with Garlic-Tofu Sauce, 132, 134
Pasta and Mushrooms, 133, 135
Penne with Broccoli, 133, 136
Perfect Pizza from Your Slow Cooker, 138, 140
Pineapple Pepper Chili, 84, 87
Pumpkin and White Bean Lasagna, 132, 134–35
Seeded and Stuffed Carnival Squash, 138, 140
Shellfish Jambalaya, 125, 127
Spanish Quinoa, 137, 140
Sweet and Sour Smoked Tofu, 125, 128–29
Tempeh Braised with Figs and Port Wine, 125, 129
Thai Curry Tofu and Veggies, 125, 128
Three-Cheese Vegetarian Spaghetti, 133, 135

pork
Apple Cranberry Pork Roast, 94, 96
Asian Pork Roast, 94, 96–97
Asian Ribs, 100, 102
Barbecued Pork Chops, 95, 98
Coddled Ham, 101, 103
Easiest Ribs, 99, 100
Easy Maple Barbecue Pulled Pork Shoulder, 95, 97
Easy Pork Roast, 94, 96
Ham and Cabbage Casserole, 101, 103
Ham and Scalloped Potatoes, 101, 103
Hawaiian Pork Roast, 94, 96
Holiday Ham, 101, 103
Honey Mustard Ribs, 100, 102
Orange-Glazed Ham, 101, 103
Pork and Sweet Potato Dinner, 95, 97
Pork Chops and Vegetables in Mushroom Gravy, 95, 98
Pork Chops Braised with Sauerkraut, 99, 100
Pork Chops with Apples, 99, 100
Pork Chops with Sweet Potatoes, 99, 100
Pork Loin with Honey Mustard, 95, 97
Slow Cooker Shredded Pork, 95, 97
Smoked Ham Hocks with White Beans, 100, 102
Southern Stuffed Pork Chops, 95, 98
Stuffed Pork Chops, 95, 98
Thai Curry Pork, 100, 102

poultry
Apricot Chicken, 114, 116
Baked Whole Chicken, 104–5, 107
Barbecued Turkey Thighs, 119, 121
Braised Turkey Wings with Mushrooms, 118, 121
Chicken and Dumplings, 115, 116–17
Chicken Cacciatore, 115, 117
Chicken with Root Vegetables, 104, 106
Cornish Game Hens and Wild Rice, 115, 117
Cranberry Barbecued Turkey, 119, 121
Cranberry Chicken Breasts, 107, 108
Drumsticks with Hoisin and Honey, 115, 117
Easiest Lean Artichoke Chicken Breasts, 105, 107
Easy Asian Sweet Chili, 113, 114
In-a-Pinch Pesto Chicken and Mushrooms, 107, 108
Lean and Green Stuffed Peppers, 122–23, 124
Lean Lemon-Apricot Chicken Breasts, 105, 107
Lemon, Rosemary, and Garlic Chicken Breasts, 109, 110
Mom's 1960s Chicken Redux, 109, 114
Peanutty Thai Chicken, 112, 114
Santa Fe Chicken, 107, 108
Savory Slow-Cooked Meat Loaf, 79, 81
Savory Slow Cooker Tender Turkey Drumsticks, 115, 120
Savory Turkey and Rice, 119, 122
Seriously Simple Chicken Chili, 112, 114
Slow Cooker Chicken Mole, 115, 116
Spinach, Basil, and Feta-Stuffed Chicken Rolls with Pignoli, 113, 114
Sweet and Saucy Free-Range Chicken Thighs, 114, 116
Sweet and Sour Chicken Breasts, 109, 111
Turkey and Fruit Sweetened Cranberry Sauce Supper, 115, 120
Turkey Dinner, 115, 121
Turkey Meat Loaf, 122, 124
Turkey Tortilla Pie, 119, 122

sausage
Green Beans with Smoked Sausage, 101, 103
Mix and Match Jambalaya, 125, 139
Sausage with Apples and Onions, 101, 104
Slow Cooker Sausage and Lima Beans, 101, 104

veal
Osso Buco, 94, 96
Roast Veal Shoulder, 93, 94

Mangoes
Caribbean Mango Black Beans, 199–200, 203
Juice-Sweetened Tropical Fruit Compote, 219, 224
Mango Coconut Rice Pudding, 226, 230
Manhattan Braised Halibut Steaks, 124, 126
Maple syrup
Easy Maple Barbecue Pulled Pork Shoulder, 95, 97
Maple Cider, 246, 252
Maple Custard, 229, 231
Maple Glazed Corned Beef with Vegetables, 85, 90–91
Maple Pecan Granola, 38, 40
Maple Pumpkin Custard, 231, 232
Maple-Sweetened Pumpkin-Spiced Latte, 259, 260
Ma Po Tofu, 139, 141
Marmalade
Balsamic Onion Marmalade, 17, 22
Marmalade-Glazed Carrots, 186, 193
Mashed Potato and Edamame Burrito Filling, 72, 75
Meatballs
Cranberry Meatballs, 29, 33
Low-Carb Sesame Turkey Meatballs, 29–30, 33
Party Meatballs, 28, 33
Meatless Sausage and Mushroom Ragu, 132, 134
Meat loaf
Savory Slow-Cooked Meat Loaf, 79, 81
Turkey Meat Loaf, 122, 124
Mediterranean Stuffed Grape Leaves, 34, 37
Mega Omega Piquant Artichoke, Olive, and Anchovy Sauce, 12, 15
Memorable Gingered Peaches and Blues Sauce, 12, 15
Mexican Dip, 31, 37
Mexican Egg Scramble, 47, 49
Mighty Minestrone, 148, 151
Milk
evaporated skim, 223
fat in, benefits of, 228
organic, 228
in tea, 257
Minestrone
Chicken Minestrone, 145, 151

278 • THE LITTLE SLOW COOKER COOKBOOK

Mighty Minestrone, 148, 151
	Spring Minestrone with Pesto Parmesan, 148, 151
Mint Tea, Lemon, 256, 259
Mix and Match Jambalaya, 125, 139
Mixed Berry and Almond Granola, 38, 40
Mixed Squash Casserole, 198, 202
Mocha, 261, 264
	Hot Cinnamon Mocha, 261, 264
Mochacchino Cheesecake, 241, 244
Mockahlua, 262
Mole, Slow Cooker Chicken, 115, 116
Mom's 1960s Chicken Redux, 109, 114
Moroccan Braised Lamb Shanks in Fresh Tomatoes and Red Wine, 85, 91–92
Mulled Grape Cider, 250, 253
Mulled Non-Wine, 250, 253
Mulled Wine, 251, 253
Mushrooms
	Braised Turkey Wings with Mushrooms, 118, 121
	Chick'n Mushroom Casserole, 112, 114
	Condensed Cream of Mushroom Soup, 7, 14
	Cream of Mushroom Soup, 149, 158
	Gourmet Mushrooms, 34, 37
	Hot and Sour Soup, 143, 150
	In-a-Pinch Pesto Chicken and Mushrooms, 107, 108
	Ma Po Tofu, 139, 141
	Meatless Sausage and Mushroom Ragu, 132, 134
	Mushroom Lasagna with Garlic-Tofu Sauce, 132, 134
	Mushroom Pot Roast, 77, 78
	Pasta and Mushrooms, 133, 135
	Philadelphia-Style Cheesy Portobello Sandwich, 70, 75
	Pork Chops and Vegetables in Mushroom Gravy, 95, 98
	Turkey Mushroom Soup, 149, 151
	Zested and Light Lemon-Garlic Tilapia with Roasted Shiitakes, 125, 128

N

Naturally fermented foods, 167
New England Boiled Dinner, 85, 90
New England Corned Beef and Cabbage, 84, 90
New York Style Cheesecake, 240–41, 244
No-Cream Leek and Potato Soup, 154, 158
Noodles
	Chicken Noodle Soup, 143–44, 150
	Turkey Noodle Soup, 144, 150
Northern Bean Soup, 155, 159
Not Your Grandma's Green Beans, 177, 182
Nutrient density, defined, 148, 161–62
Nuts. See also specific nuts
	Cranberry Orange Nut Bread, 58, 61
	Fruit 'n Nutty Overnight Breakfast Groats, 41, 42–43
	Low-Sugar Coco-Nutty Rice Pudding, 226, 230
	Spiced Nuts, 28, 32
	Sweet and Spicy Nuts, 25, 32
	Whole-Grain Crunchy Party Mix, 24, 26–27

O

Oat Bran Bread, 55, 56
Oats
	Apple Oatmeal Breakfast Pudding, 39, 40
	Basic Granola, 38, 40
	Big Pot of Oatmeal, 41, 44
	Breakfast Grains, 39, 40
	Carrot Cake and Zucchini Bread Oatmeal, 41, 44–45
	Maple Pecan Granola, 38, 40
	Mixed Berry and Almond Granola, 38, 40
	Oat Bran Bread, 55, 56
	Pumpkin Pie Oatmeal, 41, 45
	Raspberry Yogurt Oatmeal, 45, 46
Okra
	Veggie Gumbo with Cheater Roux, 162, 168
Old-Fashioned Vegetable Soup, 156, 164
Olives
	black
		health benefits of, 12
		Mega Omega Piquant Artichoke, Olive, and Anchovy Sauce, 12, 15
	Kalamata, facts about, 113
Onions
	Asian-Style Winter Stew, 171, 174
	Balsamic Onion Marmalade, 17, 22
	Cayenne Caramelized Onions, 185, 192
	Chicken with Root Vegetables, 104, 106
	Corn with Peppers and Onions, 176, 179
	Fresh and Light Summer Medley with Feta, 190, 196
	health benefits of, 76, 120, 185
	Onion Soup, 152, 158
	Onion Soup Mix, 7, 14
	Orange Onion Pot Roast, 78, 80
	Red Cabbage, Green Apple, and Sweet Onion, 191, 197
	Sausage with Apples and Onions, 101, 104
	Thai Curry Tofu and Veggies, 125, 128
	Vegetable Medley, 191, 197
Orange juice
	Beets with Ginger and Orange, 187, 193
	Citrus Cider, 247, 252
	Citrus Rum BBQ Sauce, 7, 14
	Cranberry Orange Cider, 247, 252
	Fruit Tea, 255, 258
	Orange Beets with Walnuts, 187, 193
	Wassail, 253, 254
Orange marmalade
	Orange-Glazed Ham, 101, 103
	Orange Onion Pot Roast, 78, 80
Oranges
	Citrusy Rosemary Breakfast Bread, 62, 67
	Cranberry Orange Nut Bread, 58, 61
	Fruit Tea, 255, 258
	Hot Rum and Fruit Punch, 254, 258
	Lower-Sugar Raisin-Orange Pumpkin Pie Pudding, 226, 230
	Real Deal Beef Stew with Orange and Clove, 76, 78
	Turkey and Fruit Sweetened Cranberry Sauce Supper, 115, 120
	Wassail Rum Punch, 254, 258
Osso Buco, 94, 96
Oysters
	Gifts from the Sea Chowder, 172, 175

P

Pantry basics
	Dumplings, 21, 23
	fruit-based
		Apple Butter, 16, 22
		Coconut Lemon Curd, 13, 15
		Fall Harvest Fruit Butter, 16, 22
		Lightly Sweetened Autumnal Fruit Butter, 13, 22
		Perfect Pumpkin Puree, 16, 22

INDEX • **279**

sauces
- Blueberry-Balsamic Meatball Sauce with Rosemary, 8, 15
- Chili Sauce, 8, 14
- Citrus Rum BBQ Sauce, 7, 14
- Easy Pasta Sauce, 9, 15
- Homemade Smoky Ketchup, 8, 14
- Mega Omega Piquant Artichoke, Olive, and Anchovy Sauce, 12, 15
- Memorable Gingered Peaches and Blues Sauce, 12, 15
- Pesto, 12, 15
- Slow Cooked Two-Tomato and Spicy Turkey Sausage Sauce, 9, 15
- Vegetarian Spaghetti Sauce, 9, 15

soups, stocks, and broth
- Beef Stock, 6, 10
- Chicken Stock, 6, 11
- Condensed Cream of Mushroom Soup, 7, 14
- Freshest Vegetable Broth, 6–7, 14
- Onion Soup Mix, 7, 14

vegetarian
- All-Occasion Roasted Garlic, 17, 22
- Apple Sage Sausage, 19–20, 23
- Balsamic Onion Marmalade, 17, 22
- Beefy Seitan, 19, 23
- Butter Chick'n, 18, 23
- Chick'n Seitan, 18–19, 23
- Dry Beans from Scratch, 18, 22
- Preserve-the-Harvest Diced Tomatoes, 17, 22
- Tea-Scented Tofu, 20, 23
- Versatile Lean and Easy Chicken Base, 21, 23

Parsnips
- Autumnal Rich-Roots Medley Potatoes, 205, 208
- Glazed Root Vegetables, 186, 193
- health benefits of, 205
- Parsnip and Carrot Medley, 186, 193

Party Meatballs, 28, 33

Party mixes
- healthier versions of, 24
- Whole-Grain Crunchy Party Mix, 24, 26–27

Pasta
- Baked Ziti, 132, 135
- Chicken Noodle Soup, 143–44, 150
- Mushroom Lasagna with Garlic-Tofu Sauce, 132, 134
- Pasta and Mushrooms, 133, 135
- Penne with Broccoli, 133, 136
- Pumpkin and White Bean Lasagna, 132, 134–35
- Smoked Tofu and Stars Soup, 143, 150
- Smoky Mac and Cheese, 200, 203
- Three-Cheese Vegetarian Spaghetti, 133, 135
- Turkey Noodle Soup, 144, 150

Peaches
- Antioxidant-Burst Raspberry Peach Cobbler, 233, 238
- Hot Spiced Fruit, 218, 224
- Memorable Gingered Peaches and Blues Sauce, 12, 15
- Peach Almond Breakfast Polenta, 41, 43
- Peach Cobbler, 233, 238
- Peaches with Butterscotch Sauce, 215, 217
- Peaches with Dumplings, 215, 217

Peanut butter
- Peanut Butter Cheesecake, 241, 244
- Peanutty Thai Chicken, 112, 114
- Rich and Creamy Sweet Potato Peanut Bisque, 161, 168

Subtly Spicy Peanut Fondue, 4, 35

Pears
- Brandied Fruit, 219, 224
- Delicata Squash and Pear Soup, 160, 168
- Earl Grey Poached Pears, 211, 216
- Fall Harvest Fruit Butter, 16, 22
- Gingered Honey Pears with Cinnamon Sticks, 214–15, 217
- Hot Spiced Fruit, 218, 224
- Hot Spiced Pears, 217, 218
- Lightly Sweetened Autumnal Fruit Butter, 13, 22
- Pear and Cardamom French Toast Casserole, 47, 48
- Poached Pears in Red Wine, 214, 216

Peas. See also Split peas
- Old-Fashioned Vegetable Soup, 156, 164

Pecans
- Acorn Squash Stuffed with Cranberry-Pecan Rice, 194, 197
- Atomic Tofu Pecan Loaf, 130, 132
- Candied Carrots and Pecans, 185, 192
- Maple Pecan Granola, 38, 40
- Spiced Nuts, 28, 32
- Sugared Pecans, 28, 32
- Sweet and Spicy Nuts, 25, 32

Penne with Broccoli, 133, 136

Peppermint Hot Cocoa, 261, 264

Peppers

bell
- Chock-Full-of-Veggies Cornbread, 63, 67
- Corn with Peppers and Onions, 176, 179
- Fajitas, 65, 73
- Fresh and Light Summer Medley with Feta, 190, 196
- Garlic Spinach with Roasted Reds, 190, 193
- health benefits of, 123, 190
- Lean and Green Stuffed Peppers, 122–23, 124
- Pineapple Pepper Chili, 84, 87
- Scrambled Tofu with Peppers, 49
- Stuffed Peppers with Beef and Corn, 83, 84
- Thai Curry Tofu and Veggies, 125, 128
- Vegetable Medley, 191, 197

hot
- capsaicin in, 162
- Habanero-Spiked "Red Hot" Cider, 246, 248

Perfect Pizza from Your Slow Cooker, 138, 140

Perfect Pumpkin Puree, 16, 22

Pesto, 12, 15
- Burst of Flavor Butternut Squash and Pesto Panini Filling, 72, 75
- In-a-Pinch Pesto Chicken and Mushrooms, 107, 108
- Spring Minestrone with Pesto Parmesan, 148, 151

Philadelphia-Style Cheesy Portobello Sandwich, 70, 75

Pick-Your-Pleasure Breakfast Rice Pudding, 41, 42

Pies, savory
- From-the-Pantry Pot Pie, 4, 129–30, 132
- Slow-Cooked Shepherd's Pie, 84, 87
- Turkey Tortilla Pie, 119, 122

Pimiento Cheese Fondue, 35, 37

Pineapple
- Brandied Fruit, 219, 224
- choosing and preparing, 214
- Fresh Pineapple with Coconut Lime Rum Sauce, 214, 217
- Fruited Tapioca, 220, 224
- Golden Fruit Compote, 219, 224
- health benefits of, 214
- Hot Spiced Fruit, 218, 224

280 • THE LITTLE SLOW COOKER COOKBOOK

Juice-Sweetened Tropical Fruit Compote, 219, 224
Pineapple Pepper Chili, 84, 87
White Fruit Cake, 237, 243
Pineapple juice
    Fruit Tea, 255, 258
Pine nuts
    Broccoli and Bacon with Pine Nuts, 184, 192
    Spinach, Basil, and Feta-Stuffed Chicken Rolls with Pignoli, 113, 114
Pizza
    Perfect Pizza from Your Slow Cooker, 138, 140
Plums
    Brandied Fruit, 219, 224
Poached Pears in Red Wine, 214, 216
Po'Boy, Veggie New Orleans, 70, 75
Polenta, Peach Almond Breakfast, 41, 43
Pomegranate Lamb, 85, 92
Pork
    Adobo Stew, 163, 169
    Apple Cranberry Pork Roast, 94, 96
    Asian Pork Roast, 94, 96–97
    Asian Ribs, 100, 102
    Barbecued Pork Chops, 95, 98
    Brunswick Stew, 170
    Coddled Ham, 101, 103
    Easiest Ribs, 99, 100
    Easy Maple Barbecue Pulled Pork Shoulder, 95, 97
    Easy Pork Roast, 94, 96
    Ham and Cabbage Casserole, 101, 103
    Ham and Scalloped Potatoes, 101, 103
    Hawaiian Pork Roast, 94, 96
    Holiday Ham, 101, 103
    Honey Mustard Ribs, 100, 102
    Orange-Glazed Ham, 101, 103
    Pork and Sweet Potato Dinner, 95, 97
    Pork Chops and Vegetables in Mushroom Gravy, 95, 98
    Pork Chops Braised with Sauerkraut, 99, 100
    Pork Chops with Apples, 99, 100
    Pork Chops with Sweet Potatoes, 99, 100
    Pork Loin with Honey Mustard, 95, 97
    Slow Cooker Shredded Pork, 95, 97
    Smoked Ham Hocks with White Beans, 100, 102
    Southern Stuffed Pork Chops, 95, 98
    Split Pea and Ham Soup, 156, 159
    Stuffed Pork Chops, 95, 98
    Thai Curry Pork, 100, 102
Potatoes. See also Hash browns; Sweet potatoes
    Asian-Style Winter Stew, 171, 174
    Au Gratin Salmon and Potato Bake, 124, 126
    Baked Potatoes, 204, 208
    Creamy Potato Soup, 152, 158
    German Potato Salad, 142, 147
    Ham and Scalloped Potatoes, 101, 103
    Hamburger Casserole, 83, 84
    Mashed Potato and Edamame Burrito Filling, 72, 75
    No-Cream Leek and Potato Soup, 154, 158
    Rosemary Potato Soup, 152, 158
    Saucy Cream Cheese Potatoes, 204, 208
Pot Pie, From-the-Pantry, 4, 129–30, 132
Pot roast
    Braised Beef in Red Wine, 78, 80
    Mushroom Pot Roast, 77, 78
    Orange Onion Pot Roast, 78, 80
    Tangy Tomato Grass-Fed Pot Roast, 76–77, 78

Preserve-the-Harvest Diced Tomatoes, 17, 22
Prunes
    Hot Spiced Fruit, 218, 224
Puddings
breakfast
    Apple Oatmeal Breakfast Pudding, 39, 40
    Eggy Spicy Whole-Grain Breakfast Bread Pudding, 39, 40
    Pick-Your-Pleasure Breakfast Rice Pudding, 41, 42
dessert
    Antioxidant-Rich Sweet Potato Carrot Pudding, 222, 225
    Brown Sugar Rice Pudding, 223, 230
    Caramel Bread Pudding, 227, 230
    Carrot Pudding, 222, 225
    Chocolate Bread Pudding, 227, 230
    Chocolate Pudding, 221, 225
    Cinnamon Eggnog Bread Pudding, 227, 230
    Fruited Tapioca, 220, 224
    Indian Pudding, 227, 231
    Low-Cal Cocoa Tapioca, 220, 225
    Lower-Sugar Raisin-Orange Pumpkin Pie Pudding, 226, 230
    Low-Sugar Coco-Nutty Rice Pudding, 226, 230
    Mango Coconut Rice Pudding, 226, 230
    Pumpkin Pie Pudding, 221–22, 225
    Pumpkin Pudding, 221, 225
    Rice Pudding, 223, 230
    Steamy, Creamy, High-Calcium Chai Pudding, 222, 225
    Strawberry Bread Pudding, 227, 231
    Tapioca Pudding, 219, 224
    Tapioca Pudding for Two, 220, 224
    Turkish Delight Tapioca Pudding, 220, 224
savory
    Corn Pudding, 176, 182
Pumpkin
    Fall Harvest Fruit Butter, 16, 22
    health benefits of, 226
    Lower-Sugar Raisin-Orange Pumpkin Pie Pudding, 226, 230
    Maple Pumpkin Custard, 231, 232
    Maple-Sweetened Pumpkin-Spiced Latte, 259, 260
    Perfect Pumpkin Puree, 16, 22
    Pumpkin and White Bean Lasagna, 132, 134–35
    Pumpkin Pie Oatmeal, 41, 45
    Pumpkin Pie Pudding, 221–22, 225
    Pumpkin Pudding, 221, 225
    Whole Wheat Pumpkin Gingerbread, 64, 67
Punch
    Cider Tea Punch, 251, 253
    Cranberry Punch, 255, 258
    Hot Rum and Fruit Punch, 254, 258
    Spiced Raspberry Punch, 254, 258
    Thanksgiving Punch, 255, 258
    Wassail Rum Punch, 254, 258
Pungent, Light, and Clear Thai Seafood Stew, 162, 169

Q

Queso Dip, 31, 36
Quiche, Broccoli-Bacon-Colby, 51, 53
Quick Sesame Teriyaki Lettuce Wraps, 69, 74
Quick Stroganoff, 79, 82
Quinoa
- Cranberry Vanilla Quinoa, 41, 44
- Spanish Quinoa, 137, 140

R

Ragu, Meatless Sausage and Mushroom, 132, 134
Raisins
- Baked Apples with Raisins, 210, 216
- Fruit-Stuffed Acorn Squash, 194, 197
- Golden Fruit Compote, 219, 224
- Lightly Sweetened Autumnal Fruit Butter, 13, 22
- Lower-Sugar Raisin-Orange Pumpkin Pie Pudding, 226, 230
- Rum Raisin Bananas, 217, 218
- White Fruit Cake, 237, 243

Raspberries
- Antioxidant-Burst Raspberry Peach Cobbler, 233, 238
- Layered Crepe Dessert, 242, 245
- Raspberry Iced Tea, 256, 259
- Raspberry Yogurt Oatmeal, 45, 46
- Spiced Raspberry Punch, 254, 258

Raspberry liqueur
- Raspberry Cappuccino, 260, 264

Red Cabbage, Green Apple, and Sweet Onion, 191, 197
Resveratrol
- health benefits of, 251
- sources of, 161

Rhubarb Flummery, 217, 218
Ribs. See also Short Ribs
- Asian Ribs, 100, 102
- Easiest Ribs, 99, 100
- Honey Mustard Ribs, 100, 102
- Thai Curry Pork, 100, 102

Rice
- Acorn Squash Stuffed with Cranberry-Pecan Rice, 194, 197
- Basic Fuss-Free Risotto, 136, 140
- Breakfast Risotto, 41, 43
- Broccoli Rice Casserole, 181, 189
- Brown Sugar Rice Pudding, 223, 230
- Cheesy Broccoli Rice, 201, 203
- Chicken Rice Soup, 144, 151
- Creamy Butternut Squash Risotto, 201, 203
- Lentils and Rice, 137, 140
- Low-Sugar Coco-Nutty Rice Pudding, 226, 230
- Mango Coconut Rice Pudding, 226, 230
- Pick-Your-Pleasure Breakfast Rice Pudding, 41, 42
- Rice Pudding, 223, 230
- Savory Turkey and Rice, 119, 122
- Simple White Rice, 201, 203

Rich and Creamy Sweet Potato Peanut Bisque, 161, 168
Risotto
- Barley Risotto, 201, 203
- Basic Fuss-Free Risotto, 136, 140
- Breakfast Risotto, 41, 43
- Creamy Butternut Squash Risotto, 201, 203

Roast Veal Shoulder, 93, 94
Rosemary
- Blueberry-Balsamic Meatball Sauce with Rosemary, 8, 15
- Citrusy Rosemary Breakfast Bread, 62, 67
- Rosemary Lamb Stew, 166, 169
- Rosemary Potato Soup, 152, 158

Rum
- Citrus Rum BBQ Sauce, 7, 14
- Fresh Pineapple with Coconut Lime Rum Sauce, 214, 217
- Hot, Spiked, and Buttered Spiced Cider, 247, 252
- Hot Buttered Rum, 254, 258
- Hot Rum and Fruit Punch, 254, 258
- Rum Raisin Bananas, 217, 218
- Slightly Drunken Apples, 210, 213
- Wassail Rum Punch, 254, 258

Russian Tea, 256, 259

S

Sage
- Apple Sage Sausage, 19–20, 23
- Holiday Tempeh and Sage Loaf, 131, 132

Salads
- German Potato Salad, 142, 147
- Lean and Easy Taco Salad, 142, 146

Salmon
- Au Gratin Salmon and Potato Bake, 124, 126
- Dilled Salmon Dijon, 123, 124
- Lemon-Poached Salmon Fillets, 123, 124
- Tomato Salmon Bisque, 173, 175
- wild vs. farmed, 123

Salsa
- Santa Fe Chicken, 107, 108

Sandwiches
- Asian Tempeh Lettuce Wraps, 69–70, 74
- Burst of Flavor Butternut Squash and Pesto Panini Filling, 72, 75
- Fajitas, 65, 73
- French Dip, 65, 74
- Greek Sandwich Filling, 68, 74
- Loaded Sloppy Joe with a Kick, 69, 74
- Mashed Potato and Edamame Burrito Filling, 72, 75
- Philadelphia-Style Cheesy Portobello Sandwich, 70, 75
- Quick Sesame Teriyaki Lettuce Wraps, 69, 74
- Shredded Beef, 68, 74
- Simplest Beefy Tacos, 68, 74
- Tempeh Tornado, 71, 75
- Texas-Style Tofu Taco Filling, 71, 75
- Veggie New Orleans Po'Boy, 70, 75

Santa Fe Chicken, 107, 108
Sauces
- Blueberry-Balsamic Meatball Sauce with Rosemary, 8, 15
- Chili Sauce, 8, 14
- Citrus Rum BBQ Sauce, 7, 14
- Easy Pasta Sauce, 9, 15
- Homemade Smoky Ketchup, 8, 14
- Mega Omega Piquant Artichoke, Olive, and Anchovy Sauce, 12, 15
- Memorable Gingered Peaches and Blues Sauce, 12, 15
- Pesto, 12, 15
- Slow Cooked Two-Tomato and Spicy Turkey Sausage Sauce, 9, 15
- Vegetarian Spaghetti Sauce, 9, 15

Saucy Cream Cheese Potatoes, 204, 208
Sauerkraut
- Chunky German Sausage and Sauerkraut Stew, 167, 169
- as naturally fermented food, 167
- Pork Chops Braised with Sauerkraut, 99, 100

282 • THE LITTLE SLOW COOKER COOKBOOK

Sausage
    Apple Sage Sausage, 19–20, 23
    Cabbage Soup with Kielbasa, 149, 151
    Chunky German Sausage and Sauerkraut Stew, 167, 169
    Corn-Tastic Tex-Mex Loaf, 130
    Green Beans with Smoked Sausage, 101, 103
    Meatless Sausage and Mushroom Ragu, 132, 134
    Mexican Egg Scramble, 47, 49
    Mix and Match Jambalaya, 125, 139
    Pear and Cardamom French Toast Casserole, 47, 48
    Sausage with Apples and Onions, 101, 104
    Savory Cheddar Sausage Bread, 64, 67
    Shellfish Jambalaya, 125, 127
    Slow Cooked Two-Tomato and Spicy Turkey Sausage Sauce, 9, 15
    Slow Cooker Sausage and Lima Beans, 101, 104
    Soy Chorizo Black Bean Stew, 167, 174
    turkey, benefits of, 9
Savory Cheddar Sausage Bread, 64, 67
Savory Slow-Cooked Meat Loaf, 79, 81
Savory Slow Cooker Tender Turkey Drumsticks, 115, 120
Savory Turkey and Rice, 119, 122
Scallops
    Gifts from the Sea Chowder, 172, 175
Scrambled Tofu with Peppers, 49
Scrumptious Strawberry Cornbread, 63, 67
Seeded and Stuffed Carnival Squash, 138, 140
Seitan
    Beefy Seitan, 19, 23
    Chick'n Cacciatore, 131, 132
    Chick'n Mushroom Casserole, 112, 114
    Chick'n Seitan, 18–19, 23
    From-the-Pantry Pot Pie, 4, 129–30, 132
    Kung Pao Chick'n, 137, 140
    Mix and Match Jambalaya, 125, 139
    Shellfish Jambalaya, 125, 127
    Veggie New Orleans Po'Boy, 70, 75
Seriously Simple Chicken Chili, 112, 114
Sesame seeds
    Low-Carb Sesame Turkey Meatballs, 29–30, 33
    Quick Sesame Teriyaki Lettuce Wraps, 69, 74
Shallot Apple Brussels Sprouts, 181, 183
Shellfish. See also Fish
    Corn Chowder with Crab, 173, 175
    Easy Manhattan Clam Chowder, 173, 175
    Gifts from the Sea Chowder, 172, 175
    Light Louisiana Creole Shrimp Soup, 161–62, 168
    Pungent, Light, and Clear Thai Seafood Stew, 162, 169
    Shellfish Jambalaya, 125, 127
    Shrimp Chowder, 173, 175
    Sweet and Sour Shrimp, 125, 127
    Szechuan Shrimp, 125, 127
Shepherd's Pie, Slow-Cooked, 84, 87
Short Ribs, 79, 83
    Barbecued Short Ribs, 79, 82
Shredded Beef, 68, 74
Shrimp
    Gifts from the Sea Chowder, 172, 175
    Light Louisiana Creole Shrimp Soup, 161–62, 168
    Pungent, Light, and Clear Thai Seafood Stew, 162, 169
    Shrimp Chowder, 173, 175
    Sweet and Sour Shrimp, 125, 127
    Szechuan Shrimp, 125, 127
Side dishes

apple
    Chunky Applesauce, 206, 208
    Cranberry Applesauce, 206, 209
    Red Cabbage, Green Apple, and Sweet Onion, 191, 197
    Shallot Apple Brussels Sprouts, 181, 183
    Stewed Apples, 206, 209
    Warm Applesauce, 206, 208
Asparagus Side Dish, 180, 183
bean
    Baked Beans, 198, 202
    Caribbean Mango Black Beans, 199–200, 203
    Chana Saag, 200, 203
    Fantastic Mexi Beans, 199, 203
    Lima Beans, 199, 202
    Vegetarian Baked Beans, 198–99, 202
beet
    Beets with Ginger and Orange, 187, 193
    Fresh Sweet 'n Sour Beets, 187, 193
    Orange Beets with Walnuts, 187, 193
broccoli
    Asian Broccoli, 181, 183
    Broccoli and Bacon with Pine Nuts, 184, 192
    Broccoli Casserole, 181, 188
    Broccoli Rice Casserole, 181, 189
    Cheesy Broccoli Rice, 201, 203
Brussels sprouts
    Balsamic Brussels Sprouts, 180, 183
    Shallot Apple Brussels Sprouts, 181, 183
cabbage
    Bavarian Cabbage, 184–85, 192
    Braised Red Cabbage, 184, 192
    Red Cabbage, Green Apple, and Sweet Onion, 191, 197
carrot
    Candied Carrots and Pecans, 185, 192
    Glazed Root Vegetables, 186, 193
    Marmalade-Glazed Carrots, 186, 193
    Parsnip and Carrot Medley, 186, 193
    Vodka and Dill-Glazed Baby Carrots, 186, 193
cauliflower
    Curried Cauliflower, 184, 192
corn
    Corn Pudding, 176, 182
    Corn with Peppers and Onions, 176, 179
    Creamy Corn, 176, 178
    Fresh Chili Lime Cob Corn, 176, 182
Eggplant Curry, 198, 202
grain
    Barley Risotto, 201, 203
    Cheesy Broccoli Rice, 201, 203
    Creamy Butternut Squash Risotto, 201, 203
    Curried Couscous, 204, 207
    Simple White Rice, 201, 203
    Smoky Mac and Cheese, 200, 203
green bean
    Green Bean Casserole, 180, 183
    Not Your Grandma's Green Beans, 177, 182
    Southern Beans, 180, 183
    Tangy Beans, 177, 182
greens
    Chana Saag, 200, 203
    Garlic Spinach with Roasted Reds, 190, 193
        Spinach Parmesan Casserole, 184, 192
    leeks
    Braised Leeks with Vinaigrette, 185, 192

INDEX • 283

mixed-vegetable
    Easiest Vegetable-Surprise Dish, 190, 197
    Fresh and Light Summer Medley with Feta, 190, 196
    Vegetable Medley, 191, 197
onion
    Cayenne Caramelized Onions, 185, 192
    Red Cabbage, Green Apple, and Sweet Onion, 191, 197
parsnip
    Autumnal Rich-Roots Medley Potatoes, 205, 208
    Glazed Root Vegetables, 186, 193
    Parsnip and Carrot Medley, 186, 193
potato
    Au Gratin Potatoes, 205, 208
    Autumnal Rich-Roots Medley Potatoes, 205, 208
    Baked Potatoes, 204, 208
    Easy Cheesy Potato Casserole, 204, 208
    Holiday Sweet Potato Casserole, 205–6, 208
    Saucy Cream Cheese Potatoes, 204, 208
squash
    Acorn Squash, 191, 197
    Acorn Squash Stuffed with Cranberry-Pecan Rice, 194, 197
    Butternut Squash Puree, 195, 197
    Creamy Butternut Squash Risotto, 201, 203
    Creamy Zucchini Casserole, 195, 202
    Fruit-Stuffed Acorn Squash, 194, 197
    Italian Zucchini, 198, 202
    Mixed Squash Casserole, 198, 202
    Spice-Rubbed Spaghetti Squash, 195, 202
    Squash Casserole, 191, 197
tomato
    Stewed Tomatoes, 177, 182
    Summer Stewed Tomatoes, 177, 182
Simplest Beefy Tacos, 68, 74
Simple Veal Stew, 166, 169
Simple White Rice, 201, 203
Slightly Drunken Apples, 210, 213
Sloppy joes
    Loaded Sloppy Joe with a Kick, 69, 74
    Tempeh Tornado, 71, 75
Slow Cooked Two-Tomato and Spicy Turkey Sausage Sauce, 9, 15
Slow Cooker Chicken Mole, 115, 116
Slow Cooker Chocolate Cake, 236–37, 239
Slow Cooker Custard, 228, 231
Slow Cooker Poached Eggs, 50, 53
Slow cookers
    cleaning, 143
    retrieving hot inserts from, 228
Slow Cooker Sausage and Lima Beans, 101, 104
Slow Cooker Shredded Pork, 95, 97
Smoked Ham Hocks with White Beans, 100, 102
Smoked Tofu and Stars Soup, 143, 150
Smoky Mac and Cheese, 200, 203
Smothered Steak, 79, 82
Soups. See also Broth; Stews; Stocks
    Bean and Vegetable Soup, 156, 159
    Beef Barley Soup, 142, 150
    Beef Borscht, 172, 175
    Black Bean Soup, 154, 159
    Broccoli-Cheese Soup, 157, 168
    Cabbage Soup with Kielbasa, 149, 151
    Chicken Corn Soup, 144, 150
    Chicken Minestrone, 145, 151
    Chicken Noodle Soup, 143–44, 150
    Chicken Rice Soup, 144, 151
    Chicken Soup with Wild Rice, 145, 151
    Condensed Cream of Mushroom Soup, 7, 14
    Corn Chowder with Crab, 173, 175
    Cream of Mushroom Soup, 149, 158
    Cream of Unpotato Soup, 152–53, 158
    Creamy Potato Soup, 152, 158
    Curried Coconut Cream of Cauliflower Soup, 160, 168
    Delicata Squash and Pear Soup, 160, 168
    Easy Manhattan Clam Chowder, 173, 175
    Gifts from the Sea Chowder, 172, 175
    Ground Sirloin Borscht, 172, 175
    Hot and Sour Chinese Vegetable Soup, 157, 168
    Hot and Sour Soup, 143, 150
    Lean Dried Apricot, Chicken, and Wild Rice Soup, 145, 151
    Light Louisiana Creole Shrimp Soup, 161–62, 168
    Loaded Split Pea Sweet Potato Soup, 153, 158
    Lo-Cal Caribbean Black Bean Soup, 154–55, 159
    Mighty Minestrone, 148, 151
    No-Cream Leek and Potato Soup, 154, 158
    Northern Bean Soup, 155, 159
    nutrient density of, 148, 162
    Old-Fashioned Vegetable Soup, 156, 164
    Onion Soup, 152, 158
    Onion Soup Mix, 7, 14
    Rich and Creamy Sweet Potato Peanut Bisque, 161, 168
    Rosemary Potato Soup, 152, 158
    Shrimp Chowder, 173, 175
    Smoked Tofu and Stars Soup, 143, 150
    Split Pea and Ham Soup, 156, 159
    Split Pea and Lentil Soup, 155, 159
    Spring Minestrone with Pesto Parmesan, 148, 151
    Sweet Tooth–Buster Sweet Potato Apple Soup, 153, 158
    Tomato Salmon Bisque, 173, 175
    Turkey Mushroom Soup, 149, 151
    Turkey Noodle Soup, 144, 150
    Veggie Gumbo with Cheater Roux, 162, 168
    for weight loss, 161–62
    What's in the Freezer Veggie Soup, 156–57, 165
Southeast Asian Coconut Custard, 229, 231
Southern Beans, 180, 183
Southern Stuffed Pork Chops, 95, 98
Soy Chorizo Black Bean Stew, 167, 174
Spaghetti, Three-Cheese Vegetarian, 133, 135
Spaghetti squash
    health benefits of, 195
    Spice-Rubbed Spaghetti Squash, 195, 202
Spanish Quinoa, 137, 140
Spiced Apples, 211, 216
Spiced Apple Wine, 251, 253
Spiced Candied Apples and Yams with Raw Chocolate Drizzle, 211, 216
Spiced Cider, 246, 252
Spiced Nuts, 28, 32
Spiced Raspberry Punch, 254, 258
Spiced Tea, 256, 259
Spice-Rubbed Spaghetti Squash, 195, 202
Spicy Hash Browns, 51, 53
Spinach
    Eggs Florentine, 50, 53
    Garlic Spinach with Roasted Reds, 190, 193
    health benefits of, 190
    Spinach, Basil, and Feta-Stuffed Chicken Rolls with Pignoli, 113, 114

Spinach Artichoke Dip, 29, 33
Spinach Dip, 31, 36
Spinach Parmesan Casserole, 184, 192
Split peas. See also Peas
    Loaded Split Pea Sweet Potato Soup, 153, 158
    nutrients in, 155
    Split Pea and Ham Soup, 156, 159
    Split Pea and Lentil Soup, 155, 159
Spoonbread, Cheesy, 24
Spring Minestrone with Pesto Parmesan, 148, 151
Spring mix, 126
Squash. See Acorn squash; Butternut squash; Zucchini
    Delicata Squash and Pear Soup, 160, 168
    Mixed Squash Casserole, 198, 202
    Seeded and Stuffed Carnival Squash, 138, 140
    Spice-Rubbed Spaghetti Squash, 195, 202
    Squash Casserole, 191, 197
Steak
    Beef with Gravy, 79, 82
    Fajitas, 65, 73
    Quick Stroganoff, 79, 82
    Smothered Steak, 79, 82
    Steak Rollups with Asparagus, 79, 81
    Swiss Steak, 79, 81
Steamy, Creamy, High-Calcium Chai Pudding, 222, 225
Stewed Apples, 206, 209
Stewed Tomatoes, 177, 182
Stews
    Adobo Stew, 163, 169
    Asian-Style Winter Stew, 171, 174
    Belgian Beef Stew, 163, 169
    Brunswick Stew, 170, 174
    Chunky German Sausage and Sauerkraut Stew, 167, 169
    Curried Mulligatawny Lamb Stew, 166, 169
    Hard Cider and Cabbage Stew, 171, 174
    Hearty Chicken Stew, 167, 169
    Pungent, Light, and Clear Thai Seafood Stew, 162, 169
    Real Deal Beef Stew with Orange and Clove, 76, 78
    Rosemary Lamb Stew, 166, 169
    Simple Veal Stew, 166, 169
    Soy Chorizo Black Bean Stew, 167, 174
    Szechuan Chicken Stew, 170, 174
    Tofu Bouillabaisse, 157, 168
    Vegetable-Loaded Beef and Barley Stew, 163, 169
    Veggie-Rich Asian Chicken Stew, 170, 174
    White Bean and Kale Stew, 171, 174
Stocks. See also Broth
    Beef Stock, 6, 10
    broths vs., 7
    Chicken Stock, 6, 11
Strawberries
    Scrumptious Strawberry Cornbread, 63, 67
    Strawberry Bread Pudding, 227, 231
    Strawberry Chocolate Crumble, 240, 244
    Strawberry-Lime Granita, 4, 242
    Strawberry Sourdough Bread Pudding, 40, 42
Stroganoff, Quick, 79, 82
Stuffed Peppers with Beef and Corn, 83, 84
Stuffed Pork Chops, 95, 98
Subtly Spicy Peanut Fondue, 4, 35
Sugar
    Cinnamon Sugar, 206
    Vanilla Sugar, 237
Sugared Pecans, 28, 32

Sulfur dioxide, as preservative, 105
Summer Stewed Tomatoes, 177, 182
Sunflower seeds
    Seeded and Stuffed Carnival Squash, 138, 140
Sweet and Saucy Free-Range Chicken Thighs, 114, 116
Sweet and Sour Chicken Breasts, 109, 111
Sweet and Sour Chicken Wings, 30, 33
Sweet and Sour Hot Dog Bites, 30, 33
Sweet and Sour Shrimp, 125, 127
Sweet and Sour Smoked Tofu, 125, 128–29
Sweet and Spicy Nuts, 25, 32
Sweet potatoes
    Antioxidant-Rich Sweet Potato Carrot Pudding, 222, 225
    Autumnal Rich-Roots Medley Potatoes, 205, 208
    health benefits of, 153, 161, 222
    Holiday Sweet Potato Casserole, 205–6, 208
    Loaded Split Pea Sweet Potato Soup, 153, 158
    Pork and Sweet Potato Dinner, 95, 97
    Pork Chops with Sweet Potatoes, 99, 100
    Rich and Creamy Sweet Potato Peanut Bisque, 161, 168
    Spiced Candied Apples and Yams with Raw Chocolate Drizzle, 211, 216
    Sweet Tooth–Buster Sweet Potato Apple Soup, 153, 158
Swiss Steak, 79, 81
Swordfish Braised with Thai Green Curry, 124, 126
Szechuan Chicken Stew, 170, 174
Szechuan Shrimp, 125, 127

T

Taco Dip, 31, 37
Tacos
    Lean and Easy Taco Salad, 142, 146
    Simplest Beefy Tacos, 68, 74
    Texas-Style Tofu Taco Filling, 71, 75
Tangy Beans, 177, 182
Tangy Tomato Grass-Fed Pot Roast, 76–77, 78
Tapioca
    Fruited Tapioca, 220, 224
    Low-Cal Cocoa Tapioca, 220, 225
    Tapioca Pudding, 219, 224
    Tapioca Pudding for Two, 220, 224
    Turkish Delight Tapioca Pudding, 220, 224
Tart cherry supplement, health benefits of, 77
Tea
    black, health benefits of, 257
    Chai Tea, 257, 259
    Cider Tea Punch, 251, 253
    Earl Grey Poached Pears, 211, 216
    Fruit Tea, 255, 258
    Lemon Mint Tea, 256, 259
    Lower-Cal Vanilla Bean Chai, 257, 259
    milk in, 257
    Raspberry Iced Tea, 256, 259
    Russian Tea, 256, 259
    Spiced Tea, 256, 259
    Tea-Scented Tofu, 20, 23
    Tea "Thyme" Lemon Blondies, 235, 239
    Tropical Tea, 255, 258
Tempeh
    Asian Tempeh Lettuce Wraps, 69–70, 74
    Holiday Tempeh and Sage Loaf, 131, 132
    Tempeh Braised with Figs and Port Wine, 125, 129
    Tempeh Tornado, 71, 75
Teriyaki Lettuce Wraps, Quick Sesame, 69, 74

Texas-Style Tofu Taco Filling, 71, 75
Thai Curry Pork, 100, 102
Thai Curry Tofu and Veggies, 125, 128
Thanksgiving Punch, 255, 258
Three-Alarm Chili, 84, 86
Three-Cheese Vegetarian Spaghetti, 133, 135
Tilapia
    health benefits of, 128
    Zested and Light Lemon-Garlic Tilapia with Roasted Shiitakes, 125, 128
Tofu
    Atomic Tofu Pecan Loaf, 130, 132
    Butter Chick'n, 18, 23
    Corn-Tastic Tex-Mex Loaf, 130
    Hot and Sour Soup, 143, 150
    Ma Po Tofu, 139, 141
    Mix and Match Jambalaya, 125, 139
    Mushroom Lasagna with Garlic-Tofu Sauce, 132, 134
    Scrambled Tofu with Peppers, 49
    Smoked Tofu and Stars Soup, 143, 150
    Sweet and Sour Smoked Tofu, 125, 128–29
    Tea-Scented Tofu, 20, 23
    Texas-Style Tofu Taco Filling, 71, 75
    Thai Curry Tofu and Veggies, 125, 128
    Tofu Bouillabaisse, 157, 168
    Weekend Tofu and Hash Brown Breakfast Casserole, 47, 49
Tomatoes
    Chick'n Cacciatore, 131, 132
    Chili Sauce, 8, 14
    Clean and Tasty Pizza Fondue, 35, 37
    Fajitas, 65, 73
    Fresh and Light Summer Medley with Feta, 190, 196
    Garlic Spinach with Roasted Reds, 190, 193
    Homemade Smoky Ketchup, 8, 14
    Moroccan Braised Lamb Shanks in Fresh Tomatoes and Red Wine, 85, 91–92
    Preserve-the-Harvest Diced Tomatoes, 17, 22
    selecting, 17
    Slow Cooked Two-Tomato and Spicy Turkey Sausage Sauce, 9, 15
    Stewed Tomatoes, 177, 182
    Summer Stewed Tomatoes, 177, 182
    Tangy Tomato Grass-Fed Pot Roast, 76–77, 78
    Tomato-Herb Bread, 55, 57
    Tomato Salmon Bisque, 173, 175
    Vegetable Medley, 191, 197
    Vegetarian Spaghetti Sauce, 9, 15
Tortillas
    Breakfast Burritos, 50, 53
    Corn-Tastic Tex-Mex Loaf, 130
    Mashed Potato and Edamame Burrito Filling, 72, 75
    Simplest Beefy Tacos, 68, 74
    Turkey Tortilla Pie, 119, 122
Trail mix
    Dark Chocolate Trail Mix for a Crowd, 25, 32
    as healthy snack, 25
Tropical Tea, 255, 258
Turkey
    Barbecued Turkey Thighs, 119, 121
    Braised Turkey Wings with Mushrooms, 118, 121
    Clean and Tasty Pizza Fondue, 35, 37
    Cranberry Barbecued Turkey, 119, 121
    free-range, 120

    Lean and Easy Taco Salad, 142, 146
    Lean and Green Stuffed Peppers, 122–23, 124
    Low-Carb Sesame Turkey Meatballs, 29–30, 33
    as protein source, 120
    Savory Slow-Cooked Meat Loaf, 79, 81
    Savory Slow Cooker Tender Turkey Drumsticks, 115, 120
    Savory Turkey and Rice, 119, 122
    Turkey and Fruit Sweetened Cranberry Sauce Supper, 115, 120
    Turkey Dinner, 115, 121
    Turkey Meat Loaf, 122, 124
    Turkey Mushroom Soup, 149, 151
    Turkey Noodle Soup, 144, 150
    Turkey Tortilla Pie, 119, 122
Turkey sausage
    benefits of, 9
    Green Beans with Smoked Sausage, 101, 103
    Slow Cooked Two-Tomato and Spicy Turkey Sausage Sauce, 9, 15
Turkish Delight Tapioca Pudding, 220, 224
Turnips
    Asian-Style Winter Stew, 171, 174
    Chicken with Root Vegetables, 104, 106
    health benefits of, 90
    Maple Glazed Corned Beef with Vegetables, 85, 90–91
    New England Boiled Dinner, 85, 90
    New England Corned Beef and Cabbage, 84, 90

V

Vanilla
    Cranberry Vanilla Quinoa, 41, 44
    Lower-Cal Vanilla Bean Chai, 257, 259
    Vanilla Sugar, 237
    Vanilla Upside-Down Cake, 237, 239
Veal
    Osso Buco, 94, 96
    Roast Veal Shoulder, 93, 94
    Simple Veal Stew, 166, 169
Vegetables. See also specific vegetables
    Bean and Vegetable Soup, 156, 159
    Chock-Full-of-Veggies Cornbread, 63, 67
    Easiest Vegetable-Surprise Dish, 190, 197
    Freshest Vegetable Broth, 6–7, 14
    Glazed Root Vegetables, 186, 193
    Hot and Sour Chinese Vegetable Soup, 157, 168
    Maple Glazed Corned Beef with Vegetables, 85, 90–91
    Old-Fashioned Vegetable Soup, 156, 164
    Pork Chops and Vegetables in Mushroom Gravy, 95, 98
    Thai Curry Tofu and Veggies, 125, 128
    Vegetable-Loaded Beef and Barley Stew, 163, 169
    Vegetable Medley, 191, 197
    Veggie Gumbo with Cheater Roux, 162, 168
    Veggie New Orleans Po'Boy, 70, 75
    Veggie-Rich Asian Chicken Stew, 170, 174
    What's in the Freezer Veggie Soup, 156–57, 165
Vegetarian Baked Beans, 198–99, 202
Vegetarian Spaghetti Sauce, 9, 15
Versatile Lean and Easy Chicken Base, 21, 23
Vinaigrette, Braised Leeks with, 185, 192
Vodka
    Mockahlua, 262
    Vodka and Dill-Glazed Baby Carrots, 186, 193

W

Walnuts
- Cinnamon Walnuts, 25, 32
- Cranberry Orange Nut Bread, 58, 61
- health benefits of, 187
- Orange Beets with Walnuts, 187, 193

Warm Applesauce, 206, 208
Wassail, 253, 254
- Clean Classic Wassail, 250, 253
- Wassail Rum Punch, 254, 258

Weekend Tofu and Hash Brown Breakfast Casserole, 47, 49
Weight loss, soups for, 161–62
Western Omelet, 49, 52
What's in the Freezer Veggie Soup, 156–57, 165
Wheat Bread, Honey, 56, 64
Wheat germ
- Breakfast Grains, 39, 40

White Bean and Kale Stew, 171, 174
White Bread, 54, 56
White Fruit Cake, 237, 243
Whole Grain Bread, 54–55, 56
Whole-Grain Crunchy Party Mix, 24, 26–27
Wholesome Chocolate Chip Banana Bread, 59, 66
Whole Wheat Bread, 54, 56
Whole Wheat Pumpkin Gingerbread, 64, 67
Wild rice
- Chicken Soup with Wild Rice, 145, 151
- Cornish Game Hens and Wild Rice, 115, 117
- Lean Dried Apricot, Chicken, and Wild Rice Soup, 145, 151

Wine
- Beef Burgundy in Hunter Sauce, 77, 78
- Braised Beef in Red Wine, 78, 80
- Double Blackberry Brandy Wine, 251, 253
- Moroccan Braised Lamb Shanks in Fresh Tomatoes and Red Wine, 85, 91–92
- Mulled Wine, 251, 253
- Poached Pears in Red Wine, 214, 216
- red, resveratrol in, 251
- Spiced Apple Wine, 251, 253
- Tempeh Braised with Figs and Port Wine, 125, 129
- Wine-Braised Artichokes, 34, 37

Wraps
- Asian Tempeh Lettuce Wraps, 69–70
- Quick Sesame Teriyaki Lettuce Wraps, 69, 74

Y

Yogurt Oatmeal, Raspberry, 45, 46

Z

Zested and Light Lemon-Garlic Tilapia with Roasted Shiitakes, 125, 128
Zesty Citrus Catfish Fillets, 124, 126
Ziti, Baked, 132, 135
Zucchini
- Carrot Cake and Zucchini Bread Oatmeal, 41, 44–45
- Chock-Full-of-Veggies Cornbread, 63, 67
- Creamy Zucchini Casserole, 195, 202
- Fresh and Light Summer Medley with Feta, 190, 196
- Italian Zucchini, 198, 202
- Mixed Squash Casserole, 198, 202
- Zucchini Bread, 58–59, 66